DARK PATTERNS, DECEPTIVE DESIGN, AND THE LAW

This book provides essential insights on dark patterns and AI-powered deceptive design for anyone who wants to understand and challenge the pervasive influence of these hidden forces shaping our digital experiences.

These hidden design strategies – from personalised user interface triggers to sophisticated backend systems – are often used to manipulate user behaviour in ways that benefit businesses at the expense of users. With advanced profiling driven by AI, these deceptive techniques can tailor digital environments to each user, raising significant questions about privacy, control and the boundaries of digital design.

The book examines the response of regulators, from the GDPR, Digital Services Act and AI Act in the EU to emerging frameworks in the USA, Brazil and India. Through real-world examples, it explains how these laws fail to address deceptive design practices and explores the implications for privacy, autonomy and consumer protection in the digital age.

By uncovering the complex layers of modern deceptive design, this book equips readers with the knowledge to recognise these tactics and consider their impact on user choice and trust. It is essential reading for legal professionals, digital rights advocates, designers, and anyone invested in fair digital practices.

Dark Patterns, Deceptive Design, and the Law

*AI's Hidden Influence on
Our Digital Experience*

MR Leiser

•HART•

OXFORD • LONDON • NEW YORK • NEW DELHI • SYDNEY

HART PUBLISHING

Bloomsbury Publishing Plc

Kemp House, Chawley Park, Cumnor Hill, Oxford, OX2 9PH, UK

1385 Broadway, New York, NY 10018, USA

Bloomsbury Publishing Ireland Limited, 29 Earlsfort Terrace, Dublin 2, D02 AY28, Ireland

HART PUBLISHING, the Hart/Stag logo, BLOOMSBURY and the Diana logo are
trademarks of Bloomsbury Publishing Plc

First published in Great Britain 2025

1

A catalogue record for this book is available from the British Library.

A catalogue record for this book is available from the Library of Congress.

Library of Congress Control Number: 2025941364

ISBN: PB: 978-1-50998-711-5
       ePDF: 978-1-50998-708-5
       ePub: 978-1-50998-709-2

Typeset by Compuscript Ltd, Shannon
Printed and bound in Great Britain by CPI Group (UK) Ltd, Croydon CR0 4YY

For product safety related questions contact productsafety@bloomsbury.com

To find out more about our authors and books visit www.hartpublishing.co.uk.
Here you will find extracts, author information, details of forthcoming events
and the option to sign up for our newsletters.

FOREWORD

In 2010, I needed a fun title for a presentation I was planning to give at the UX Brighton Conference, and I thought the term 'Dark Patterns' sounded pretty cool. A bit 'Star Wars' or 'Harry Potter'-esque, and in keeping with other terms like 'Dark Money' or 'Dark Matter'. It amazes me that the concepts I put forward in that presentation are now the subject of considerable academic research at the intersection of design, psychology, behavioural economics, and law. Recently, a friend told me that their kids were taught about dark patterns in elementary school. I'd have spent a lot more time and care choosing the name had I known it would be so popular. Today, I prefer to call them 'manipulative' or 'deceptive patterns', but since many people in the legal domain still call them 'dark patterns', it seems like that term is here to stay.

In 2010, I worked at a design agency called Clearleft, where one of the main things we provided to our clients was a 'User Interface (UI) pattern library' – code components and design specifications that defined particular chunks of UI that could be fitted together like Lego to create the front end of a website or an app, like the 'navigation bar', 'header', 'footer' and so on. That was the focus of my day-to-day work, and my focus on UI design framed my thinking in my campaign against manipulation, deception and coercion online.

When I came up with the term, the most problematic patterns I found tended to exist in the UI, so defining them as existing in this design layer seemed worthwhile. Fourteen years later, this focus on the UI has been carried through into legislation and regulation worldwide. However, while legislation adopted this focus on the UI, the world has moved on. Since 2010, the software we use every day has become increasingly complex. It's bigger, it's smarter, and there's a whole lot more of it. While this makes it more valuable, it also provides new opportunities for harmful business practices. Today, software manages most of our lives. Software decides if we're eligible for insurance or job roles, tells us when to exercise or go to bed, recommends which partners to go on dates with, and gives us mental health guidance when those relationships go wrong. Software decides what advertisements to show us and what products and prices to show us when shopping. Few aspects of our lives are free from its reach.

Along with the incredible spread of software into our lives, another change is the role and framing that software is given in tech businesses. It used to be the case that software was complex to build, and launching, scaling and maintaining a useful software product was the top-level goal – the pinnacle of achievement that would bring you success in the marketplace. The competition was so thin that you could build something that was pretty crappy to use and you'd still attract customers because you were the only game in town. You'll know what I mean if you remember how infuriatingly tricky it was to program your VHS recorder or fax machine. In the 1990s and early 2000s, there was a huge push to use insights from HCI and psychology to make software easier to use. But in the 2010s and 2020s, the framing changed again. Ease of use became a boring standard – just a hygiene factor – and software's role as a tool for persuasion and influence came to the forefront. Today, savvy tech businesses see software as a tool that allows them to profile, persuade and influence users. So, the challenge of making software itself isn't the final frontier anymore – it's human psychology and the science of influencing human decision-making. In 2018, researchers working with StubHub published a paper that casually mentioned that their 'experiment included several million users who visited the site over ten days'.[1] The sheer scale and speed of this sort of psychology experiment – to ascertain what kind of design would best influence consumers to spend more – has never before been possible in humanity's history. If they were academics, they would have been required to run their experimental plans via an ethics committee before they could run that study. In industry, no such guardrails are in place.

I'm reminded of philosopher Nick Bostrom's thought experiment of the 'paperclip maximiser'. It's like a sci-fi short story. A brilliant AI system aims to manufacture paper clips and maximise the output. Without considering the consequences, the machine decides that humans are merely an obstruction to creating more paper clips, so the era of humanity ends.[2]

Modern tech businesses build software to maximise one type of human behaviour or another. Engagement, purchasing, sharing, consuming, and data creation all lead to the key prize: revenue and growth. Harmful consequences are often ignorantly or wilfully ignored. This is the problem we face, and we need to grasp it before it grabs us.

In 1999, Stewart Brand put forward the concept of 'pace layering' – the idea that society operates at different pace levels. For example, the natural world moves slowly, human culture moves faster, governance moves faster still, and commerce moves faster than all three. Brand saw pace layering as good, describing it as 'The order of civilization. The fast layers innovate; the slow layers stabilise. The whole combines learning with continuity'.[3]

So, is our system of pace layers starting to break and run out of control? While we don't want our laws to be different when we wake up every morning, we also don't want them to be out of touch with the increasingly accelerating layer of technology. We're at a point now where tech companies are capitalising on the fact that legislators and regulators simply can't keep up with their business practices. If they move fast enough, they can get away with things that wouldn't be allowed if we could scrutinise what they were doing then. The consequences include user harm (eg financial loss, addiction, time wasted, extracted consent and unwanted contractual obligations) and marketplace harm (eg anti-competitive behaviour that harms small businesses and creates lock-in for giant monopolies).

Add AI systems to the mix, and we will have a new accelerant – and much more complexity. We're looking towards a future where software will not only manage our lives but also be able to learn, adapt and work towards strategic objectives – as if it were an entire commercial business of people and processes encapsulated in software form. An AI system has the potential to be a perfect team of employees – one that doesn't complain, doesn't get distracted or 'push back' against harmful ideas, and has a pure, unadulterated focus on its objectives to maximise and grow the business. Its complexity also gives businesses a vast, dark forest of code in which to hide manipulative, deceptive and coercive decision-making processes, making it hard for external auditors, regulators – and even the business owners – to discern precisely how and why it makes decisions the way it does.

Mark Leiser's *Dark Patterns, Deceptive Design, and the Law* arrives at a pivotal moment. The rapid evolution of technology and its manipulation of human behaviour outpace the ability of laws and ethics to keep up. This book is essential for anyone seeking to understand and combat the sophisticated tactics shaping our digital lives.

Dr Harry Brignull
East Sussex 2025

PREFACE

I consider myself a 'regulatory theorist', or a legal academic who looks at what laws are meant to do, what they actually do, and where they go awry. This stance often feels like sitting astride a *very* high horse with no reins, galloping into a chaotic battlefield armed with pointed critiques of what everyone else is doing wrong. In fairness, the metaphor is fitting – my career thus far involves considering the intended and unintended consequences of laws, especially when they are aimed at the towering behemoths of Big Tech. Generally, though, I am sceptical of the law's ability to achieve what it says on the tin. Most laws come with aspirational objectives. In reality, loopholes big enough to fit a Tesla through and unintended consequences lurk in the annexes. This book, therefore, is not a triumphalist hymn to regulation but an exploration of its messy, frustrating intersection with technology and human behaviour.

One of the moments that sparked my journey into this quagmire occurred during a public lecture on disinformation at the University of Malta. It was one of the worst storms the island had ever seen – so bad that fish were leaping out of the ocean onto bridges, an event that delighted local fishermen but left me wondering if I should have packed a canoe. My colleague, Dr Mireille Caruana, hosted me, but her hospitality was interrupted when her house was struck by lightning. The explosion took out her television, filling the room with an eerie flair. During the downtime caused by this apocalyptic weather event, I picked up a book on consumer law from her shelf. It was at this moment that I discovered a peculiar resonance between its ideas and my professional outputs thus far.

For years, I have been fascinated by the gap between how consumers are presumed to behave and how we *actually* behave. The law, particularly in contract and consumer protection, has operated under the illusion that people are rational actors, diligently reading terms and conditions and making decisions with the cold logic of Star Trek's Mr Spock. Spoiler alert: we do not. Much of what I covered in my doctoral thesis seemed to be bubbling up in consumer law dialogues, which made me want to dive deeper into the theories about consumer behaviour and how the law frequently gets it wrong. Over that academic year, I read extensively on the topic, and those ideas form the theoretical backbone of much of what you'll find in this book. However, consumer behaviour is not just a theoretical curiosity. It's also the playground of some of the most insidious forms of manipulation we encounter today. Enter dark patterns.

I've always been a fan of mentalists and psychological illusionists like Derren Brown, who can nudge people into making choices they believe are their own. Watching these performances is thrilling and unnerving and reminds me how easily our minds can be steered. Dark patterns operate on the same principles but with far less entertainment value and far more harm. These manipulative design techniques exploit psychological triggers, such as urgency, guilt, or social proof, to guide users into decisions that benefit businesses – and often harm consumers.

Allow me to provide a brief taxonomy of these patterns to set the stage. Coercive patterns are among the most common and effective. Consider the ubiquitous countdown timers urging you to 'Act Now!' before the deal of a lifetime disappears. These patterns create a false sense of urgency, pressuring users into hasty decisions. Obstructive patterns, on the other hand, are designed to frustrate. If you've ever attempted to cancel a subscription only to be confronted with labyrinthine processes that rival Kafka's worst nightmares, you've encountered this category. Then there are the deceptive patterns – design choices that intentionally mislead. These are the dark wizards of the interface world, hiding opt-out options in the digital equivalent of a broom cupboard or presenting information in ways that confuse rather than clarify. Finally, manipulative patterns exploit our social instincts. From guilt-inducing 'Are you sure you want to leave?' prompts to fake reviews and social proof, these tactics prey on our psychological vulnerabilities.

The problem with dark patterns is that they don't just exploit our cognitive biases; they institutionalise them. They weave manipulation into the very fabric of our digital lives. And here lies the rub: regulation, as it currently stands, is woefully ill-equipped to address this. The GDPR, heralded as a silver bullet for Big Tech's excesses, has been more like a well-meaning but slightly inept guardian. While it has achieved some successes, such as increasing transparency around data collection, it has not lived up to its initial promises. The fact that the EU has had to churn out an entire library of new regulations – the Digital Services Act, the AI Act, the Data Act – suggests that policymakers know this too. And yet, in many law schools, information technology law remains an afterthought, with data protection dominating the curriculum to an almost absurd degree. This overconcentration has led to a peculiar myopia where GDPR specialists demand to regulate AI as if consent boxes and privacy notices can solve the challenges of algorithmic opacity and automated decision-making.

This book argues that dark patterns and deceptive design extend beyond user interfaces and consumer protection. They are embedded in system architecture, shaping choices, triggering nudges, and influencing behaviour. These manipulations operate beneath the surface – within algorithms, data pipelines, and business models that prioritise engagement, conversion, and profit. Dark patterns are merely the visible tip of a broader system of deceptive design.

This topic is both complex and compelling because it spans multiple disciplines. Understanding and regulating deceptive design requires insights from behavioural economics, psychology, computer science, and law – yet these fields often operate in silos. Lawyers draft regulations based on outdated behavioural models, designers create interfaces without considering legal consequences, and technologists build systems prioritising efficiency over fairness. Consumer protection authorities view big tech differently from data protection authorities under the law. In one silo, you are a consumer; in another, you are a data subject. These are not the same.

It is tempting to believe that regulation alone can solve the problems of dark patterns and deceptive design, but I remain sceptical. While maximising opportunities for enforcement is necessary, the law alone is insufficient. We require a more profound shift in how we perceive technology, design, and their societal impact – rethinking the norms, values, and incentives that shape digital ecosystems. This involves questioning whether increased engagement is beneficial or if user autonomy can coexist with business models built on manipulation. The law is one tool; education, advocacy, and innovation are equally vital in resisting deceptive design.

This book is the product of academic inquiry, professional experience, and personal curiosity. It stems from a stormy day in Malta, years of wrestling with regulatory theory, and a fascination with the psychology of persuasion. It is also a call to arms – an invitation to examine the digital spaces we navigate critically. Whether you are a lawyer, designer, technologist, or concerned citizen, I hope you find something here that challenges or inspires you. And if you're paying attention, you might spot a few Easter eggs – small rewards for the curious, much like the subject of this book itself. If not, perhaps I'll see you at a Derren Brown show, where at least the manipulation is honest.

Dr Mark Leiser
Scotland 2025

ACKNOWLEDGEMENTS

Writing a book about dark patterns and deceptive design has been both a maze and a mirror – an exercise in exploring the deceptive twists of technology while reflecting on the people who helped me navigate this journey. First and foremost, I sincerely thank Professor Andrew Murray, Head of the Law School and Professor of Information Technology Law at the London School of Economics. Andrew, you have been my mentor, advisor, and close friend through this process. Your insights are unparalleled, your advice unfailingly wise, and your sense of humour much needed. I appreciate the time you took out of your day to read chapters of this book.

A close second are all the people at Bloomsbury/Hart Publishing, particularly Verity Stuart and my editor, Roberta Bassi. Your feedback has undoubtedly made this a much better book. I appreciate the opportunity you provided and your support in bringing it to fruition.

To Dr Mireille Caruana of the University of Malta: Thank you for accidentally nudging me into consumer law. Your 'detour' led me exactly where I needed to go – right into the heart of this work. Special thanks to my partners managing the LSD Enforcement Database at Deceptive. Design – Dr Cristiana Santos and Kosha Doshi. I would also like to thank Yordanka Ivanova and Irina Orssich of the European Commission and now the AI Office for their trust in me over the summer of 2024 to write a background report on the constitutive elements of Article 5(1)(a) and (b) of the EU's AI Act. Much of this work appears (in condensed form) in the AI Office's Guidelines on Prohibitions.

I extend my deepest gratitude to my reviewers: Mr Rohit Hebbale Ramkumar, my former Advanced Masters student who is now the AI Compliance Officer and DPO at Eltemate. Thank you for your sharp critiques and fresh perspective, which strengthened this book. I also wish to express my gratitude to Ms Saba Şahika Tahmaz Üzeltürk of Yeditepe University for her assistance with the book's visuals. My heartfelt thanks go to Marie Potel-Saville at Fair Patterns for her feedback on elements of

Chapter 8 and her tireless work to make digital spaces more equitable. Likewise, I appreciate my former student, Ms Vera Nuijens, for providing valuable feedback on Chapter 8.

To all the students, organisations, regulators, and civil society groups who have welcomed me into their offices or video conferences to discuss the dangers of dark patterns and deceptive design: thank you for listening, challenging, and inspiring me. I would also like to extend my gratitude to Egelyn Braun at the European Commission, Dries Cuijpers of the Dutch ACM, and Finn Lützow-Holm Myrstad, Director of Digital Policy at the Norwegian Consumer Council, for your commitment to holding platforms accountable and fostering a fairer digital landscape.

Most importantly, I cannot thank Dr Harry Brignull, the original crusader against dark patterns, enough. Your feedback and encouragement have fundamentally shaped the very core of this book. Thank you for generously sharing your time, insights, and unwavering commitment to exposing and dismantling deceptive design.

Finally, to George Green. Your understanding and unwavering patience have made this book possible. You've been my anchor when the world felt overwhelming and my greatest champion when I needed it most. Thank you for every moment you reminded me to breathe, laugh, and keep going.

With appreciation,
Mark

DARK PATTERNS VS DECEPTIVE DESIGN TERMINOLOGY EXPLAINED

In 2010, Dr Harry Brignull coined the term 'dark patterns' to describe a 'user interface that has been carefully crafted to trick users into doing things, such as buying overpriced insurance with their purchase or signing up for recurring bills'.[1] After registering darkpatterns.org, he made available a 'pattern library with the specific goal of naming and shaming deceptive user interfaces'.[2] Based on Brignull's work, **user interface dark patterns** represent open and overt manipulative tactics that directly influence user decision-making. Thus, these patterns are quickly identified, such as when designers deliberately obscure or hide an unsubscribe button. Dr Cristiana Santos and I argued in an academic paper that **darker patterns** are more subtle and elusive. These patterns employ persuasive design techniques to exploit user vulnerabilities or biases, leading to outcomes like hidden fees or misleading advertising. Users often realise the consequences of these patterns only after the fact. The **darkest patterns** involving more complex tactics are found in the **system architecture.** The term 'deceptive design' covers all three.

Deceptive design strategies range from deterministic systems, which use advanced coding to ensure specific outcomes, to stochastic (non-deterministic) systems, where outputs vary unpredictably, as seen in machine learning models. Unlike traditional dark patterns that can be mapped in flowcharts, these complex techniques defy straightforward analysis.

Manipulative design exists on a spectrum, from visible dark patterns to deeply embedded, opaque tactics. While legal frameworks regulate explicit manipulations, many deceptive strategies operate beyond these rules, hidden in algorithmic processes and subtle interface nudges.

Figure 1 What Deceptive Design Entails

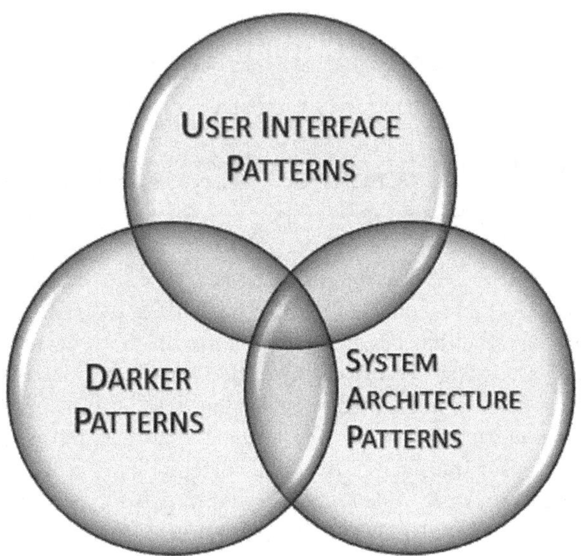

Deceptive design spans user interfaces, system architectures, and machine learning, systematically exploiting user vulnerabilities to shape behaviour.

Addressing these evolving manipulations requires robust regulation, ethical design principles, and technological scrutiny. Recognising deceptive design in its full scope is essential for protecting user autonomy, ensuring transparency, and preventing exploitation – especially for vulnerable populations.

Finally, I recognise that some readers view the term 'dark patterns' as perpetuating racial stereotypes. This racialised language was one of the reasons behind the shift to 'deceptive patterns' on the deceptive.design website. However, 'dark patterns' has become an established legal term in Europe. Therefore, I have used it here to reflect its official usage in legal frameworks.

TABLE OF CONTENTS

PART ONE
DARK, DARKER, AND DARKEST PATTERNS

PART THREE
THE FIGHT AGAINST DARK PATTERNS
AND DECEPTIVE DESIGN

Dark, Darker, and Darkest Patterns

1

A Frightening Future
Awaits, Unless …

1.1. Introduction

The algorithm is patient, the data plentiful, and the user unsuspecting. Every click, typo, or hesitation becomes a breadcrumb leading to a profile – crafted not to serve the user but to serve those who profit from knowing them better than they know themselves. Vulnerability becomes currency in the opaque interplay of AI and ambition, and autonomy is its price. What happens when the systems we've built to assist us become architects of our exploitation? These systems do not simply reflect human intent; they amplify it, automating the biases, ambitions, and greed embedded in their design. The question is no longer whether such technologies can serve humanity but whose humanity they serve – and at what cost? To understand the stakes, consider three stark examples of AI systems that optimise profit while eroding autonomy and fundamental rights.

Jessica, a typical teenager, visits Facebook to play a game promising to reveal what *spirit animal* she most likely relates to. Her mum reprimands her from upstairs, 'Put your phone away and get back to doing your homework!' Jessica duly complies and visits her school's online repository to download her homework. Her first assignment of the day is to complete a science report. She uses the same cloud-based processor her school has made available for three years, typing out the definition of a proton, its relationship with electrons, and the number of neutrons. A squiggly red line indicates a spelling mistake. She corrects it and moves on to the next part of the assignment. She visits a science website to learn about protons and their function in atoms. Much of the language is too complex for her. She struggles

> to comprehend it, so she searches for 'atoms made easy' via Google. She makes a mistake typing in the search term, but the search giant catches it and provides results that reflect the correct spelling.

The slow typing speeds, the typos, the search term, and the mistakes are all data points – or titbits of information that, on their own, do not reveal much. A 'black box' somewhere knows something that Jessica, her parents, and her teachers might not: Jessica generated data points that match the profile of someone with difficulties writing words properly, poor spelling, and decoding abilities. An algorithm or an AI system has 'learned' that Jessica, who has only begun writing a simple report for her science class, might have learning challenges or even a disorder. When put together, these data points form a profile of someone with a learning disability. This revelation, while potentially helpful for Jessica's educational needs, also raises serious concerns about potential exploitation. What happens when a commercial actor or an organisation of the state takes advantage of this inferred diagnosis? What if she is deemed unworthy or eugenically undesirable?

But the algorithm is not done. Later, when Jessica signs up for a new app, Jessica is asked to agree to the terms and conditions of the privacy policy. This is a crucial moment, as understanding and agreeing to these policies can help protect Jessica's personal information and ensure it is used responsibly.

Privacy Policy:

> **Data Utilization and Exfiltration Protocol:** Pursuant to the stipulations delineated herein, your data subsets may be subject to aggregation, analysis, and extrapolation by designated processors. Data fiduciary duties bind these processors and employ cryptographically secure data obfuscation techniques, ensuring the non-identifiability of your personage. This robust security measure is in place to protect your data. Notwithstanding the aforementioned, data may be disseminated to third-party contingents upon the condition of explicit consent, which shall be subsumed under the auspices of tacit approval unless otherwise revoked in a manner consistent with the procedural dictates outlined in Section 8, Subsection 3, Paragraph ii of this document. Furthermore, all data transactions are conducted strictly to the principles of minimisation, whereby only the requisite data parcels necessary to fulfil transactionally pertinent obligations are processed. Compliance with this protocol is subject to periodic audits by an independent certifying body to ascertain adherence to statutorily mandated data protection edicts.

The intentionally complex and verbose privacy policy is presented to Jessica after the system aggregates all her data points and determines that she matches the profile of someone with dyslexia. The policy is then personalised to exploit Jessica's vulnerability. It's not just the language used; the policy is automated and personalised to take advantage of what the machine was designed to identify: Jessica's vulnerability.

Now imagine the following scenario:

Harriet is quickly approaching the first anniversary of her grandpa's passing. The memory of her grandfather, a lovely, thoughtful man with reading glasses perched on his nose above a soft and gentle smile, is still fresh in her mind. Today, however, her emotions are not about reminiscing. She is dealing with an online e-commerce site whose delivery did not arrive on time. Her frustration turns to anger when she realises the only means of engaging with the company's customer service department is through an online chatbot. Reluctantly and begrudgingly, she initiates the conversation, expecting to type a barrage of complaints about breaching the agreed delivery times. Instead, a digital avatar appears – an older adult, a grandfatherly cardigan-wearing figure with a slightly stooped posture and a calm-reassuring voice, asks how he can help Harriet with her problem. Harriet's demeanour changes and deference appears as she unconsciously acknowledges the customer service agent's seniority and experience. She considers him wise and worthy of her respect, not because of his ability to solve customer service issues, but because of her middle-class upbringing; respecting elders was not just taught but expected.

Harriet did not comprehend that her grandfather's obituary was posted online, doubling up as data pumped into an AI model that predicts when Harriet might be most susceptible to digital manipulation. Nor did she realise that Grandpa Harry's profile pic was scraped from her Facebook account before she went to university. Nor did Harriet immediately grasp that her customer service agent was not real; he was an AI-generated agent. On closer inspection, she noticed the chat window's disclaimer that the customer service agent was synthetic. But at this point, she was locked into the agent – artificial or not, she could not get angry at this lovely, old 'man' who reassured her in his grandfatherly voice that delivery had indeed been made. Her package was left with her neighbour, 'a lovely lady named Mrs Wilson'.

Beneath the website's chat window is a complex system architecture that collects, stores, and aggregates personal information about Harriet, her social connections, and an unsupervised machine-learning system that feeds, in part, on publicly available information from the internet. Another system generates avatars based on those insights. Not only did the system know that Harriet's grandfather had passed from an online obituary, but that it was coming up on the first anniversary of his death. From their interaction history, it was 'learned' that grandfather and granddaughter were close and that she might be more susceptible to remaining a customer if presented with an avatar resembling her grandpa. Although it is transparent that Harriet communicated with an AI-generated customer service agent, the system that *chooses* what that avatar looks and sounds like is not. The chatbot is personalised based on her profile as potentially vulnerable. The dialogue is designed to take advantage of her situation, and the avatar manifests itself in a manner unique to Harriet.

Finally, consider the following example:

Roberta enjoys a night out with her colleagues after work. At the end of the evening, after a couple of glasses of wine, she catches a train that takes her home. Realising her stop was approaching, she ordered a taxi via an app on her mobile phone to take her from the train station to her apartment. Usually, she walks, but on this occasion, it is raining and cold outside, and she feels a little tipsy. She notices that her preferred app is pricing taxis slightly higher than usual. Normally, she would shop around a little for another cab, but she just noticed that her battery is down to 4 per cent, so she wants to ensure a taxi awaits her upon arrival at the train station. She booked the taxi at a rate 20 per cent higher than would typically be expected at this time. But it's Friday night, wet outside, and she wants to get home. The media have recently reported an increase in crime along her route. It's prudent not to risk it. Better safe than sorry. Roberta did not notice that the font size of her battery level had increased slightly, bringing it to her attention. Nor did she realise she had a 10 per cent battery just a few minutes ago. Had she gone onto another app, she might have noticed that another cheaper taxi company had cars standing by. She did not

> recognise that the pricing she was provided was unique to her – calculated considering her location data (pub, train, train station), weather data (cold and rainy), and purchase history (a couple of glasses of wine). Nor was she aware that an analysis of her browsing history determined that she might feel vulnerable when walking home, thanks to those news stories about crime in the neighbourhood.

Roberta's data, combined with the taxi app's personalised pricing offered to her as a consumer, facilitated manipulating the physical representation of her phone's battery level on the user interface via malicious coding in the phone's system architecture. It took multiple forms of deceptive design to get to the point where Roberta overpaid for her taxi. Would she have undertaken to hire a taxi without the deception? Most certainly. However, would she have undertaken to take *this* taxi at a 20 per cent premium to others available on the market without the deceptive design affecting her choices? Probably not. But where was the deception? One might argue that the system was designed to manipulate Roberta into paying a premium.

These three examples reveal the *convergence* of data, algorithmic profiling, and machine learning into systems that deceive us into doing something we might not ordinarily want to do. Deceptive design elements are present in data collection and processing, profiling and automated decision-making, and manifestation of the user interface or user experience. These might not be possible yet, but do we want these happening worldwide?

And what if I told you that, despite a plethora of laws and acts to bring big tech to heel, not even one is empowered by lawmakers to regulate the deceptive design found embedded in the system architecture? Across the entirety of the *digital design acquis*, only deceptive design in the *user interface* is prohibited. Even worse, under the flagship law of the European Union (hereafter, EU) regulating big tech, the Digital Services Act (hereafter, DSA) only applies to a narrowly defined group of 'online platforms'.[1]

Yet a far bigger problem is that consumer protection, data protection, platform and AI regulation do not provide an answer to these issues on their own. Unfortunately for EU citizens, this is how the scope of each significant law regulating technology has been compartmentalised. EU data protection law only looks after 'data subjects', consumer protection only applies to 'consumers', and the flagship AI Act only regulates 'AI systems'. Lawmakers have opted out of a systems-wide approach to regulating big tech, opting for a more 'siloed' approach.

This poses a few problems. First, the processing of personal data in the EU does not have to rely on the consent of the data subjects. The legitimate interests ground of the GDPR acts as a broad lawful basis, extending cover to companies in the business of extracting value from personal data (whether this complies with the fairness and transparency principles of the GDPR is another story).[2] Thus, a company seeking to profit from exploiting data analytics would theoretically have a legitimate interest in grabbing as much data as possible to train its artificial intelligence (AI). Second, consumer law can be slow and difficult to enforce. Take, for example, the general prohibition on unfairness found in the Unfair Commercial Practices Directive.[3] To fall foul of this provision, enforcers would have to prove that the (a) practice in question was a commercial one, (b) that it took place between a business and a consumer, (c) that it is contrary to the requirements of professional diligence of the profession accused of the unfair practice, and that it (d) materially distorts or is likely to distort the (e) economic behaviour about the product of the (f) average consumer or the average consumer of a group if the commercial practice is directed to a group of consumers.

That is much stuff to prove. What, for example, does a consumer do to prove that a business caused a 'material distortion'? How does a consumer prove their behaviour was typical of the 'average consumer'?

Most consumers do not take action to enforce their rights. The consumer protection authorities do the hard work. However, consider the following: First, a study by the Dutch Consumer Protection Authority (ACM), in conjunction with the European Commission, determined that 40 per cent of all websites used 'dark patterns' to trick consumers.[4] In another study dubbed a 'mystery shopping exercise', the European Commission determined that 97 per cent of all websites used at least one deceptive technique.[5] Scholarly investigations have revealed the pervasive use of deceptive design practices across various digital platforms, encompassing social media networks, e-commerce sites, mobile applications, and video games.[6]

However, an academic named Martin Samek of Charles University determined that consumer protection authorities in Eastern Europe were paid little more than the national minimum wage and had little to no experience working with digital technologies.[7] There is quite a gap between the number of websites undertaking some deceptive design technique and the number of qualified experts capable of determining the deception and how it influences consumers. These deceptive designs are so prevalent that enforcers cannot do their jobs properly.

How did we get here? As I will outline in the next section, three trends also converged, giving rise to a superstorm of techniques to trick users into doing something that they would not normally do: first, the increase in tracking and persuasion technologies (or, if you are a disciple of Suzanna Zuboff, Surveillance Capitalism[8]); second, the standardisation of design techniques commonly deployed in the user interface to capture user attention, increase engagement, and show compliance with legal rules and requirements; finally, increased legal obligations to show, for example, that users consented to data processing were imposed on platforms, websites and app developers. For extra spice, add a healthy dash of competition among platforms to capture a limited number of users. In this superstorm, designers almost inevitably adopted 'dark patterns 'to trick and deceive users.

1.2. When and why 'Patterns' Went 'Dark'

> Dark Arts are underhanded, deceptive, or manipulative techniques used to achieve one's goals in politics, business, or other areas. These are often considered unethical or morally dubious strategies.

Before presenting the first conference paper on the topic, Dr Harry Brignull worked on the concept and terminology of 'dark patterns' for a while, relying on others in his field for examples of tricks websites use to get users to do something that goes against their interests.[9] Others working in different disciplines deployed terminology like 'nudging',[10] 'choice architecture',[11] and more recently, 'sludging'.[12] Behind some of this was a change in thinking about economic modelling.

As it happened, the turn of the century saw an academic migration away from twentieth-century economic theories of human beings as rational actors and more nuanced modelling of actual human behaviour. Nobel Prize in Economics Winners like Richard Thaler, regulatory theorists like Cass Sunstein, and cognitive psychologists like Nobel Prize Winner Daniel Kahneman theorised that humans are not the all-knowing, emotionless, and utility-maximising agents rational theorists claimed.

Rather than Mr Spock, humans are more akin to Homer Simpson – lazy, emotional, impulsive, irrational beings who rarely make optimal decisions. A body of scholarly work suggested that humans use mental shortcuts called heuristics to make decisions across varied fields like health and financial well-being, retirement planning, and dietary choices. We even use these heuristics when deciding our security and what political party to vote for. Kahneman and his research partner, Amos Tversky, argued that many shortcuts result in poor decision-making, systematic errors, and biases.[13] Their academic opposition, Gerd Gigerenzer, led a school of thought that humans use *fast and frugal* heuristics. These generally serve humanity well.[14] For the *fast and frugal* school, environmental factors are more responsible for humans' bad decisions than we default to using mental shortcuts during moments of uncertainty.

The *heuristics and biases* and the *fast and frugal* schools led to a voluminous amount of work showcasing how regulators can use design tactics to 'nudge' people to make better decisions. To collect more tax receipts, better design correspondence with taxpayers is needed. If policymakers are concerned about a shortage of organ donors, change the design of your organ donation form. To overcome inertia among workers, make them opt-out of their pension plan rather than relying on them to opt-in. Want people to get more exercise? Design your buildings, town centres, and urban spaces to get them walking. The list goes on.

Unfortunately, many of this work's insights were leaned into by businesses and integrated into narratives around how to get potential customers to engage, stay on their platforms, and do what the corporation wanted. The good intentions behind Thaler and Sunstein's work (helping policymakers implement inexpensive changes to existing design strategies to achieve better regulatory outcomes) were hijacked by corporations seeking to use similar insights in design to get users to do something that benefitted the platform at the user's expense. Academic work lamenting over 'hypernudging',[15] the personalisation of stylised nudges in the online environment, increased awareness of the pervasiveness of AdTech and digital marketing tools, and the anger at the Edward Snowden revelations about the extent of state surveillance and the Cambridge Analytica scandal started international dialogues on the capabilities of technologies to collect, profile, and process individuals' data, as well as the role of private platforms management over the digital equivalent to the town square.[16]

European legislators, sensing not only frustration from the electorate over US government spying and increased state insecurity over several terrorist attacks around the world, began legislating a limited set of electronic privacy protections and individual rights from state-sponsored surveillance,[17] provided an updated set of business rules and obligations to tech companies seeking access to or operating within the EU Single Market,[18] provided the security services and law enforcement agencies with a proportional legal framework for the interference with fundamental rights and freedoms as bestowed to every citizen under the EU Charter and enhanced existing legal regimes for the processing of *personal data.*

The General Data Protection Regulation (GDPR), enacted in 2018, is the EU's flagship law regarding the processing of personal data. For some, the GDPR is a prohibitive regime: No one is permitted to process personal data unless they have a lawful basis for doing so and comply with an exhaustive list of 'data protection principles'. For others, the GDPR is facilitative. Two of the GDPR's objectives concern the free movement of personal data around the European Union. One is explicit. The other prohibits member states from imposing barriers to the free movement of personal data. The last objective focuses on respecting the fundamental right to data protection. The truth probably lies somewhere in the middle: the GDPR is about the free movement of personal data around the European Union in a manner that respects fundamental rights. At its heart, EU data protection regime supporters believe the GDPR is about *informational self-determination* or *control* over what happens to your data. For the cynics and businesses in data processing, the theory of control is overstated. Anyone can process personal data if they satisfy one of six lawful bases before doing so (and comply with some limited principles). Only one – 'consent' – provides data subjects with control over their data. The other five are context-specific – is processing necessary for the performance of a contract? Is there a national rule mandating the processing of personal data? Is it in the public interest to process personal data? Does a data controller have a legitimate interest in processing your data? Is processing necessary in the vital interests of the data subject?

Consent is, however, required for processing data that might reveal special categories of sensitive information about a person. Location data is not, per se, sensitive on its own. But if it demonstrates that you visited a mosque every Friday or a church on Sunday, one could infer your religion. A photograph is not *de facto* sensitive data but might reveal someone's racial characteristics. A record of your grocery purchases might reveal your religious affiliation (halal or kosher food), your sexual health (pregnancy tests, condoms), and health information (frequency of tobacco and alcohol purchases). Because we must provide it to function in the modern world, consent is arguably the most crucial lawful basis of the EU's data protection regime. With the proliferation of mobile devices, social media networks, and apps in modern society, almost all aspects of digital technologies operate under a legal requirement to obtain consent before processing personal data and an obligation to prove that they received it if the regulator ever audits.[19]

The conundrum designers faced during the growth of the information economy is almost worthy of empathy. There was considerable competition in the marketplace as platforms fought for primacy, pressure to attract users to lock in network effects, and a legal obligation to obtain consent before processing personal data. Making user consent *easy* to get seems a natural and logical step for a designer tasked with complying with a legal obligation and increasing user engagement. Why place barriers in the user interface when nudging users to consent is an alternative?

The problem is that 'consent' has a specific meaning. The GDPR requires consent to be freely given, specifically informed, and unambiguous.[20] It is also tied to the purpose principle. Consent is only valid when the data subject is made aware of the specific purpose of the processing. Rushing people through the process might increase engagement, but it does not allow for the intended reflection needed to exercise control over how one's data is processed. As designers developed solutions to the consent conundrum, a race to the bottom resulted in the design that made obtaining consent incredibly easy.

The evolution from designing for ease of use to employing manipulative techniques illustrates a significant shift in design ethics. As companies competed to streamline user experiences, including obtaining consent, the line between simplification and deception blurred. This shift was driven by intense competition among platforms and websites, each vying to minimise user resistance to consent processes. However, this competitive drive led to the widespread adoption of deceptive practices or 'dark patterns' to secure user consent. Often barely noticeable to the average user, these techniques effectively coerced consent rather than genuinely obtaining it, compromising the informed and voluntary agreement principle. Thus, what began as an endeavour to enhance user engagement evolved into a manipulation strategy.

Based on how commonplace the term 'dark patterns' has become, one would be forgiven for believing that Harry Brignull is a boisterous, self-serving advocate for ethical web design. On the contrary, he is remarkably humble and unassuming. He is the opposite of Max Schrems, a vocal privacy advocate and active litigator. Until recently, he was a pensions company's user experience and innovation director. He has no formal legal training and does the 'ethicist' part of his job in his spare time. Although he never worked as a web designer, coining the phrase 'dark patterns'[21] and thus setting off a decade of regulatory reform across continents and jurisdictions will be part of his legacy.

Harry is a remarkable character. One only must speak to him briefly to see his evident passion for fairer design. By deploying the term 'dark pattern', Harry spoke in the language of designers. His terminology was also adopted by lawyers. This decision was instrumental in getting dialogue from others working in the space who shared Harry's frustrations with a growing number of unethical design practices. An essential aspect of this dialogue is using the word 'pattern'. A *user interface design pattern* is a common and reusable solution to a standard and recurring problem designers must solve in the user interface. In other words, when a designer is plagued with a task (x), they look for examples of how other designers solved x. Eventually, these patterns become standard practices among user interface (UI) and user experience (UX) designers. In this sense, the task is solved by design-based means.

Like the dark arts, Harry was concerned that underhanded, deceptive, or manipulative 'dark' patterns were implemented to solve a variety of user interface-related tasks. Dark patterns represent a critical concept within digital design, particularly concerning user interfaces and user experiences across various platforms. This term encapsulates a range of manipulative techniques employed to subtly or overtly influence user decisions and actions in ways that benefit the service provider, often at the user's expense. At its core, a dark pattern is designed to deceive, coerce, or manipulate users into making decisions they might not have made if presented with transparent, straightforward choices. The essence of dark patterns lies in their capacity to exploit cognitive biases and psychological vulnerabilities, harnessing these human factors to steer behaviours in a predetermined direction dictated by the design's architects – typically for commercial or data extraction purposes.

Dark patterns do not operate in isolation; they are part of broader strategies to maximise engagement, boost conversions, or push profitable actions at users' expense. They nudge users into consenting to unnecessary data collection, trick them into subscriptions, or steer them through convoluted paths to unintended outcomes. These tactics exploit behavioural psychology, using interfaces that bypass rational thought and trigger automatic responses. The goal is to shape a digital environment where choices feel voluntary but are subtly engineered. Dark patterns embed themselves within digital ecosystems, exploiting individual vulnerabilities and reinforcing systemic biases. Algorithms may selectively show or hide information based on demographics, perpetuating stereotypes or prioritising profit over fairness. This exacerbates social and economic inequalities, as vulnerable groups face greater risks of deception and financial harm. Additionally, these manipulative designs thrive on digital illiteracy, making it harder for users to detect or resist them.

1.3. Dark Patterns and the Law

As digital technologies drive innovation and connectivity, they also introduce risks and potential misuse. Regulators aim to curb the most harmful deceptive designs, ensuring fairness, transparency, and respect for user autonomy. Deceptive design goes beyond surface-level tricks like misleading buttons or hidden terms. As illustrated in this chapter's examples, deception often lies deep within algorithms and data processing, sometimes powered by AI. These opaque manipulations – dubbed the 'darkest' patterns – pose significant challenges for regulators and consumers, requiring specialised knowledge and tools for detection.

Regarding legality and regulation, the emergence and proliferation of dark patterns have drawn the attention of lawmakers and regulatory bodies.[22] For example, the Federal Trade Commission (FTC) has intensified efforts to combat dark patterns – tactics companies use to manipulate consumer behaviour. These practices include subscription traps, where consumers are misled or obstructed when trying to cancel services, and junk fees, where hidden costs are revealed only at the final stages of a transaction. The FTC's new 'Click to Cancel' Rule, part of the updated Negative Option Rule, addresses deceptive subscription practices by requiring sellers to ensure transparency, truthfulness, and ease in subscription cancellations.[23] This rule targets common issues where consumers face unclear terms, unauthorised charges, and deliberate obstacles to cancel subscriptions. Sellers must provide accessible, clear information before sign-up, prove consumer awareness of subscription terms, and offer a cancellation process as straightforward as sign-up.

Non-compliance risks liability for civil penalties and redress, reinforcing consumer autonomy and deterring manipulative business practices that exploit consumer inertia or confusion. The rule signals an FTC commitment to consumer rights and transparency in digital transactions.[24]

The FTC's enforcement actions against major companies such as Amazon, Adobe, and Vonage highlight the agency's focus on ensuring transparency and preventing companies from using manipulative interfaces to trap consumers into unwanted services or payments. The FTC's proposed rules, including a 'click-to-cancel' provision and a ban on hidden fees, aim to make subscription models and online interfaces more straightforward for consumers. The agency is also addressing the emerging use of AI in perpetuating dark patterns, ensuring that digital manipulation through personalised interfaces and algorithms does not undermine consumer rights. The FTC's proactive regulatory and enforcement efforts reflect a commitment to protecting consumers from deceptive designs and fostering a fairer digital marketplace.[25]

On 4 September 2024 the California Privacy Protection Agency (CPPA) issued an Enforcement Advisory on Avoiding Dark Patterns: Clear and Understandable Language, Symmetry in Choice. It urged businesses to ensure user interfaces clearly and symmetrically present consumer choices – such as opt-outs. The California Consumer Privacy Act (CCPA) defines dark patterns as interfaces undermining consumer autonomy or privacy rights. For example, opt-out data-sharing options must be clear and balanced; ambiguity may constitute a dark pattern. The Advisory also warns businesses may unintentionally create dark patterns if their interfaces impair consumer decision-making. In other words, the focus is on the design's effect, not the intent. The Advisory does not reference any specific enforcement actions taken by the CPPA but provides insights drawn from the agency's enforcement activities under California law.[26] Colorado Privacy Act[27] and, most recently, also into Indian law.[28]

1.4. Manipulation Beneath the Interface

At the start of this chapter, I outlined three examples of how developers can manipulate users into doing something they would not ordinarily do but for deception. But notice there were no visual tricks, confusing buttons, or subscription traps. These are forms of deceptive design rooted in AI-capable design techniques we already know exist. The capability of AI to personalise deception based on individual psychological profiles calls for an urgent reassessment of design standards and legal boundaries. The challenge lies in identifying these manipulations and crafting laws that can adapt to the complexities of AI technologies that operate at a level often invisible to the user. By acknowledging the depth of deceptive design and the sophisticated use of AI, stakeholders can better safeguard user autonomy against the increasingly subtle forces shaping user behaviour in the digital realm.

Down the street from where I have undertaken most of my research on dark patterns is a wonderfully capable academic based at Utrecht University, Dr Cristiana Santos. We published a paper outlining that the most deceptive design in the user interface is visible and recognisable to users as a dark pattern.[29] We also started analysing enforcement measures from consumer, competition, and data protection authorities and convinced Harry Brignull to host our enforcement database on his website.[30] During our dialogues, we convinced Harry that deceptive design was much broader than user interface dark patterns and extended beneath the user interface. Harry was publishing his book, directed at designers, about the manipulative practices that have become commonplace in their profession. He titled his book *Deceptive Patterns*, making large chunks available for free on his website.[31] An excellent read, the ethos behind rebranding the darkpatterns.org website as deceptive patterns were primarily to address dark patterns beneath the surface of the user interface embedded in the architecture and the systems that feed the interface.

My work with Dr Cristiana Santos and our collaboration with Harry Brignull on redefining dark patterns highlights a crucial shift in digital design discourse. Expanding the scope to deceptive design beneath the user interface acknowledges manipulation beyond visible tricks. Our initiative to track enforcement actions and engage the design community through resources like Brignull's book reflects a proactive stance against these practices. The digital landscape has evolved, with the current datafication phase relying on AI to extract value from vast datasets. While AI enhances efficiency, it facilitates manipulation through visible and hidden mechanisms. Dark patterns are just one aspect of deceptive design, which operates deep within digital architectures, subtly shaping user behaviour.

Market competition fosters innovation but also encourages manipulative practices. Companies may push legal boundaries, using dark patterns to influence choices or covertly harvesting data. This manipulation affects not just consumer behaviour but broader societal norms. Lawmakers must balance regulation with technological progress, ensuring fairness and transparency. Understanding both surface-level and systemic manipulations is paramount. Like a house's strength lies in its foundation, digital integrity depends on underlying architectures. Regulators must go beyond UI-based dark patterns and address deeper deceptive design issues to protect consumers, safeguard democratic processes, and maintain digital trust.

As we advance, this book will adopt the following terminology: Generally speaking, 'dark patterns' refers to manipulative design in the user interface. In contrast, 'deceptive design' goes beyond just *user interface dark patterns*. Think of an iceberg.[32] Dark patterns are the tip of the iceberg – the things that you see, you know, that are there. Deceptive design is *both* user interface dark patterns and the things you cannot see – the manipulation beneath the interface. There is overlap. Dark patterns should be seen as a subset of deceptive design techniques. Still, I have tried to keep this distinction to help readers understand what is at stake when interfaces and systems are designed without considering the implications of their use.

This distinction between dark patterns and deceptive design is critical, highlighting the multifaceted nature of manipulation within digital environments. As the more visible manifestations of deceptive practices, dark patterns alert users and regulators to the surface-level tricks that can often be addressed with direct regulatory measures. However, deceptive design is more profound, encapsulating these visible manipulations and the more insidious ones buried within the algorithms and system architectures that support user interfaces. This deeper layer of manipulation is more challenging to detect and regulate because it operates beneath the observable surface, often exploiting psychological principles and data-driven insights to shape user behaviour in ways that are not immediately apparent.

Addressing these challenges requires a comprehensive approach that combines technological savvy, psychological insight, and legal frameworks. As AI technologies evolve, the capability to personalise deceptive strategies to exploit individual vulnerabilities becomes a significant regulatory concern. Developing legislative tools like the EU's AI Act is a step in the right direction.[33] Still, there is a pressing need for ongoing collaboration between technologists, designers, psychologists, and legal experts to ensure these tools remain effective against an ever-evolving backdrop of AI capabilities. We can only protect user autonomy and promote a digital landscape that respects user rights and fosters transparency and fairness through such interdisciplinary efforts.

As digital spaces become increasingly central to daily life, correctly understanding, exposing, and regulating deceptive design becomes a technical challenge and a societal imperative. Understanding dark patterns also involves recognising the implications of digital design. It calls for a critical examination of how technologies shape human behaviour and the responsibilities of those who create and deploy these technologies and reflects a junction in digital regulation. The intersection of design, psychology, technology, and law raises questions about the future of human autonomy in the digital age.

1.5. Some Limitations

The term 'dark patterns' transcends various potentially unlawful practices under existing laws, such as unfair commercial practices, violations of the GDPR's transparency principle, or breaches of consumer consent requirements. However, labelling a practice as a 'dark pattern' does not automatically render it illegal. Judicial interpretation and associated legal tests, which I explore in later chapters, are essential to determine the legality of such designs. This requires readers to remember that while 'dark patterns' and 'deceptive design' may suggest unlawful practices, each instance requires meticulous legal scrutiny to classify it as illegal.

Second, typologies[34] employed to differentiate and categorise deceptive patterns can obscure the definition of deceptive design as understood by leading figures within the design community.[35] Instead of proposing a new typology and crafting unique terminology, I have chosen to lean into the definition of commercial dark patterns as articulated by the Office of Economic Development (OECD):[36]

> Dark commercial patterns are business practices employing elements of digital choice architecture, particularly in online user interfaces, that subvert or impair consumer autonomy, decision-making or choice. They often deceive, coerce or manipulate consumers and are likely to cause direct or indirect consumer detriment in various ways. However, it may be difficult or impossible to measure such detriment in many instances.

Third, I use 'deceptive design' broadly.[37] This term covers techniques in both the user interface and system architecture designed to manipulate, persuade, deceive, and even foster addiction. With a coded foundation, these methods go beyond surface-level design. Scholarly interest in deceptive design has grown significantly, evolving from early classifications of UI-based dark patterns to broader system-level influences. While foundational works are cited in earlier chapters, the interdisciplinary nature of this field means some contributions are inevitably omitted due to scope and word limits. This does not diminish their importance but reflects the challenge of comprehensive coverage. With the DSA and AI Act still in the early stages, uncertainty remains around implementation, including future Codes of Practice and Guidelines. Few legal precedents exist to clarify their interpretation. My analysis in Part One, particularly regarding Article 25 DSA, is based on preliminary interpretations open to future scrutiny. This book highlights the evolving nature of these regulations and the complexities of their enforcement. Chapter two sets expectations for readers, outlining the terminological, scholarly, and legal landscapes shaping deceptive design.

1.6. The Book's Structure

This book is constructed as follows: There are three parts to this book. Part One contains chapter two, which serves as an introductory exploration into the landscape of digital design. It begins with a historical overview of design ethics. It traces the transition from user-centric principles emphasising user empowerment and satisfaction to the rise of manipulative design tactics to exploit users for commercial gains. The chapter introduces the concept of 'dark patterns'. The discussion progresses to categorising various dark pattern typologies, illustrating each with examples from different digital platforms. These typologies include misleading navigation, hidden costs, bait-and-switch tactics, and unsolicited subscription traps. The role of artificial intelligence in refining and implementing dark patterns is also explored, emphasising how AI enhances the capability of these designs to manipulate user behaviour at scale. This chapter also presents case studies from industries such as social media, e-commerce, and digital advertising to demonstrate how pervasive and impactful these deceptive practices can be. It concludes by discussing the implications of dark patterns on user behaviour and societal norms, setting a critical tone for the need for legal considerations and regulatory interventions in digital design.

Building on chapter one, chapter two explores the harms caused by dark patterns, beginning with their impact on user autonomy. It explains how these designs undermine informed decision-making, violating user agency. The chapter also examines how deceptive design erodes trust, making users wary of digital interfaces, which can reduce engagement and impact digital commerce. An economic analysis highlights how dark patterns distort market competition by undermining informed consent, crucial for fair competition and consumer protection. This chapter sets the foundation for discussions on regulatory responses and the complexities governing manipulative digital practices.

Chapter three critically analyses regulatory responses, covering efforts by consumer protection authorities, data regulators, and competition enforcers. It examines cookie consent mechanisms, showing how dark patterns have subverted transparency goals. The chapter critiques compliance failures, including deceptive consent management platforms and manipulative interface designs that nudge users toward data sharing. It also explores broader legal frameworks, such as the EU's Unfair Commercial Practices Directive and the FTC Act, which classify dark patterns as misleading and aggressive. Enforcement challenges – proving intent, subtlety of manipulation, and cross-border complexities – are discussed alongside case studies of actions against Google, Facebook, and Amazon. The chapter also highlights how dark patterns reinforce market power by locking in consumers and disadvantaging competitors. It concludes by calling for more vigorous enforcement, harmonised regulations, and deeper insights into digital manipulations to ensure consumer autonomy and fair competition.

Chapter four examines the EU's regulatory response, focusing on the DSA, DMA, Data Act, GDPR, ePrivacy Directive, and UCPD. It assesses their effectiveness in protecting user autonomy, particularly Article 25 of the DSA, which targets manipulative interface design. While the DSA promotes transparency, enforcement challenges persist due to broad language, regulatory overlaps, and difficulty addressing system-level manipulations. The DMA tackles gatekeeper dominance but prioritises market fairness over consumer protection, leaving gaps. The Data Act ensures fair data access in IoT but lacks provisions against manipulative practices in smart devices. The chapter critiques these frameworks' limitations in regulating non-traditional interfaces like virtual assistants, which embed manipulative tactics beyond UI protections. It underscores the need for integrated, adaptive regulation, refining Article 25 DSA and leveraging the AI Act's prohibitions on psychological manipulation under Articles 5(1)(a) and 5(1)(b) to address AI-driven deceptive design.

Part Two examines the evolution of dark patterns from visible UI manipulations to systemic tactics embedded in digital architectures. Chapter five categorises system architectures into *Triggered UI, complex deterministic, and non-deterministic* systems, explaining how they enable increasingly sophisticated manipulation. Triggered UI relies on simple logic, complex deterministic systems use intricate algorithms, and non-deterministic systems adapt dynamically through AI. As these systems grow more opaque, detecting manipulation becomes harder. Case studies in e-commerce, social media, and gaming illustrate cognitive bias exploitation through personalised pricing, algorithmic recommendations, and reinforcement loops, fostering dependency while eroding autonomy. Existing regulations like the DSA and GDPR primarily address surface-level manipulations, leaving deeper systemic exploitation unchecked. The chapter argues for expanded regulatory scrutiny, mainly refining Article 5(1)(a) and (b) to counter deceptive design's increasing sophistication.

Chapter six explores AI-powered deceptive design, where manipulation shifts from UI tricks to hidden, algorithmic tactics. Adaptive AI systems exploit cognitive biases invisibly, learning from user behaviour to deploy tailored manipulations like emotional nudges and dynamic pricing. Case studies reveal AI-driven distortions in shopping, finance, and other digital services, causing economic and psychological harm. The chapter critiques the EU AI Act's Article 5(1)(a) for its high threshold of proving intent and significant harm, which may allow subtle manipulative practices to persist. It calls for more substantial transparency, explainability, and proactive enforcement to regulate surface-level UI and deeper system architectures that drive digital exploitation.

Chapter seven examines how digital systems exploit vulnerabilities across informational, psychological, and systemic dimensions, mainly targeting children, the elderly, and socioeconomically disadvantaged groups. AI-driven platforms personalise manipulative tactics, amplifying harm and deepening inequalities. The chapter critiques Article 5(1)(b)'s high intervention threshold, questioning its ability to protect vulnerable users. Case studies highlight addictive design traps for children and financial coercion targeting elderly users. Existing legal frameworks often fail to address the cumulative effects of manipulation. The chapter advocates for a regulatory approach integrating fairness, inclusivity, and proactive safeguards to counter systemic exploitation beyond overt harm.

Part Three synthesises the book's key insights, tracing digital manipulation's evolution from overt UI-level dark patterns to covert, AI-driven systemic strategies. Chapter eight examines how platforms exploit cognitive biases using adaptive tools like Large Action Models (LAMs) to manipulate decisions while bypassing regulatory safeguards. It reviews legal frameworks such as the GDPR, DSA, and UCPD, assessing their strengths and limitations in combating manipulation. Case studies and judicial rulings highlight how these laws address transparency, consent, and fairness while emerging solutions like behavioural audits and technical tools offer new detection methods. The chapter concludes with a call for systemic reform, proposing a Digital Fairness Act to mandate fairness audits, algorithmic transparency, and protections for vulnerable users, ensuring ethical platform operations.

An Afterword reflects on recent developments and ties everything together. The book does not offer simple solutions but underscores the complexity of regulating digital environments. It calls for coordinated efforts to enhance transparency and protection, aiming for a safer digital future. Raising awareness and inspiring reform contributes to ongoing discussions on strengthening legal frameworks to address digital manipulation effectively.

2

Deceptive Techniques and their Associated Harms

2.1. Introduction

The previous chapter highlighted deceptive design's pervasive influence in shaping user behaviour, revealing how digital entities engineer interactions to nudge, influence, or coerce users in ways that prioritise corporate interests over autonomy. This chapter reframes dark patterns as more than mere annoyances, positioning them as urgent legal and regulatory concerns. These manipulative strategies erode trust in digital interactions, demanding stronger enforcement and a recalibrated regulatory focus. While frameworks exist, their effectiveness is undermined by weak enforcement and failure to target the most exploitable points in digital design.

At the outset, it is crucial to emphasise that user interface dark patterns are not isolated incidents but rather pervasive in various digital platforms and services, particularly those involving subscriptions, privacy settings, and online purchases. Reports from organisations like the International Consumer Protection and Enforcement Network (ICPEN) and the Federal Trade Commission (FTC) underscore the widespread use of these manipulative design practices that deceive or coerce users into making unintended decisions.[1] For instance, an ICPEN report found that 75.70 per cent of traders in a sweep of 642 used at least one dark pattern, with 66.82 per cent employing multiple dark patterns. In a mystery shopper exercise undertaken by the European Commission, 97 per cent of popular websites and apps used by EU consumers deploy at least one form of dark pattern.[2] A study by Princeton University revealed that dark patterns are widespread in e-commerce, with 11.1 per cent of 11,000 analysed shopping websites containing at least one dark pattern.[3] Among the types of dark patterns, urgency tactics like countdown timers were widespread, appearing in 393 instances across 361 websites. A 2024 report from the Swedish Consumers' Association examined the cancellation processes of 20 digital entertainment and news services in Sweden, revealing the use of dark patterns obstructing consumers from unsubscribing. The report identified five main tactics – adding unnecessary steps, creating dead ends, using visual interference, toying with emotions, and employing misleading wording – while advocating for legislative changes to simplify cancellations, requiring explicit consent for subscription renewals, and mandating notifications for inactive subscriptions.[4]

The FTC's report exposed the sophistication and prevalence of dark patterns, showing how they exploit cognitive biases to manipulate consumer behaviour. Examples include hidden costs revealed late in transactions, false claims of product popularity to create urgency, and pre-selected options coercing consent. The report highlighted companies using A/B testing to refine these tactics, increasing their effectiveness. Furthermore, dark patterns extend beyond web interfaces to mobile apps and emerging technologies like AR and VR, where manipulation risks are more significant. Companies deploy multiple dark patterns simultaneously, intensifying consumer harm and embedding these practices across the digital ecosystem. The prevalence of such tactics underscores the extensive reliance on deceptive practices in online shopping to manipulate consumer behaviour.

Regulatory bodies like the FTC and enforcement networks like ICPEN have increasingly focused on addressing these insidious tactics. Their efforts aim to shield consumers from designs that, while often subtle, result in significant consequences such as financial exploitation, privacy infringements, and an erosion of trust in digital services. The detrimental effects extend beyond individual interactions, compromising confidence in digital platforms and undermining the development of a transparent and equitable online environment. By distorting market dynamics and circumventing informed consent, dark patterns hinder efficient resource allocation, contributing to widespread economic inefficiencies. Consumers are routinely subjected to hidden fees, unwanted subscriptions, and inflated prices, systematically impairing their ability to make informed decisions. This erosion of autonomy not only degrades user experiences but also disrupts fair competition, perpetuating inefficiencies that ripple across the broader digital economy.

Chapter two explores these practices' profound and often insidious harms with this foundational understanding. It investigates the impacts of dark patterns by drawing upon interdisciplinary research from psychology, economics, human-computer interaction (HCI), digital design, and artificial intelligence. This interdisciplinary approach is essential for understanding manipulative practices and developing solutions prioritising user rights and digital equity. Through case studies and analysis, the chapter explores strategies for mitigating these harms and fostering a fairer digital environment. It begins by examining how deceptive design undermines user autonomy and dignity. Autonomy, central to personal freedom, is eroded through misleading information, pre-selected defaults, and manipulative prompts that exploit cognitive biases. These tactics strip users of control, reshaping behaviours to benefit corporate interests. This chapter underscores the need for transparency, fairness, and respect for user agency in digital systems.

2.2. Types of Dark Patterns (User Interface)

Scholars specialising in dark patterns have developed various typologies, taxonomies, and ontologies to classify and understand these deceptive design practices. Instead of reiterating exhaustive analyses and critiquing every existing framework, this discussion will focus on three notable classifications, beginning with a taxonomy developed by Harry Brignull, who coined the term 'dark patterns'. A taxonomy is a structured classification system that organises items or concepts into categories based on shared characteristics. It provides a hierarchical framework for understanding relationships between entities, making it easier to identify, study, and manage them systematically. In the context of deceptive patterns in digital design, a taxonomy helps categorise various manipulative tactics companies use to influence user behaviour. This categorisation provides clarity and facilitates discussion, regulation, and mitigation of such practices.

2.2.1. Brignull's Taxonomy

Brignull's taxonomy of dark patterns is particularly influential.[5] It systematically categorises manipulative design tactics based on their characteristics and intended effects. This approach helps identify and understand companies' specific methods to deceive users. By classifying these patterns, Brignull's taxonomy provided a framework for analysing how different techniques affect user behaviour and what regulatory measures might be necessary to address them.[6] His taxonomy not only aids in identifying and categorising deceptive practices but also highlights the need for greater transparency and fairness in digital design. By understanding these patterns, regulators, designers, and users could advocate for better design practices that respect user autonomy and promote trust in digital interactions. Through this structured approach, the goal was to mitigate the negative impacts of dark patterns and foster a more user-friendly digital environment.

Brignull's taxonomy identifies several critical categories in deceptive patterns, each encompassing specific tactics that exploit users' vulnerabilities.[7] The taxonomy arises from the need to identify and address how digital interfaces systematically manipulate users. These categories include sneaking, urgency, misdirection, social proof, scarcity, obstruction, and forced action. **Sneaking** refers to tactics where businesses add additional items or costs to a user's transaction without explicit consent. For example, an online retailer might add an unwanted magazine to a shopper's cart or reveal hidden costs only at the final checkout stage. This manipulative technique capitalises on users' inattention or the complexity of the transaction process to push through extra charges or products unnoticed. Another common tactic is **urgency**, which creates a false sense of time pressure to compel users to act quickly. Businesses create urgency through countdown timers that suggest a deal is about to expire or limited-time messages that evoke a sense of fleeting opportunity. These tactics leverage the psychological pressure of missing out, nudging users to make hasty decisions without thoroughly considering their options.

Misdirection exploits an interface's design and language to steer users toward choices that benefit the company, often at the user's expense. **Confirm shaming** uses guilt-inducing language to discourage users from opting out of service. **Visual interference** employs strategic design elements to hide or obscure less desirable options, making it difficult for users to make informed choices. **Trick wording** involves ambiguous or misleading language that confuses users into selecting options they might otherwise avoid. **Social proof** manipulates users by leveraging their tendency to follow the actions of others. Activity messages, such as notifications that '5 people purchased this item in the last hour,' create an illusion of popularity and urgency, encouraging users to conform to perceived social norms. Similarly, **testimonials** can influence decisions by showcasing supposedly genuine reviews, even when their authenticity is questionable. **Scarcity tactics** create a false impression of limited availability to increase the desirability of a product. Messages indicating low stock or high demand prompt users to make quick purchases out of fear of missing out.

All these manipulations exploit the natural human response to scarcity, driving users to act impulsively. By categorising deceptive patterns this way, Brignull helped designers better understand the underlying tactics of dark patterns. It also aided in educating users about potential manipulations, empowering them to make more informed decisions. His structured approach provides a comprehensive framework to analyse, critique, and ultimately mitigate the impact of dark patterns.

2.2.2. Gray, Bielova, Santos and Mildner's Ontology

Often used in computer science, information science, and artificial intelligence to model knowledge in a structured, machine-readable format, ontologies are formal representations of concepts within a domain and the relationships between those concepts. For example, an ontology for the medical domain might include concepts like 'disease,' 'symptom,' and 'treatment' and their relationships. Therefore, the following form of structuring the knowledge of deceptive design is an ontology of dark patterns proposed by Colin Gray et al.[8] The authors developed a three-level ontology with standardised definitions for 64 dark pattern types. This structure includes low-level patterns (specific user interface elements ('dark patterns'), meso-level patterns (context-agnostic strategies), and high-level patterns (broad, abstracted forms of manipulative practices). The authors argue that their ontology supports transdisciplinary engagement by providing a shared language for scholars, regulators, and legal professionals, thus facilitating empirical research, regulatory action, and legal sanctions by aligning different terminologies and contexts into a coherent framework.

Their formal structuring categorised dark patterns, elucidating their interrelationships and hierarchies. By differentiating between low-level patterns (specific manipulative interface elements), meso-level patterns (general strategies applicable across various contexts), and high-level patterns (broad categories of manipulative practices), the ontology offers a multi-layered understanding that is crucial for thorough analysis and intervention. The significance of this ontology lies in its ability to facilitate cross-disciplinary dialogue and collaboration. Scholars from different fields can use standardised definitions to ensure their research is aligned and comparable, which is vital for building a robust body of knowledge on dark patterns. Regulators can leverage the detailed classification to better identify and address specific manipulative practices in legal and policy frameworks, making enforcement more precise and effective. Legal professionals, on the other hand, can utilise the ontology to clearly define and communicate the nature of deceptive practices in legal proceedings, supporting the development of case law and legislative measures against dark patterns.

The ontology's machine-readable format enhances its applicability in computational fields. Developers and designers can integrate this structured knowledge into automated systems for detecting and mitigating dark patterns, fostering the creation of user-centric and sound digital environments. The ontology also serves as a foundational element for developing educational materials, helping to raise awareness and understanding of deceptive design among stakeholders, including the public. By promoting a unified approach, Gray et al's ontology underscores the importance of a collective effort in combating the pervasive issue of deceptive design. It encourages adopting best practices and developing new technologies and methodologies, prioritising user welfare.

2.2.3. Leiser and Santos's Classification

The third and final is the classification of deceptive design developed by me and my collaborator, Dr Cristiana Santos. Our classification refers to manipulative or exploitative design techniques embedded in the user interfaces (UIs) and system architectures of websites and apps.[9] These patterns influence user decisions and behaviour, leading to choices that users might not have made independently. It categorises visible, darker, and darkest patterns, highlighting their increasing levels of complexity and subtlety. **Visible patterns** are overt and easily recognisable manipulative practices that directly affect user decision-making. These include tactics like nagging, which repeatedly prompts users to take a particular action, and preselection, where options are pre-chosen for the user, often leading them to share more personal information or make unintended purchases. Another example is obstructive refusal or withdrawal mechanisms, where users find it difficult to decline or withdraw consent, unsubscribe from services, or navigate privacy settings. These patterns are often the focus of regulatory scrutiny due to their conspicuous nature and the immediate impact on user experience.

Darker patterns are more covert and less immediately discernible to users, requiring deeper scrutiny to uncover. These include practices like complex information presentation, where essential data such as terms and conditions or privacy policies are difficult to find or understand. Misleading practices fall under this category, involving presenting information in ways that obscure its true meaning, such as using ambiguous language or placing critical details in fine print. Fragmented data protection information, where information is spread across multiple documents or hidden behind numerous links, also exemplifies darker patterns. These techniques make it challenging for users to make informed decisions, as they must expend significant effort to access and understand the necessary information.

The **darkest patterns** are the most insidious, embedded deeply within the system architecture, and often leverage sophisticated algorithms to change user behaviour. These patterns include deterministic and stochastic approaches. Designers meticulously craft deterministic patterns to achieve specific undesirable outcomes for users by exploiting their cognitive biases and personalising their experiences based on detailed behavioural data. These are carefully hidden within the system's code, making detection possible only through comprehensive technical analysis. For instance, highly personalised recommendation systems that steer users towards unwanted actions fall under this category. On the other hand, stochastic patterns involve systems that operate as black boxes, where the outcomes for the same input can vary unpredictably. These systems, often powered by machine-learning algorithms and increasingly AI systems, adapt and change their behaviour, making it difficult for users and developers to understand or predict their functioning. Such patterns can collectively manipulate user groups or communities, using insights from their data without explicit awareness of the exploitation. An example is hyper-nudging techniques, where users receive personalised nudges based on their behavioural data to influence their decisions subtly but powerfully.

Our classification provided a framework for comprehensive understanding and addressing the diverse spectrum of deceptive design practices. Categorising dark patterns based on their visibility and detectability underscores the necessity for more nuanced and expansive regulatory approaches. This framework advocates extending oversight beyond the surface-level user interface to include the underlying system architecture, ensuring that digital systems adhere to legal standards and respect user autonomy. Such a holistic perspective is indispensable for developing robust countermeasures against the increasingly sophisticated manipulative strategies employed in the digital landscape.

2.2.4. Frameworks for Understanding and Combating Dark Patterns

Understanding the classification, typologies, taxonomies, and ontologies of dark patterns is essential for grasping the scope and complexity of these manipulative design strategies. The interdisciplinary nature of frameworks developed by Brignull, Gray et al, and me in collaboration with Dr Cristiana Santos illustrates the importance of collaborative efforts in combating deceptive design. These frameworks transcend mere categorisation, serving as foundational tools for identifying and addressing the tangible harms inflicted by dark patterns. These harms extend beyond theoretical concerns to encompass significant economic, psychological, and societal ramifications. By systematically categorising deceptive practices, these frameworks enable a deeper understanding of their impacts and provide a basis for mitigating their adverse effects.

Addressing dark patterns requires an integrative approach that combines insights from law, computer science, behavioural psychology, and design studies. Ontologies and taxonomies standardise definitions and terminology, fostering cross-disciplinary research, regulatory coordination, and legal enforcement. Thus, the detailed classification of dark patterns is not merely an academic pursuit but a practical necessity for understanding the substantial harm these practices inflict on individuals and society. These frameworks reveal manipulative design's economic, psychological, and societal consequences through systematic categorisation, providing a foundation for informed regulatory intervention and ethical design practices. As the discussion transitions to the specific harms associated with dark patterns, the foundational insights offered by these frameworks remain pivotal. They equip policymakers, designers, and researchers with the analytical tools needed to combat deceptive design and foster a digital ecosystem rooted in transparency, fairness, and respect for user autonomy.

With this in mind, Table 2.1 illustrates a taxonomy of user interface dark patterns, detailing various manipulative design practices that undermine consumer autonomy and well-being. Leaning on the European Commission's Behavioural Study into Dark Patterns,[10] the table categorises dark patterns into distinct groups: nagging, social proof, obstruction, sneaking, interface interference, disguised ads, confirm shaming, forced action, and urgency. Each variant within these categories, sourced from experts like Gray, Mathur, Brignull, and Bosch,[11] is described alongside the specific harm they inflict on users.[12] These harms range from cognitive burdens and psychological distress to economic losses and privacy violations, showcasing the extensive and multifaceted impact of dark patterns on consumers.

Table 2.1 User Interface Dark Patterns

Category	Variant	Description	Source	Typical Outcome of Harm
Nagging	N/A	Repeated requests to do something the organisation prefers	Gray	**Cognitive Burden:** Increased frustration and mental health issues such as addiction and dependency.
Social Proof	Activity messages	Misleading notice about other consumers' actions	Mathur	**Cognitive Burden:** Unnecessary expenditure of time, energy, and attention.
	Testimonials	Misleading statements from consumers	Mathur	**Loss of Trust and Satisfaction:** Reducing consumer trust in online platforms and services.

(continued)

Table 2.1 *(Continued)*

Category	Variant	Description	Source	Typical Outcome of Harm
Obstruction	Roach Motel/ difficult cancellations	Asymmetry between signing up (easy) and cancelling (hard)	Gray, Mathur	**Loss of Autonomy:** Difficult-to-find cancellation options.
	Price comparison prevention	Frustrates comparison shopping	Brignull, Gray, Mathur	**Economic Harm:** Financial loss because of inefficient allocation of products.
	Intermediate currency	Purchases in virtual currencies to obscure costs	Brignull	**Economic Harm:** Businesses charge higher prices to consumers through targeted pricing.
Sneaking	Sneak into basket	Items that consumers did not add end up in the cart	Brignull, Gray, Mathur	**Economic Harm:** Financial loss because of unintended purchases.
	Hidden Costs	Costs obscured or disclosed late in the transaction	Brignull, Gray, Mathur	**Economic Harm:** Financial loss because of hidden costs.
	Hidden Subscription / forced continuity	Unanticipated or undesired automatic renewal	Brignull, Gray, Mathur	**Economic Harm:** Financial loss due to forced continuity and difficult cancellation.

(continued)

Table 2.1 *(Continued)*

Category	Variant	Description	Source	Typical Outcome of Harm
	Bait and Switch	The consumer purchases something different from what the business initially advertised.	Gray	**Cognitive Burden:** Increased frustration and mental health issues.
Interface Interference	Hidden information / False hierarchy	Businesses visually obscure or arrange vital information to promote a specific option.	Gray, Mathur	**Privacy Violations:** Undermining consumers' privacy through default options and cookie consent.
	Preselection (default)	Pre-selected default option that is in the company's interest	Bosch, Gray	**Loss of Autonomy:** Manipulation of decision-making processes.
	Toying with emotion	Emotionally manipulative framing of the design	Gray	**Psychological Harm:** Causing stress and confusion through manipulative design.
	Trick questions	Intentional or apparent ambiguity to confuse the consumer	Gray, Mathur	**Cognitive Burden:** Increased frustration and mental health issues.

(continued)

Table 2.1 *(Continued)*

Category	Variant	Description	Source	Typical Outcome of Harm
Disguised Ad	N/A	Businesses manipulate consumers into clicking on an advertisement disguised as something else.	Brignull, Mathur	**Cognitive Burden:** Unnecessary expenditure of time, energy, and attention.
Confirm shaming	N/A	Choice framed in a way that seems to treat the consumer as dishonest/ stupid	Brignull, Mathur	**Psychological Harm:** Causing stress and confusion through manipulative design.
Forced Action	Forced Registration	Businesses deceive consumers into believing that registration is necessary.	Bosch	**Loss of Autonomy:** Manipulation of decision-making processes.
Urgency	Low stock / high demand message	Consumers falsely informed of limited quantities	Mathur	**Cognitive Burden:** Unnecessary expenditure of time, energy, and attention.
	Countdown timer / Limited time message	Opportunity ends soon with false visual information	Mathur	**Cognitive Burden:** Increased frustration and mental health issues.

2.3. Silent Harms: How Dark Patterns Undermine Users

Imagine navigating a website where a countdown clock urges you to 'Buy Now – Only 2 Left!' while hidden fees creep into your total. You try to unsubscribe but face a maze of 'Are you sure?' messages and guilt-laden prompts. Your private data is quietly shared, default options push you toward disclosure, and colourful buttons lure you into choices that aren't yours. Meanwhile, algorithms adapt, refining these manipulations to target you more precisely. These are the fingerprints of dark patterns, leaving behind lost money, stolen time, compromised privacy, and growing distrust in the digital world. Design silently shapes our online behaviour, but beneath the surface, manipulative tactics exploit and coerce. Experts warn of their measurable harms – economic loss, privacy violations, and cognitive burdens. Dark patterns strip users of genuine agency, leveraging cognitive overload and emotional manipulation to create the illusion of choice. The result isn't just frustration but a deeper erosion of trust and autonomy.[13]

2.3.1. Economic Consequences of Dark Patterns: Immediate Losses, Long-Term Burdens, and Market Distortion

Picture this: a consumer clicks through an online store, only to face surprise charges masked by flashy promotions. A guilt-laden pop-up pleads, 'Stay connected!' as they try to cancel an auto-renewed subscription. Over time, these relentless tricks erode trust, making every online purchase feel like a potential trap. Deceptive practices lead consumers to make unintended purchases, subscribe to services they do not need, or incur hidden fees. For instance, tactics like 'sneak-in-the-basket',[14] where additional items are added to the cart without explicit consent, or 'forced continuity',[15] where users are charged automatically after a free trial without sufficient warning, result in financial losses.[16] Consumers may find themselves locked into difficult-to-cancel subscriptions, incurring ongoing costs they had not anticipated. These practices distort market efficiency and lead to an inefficient allocation of resources, ultimately causing financial strain on consumers. This distrust also affects ethical businesses and discourages digital spending. For vulnerable populations, the stakes are higher. A single unexpected charge can cause financial strain, especially for those already struggling. Older adults and lower-income consumers, with fewer digital skills and resources, are hit hardest – left overcharged, overburdened, and underserved. These harms ripple outward, reinforcing economic inequality.

Dark patterns exacerbate economic harm by manipulating consumer behaviour. One such method that plays on user psychology is 'confirm shaming',[17] which uses guilt to pressure consumers into making purchases or decisions they might otherwise avoid. For example, a pop-up might suggest that not completing a purchase is akin to missing out on a great opportunity or questioning the user's intentions with phrases like 'Do not miss out!' or 'Are you sure?'. These subtle pressures coerce consumers into spending on products or services they neither need nor want, further straining their financial resources.

Moreover, the economic impact of dark patterns extends beyond immediate losses. They contribute to long-term financial detriment by fostering a culture of recurring expenses that consumers might not be fully aware of.[18] Subscription-based models exploit dark patterns to ensure continuous revenue streams from consumers.[19] For instance, a service might offer a free trial but require credit card information upfront, with the understanding that the subscription will auto-renew at the end of the trial period unless explicitly cancelled. The design of the cancellation process needs to be revised, requiring consumers to navigate multiple steps or hidden options, increasing the likelihood that they will fail to cancel in time.[20] As a result, consumers incur repeated charges that, over time, accumulate and have a substantial impact on their financial well-being.[21]

Another insidious economic harm caused by deceptive design is the distortion of pricing transparency. Practices such as hidden fees and drip pricing – where additional charges are revealed only at the last stage of the purchase process – mislead consumers about the actual cost of a product or service.[22] This lack of transparency prevents consumers from making accurate price comparisons, leading them to make suboptimal purchasing decisions. For instance, an airline ticket might initially appear cheaper than competitors, but its cost rises sharply when businesses add mandatory fees. This deceptive pricing strategy results in financial loss for consumers and distorts market competition, allowing companies that employ such tactics to dominate the market unfairly.[23]

Deceptive design does not just cost individuals a few extra dollars; it silently rewrites the rules of trust in commerce, undermining fairness and transparency. The consequences are stark: immediate financial losses, long-term burdens from hard-to-cancel services, and a marketplace that feels less like an ecosystem of opportunity and more like a minefield. As dark patterns proliferate, they exploit and entrench the vulnerabilities of those least able to afford the cost, leaving a fractured trust that threatens the very foundation of the digital economy.

2.3.2. Infringement of Fundamental Rights

Deceptive design also poses significant threats to privacy and data protection rights, compounding the economic harm experienced by consumers. Manipulative consent dialogues, default options favour extensive data sharing, and hidden privacy settings are common tactics that trick users into divulging more personal information than intended. Covert data collection undermines user privacy and exposes consumers to potential data misuse. In an age where data breaches and privacy concerns are rampant, exploiting data through deceptive design exacerbates the vulnerability of personal data, leading to further distrust in digital services. One of the primary mechanisms by which deceptive design infringes on privacy is through manipulative consent dialogues. Businesses often craft these dialogues to nudge users into agreeing to data collection and sharing practices without providing clear and transparent information about the specifics of their consent. For example, consent dialogues may use ambiguous language, pre-checked boxes, or designs that make the 'Agree' button more prominent than the 'Disagree' button, effectively steering users toward consenting. This lack of informed consent violates fundamental data protection principles, including transparency and user autonomy.

Furthermore, deceptive designs infringe upon user privacy. Tactics such as pre-checked consent boxes for data sharing, misleading privacy settings, and ambiguous language regarding data use trick users into divulging more personal information than they intend. This invasion of privacy can lead to many negative consequences, including unwanted marketing communications, data breaches, and the misuse of personal information. Exploiting consumer data through deceptive practices constitutes a direct infringement of the fundamental right to data protection, challenging the principles enshrined in European legal frameworks. Such actions undermine the foundational tenets of autonomy and accountability, necessitating a recalibration of regulatory frameworks to ensure effective enforcement mechanisms and uphold legal and ethical standards. Default settings that favour data sharing further erode privacy protections. Many digital services deliberately collect the maximum amount of data by default, requiring users to take deliberate steps to opt-out. These default settings go unnoticed by users, who may not realise that digital services collect and share their personal information extensively. This tactic exploits default bias, where individuals are likelier to stick with pre-selected options due to inertia or lack of awareness. As a result, users inadvertently expose themselves to more significant privacy risks, including data profiling, targeted advertising, and even unauthorised third-party access to their information. Hidden privacy settings are another deceptive design tactic that compromises user privacy. By burying privacy controls deep within menus or using confusing terminology, companies make it difficult for users to understand and manage their privacy preferences effectively. This obfuscation prevents users from taking control of their data, leaving them vulnerable to unwanted data collection and sharing. For instance, social media platforms may hide settings for restricting data visibility or deactivating data sharing with third-party apps, making it challenging for users to protect their personal information.

2.3.3. Cognitive, Emotional, and Psychological Toll

The cognitive and emotional toll of constant subjection to confusing interfaces, deceptive systems, overwhelming amounts of information, and repetitive prompts sap users' cognitive resources. This increased cognitive load can lead to frustration, stress, and even mental health issues such as addiction and dependency. For example, patterns like 'confirm-shaming', which guilts users into making choices, or 'nagging',[24] which repeatedly pressures users to take an action they have previously declined, create a hostile and emotionally draining user experience. Over time, these tactics can lead to significant emotional distress and a negative perception of digital interactions. The intricate designs of deceptive patterns exploit various psychological mechanisms, intensifying their cognitive burden. Cognitive load theory suggests that human working memory has limited capacity, and when overloaded, it impairs decision-making and learning. Deceptive design exploits this limitation by bombarding users with excessive information and choices, presented confusingly. This deliberate obfuscation forces users to expend more mental energy than necessary, leading to decision fatigue. When users continuously face complex navigation, unclear terms, and hidden conditions, these challenges deplete their cognitive resources, causing mental exhaustion and reducing their ability to make rational decisions.

Emotionally, the relentless use of deceptive design can foster a sense of helplessness and frustration. Confirm-shaming tactics, which use guilt to pressure users into making confident choices, prey on users' emotional vulnerabilities. For instance, a website might present an option to decline an offer with language designed to induce guilt, such as 'No, I do not want to save money.' This manipulative phrasing can make users feel inadequate or guilty for making a choice that aligns with their preferences, leading to emotional stress. Similarly, nagging patterns repeatedly remind users to perform actions they have previously opted out of, creating a sense of annoyance and frustration. This constant badgering erodes user patience and contributes to a negative emotional state. The sense of manipulation further exacerbates the emotional strain. Users recognise that companies are coercing them into actions that may not align with their best interests, leading to feelings of betrayal and mistrust. This erosion of trust affects their relationship with a particular service and generalises to their overall digital experiences, fostering a broader scepticism towards online interactions. The awareness of being deceived can also lead to anger and resentment, adding to the emotional toll.

Moreover, the repetitive nature of these interactions can lead to habituation, where users become accustomed to stress and frustration, normalising these negative experiences. This normalisation can have long-term implications for mental health, as users may start to accept high levels of cognitive and emotional strain as a regular part of their digital interactions. Over time, this habituation can contribute to chronic stress and anxiety, conditions that are known to negatively impact overall well-being.

In addition to the immediate emotional impacts, there is a risk of developing dependency on specific digital platforms due to the manipulative design of their interfaces. Features that exploit reward mechanisms, such as variable rewards seen in social media notifications or game mechanics, can create addictive behaviours. Users might find themselves compulsively checking their devices or engaging with content, driven by the unpredictable nature of these rewards. This dependency impacts not only mental health by fostering anxiety and obsessive behaviours but also disrupts other areas of life, such as sleep patterns, productivity, and real-world social interactions. Deceptive design has a profound cognitive and emotional toll, affecting users' mental health and well-being. Deliberately designing manipulative interfaces to exploit cognitive biases and emotional vulnerabilities results in a host of adverse outcomes, including stress, frustration, dependency, and a pervasive sense of mistrust in digital environments. These impacts underscore the need for greater awareness and regulation to protect users from the harmful effects of deceptive design practices.

2.3.4. Consumer Autonomy

Deceptive design fundamentally undermines consumer autonomy by manipulating decision-making processes.[25] Through misleading information, obfuscated options, and pre-selected choices, these designs restrict users' ability to make informed decisions.[26] For instance, difficult-to-find cancellation options and hidden costs prevent users from exercising their right to opt-out or make choices that align with their preferences. This erosion of autonomy is particularly concerning as it forces users to take actions that benefit the business at the expense of their interests, stripping them of control over their digital interactions. One of the primary tactics employed by deceptive design is using misleading information, such as false claims, ambiguous language, or incomplete details about products and services. For example, a common strategy is the creation of fake scarcity – messages that falsely indicate the limited availability of a product to instil a sense of urgency. Consumers, driven by the fear of missing out, may rush to purchase without thoroughly considering whether they need the product or if it represents good value. Such tactics exploit psychological triggers, leading individuals to make decisions they might regret later.

Obfuscated options are another critical element of deceptive design that undermines consumer autonomy. When options are hidden or presented convolutedly, it becomes challenging for consumers to find the information they need to make an informed choice. An example is the 'roach motel' design pattern, where getting into a subscription service is easy but frustratingly tricky. Users may have to navigate multiple pages, endure misleading prompts, and encounter ambiguous terminology to cancel a subscription. This intentional complexity dissuades users from opting out, effectively trapping them in a service they no longer want. Pre-selected choices further constrain consumer autonomy by making certain decisions the default option. Businesses configure these defaults to prioritise their interests over those of the consumer. For instance, during the sign-up process for online services, users might discover that the option to receive marketing emails is pre-selected or that businesses actively present higher-cost plans as the default choice. This subtle nudge leverages the tendency of individuals to go with default options, especially when they are in a hurry or not fully attentive. Consequently, users might end up agreeing to terms they are uncomfortable with or paying more than they intended.

Moreover, deceptive designs frequently employ dark patterns that exploit cognitive biases. Techniques such as 'confirm shaming,'[27] which guilts users into choosing a particular option, or 'forced continuity,'[28] which transitions a free trial into a paid subscription without clear notice, serve as prime examples. These tactics prey on users' emotions and cognitive limitations, pushing them into making decisions that favour the business. The result is a significant power imbalance, where the company controls the user's choices and, by extension, their digital experience.[29] The impact of these deceptive practices is particularly profound when considering vulnerable populations, such as those with lower digital literacy or those who are not native speakers of the interface language. These groups are even more susceptible to manipulation as they may lack the skills or knowledge to navigate deceptive designs effectively. As a result, they are more likely to fall prey to hidden costs, unwanted subscriptions, and data privacy infringements.

In sum, deceptive design practices infringe upon consumer autonomy by strategically manipulating decision-making processes. Misleading information, obfuscated options, and pre-selected choices systematically steer consumers towards decisions that benefit businesses at their expense. This manipulation erodes trust in digital services and highlights the urgent need for regulatory oversight to protect consumer rights and promote fair digital interactions.

2.3.5. Consumer Trust and Satisfaction

The pervasive use of deceptive design corrosively affects consumer trust and satisfaction. When users recognise that platforms or services have deceived them, it erodes their trust, leading to potential disengagement and negative word-of-mouth.[30] This distrust can also spread to other digital services, creating a broader sense of scepticism and wariness towards online interactions. Lower consumer satisfaction resulting from manipulative practices harms individual businesses and undermines the digital ecosystem, making it harder for 'ethical' businesses to compete. The loss of consumer trust has profound implications for the digital marketplace. Trust is a cornerstone of the consumer-business relationship, especially in the online environment where direct personal interaction is minimal or non-existent. When consumers feel that deceptive design tactics have betrayed their trust, they will likely become more cautious and less willing to engage with digital services. This caution can manifest in reduced usage of online platforms, reluctance to share personal information, and increased hesitancy to make online purchases. Over time, this erosion of trust can lead to a significant decline in user engagement, impacting the overall viability of digital businesses.

Moreover, the spread of distrust can have a domino effect across the digital ecosystem. When consumers encounter dark patterns on one platform, they may question the integrity of other platforms, even those that do not engage in such practices. This generalised scepticism can decrease overall digital participation as users become wary of potential manipulation and deception. This environment of distrust can stifle innovation, as new and emerging platforms may need help to gain a foothold in a market where consumers are increasingly cynical. Consumer satisfaction is intrinsically linked to trust, and dark patterns severely undermine this satisfaction. When users feel manipulated, their overall experience is tainted, leading to dissatisfaction. This dissatisfaction is not limited to a single interaction but can influence the consumer's perception of the brand. Negative experiences caused by dark patterns can lead to increased churn rates, where dissatisfied customers abandon the service in favour of alternatives. High churn rates can be particularly damaging for subscription-based services, where retaining customers is crucial for sustained revenue. The impact of dark patterns on consumer satisfaction extends beyond immediate user interactions. Negative experiences can fuel negative word-of-mouth, both online and offline. Dissatisfied consumers will likely share their negative experiences with friends and family through social media. This amplification of dissatisfaction can significantly harm a company's reputation, making it more challenging to attract new users and retain existing ones. In today's connected world, a single negative review or post can reach thousands, if not millions, of potential customers, amplifying the damage caused by dark patterns.

2.3.6. Vulnerability

Deceptive design disproportionately affects vulnerable populations, such as older people, children, lower-income individuals or those with limited digital literacy. These groups frequently demonstrate greater susceptibility to manipulative tactics and may lack the resources or knowledge to navigate complex and deceptive interfaces effectively. For instance, designs that hide essential information on smaller screens or exploit cognitive biases can harm users who rely primarily on mobile devices or are first-generation internet users. This situation exacerbates existing social inequalities and deepens the digital divide, further marginalising vulnerable populations. The impact on these groups is profound, as they often encounter significant barriers to accessing digital services and understanding the implications of their online actions. Lower-income individuals may need more financial flexibility to absorb unexpected charges or subscriptions from deceptive practices. This financial vulnerability means that even small, unintended expenditures can lead to substantial economic hardship, contributing to poverty and financial instability. Additionally, the limited availability of alternative options for digital services forces these consumers to continue using platforms that engage in deceptive practices, further entrenching their disadvantage.

Limited digital literacy exacerbates the challenges faced by vulnerable populations. Individuals with lower levels of education or those new to the internet may need to be made aware of standard deceptive practices or need more skills to identify and avoid them. For example, they might need to recognise phishing attempts, misleading consent forms, or the implications of data-sharing agreements. This lack of awareness and skill makes them prime targets for exploitation, as they are less likely to question the authenticity of deceptive prompts or understand the full consequences of their online actions. Furthermore, deceptive design practices that exploit cognitive biases, such as default settings or urgency messages, disproportionately impact these users. Cognitive biases like the status quo bias, where individuals are more likely to accept the default option, can lead to unintended subscriptions or data sharing. Similarly, urgency messages that create a false sense of scarcity or immediacy can pressure users into making hasty decisions without fully considering the consequences. These manipulative tactics take advantage of the cognitive limitations of vulnerable users, leading to decisions that may not align with their best interests.

The reliance on mobile devices among lower-income and digitally inexperienced users also heightens their susceptibility to deceptive designs. Mobile interfaces often present information in a condensed and less accessible manner than desktop interfaces. Essential details may be hidden behind multiple layers or small print, making it difficult for users to fully understand what they consent to or purchase. This interface limitation, combined with the smaller screen size and potentially slower processing speeds of lower-cost devices, creates an environment where deceptive practices can thrive unnoticed. The marginalisation of these vulnerable populations through deceptive design practices perpetuates existing social inequalities and widens the digital divide. As these users continue to face barriers in accessing and safely navigating digital environments, they experience more significant exclusion from the economic and social benefits of the digital economy. This exclusion can have long-term implications, including limited access to education, employment opportunities, and essential services increasingly moving online. Moreover, the social repercussions extend beyond individual users to affect communities and society. As vulnerable populations become more marginalised, the overall trust in digital platforms and services diminishes. This erosion of trust can deter broader community engagement with digital technologies, slowing the adoption of beneficial innovations and reducing overall societal progress. It also burdens social services and support systems, which must address the consequences of financial and emotional harm caused by deceptive practices.

2.3.7. Broader Societal Impacts

The harm caused extends beyond individual consumers to the broader society, distorting market competition by manipulating consumer choices and creating lock-in effects. The prevalence of dark patterns distorts market competition by creating unfair advantages for businesses that employ these tactics. More 'ethical' businesses prioritising transparency and trust face significant challenges in differentiating themselves when dark patterns are widespread. The manipulation of consumer choices through deceptive design lowers the overall standard for user experience and compels companies to exert even greater effort to build and maintain consumer trust. Such practices create an environment where companies employing dark patterns gain competitive advantages, thereby reducing the ability of more ethical businesses to compete fairly.[31]

In the long term, the prevalence of dark patterns can lead to a vicious cycle of mistrust and dissatisfaction. The widespread use of such tactics can erode trust in digital markets and democratic processes as consumers become increasingly sceptical of online interactions and data practices. As consumers become more aware of these deceptive practices, they may develop a generalised mistrust of digital services, even those operating ethically. This pervasive scepticism can reduce the effectiveness of legitimate marketing and engagement strategies, making it harder for all businesses to connect with consumers. The overall digital economy suffers as businesses and practices consistently erode trust, a fundamental component of online transactions. This erosion of trust affects individual businesses and hampers the growth and potential of the digital ecosystem.[32] This loss of confidence can have far-reaching consequences for the digital economy and society, undermining social welfare and economic efficiency.

In addition to harming individual privacy, deceptive design practices undermining privacy can have broader societal impacts. They contribute to a surveillance culture where extensive data collection and monitoring become normalised. This culture erodes privacy as a fundamental right and shifts the balance of power towards corporations and entities that control the data. As privacy diminishes, the potential for abuse increases, with companies leveraging personal data to manipulate consumer behaviour, influence political opinions and shape societal norms. Extensive data collection and monitoring become normalised, eroding privacy as a fundamental right. This shift in the balance of power towards corporations and entities that control data increases the potential for abuse. Companies can leverage personal data to manipulate consumer behaviour, influence political opinions, and shape societal norms. This erosion of privacy threatens democratic principles of transparency, accountability, and individual autonomy.

Dark patterns not only distort immediate consumer decision-making but can also alter long-term behavioural norms in ways that persist beyond any single interaction. By conditioning users to navigate misleading interfaces, these tactics recalibrate expectations about what constitutes a 'normal' digital experience, embedding manipulative features into the baseline of user–platform engagement. Over time, such habituation can diminish users' capacity to recognise or resist exploitative practices, effectively lowering the threshold for future manipulation. This normalisation effect gives manipulative design a durable strategic value for unscrupulous actors, allowing them to entrench asymmetries of power and influence without the need for overt coercion. As these norms crystallise, regulatory interventions face greater challenges in restoring meaningful choice and agency, since user behaviour itself has adapted to operate within a distorted environment.

Table 2.1 above comprehensively categorises user interface dark patterns, detailing their specific variants, descriptions, sources, and reported harms. As demonstrated, these manipulative designs significantly impact consumer autonomy, cognitive load, financial well-being, and emotional health. However, other research has also examined the harms of dark patterns. My long-time collaborator Dr Cristiana Santos and her co-authors identified various harms caused by dark patterns, including emotional distress, privacy loss, financial loss, weaker or distorted competition, loss of autonomy, loss of trust, loss of time, labour and cognitive burden, addiction, attentional harm, price transparency issues, and physical/bodily harm. They noted that many of these harms are interrelated, with some leading to or exacerbating others, such as addiction leading to financial loss or loss of time. Their findings indicate that dark patterns cause a wide range of individual and collective harms, often intertwined and compounding each other. These intertwined effects highlight the complexity of dark patterns' impact on users and the market. The analysis underscores the need for comprehensive approaches to address these multifaceted harms effectively.[33]

Deceptive design techniques exploit cognitive biases to influence behaviour, combining methods to invade privacy, trick users into sharing more information than intended, and mislead users about how their data will be used or shared. Furthermore, by exploiting situational vulnerabilities, *personalised* user interface dark patterns also harm competition, price transparency, and trust in the market. By manipulating user choice, they can also induce false beliefs. The cognitive and emotional toll of constant subjection to confusing interfaces and deceptive systems diverts users' attention and depletes cognitive resources. This unnecessary expenditure of time, energy, and attention results in a loss of opportunities, as users are distracted from more meaningful activities or more beneficial decisions.

2.4. Deceptive 'Systems'

As Steve Jobs noted, 'Design is how it works'.[34] While digital interfaces can enhance usability, they also enable manipulation. Traditionally, dark patterns have been linked to UI/UX design, where cognitive biases are exploited to nudge or mislead users. However, alongside Dr Santos, I argue for a broader view, encompassing both visible manipulative UI elements and deeper system architecture that shapes user behaviour before interaction even reaches the interface.[35] Like a house's structure hidden beneath its paint, deceptive design operates at multiple levels, often unseen but highly impactful.

Regulators have focused on visible dark patterns, such as pre-selected options and misleading menus, as these are easier to identify and enforce. Laws like the GDPR, UCPD, and DSA address such practices, targeting consent boxes and obfuscation tactics to improve transparency. However, Dr Santos and I introduced a tiered visibility threshold, recognising that many manipulative tactics are more subtle. These 'darker' patterns obscure essential functions, such as contract termination or consent withdrawal, requiring technical scrutiny for enforcement. The most insidious 'darkest' patterns lie in system architecture, exploiting algorithmic structures beyond users' perception. Hyper-nudging and AI-driven personalisation subtly steer behaviour using behavioural data. These tactics, embedded in a platform's foundational design, manipulate at scale while remaining difficult to detect, underscoring the need for more robust regulatory oversight.

AI-powered and algorithmic systems enable a more insidious form of deceptive design by exploiting user data and behavioural psychology. Unlike traditional manipulations confined to visible user-interface elements, AI-driven deception operates through vast personal data collection and advanced computational models that influence users in ways they often cannot consciously detect.[36] These systems process large and heterogeneous datasets to construct granular behavioural profiles, mapping not only overt preferences but also latent vulnerabilities. Such profiling enables precision-targeted manipulative strategies that adapt dynamically to each individual. For example, algorithms can identify users who respond disproportionately to urgency cues or emotionally charged appeals by analysing browsing history, interaction patterns, and contextual signals. Social media platforms are particularly effective at operationalising these insights, leveraging AI to amplify content designed to evoke strong emotional reactions. In pursuit of engagement maximisation, such systems preferentially surface material associated with heightened arousal states, such as outrage, fear, or euphoric affirmation, thereby reinforcing behavioural loops that deepen platform dependency.[37] Over time, these cycles can elevate anxiety, intensify depressive tendencies, and distort self-perception by continually reframing how individuals interpret themselves and their social environment. The embedded nature of such manipulation makes it difficult to detect or resist. Its precision, persistence, and capacity to exploit subconscious triggers render AI-driven deception both particularly harmful and uniquely challenging to mitigate.[38]

One of the most insidious aspects of AI-driven deceptive design is its ability to hide its manipulative intent. Users often fail to recognise that algorithms tailored to exploit their specific behavioural patterns shape their decisions. This lack of transparency undermines informed consent and makes it easier for users to resist or recognise the manipulation. First, AI-driven systems often rely on extensive data collection to function effectively. Users may be unaware of the extent of data collected and how companies use it. Second, AI systems can create complex and confusing user experiences by dynamically adjusting the interface based on user interactions. Such dynamic adjustments can lead to a heightened cognitive burden as users struggle to navigate ever-changing and increasingly convoluted interfaces. Such dynamic manipulations are more challenging to identify and regulate than static deceptive practices.[39]

AI-powered deceptive design disproportionately harms vulnerable populations, particularly those with lower digital literacy or socio-economic disadvantages. Less able to recognise or resist manipulation, they face greater financial loss and psychological distress, deepening social inequalities and the digital divide. Beyond individual harm, AI-driven manipulation erodes democratic processes and public trust. Micro-targeted political campaigns can distort opinion and influence elections, threatening democratic integrity. The constant sense of surveillance and manipulation fosters distrust in digital platforms, stifling innovation and slowing the adoption of beneficial technologies.[40]

2.5. System Architecture-Based Deceptive Design Techniques

System architecture-based deceptive design techniques, embedded deeply within the underlying systems rather than visible in the user interface, play a crucial role in these harms. Algorithmic bias in AI systems can reinforce and exacerbate biases in their training data, resulting in discriminatory outcomes. These outcomes are particularly harmful in contexts like hiring or loan approval, where biased algorithms perpetuate inequality and limit opportunities for marginalised groups.[41] Dark nudges are subtle cues embedded within the system architecture that guide users towards specific actions without explicit awareness. For example, an e-commerce site might use algorithmic recommendations to nudge users towards higher-priced items or subscription services, exploiting cognitive biases such as the default effect or the scarcity heuristic.[42] Hyper-personalisation leverages detailed user profiles to deliver content and advertisements that exploit individual vulnerabilities. Such practices can lead to economic harm through impulsive purchases, privacy violations due to extensive data collection, and psychological harm from constant exposure to emotionally charged content.[43] Feedback loops created by AI systems can reinforce user behaviours and preferences, often to the user's detriment. For instance, social media algorithms prioritising sensationalist content can increase polarisation and societal harm by fostering echo chambers and reducing exposure to diverse viewpoints.[44] AI-powered and algorithmic deceptive design represents a more insidious and pervasive threat than traditional deceptive practices. The deep integration of manipulative techniques within the system architecture exacerbates various harms, including economic loss, privacy violations, cognitive burden, loss of autonomy, psychological distress, and broader societal impacts.[45] When embedded manipulation operates over time, its effects extend beyond the immediate user. Patterns of altered decision-making propagate through networks, shaping market dynamics, influencing cultural norms, and constraining collective agency, ultimately re-configuring the environments in which economic, social, and political life unfolds.

2.6. Harms from AI Systems of Manipulation

Artificial Intelligence (AI) systems increasingly shape daily life, influencing social media, e-commerce, healthcare, and finance. While offering benefits, they also pose serious risks, particularly in psychological manipulation. AI's ability to exploit cognitive biases, influence decisions, and manipulate behaviour raises critical ethical and regulatory concerns. These manipulations threaten individual autonomy, mental health, societal trust, and economic stability. A primary harm of AI-driven psychological manipulation is the erosion of autonomy. Sophisticated algorithms subtly influence decisions without user awareness. Techniques like subliminal messaging, personalised nudging, and cognitive bias exploitation lead individuals to make choices they might not have made if fully informed. This covert manipulation undermines autonomy by depriving individuals of genuinely free and informed decision-making. The widespread use of AI in psychological manipulation also threatens societal trust and democratic integrity. AI-driven disinformation and fake news distort public opinion, polarise societies, and erode confidence in institutions. During elections, AI can spread false narratives, subtly influencing voter behaviour and undermining democracy. This manipulation makes it harder to distinguish truth from falsehood, severely compromising trust in media and governance. Economically, AI manipulates consumer behaviour to maximise profits, often at consumer expense. Personalised pricing exploits willingness to pay, while dark patterns trick users into unintended purchases or excessive data sharing. These tactics harm individuals and distort market competition by favouring companies that manipulate over those that prioritise ethical practices. Vulnerable populations are disproportionately affected by AI-driven manipulation. Predatory financial products exploit low-income individuals, worsening financial instability and debt. AI-driven dark patterns in healthcare can manipulate patients into unnecessary treatments, leading to physical and financial harm, particularly for those already disadvantaged.

Beyond economic and political concerns, AI manipulation undermines human dignity. By exploiting unconscious biases and emotional vulnerabilities, these systems reduce individuals to mere tools for engagement and sales. Such practices violate fundamental principles of respect and fairness, challenging ethical norms on the acceptable use of technology. Table 2.2 further illustrates how system architecture-based deceptive design exploits user vulnerabilities, causing significant economic, psychological, and societal harm.

Table 2.2 System Architecture-Based Deceptive Design Techniques and Associated Harms

Deceptive Design Technique	Description	Associated Harms
Algorithmic Bias	AI systems reinforce and exacerbate biases present in their training data.	Discriminatory outcomes in hiring, loan approval, and other critical areas perpetuate inequality and limit opportunities for marginalised groups.[46]
Dark Patterns	Subtle cues within the system architecture guide users towards specific actions without explicit awareness.	Economic exploitation through increased spending on higher-priced items or subscription services; manipulation of cognitive biases such as the default effect or scarcity heuristic.[47]
Hyper-Personalisation	Leveraging detailed user profiles to deliver highly personalised content and advertisements.	Economic harm from impulsive purchases, privacy violations through extensive data collection, and psychological damage from constant exposure to emotionally charged content.[48]

(continued)

Table 2.2 *(Continued)*

Deceptive Design Technique	Description	Associated Harms
Social media Algorithmic Feeds	AI-driven content prioritisation based on user behaviour rather than chronology.	Increased polarisation and societal harm by fostering echo chambers and reducing exposure to diverse viewpoints; loss of user autonomy in content consumption; psychological distress from sensationalist content.[49]
E-commerce Recommendation Systems	AI-driven suggestions in e-commerce to exploit user preferences and vulnerabilities.	Economic exploitation through targeted ads and purchase nudges; loss of autonomy due to manipulation of decision-making processes.
Dynamic User Interfaces	Interfaces that change based on user interactions to confuse or mislead.	Increased cognitive burden as users struggle to navigate; reduced ability to make informed decisions; frustration and potential disengagement from the platform.
Data Collection and Profiling	Extensive gathering of user data to create detailed profiles for targeted manipulation.	Privacy violations; loss of autonomy over personal information; exploitation through targeted advertising and content manipulation.
Behavioural Targeting	Use of AI to identify and exploit specific user behaviours and tendencies.	Economic harm from tailored ads that exploit vulnerabilities; increased psychological pressure from targeted emotional triggers; potential addiction to digital platforms.

(continued)

Table 2.2 *(Continued)*

Deceptive Design Technique	Description	Associated Harms
Auto-play Features	Continuous content streaming without natural stopping points.	Reduced ability to self-regulate screen time; potential addiction to content; negative impact on sleep and daily routines.
Subliminal Messaging	Techniques that subtly influence user behaviour without conscious awareness.	Undermines user autonomy; can lead to decisions that are not in the user's best interest; psychological distress from manipulative influences.

2.7. Conclusion

This chapter examined deceptive design techniques, extending beyond traditional UI dark patterns to systemic manipulative practices embedded in system architecture. It highlighted the extensive harm these tactics cause, including economic losses, privacy violations, cognitive burdens, and broader societal impacts. The chapter introduced a tiered visibility threshold, categorising dark patterns into visible, darker, and darkest forms, with the latter leveraging AI to manipulate user behaviour covertly. This discussion underscored the insidious nature of AI-driven manipulation, which exploits user data and cognitive biases, leading to significant psychological and economic harm. This chapter provides the foundation for exploring regulatory responses in chapter three. With a clear understanding of UI dark patterns and their far-reaching consequences, examining the regulatory landscape addressing these deceptive practices is vital. Insights from this chapter highlight dark patterns' significant impact on consumer behaviour, reinforcing the need for stronger protections. Accordingly, chapter three adopts a legal-analytical approach to assess existing laws combating dark patterns, evaluating their strengths and shortcomings. This analysis informs discussions on how regulations must evolve to better protect consumers. Transitioning from problem identification to regulatory response, the chapter sets the stage for exploring legal reforms and design principles. It examines the current regulatory landscape and emphasises the need for proactive measures to counter emerging deceptive practices. As digital environments evolve, regulatory frameworks must adapt to uphold consumer rights and ensure fair competition.

3

Regulatory Responses to Dark Patterns and Deceptive Design

3.1. Introduction

On 29 October 2021, the US Federal Trade Commission (FTC) issued a policy statement emphasising its commitment to enforcement against companies employing deceptive designs. Samuel Levine, Director of the FTC's Bureau of Consumer Protection, underscored this commitment by stating, 'Our report shows how more and more companies are using digital dark patterns to trick people into buying products and giving away their personal information. This report – and our cases – clearly conveys that these traps will not be tolerated'.[1] The FTC statement highlighted that dark patterns violate consumer protection laws and announced increased scrutiny to ensure transparency and fairness in digital market interfaces.[2] Subsequently, the California Privacy Protection Agency (hereafter CPPA[3]) released its draft regulations addressing dark patterns for the California Privacy Rights Act (hereafter, CPRA[4]) on 27 May 2022. The draft regulations prohibited interfaces that impair user choice or autonomy, stipulating that businesses must avoid complex or confusing language, require clear and straightforward consent mechanisms, and ensure that user interfaces do not use deceptive designs that mislead or coerce users into unwanted decisions. Across the Atlantic Ocean, the Information Commissioner's Office and the Competition and Markets Authority of the United Kingdom issued a joint paper outlining their concerns and expectations regarding dark patterns in digital services, emphasising the necessity of addressing these deceptive practices through coordinated regulatory efforts.[5] They stressed the importance of integrating privacy and competition law considerations to ensure fair and transparent online environments.

Meanwhile, across the North Sea, as discussed in the next chapter, the European Union (EU) developed a body of laws to tackle deceptive design. Key provisions of the European Union's Digital Services Act (DSA[6]) came into force on 17 February 2024, containing the first European provision directly applicable to dark patterns and deceptive design in online platforms.[7] The EU's Digital Markets Act[8] prohibited using user interface dark patterns by platforms designated as gatekeepers.[9] In March 2022, the European Data Protection Board (EDPB) issued guidelines on dark patterns in social media interfaces to help designers and users avoid manipulative practices that infringe on GDPR requirements.[10] The EDPB guidelines seek to safeguard individuals from inadvertently making decisions that could negatively impact their data rights. They advocate for interface designs that prioritise clarity, user autonomy, and strict adherence to legal requirements.

The European Commission also updated its guidance for implementing the Unfair Commercial Practices Directive (UCPD).[11] On 17 December 2021, the European Commission adopted updated guidance under the UCPD, spotlighting the growing threat of dark patterns in the digital marketplace. The guidance underscored how manipulative design tactics can deceive and exploit consumers, often skirting or violating consumer protection laws outright. By targeting these underhanded practices, the rules demanded greater transparency and fairness in how businesses interact with consumers online. Crucially, the guidance aligned with broader EU legal frameworks, including the GDPR and ePrivacy Directive, to create a cohesive defence against misleading, aggressive, and manipulative strategies designed to prey on consumer vulnerabilities.

Dr Cristiana Santos and I referred to the collective legal framework regulating dark patterns as the *digital design acquis*. One might expect such a framework to eliminate deceptive design, yet these manipulative tactics continue to evolve. This chapter examines early but crucial regulatory efforts to combat dark patterns. While regulators strive to enforce transparency, deceptive strategies often outpace enforcement. This chapter explores how consumer protection, data privacy, and competition authorities address these challenges, highlighting their strategy and the gaps that allow deception to persist. Each section underscores the evolving legal landscape of dark patterns and the critical role of regulatory bodies.

The first Section examines cookie notices and banner laws, which were initially designed for transparency but are now widely exploited for manipulation. Regulations like the GDPR and CCPA impose strict consent requirements, yet many organisations use deceptive opt-in schemes and ambiguous language to promote excessive data collection, undermining regulatory intent.

The second Section examines consumer law's role in addressing dark patterns as unfair commercial practices. The UCPD in Europe and the FTC Act in the US provide the legal foundation, yet regulators struggle to combat manipulative design tricks that exploit behavioural psychology. Proving deceptive intent remains challenging, as dark patterns are subtle and evolve rapidly. Limited resources and cross-border legal gaps further hinder enforcement, allowing manipulation to persist. Stronger legal reforms and clearer guidelines are essential to dismantling these tactics and closing regulatory loopholes.

The final Section examines how dark patterns distort competition, granting unfair advantages to certain businesses at the expense of consumers and rivals.[12] Grounded in antitrust principles, it analyses how deceptive design undermines fair competition and reviews key regulatory actions against firms using manipulative tactics. Companies have faced penalties for trapping users in services or collecting excessive data to strengthen market dominance.[13] By assessing enforcement efforts, this section evaluates the effectiveness of current laws and proposes regulatory improvements to promote fair competition.

3.2. Deceptive Design and the Exploitation of Cookie and Data Protection Laws

Cookie notices and banner laws originated in the early 2000s, driven by the rapid proliferation of digital technologies and online services that demanded regulatory frameworks to protect consumer privacy and data security. The EU's introduction of Directive 2002/58/EC, commonly known as the ePrivacy Directive,[14] marked a significant legislative effort to address the privacy concerns associated with cookies and laid the groundwork for subsequent regulations. After an amendment to the law in 2009, websites were legally obliged to obtain user consent before storing or accessing information, primarily through cookies, on their devices.[15] These measures aimed to safeguard user privacy, prevent unauthorised tracking and data collection, and empower individuals to make informed decisions by managing their cookie preferences.[16] By requiring websites to disclose their cookie practices and secure consent before processing, these regulations sought to build a transparent and accountable digital ecosystem that empowered users with control over their data.

Despite these noble intentions, the practical implementation of cookie notices and banner laws encountered significant challenges. The practical implementation of these laws often reveals a stark gap between intention and reality, raising questions about their effectiveness in protecting users.[17] Cookie laws may have emerged to enhance transparency and give users greater control over data, but deceptive practices have frequently undermined their implementation. Businesses adapted dark patterns to comply with regulations while covertly advancing their data-tracking objectives formally. Early versions of cookie notices often needed more clarity and were frequently overlooked by users, leading to widespread non-compliance and undermining the effectiveness of the regulation.[18]

In response to these issues, the EU introduced the GDPR, reinforcing and expanding the requirements for cookie consent when using personal data and introducing stricter penalties for non-compliance. Simultaneously, two things happened: first, surveillance capitalism catalysed the evolution of sophisticated AdTech tools meticulously crafted to adhere to legal frameworks while adeptly harvesting user data. These technologies employ dark patterns to manipulate user consent subtly, maximising data collection and allowing businesses to exploit personal information for targeted advertising and profit. Second, the development of design norms aimed at protecting user privacy and ensuring transparency was significantly undermined by a pervasive 'race to the bottom' in design tactics. Driven by competitive pressure to maximise data collection, businesses widely adopted dark patterns that obscure opt-outs and mislead users. These practices undermine the law's intent, eroding trust and compromising consumer autonomy.

That competitive descent pressured designers to operate at the edge of legality. Santos, Gray, Bielova, and Ahuja critically analysed the tension between GDPR-compliant consent banners and usability principles in human-computer interaction. Using heuristic evaluation, they demonstrated how common design choices often fall short of legal standards for unambiguous, informed, and freely given consent, frequently embedding dark patterns that nudge users toward less privacy-protective options.[19]

By aligning usability heuristics with GDPR requirements, the authors highlighted the need to bridge legal and design disciplines to create consent interfaces that genuinely uphold user autonomy. They called for a shift toward transparent, neutral, and accessible consent banners, ensuring compliance while enhancing usability and reinforcing legal integrity.

3.2.1. Conflicts with Data Protection Laws

Emerging dark patterns exploiting cookie regulations present significant conflicts with established data protection frameworks, particularly the ePrivacy Directive and the GDPR. These conflicts arise from manipulating user consent and undermining transparency and informed decision-making processes mandated by these laws.[20] The GDPR requires individuals to consent freely, specifically, in an informed manner, and unambiguously.[21] Furthermore, the GDPR emphasises user autonomy *through* transparency,[22] mandating that organisations clearly and quickly explain how they will use individuals' data.[23]

One critical aspect is the readability and clarity of consent information. According to research by Soe et al, many cookie consent notices are designed to be complex and challenging to understand, thereby discouraging users from reading them thoroughly and making informed decisions.[24] This complexity often relies on lengthy text and legal jargon that average users struggle to interpret. Manipulation extends to consent interface design, where studies reveal that websites use colour contrast and button placement to steer users toward accepting cookies. The 'accept' button is typically bold and prominent. At the same time, the 'reject' option is muted or buried under multiple clicks, exploiting users' tendency to choose the most straightforward path – undermining genuine consent. Additionally, cookie retention often far exceeds necessity, with many stored for over a year, contravening the GDPR's requirement to limit data storage to its intended purpose.[25]

Another prominent issue scholars have identified regarding privacy and data protection: The misuse of consent management platforms (CMPs).[26] These platforms, theoretically designed to help websites comply with GDPR, often employ dark patterns. For instance, research has shown that 60 per cent of default notices from major CMPs contain at least one form of manipulative design.[27] These include pre-ticked boxes for consent, hiding rejection options behind multiple clicks, or presenting consent options in a confusing manner that nudges users towards acceptance.[28] Such practices violate the GDPR requirement that consent mechanisms be transparent and straightforward.[29] A study by Nyquist and Hildebrand highlighted how dark patterns in cookie consent interfaces can deceive users into giving more consent than necessary. Their research revealed that many websites use small notices or full-page popups to obscure user choices, thereby pressuring users into consenting to all cookies to continue using the site, violating Article 4(11) GDPR.[30]

The GDPR empowers users with enhanced controls over what it means to consent to data processing and places obligations on data controllers to ensure transparency in how they use a data subject's data. However, dark patterns subvert these goals by coercing users into consent without genuine understanding. Such practices, explicitly prohibited under the GDPR, undermine users' ability to make free and informed choices about their data.[31] Dark patterns erode user trust in online services and the broader digital ecosystem. When users feel deceived, confidence in platforms deteriorates, undermining long-term engagement. Beyond violating legal requirements, these manipulative practices weaken the trust essential for sustainable user-platform relationships.[32]

The economic impact of dark patterns and GDPR non-compliance is substantial. While the GDPR imposes fines of up to 4 per cent of annual global turnover for serious violations, companies weigh these penalties against the lucrative gains from data exploitation. For some, the potential profits justify the risk. However, regulatory enforcement and escalating fines highlight deceptive practices' financial and reputational costs, reinforcing the need for strict compliance with data protection laws.[33] The economic incentives behind dark patterns are straightforward – platforms profit from data collection, fuelling persistent manipulative practices despite regulatory risks. Weak enforcement often makes fines a mere cost of doing business in the EU, reinforcing this behaviour. However, companies must weigh short-term gains against long-term costs, including escalating penalties, legal scrutiny, and eroding consumer trust.

3.2.2. Geographical Inconsistencies in GDPR Application

Another conflict arises from the geographical inconsistencies in the application of GDPR. Websites from different regions exhibit varying levels of compliance, often influenced by local regulations and enforcement rigour. For example, websites in the UK and France show better compliance with GDPR, providing explicit consent options and using precise language. However, even these websites sometimes include pre-ticked boxes, which subtly coerce users into consenting. While the GDPR aims to harmonise standards for protecting data, the reality is that enforcement and compliance levels vary. This disparity allows some websites to exploit loopholes or less stringent enforcement in certain regions, thereby perpetuating dark patterns.[34] In contrast, South African websites frequently assume implicit consent, presenting users with no natural choice, a clear violation of GDPR standards that could lead to significant data protection issues for users interacting with these sites.[35]

The United States's approach to protecting consumer privacy presents another complex scenario. Without a federal equivalent to the GDPR, compliance varies widely. Some US-based websites offer clear consent options, while others do not adhere to the transparency and explicit consent standards associated with the GDPR. This lack of uniformity challenges global users and underscores the need for harmonised international data protection standards.[36] The inconsistency in compliance among US websites often results in extensive data collection that conflicts with GDPR principles. The CCPA represents a key shift in US cookie regulations, granting consumers rights to transparency, control, and opting out of data sales. Like the GDPR, it mandates clear and accessible notices, yet enforcement challenges persist.

The battle over cookie notices resembles a strategic chess match, with regulators tightening enforcement while companies devise new evasive tactics. Through convoluted language, misleading opt-ins, and manipulative layouts, businesses have refined data collection into deceptive art. Regulators are responding with sharper enforcement, but without robust follow-through, rules remain paper tigers. Bold, uncompromising action is needed to curb these practices. Addressing dark patterns requires both regulatory efforts and user empowerment to resist manipulation. A digitally aware public, capable of spotting pre-ticked boxes and buried opt-outs, is far harder to deceive. The evolution of cookie notices reflects a broader struggle between technological advances and corporate responsibility. The GDPR has raised the stakes, forcing companies to answer fundamental questions: Why are you tracking me? For how long? Who else gets access?

3.2.3. Enforcement

The enforcement of data protection laws by authorities such as CNIL (Commission Nationale de l'Informatique et des Libertés) and other Data Protection Authorities (DPAs) across Europe demonstrates a robust approach to addressing violations, particularly concerning the misuse of consent mechanisms and dark patterns. Authorities have emphasised that consent under Article 6(1)(a) GDPR must be given freely, specifically, in an informed manner, and unambiguously as per Article 4(11). Various cases highlight the significant penalties and corrective measures imposed on major tech companies for non-compliance. One notable case is CNIL's enforcement action against Google in 2019. Google was fined €50 million for insufficient consent policy information and misuse of personal data in ad personalisation. CNIL found that Google's consent process lacked transparency, with information scattered across multiple documents and the options to refuse consent not being as easily accessible as those to consent. This decision emphasised the GDPR's requirement for clear and accessible information and highlighted the manipulative nature of consent mechanisms employed by Google.[37] In 2020, CNIL again sanctioned Google, a total of €100 million,[38] and Amazon €35 million,[39] for deploying tracking cookies without valid user consent. Authorities imposed sanctions after determining that both companies deployed cookies on users' devices without securing prior consent or providing sufficient information. Their cookies also continued to track users even after they indicated they did not wish to allow tracking. CNIL also sanctioned Facebook in 2022, imposing a penalty of €60 million for similar reasons. Facebook's interface made accepting all cookies significantly easier than refusing them.[40] This practice violated the principle that consent must be as easy to withdraw as it is to provide, reinforcing that dark patterns in consent mechanisms are unlawful under the GDPR.

Another significant enforcement action involved the Belgian Data Protection Authority (DPA) in 2022, which fined the Interactive Advertising Bureau (IAB) Europe €250,000. The IAB's Transparency and Consent Framework (TCF), widely used across the ad tech industry to collect user consent for data processing, was non-compliant with the GDPR. The Belgian DPA determined that the TCF did not provide transparent and specific information regarding the processing purposes and did not ensure that users gave their consent freely. This decision underscores the regulatory focus on ensuring that consent frameworks do not employ dark patterns that could mislead users about their data protection rights.[41]

These enforcement actions reflect a broader trend of increased regulatory scrutiny and the imposition of substantial fines for non-compliance with data protection laws. The recurring themes in these cases include using dark patterns to manipulate consent, the lack of transparency in providing information about data processing, and the failure to make consent mechanisms straightforward and accessible. DPAs across Europe are collaborating to tackle these issues, emphasising the importance of a unified approach to enforcement. The European Data Protection Board (EDPB) has also played a crucial role in coordinating cross-border enforcement actions and issuing guidelines to clarify GDPR requirements. For example, the EDPB's guidelines on consent emphasise that organisations must obtain permission through affirmative action and cannot infer it from pre-ticked boxes or inactivity. These guidelines help organisations across the EU adopt best practices in acquiring and managing user consent, thereby minimising the risk of using dark patterns.[42] The Dutch Data Protection Authority, Autoriteit Persoonsgegevens, developed a structured approach to calculating fines for GDPR violations, categorising violations into four levels of severity and corresponding acceptable ranges. This structured approach is part of a broader effort to ensure that enforcement is consistent and proportionate to the seriousness of the infractions. For instance, serious breaches involving deliberate misuse of user data or substantial harm to individuals' rights attract higher penalties. This methodology ensures that fines effectively deter violations and transparently explains how authorities make enforcement decisions.[43]

3.3. Consumer Law and Deceptive Design

Imagine a consumer drawn to a 'Limited-Time Offer' that never expires. The UCPD protects individuals from deceptive tactics while recognising that some industries thrive on bold sales techniques that do not require micro-regulation. At its core, the Directive prohibits *unfair* commercial practices that distort consumer decision-making, categorising them into misleading actions, misleading omissions, and aggressive practices. A retailer inflating prices to promote fake discounts exemplifies misleading actions, while omitting key subscription costs constitutes a misleading omission. Aggressive tactics, such as pressuring vulnerable consumers, further highlight the need for enforcement. Annex I of the UCPD strengthens compliance by blacklisting 31 inherently unfair practices, from bait advertising to false professional endorsements. For instance, sending deceptive invoices disguised as overdue payments is explicitly outlawed. Picture a scenario where unscrupulous actors inundate a user with invoices for a service, cleverly disguising them to look like overdue payments – a tactic expressly forbidden in the Directive. Thus, this blacklist serves as a beacon of clarity for regulators and businesses alike, providing unambiguous benchmarks for compliance and enforcement.

The UCPD's emphasis on transparency and honesty in commercial communications further underpins its philosophy. It requires that consumer information is presented accurately and without deception. This principle is not simply about semantics but addresses a critical power imbalance. In a digital age where businesses deploy complex algorithms to tailor offers and obscure critical terms, the Directive protects the average consumer – defined by the CJEU as reasonably informed, observant, and circumspect – from being misled.[44] Moreover, the Directive provides a structured approach to determining unfairness. Factors such as the practice's impact on the average consumer's economic behaviour and its potential to cause detriment play pivotal roles in enforcement decisions. The 'average consumer' standard is not static but contextual, evolving to account for vulnerable groups and specific circumstances, such as children or those in financial distress. For instance, regulators would assess a payday loan advertisement targeting individuals facing economic hardship through a lens that accounts for their heightened susceptibility.

Enforcement remains primarily in the hands of national authorities tasked with upholding the Directive's principles within their jurisdictions. These authorities can investigate and sanction businesses that violate the Directive, ensuring a harmonised approach across the EU's member states. Despite this decentralised enforcement, the Directive fosters consistency, balancing the flexibility of local applications with the overarching goal of maintaining high consumer protection standards. The UCPD is not merely a legal instrument but a living framework that reflects the dynamic between consumer rights and commercial interests. Its provisions function as a sword and a shield – proactively delineating boundaries for businesses while reacting decisively against violations.

Meanwhile, the FTC Act in the United States is structured to empower the Federal Trade Commission (FTC) to prevent unfair methods of competition and unfair or deceptive acts or practices in commerce.[45] The Act establishes the FTC as an independent agency with broad authority to enforce antitrust and consumer protection laws.[46] It includes provisions that define and prohibit unfair or deceptive acts or practices, with Section 5 as the cornerstone, prohibiting 'unfair or deceptive acts or practices in or affecting commerce'. The FTC Act grants the Commission investigative powers, including conducting investigations, requiring reports, and issuing subpoenas.[47] It also provides the FTC with enforcement mechanisms such as cease-and-desist orders, administrative proceedings, and civil penalties. Furthermore, the Act allows for rulemaking to define and prevent specific unfair practices and facilitates cooperation with other agencies and international bodies.[48] The FTC Act's structure aims to protect consumers and maintain fair competition, with the FTC's Bureau of Consumer Protection and Bureau of Competition playing central roles in implementing and enforcing the Act's provisions.

The UCPD and the FTC Act aim to protect consumers from deceptive and unfair business practices, but they operate within different regulatory frameworks and scopes. The UCPD provides a harmonised legal framework across EU member states, explicitly prohibiting unfair commercial practices through clearly defined categories and a blacklist of prohibited practices, ensuring uniform enforcement by national authorities. In contrast, the FTC Act empowers the Federal Trade Commission to prevent unfair or deceptive acts in commerce, granting it broad investigative and enforcement powers to address deceptive practices. While the UCPD sets out specific unfair practices in all circumstances, the FTC Act relies on a broader interpretation of unfair or deceptive practices, allowing for more flexible and case-by-case enforcement. Both frameworks curb manipulative design practices. However, the UCPD's detailed provisions and uniform application across the EU contrast with the FTC's more discretionary and flexible approach in the US.

The UK's Competition and Markets Authority (CMA) is an independent non-ministerial government department responsible for promoting competition and preventing anti-competitive activities, including misleading and unfair commercial practices. Unlike the UCPD in the EU, which provides a harmonised framework across EU member states, the CMA operates within the UK's domestic legal context. The CMA applies the Consumer Protection from Unfair Trading Regulations 2008, which mirrors the principles of the UCPD while tailoring them to UK law. The CMA's approach combines elements of both the UCPD's specific prohibitions and the FTC's broad enforcement powers. While the FTC enforces US federal law with a broad scope of authority, the CMA focuses on ensuring fair competition and consumer protection within the UK, often addressing market-wide issues and systemic practices through investigations, market studies, and enforcement actions. This integrated approach makes the CMA's regulatory framework distinct, combining competition and consumer protection roles within a single body, compared to the more specialised focus of the FTC and the EU's coordinated but nationally implemented UCPD framework.

3.3.1. Definition and Scope of Unfair Commercial Practices

The UCPD creates a robust framework to shield EU consumers from unfair, misleading, and aggressive business practices across advertising, marketing, and sales in business-to-consumer transactions. Article 2 UCPD lays the groundwork with its precise definitions of 'consumer,' 'trader,' and 'product,' setting the stage for its sweeping reach across industries. Article 5 strikes the heart of the matter with a blanket ban on unfair commercial practices, while Articles 6 and 7 sharpen the focus, targeting misleading actions and omissions with surgical precision. Articles 8 and 9 tackle aggressive tactics head-on, outlawing coercion and undue influence. For those who prefer specifics, Annex I delivers a no-nonsense blacklist of 31 practices deemed unfair in any context, giving regulators and businesses an unequivocal playbook to follow. Enforcement of the UCPD lies in the hands of national authorities in each member state, tasked with monitoring compliance, investigating breaches, and imposing penalties. By harmonising consumer protection laws across the EU, the Directive eliminates legal fragmentation. It guarantees robust consumer safeguards in every member state, building trust and ensuring fair competition across the internal market.[49]

3.3.2. How Dark Patterns are Classified as Unfair Commercial Practices

Dark patterns risk classification as unfair commercial practices because their inherently deceptive and manipulative nature violates the Directive's core principles of fairness, transparency, and consumer autonomy. Misleading actions and omissions that distort or are likely to distort the economic behaviour of the average consumer are prohibited.[50] Dark patterns often fall into these categories by presenting information that confuses consumers, hides crucial details, or creates a false impression of the transaction. For example, pre-ticked boxes for agreement to the terms and conditions or payment subscriptions exploit consumers' inattentiveness, resulting in users inadvertently agreeing to additional services or data collection. These practices contravene the explicit, informed consent requirement and specific, unambiguous information.[51] Coercive tactics that impair consumers' ability to make free choices, such as persistent popups or countdown timers that pressure users into hurried decisions can also amount to aggressive practices.[52] Other patterns are identifiable as UCPD violations due to their direct alignment with unfair practices outlined in the Directive and its Annex I blacklist.[53]

Determining whether a dark pattern constitutes a UCPD violation involves assessing the practice against specific criteria, such as the clarity, accuracy, and completeness of the information provided to consumers and the practice's potential to distort the economic behaviour of an average consumer. Regulatory authorities evaluate the context in which the information appears, examining the design and functionality of the user interface and the ease with which consumers can access and understand relevant details. This comprehensive assessment ensures that the presentation of information is clear and that the design or functionality of the interface does not mislead consumers. For example, 'hidden costs', where businesses disclose additional charges only at the final stages of a transaction, contravene the Directive's requirements for transparency and informed consumer choice.[54] Accordingly, this would amount to a misleading omission. Regulators also scrutinise practices such as urgency tactics with countdown timers that pressure consumers into making quick decisions of their aggressive nature.[55]

Annex I further supports classifying some dark patterns as unfair practices without determining whether an average consumer would have made the same decision. Several dark patterns align with these blacklisted practices, such as 'Limited-Time Offer', creating unwarranted urgency and pressuring consumers into making immediate purchasing decisions without adequate consideration. Using such tactics to manipulate consumer behaviour directly contradicts the Directive's aim to protect consumers from exploitation and ensure fair market practices. Additionally, the *New Deal for Consumers* reform package highlighted the importance of addressing the digitalisation of commerce and the advanced techniques companies use to influence consumer behaviour, such as algorithm-driven personalisation and other methods that can subtly affect consumer decisions without direct deception. By classifying dark patterns as unfair commercial practices, the UCPD, in theory, provides a robust legal framework to combat deceptive techniques and uphold consumer rights across increasingly complex digital marketplaces.

My former master's student, Wen-Ting Yang, developed a hierarchical taxonomy of dark patterns, as illustrated below. This taxonomy aligns closely with the UCPD by highlighting how these manipulative tactics can mislead and coerce consumers, distorting their economic behaviour.[56] The taxonomy categorises dark patterns into four primary levels: active misleading actions, passive misleading omissions, undesirable imposition, and undesirable restriction. Each level includes specific tactics such as misleading information, hidden costs, pressured selling, and forced continuity. These tactics map onto the UCPD's provisions prohibiting practices likely to materially distort the economic behaviour of the average consumer.[57]

Similarly, passive misleading omissions, such as hiding critical information or delaying provision, align with the UCPD's stance against practices that omit essential information, thereby misleading consumers. Undesirable impositions, including pressure selling and sneak-into-basket tactics, mirror aggressive practices under the UCPD that exert undue pressure on consumers. Finally, undesirable restrictions like making cancellations difficult or using roach motels align with practices that exploit consumer vulnerabilities and hinder their ability to make informed choices. By categorising these dark patterns, the Yang & Leiser taxonomy provides a structured approach to understanding and regulating these practices within the UCPD framework, ensuring comprehensive consumer protection against subtle and overt forms of manipulation.[58]

Yang & Leiser's four-level hierarchical taxonomy & corresponding types of dark patterns			
Category		**Type**	**Explanation**
Information Asymmetry	Active Misleading Actions — Misleading Information	Testimonials of Uncertain Origin	Misleading users by providing them with false, confounding, deceiving, or exaggerated information
		Scarcity	Misleading users by providing them with false, confounding, deceiving, or exaggerated information
		Friend Spam	Misleading users by providing deceiving information
		Fake Countdown Timers	Misleading users by providing them with fraudulent information
		Limited-time Messages	Misleading users by providing them with deceiving or exaggerated information
	Misleading Presentation	Trick Questions	Misleading users through wording
		Misdirection (Visual Interference)	Misleading users by using visual interference
	Passive Misleading Omissions — Hiding Information	Price Comparison Prevention	Misleading users by withholding clear and comprehensible price information

(continued)

(Continued)

Yang & Leiser's four-level hierarchical taxonomy & corresponding types of dark patterns				
Category			**Type**	**Explanation**
		Delaying Provision	Hidden Costs	Delaying price information provisions
Free Choice Repression	Undesirable Imposition	Pressure Imposing	Pressured Selling (Repeated Popup Dialogs or Confirm Shaming)	Imposing pressure on users through repeated inquiries or wordings that make users experience guilt or shame
		Forced Acceptance	Sneak into Basket	Compelling consumers to accept the uninvited products by directly placing the products in their shopping carts
			Privacy Zuckering (Easy to Register)	Compelling consumers to accept the undesirable subscription by using tricks that thrust them towards subscriptions
			Forced Continuity (Hidden Subscription)	Compelling consumers to continue the subscription by renewing their membership subtly

(continued)

(Continued)

Yang & Leiser's four-level hierarchical taxonomy & corresponding types of dark patterns			
Category		**Type**	**Explanation**
		Bait and Switch	Compelling users to accept a particular arrangement by manipulatively navigating them away from their original objective regardless of their willingness
		Disguised Advertisement	Compelling users to view an advertisement by manipulatively navigating them away to a location that they did not expect to reach, regardless of their willingness
	Undesirable Restriction	Restricting Specific Users	Forced Action (Enrol to Access, Pay to Skip, and Accept to Access)	Restricting unpaid or unsubscribed users from options such as content access or skipping advertisements
		Restricting Specific Actions	Roach Motel (Hard to Cancel)	Making specific actions such as unsubscribing more complicated than needs to be

3.3.3. Challenges in Identifying and Regulating Dark Patterns under EU Consumer Law

The UCPD's consumer-centric approach is a key strength, as regulators need not prove intent to classify a practice as unfair. Instead, the focus is on whether a commercial practice materially distorts consumer behaviour. This design allows enforcement against manipulative tactics, even when no deceptive intent is evident, addressing the complexity of modern marketing strategies and subtle dark patterns. Since many exploit psychological principles or are embedded in digital interfaces, proving intent would be impossible. By prioritising impact over motivation, the UCPD ensures broad consumer protection. However, the Directive's broad definitions of misleading and aggressive practices create enforcement inconsistencies. The concept of 'material distortion' is context-dependent, and the reliance on the 'average consumer' standard overlooks cultural, educational, and technological differences. Additionally, the UCPD primarily targets surface-level manipulations in user interfaces, missing deeper deceptive strategies within system architectures and algorithmic processes. These gaps demand a shift toward a more adaptive regulatory framework that embraces clear, actionable guidelines and redefines what constitutes an *unfair* dark pattern in the rapidly evolving digital marketplace.

Assessing infractions under the UCPD is complex due to the evolving nature of commercial practices, particularly in digital markets. A key challenge lies in the subjective interpretation of 'misleading' or 'aggressive' practices, which depend on context and consumer perception. Variations in digital literacy, cultural norms, and consumer behaviour across EU member states further complicate enforcement. The rapid advancement of digital technologies, including personalised algorithms and behavioural targeting, increasingly blurs the line between legitimate persuasion and unfair manipulation. Regulators must continuously refine their understanding and guidelines to keep pace, demanding expertise at the intersection of law and technology.

Additionally, the cross-border nature of digital commerce introduces jurisdictional complexities, as practices that might be compliant in one member state could infringe regulations in another, necessitating coordinated enforcement actions and harmonised interpretation of the UCPD provisions. The enforcement process also faces the challenge of proving causation, particularly with dark patterns that subtly influence consumer behaviour without overt deception, making it difficult to demonstrate that the practice significantly distorts a consumer's economic behaviour. These challenges necessitate a dynamic and multifaceted approach to regulation, encompassing continuous monitoring, robust cross-border cooperation, and an adaptable legal framework that can effectively address the intricacies of modern commercial practices.

The EU's consumer law acquis provides a strong framework for protecting consumers and ensuring fair market practices through directives like the UCPD, UCTD, and CRD. Article 11 UCPD allows entities with a legitimate interest to challenge unfair commercial practices, enabling courts or authorities to prohibit dark patterns without requiring proof of harm. This pre-emptive approach safeguards consumers from manipulation before damage occurs. Recent updates also enhance remedies, granting affected consumers compensation, price reductions, or contract termination. Contractual fairness protections further counter manipulative design tactics by invalidating unfair terms and preventing their enforcement. Member states must implement deterrents against repeated violations, fostering a dissuasive legal environment. Consumer organisations and public bodies play a critical role in ensuring compliance, while recent amendments introduce more substantial penalties, reinforcing enforcement and accountability.[59]

The framework for protecting consumer interests gains additional strength through mechanisms that allow authorities or associations to seek court orders to halt unlawful practices that harm collective consumer interests. These mechanisms are particularly critical in addressing the cross-border nature of digital commerce, ensuring that national boundaries do not constrain enforcement efforts. Regulatory networks also facilitate coordinated EU-wide enforcement by empowering consumer protection authorities to tackle widespread infringements effectively, especially those with a Union dimension.[60] Additionally, new provisions introduce class action litigation, enabling collective redress for consumers and providing a more potent mechanism for addressing widespread violations.[61] These measures enhance the deterrent effect, promote compliance, and ensure consumers access effective remedies. Together, these interconnected tools establish a comprehensive enforcement regime capable of addressing the evolving challenges in consumer protection.[62]

3.3.4. Challenges in Identifying and Regulating Dark Patterns under Section 5 of the FTC Act

Identifying and regulating dark patterns under section 5 of the FTC Act presents significant challenges, although establishing intent is not always necessary for a practice to be deemed unfair or deceptive. The FTC Act primarily focuses on the likelihood of a practice causing substantial injury to consumers, which they cannot reasonably avoid, and that is not outweighed by countervailing consumer benefits or competition.[63] This consumer-centric approach allows for classifying practices as unfair or deceptive based on their effects, regardless of the intent behind them. This consumer-centric approach allows for classifying practices as unfair or deceptive based on their effects, regardless of the intent behind them. However, proving deceptive intent can be particularly challenging given the sophistication of modern digital marketing strategies and the subtle nature of dark patterns. These tactics often rely on psychological principles and design elements that influence consumer behaviour in ways that are not immediately apparent, complicating the demonstration that a trader intentionally sought to deceive. The complexity of digital environments further exacerbates this challenge, as manipulative practices often reside deep within user interfaces or algorithms. Consequently, regulators must rely on thorough analyses of a practice's design, implementation, and consumer impact rather than establishing intent. This approach emphasises the FTC Act's broad protective scope, focusing on harmful outcomes to safeguard consumer interests.

The limitations of current legal definitions and thresholds for unfair or deceptive practices under the FTC Act create significant challenges in effectively regulating and addressing emerging manipulative tactics, especially in the digital realm. While the FTC Act provides a framework for addressing deceptive and unfair practices, these definitions can be vague and open to interpretation, leading to inconsistencies in enforcement. For instance, what constitutes 'substantial injury' or whether a practice is 'reasonably avoidable' can vary widely depending on the context and subjective perceptions of regulators and courts. The Act's reliance on the concept of a reasonable consumer, who is assumed to possess average understanding and judgment, further complicates matters, as consumer understanding and expectations can differ significantly based on cultural, educational, and technological factors. This variability makes it challenging to apply a uniform standard, especially when dealing with sophisticated dark patterns that exploit nuanced psychological triggers and advanced technological interfaces. Additionally, the FTC Act's focus on visible practices within the user interface may overlook more covert manipulative tactics embedded within the system architecture or algorithmic processes, which are harder to detect and prove. These limitations necessitate a more dynamic and adaptive regulatory framework that can address the evolving landscape of digital commercial practices, providing more specific guidelines and thresholds for what constitutes an unfair or deceptive dark pattern in digital marketplaces.

Determining the relevant aspects of infractions under the FTC Act is further complicated by the nuanced and evolving nature of commercial practices, particularly in the digital domain. A primary challenge is the subjective interpretation of what constitutes an 'unfair' or a 'deceptive' practice, as these definitions rely heavily on context and the perception of a reasonable consumer. The diversity of consumer profiles, varying levels of digital literacy, and cultural differences across the United States complicate assessing what an average consumer might find misleading or coercive. Furthermore, the rapid advancement of digital technologies and sophisticated marketing techniques, such as personalised algorithms and behavioural targeting, blurs the line between legitimate persuasion and unfair manipulation. Regulatory authorities must continually update their understanding and guidelines to keep pace with these developments, requiring substantial expertise in both legal and technological domains.

Additionally, the cross-border nature of digital commerce introduces jurisdictional complexities. Practices that might comply with one state's laws could violate those of another, necessitating coordinated enforcement actions and a harmonised interpretation of the FTC Act's provisions. The enforcement process also faces the challenge of proving intent and causation, particularly with dark patterns that subtly influence consumer behaviour without overt deception, making it difficult to demonstrate that the practice significantly distorts a consumer's economic decisions. These challenges necessitate a dynamic and multifaceted approach to regulation, encompassing continuous monitoring, robust cross-border cooperation, and an adaptable legal framework that can effectively address the intricacies of modern commercial practices.

3.3.5. Enforcement

Enforcing laws restricting dark patterns in Europe is challenging due to these manipulative tactics' sophisticated and evolving nature. The broad definitions within the UCPD and varying interpretations of what constitutes misleading or aggressive practices complicate enforcement efforts. The reliance on the 'average consumer' standard further complicates matters, as understanding and expectations of what amounts to an average consumer vary widely across different contexts. The cross-border nature of digital commerce introduces additional complexities, requiring coordinated enforcement and harmonised interpretations of the UCPD. The European Commission introduced efforts such as the DSA and the DMA, in part, to address these gaps, but they face challenges in covering the full spectrum of deceptive design, highlighting the need for a dynamic and adaptive regulatory approach to ensure adequate consumer protection.

Enforcement issues related to dark patterns under section 5 of the FTC Act and within the broader regulatory landscape pose significant challenges, given these deceptive practices' sophisticated and evolving nature. Dark patterns often fall into a legal grey area that complicates enforcement efforts. Identifying and proving the intent behind these patterns is difficult because businesses weave them into complex system architectures and algorithms, making them less visible and more challenging to regulate. The variability in consumer perceptions and the nuances in defining what constitutes 'unfair' or 'deceptive' practices compound the issue and can lead to inconsistent enforcement across jurisdictions. The FTC has historically focused on explicit and overt deceptive practices but faces challenges addressing more subtle and insidious dark patterns.

Recent regulatory actions, such as those by the CMA and other international bodies, highlight the need for a more robust and dynamic framework to adapt to new technological developments and provide clear guidelines to prevent manipulative designs. These actions underscore the importance of cross-border cooperation and the integration of technical expertise in regulatory practices to detect and combat dark patterns effectively. However, the current legal frameworks, including the DSA, DMA, and AI Act, although comprehensive, still struggle to fully address the most profound and most covert dark patterns embedded in digital architectures, necessitating continuous updates and enhanced enforcement strategies to protect consumer autonomy and ensure fair digital marketplaces.

The EDPB's WhatsApp binding decision highlights the critical need for rigorous enforcement against dark patterns that mislead users regarding their data. This decision required WhatsApp Ireland Limited to rectify user interfaces and practices to ensure compliance with GDPR principles, specifically targeting deceptive design elements that obscure user choices and consent processes.[64] The EDPB guidelines on deceptive design patterns in social media platform interfaces[65] (discussed at length in chapter eight) and the binding decision regarding WhatsApp Ireland Limited collectively emphasise the need for stringent enforcement mechanisms to tackle deceptive design practices effectively. The guidelines delineate specific design patterns that mislead users into making decisions that are not in their best interest, violating the principles of transparency, fairness, and data minimisation.[66] These guidelines are responsive to enforcement actions like the binding decision as they provide a structured approach for identifying and addressing deceptive practices.

The EDPB's decision also mandates that national supervisory authorities (SAs), like the Irish Supervisory Authority (IE SA), enforce compliance by imposing administrative fines and other corrective measures that are effective, proportionate, and dissuasive. The binding decision required the IE SA to recalibrate its final decision to ensure that WhatsApp IE's practices align with the GDPR's core principles.

3.4. Unfair Competition and Deceptive Practices

Unfair competition laws, including those in the European Union, aim to protect consumers and ensure fair market practices by addressing deceptive or unjust business tactics that distort marketplace dynamics. Thus, design strategies that manipulate or mislead users to achieve specific outcomes that benefit the business reduce overall consumer welfare and market efficiency. Shifting the focus from competing on product quality and price to exploiting consumer vulnerabilities through deceptive design can weaken competition. For example, a company that uses a design that makes it difficult to cancel a subscription service locks users into continued use and payment, preventing competitors from gaining these customers.

This practice skews the competitive landscape by artificially inflating the company's user base and retention rates, inflating its market share at the expense of competitors who engage in fairer practices. Moreover, deceptive design can effectively lock users into a specific service or product ecosystem, making it difficult for competitors to attract these users. For example, an e-commerce platform may employ urgency tactics such as countdown timers or limited-time offers to encourage users' swift purchasing decisions, thereby minimising competitors' chance to present potentially better deals or more appropriate alternatives. Exploitative design appears in cases like the CMA's investigation into online hotel booking platforms, where false scarcity and misleading rankings manipulated consumer choices by creating a false sense of urgency, limiting their ability to compare options, and increasing search costs.[67] Such practices can lead to a 'race to the bottom' where businesses compete on who can use these manipulative tactics most effectively rather than improving their product offerings or services.[68]

By manipulating user behaviour, companies can artificially inflate their market position, making it harder for new entrants or smaller competitors to gain a foothold. The result is often a market characterised by poor product quality, higher prices, and reduced innovation.[69] Established companies with extensive resources can invest in sophisticated, deceptive designs that smaller competitors cannot match, creating barriers to entry. Furthermore, when businesses manipulate users into sticking with a particular service or product, the market dynamic shifts, reducing the natural churn that would otherwise benefit competition and innovation. They undermine trust with their users and within the market. Trust is a crucial component of healthy competition as it ensures that businesses compete based on the quality and value of their offerings rather than through manipulative tactics. Deceptive practices erode trust, leading to a market where success is determined more by who can better exploit user vulnerabilities than by providing the best product or service.[70]

Moreover, unfair competitive practices stifle innovation. When businesses rely on dark patterns and deceptive designs to retain users, there is less incentive to improve their products or services genuinely.[71] Competitors who might offer more innovative or higher-quality alternatives find it challenging to attract users who are effectively trapped in another service's ecosystem.[72] This situation leads to market stagnation, where dominant players maintain their position through superior offerings and manipulative retention strategies.[73] In academic discourse, it is crucial to understand the impact of design manipulation on competitive dynamics. Research that combines insights from behavioural economics, human-computer interaction, and market competition can provide a comprehensive framework for identifying and addressing these deceptive practices.[74] By highlighting the competitive distortions caused by dark patterns and deceptive design, scholars can advocate for strategies and policies that promote a fairer and more transparent marketplace. Fostering a competitive environment prioritising innovation, quality, and ethical behaviour is essential for maintaining the market's integrity and encouraging genuine progress.[75]

3.4.1. Unfair Competition in Digital Markets

Unfair competition in digital markets refers to practices that distort the competitive landscape, often through manipulative strategies. Dark patterns and deceptive design are prominent examples of such practices, designed to mislead or coerce users into actions that benefit the business employing them, frequently at the expense of competitors. These patterns are not merely inconveniences but strategic tools to lock in customers, artificially inflate usage statistics, and create barriers to entry for competitors. For instance, a streaming service might obscure the cancellation process to reduce churn rates, thereby maintaining a more extensive subscriber base than it might otherwise deserve based on the quality of its content alone. The legal principles governing fair competition, including antitrust laws and competition law, aim to maintain a level playing field in the marketplace by preventing practices that distort competition and harm consumers.

Antitrust laws promote competition and curb monopolistic behaviours, particularly in jurisdictions like the United States.[76] These laws prohibit agreements or practices that restrict free trading and competition between businesses, such as price-fixing, market division, and monopolistic mergers. In the context of digital markets, applying these laws is increasingly scrutinised as large technology companies often engage in behaviours that could appear anti-competitive. In the European Union, competition law aims to prevent the abuse of market power and ensure that competition remains fair and open. EU competition law prohibits anti-competitive agreements and abusing dominant positions.[77] Discussed later in the next chapter, Article 13(6) DMA prohibits gatekeepers – large online platforms with significant market influence – from designing manipulative interfaces to bypass the DMA's obligations, ensuring transparency, fairness, and non-discrimination while preventing the use of dark patterns to gain unfair advantages or evade regulations.

3.4.2. Regulatory Actions

Several notable examples of cases deemed unfair competitive practices involving dark patterns exist. In the online hotel booking sector, the CMA found that platforms used misleading claims about room availability and popularity to rush consumers into booking decisions, thus artificially inflating their market position. These practices harmed consumers and distorted the competitive landscape by creating barriers to entry for other firms that did not engage in such deceptive tactics.[78] Similarly, the CMA identified issues with drip pricing and insufficient price transparency in the car rental industry, where the booking process obscured additional costs until the final stages.[79] This practice misled consumers about the actual cost of rentals and disadvantaged competitors who provided more precise pricing information. Another notable case centres on the practices of dominant online platforms such as Google and Facebook, which employed default settings and intricate privacy configurations to curtail consumer autonomy over personal data. By leveraging their substantial market power, these platforms entrenched their dominance, utilising dark patterns within their user interfaces to subtly manipulate consumer consent and data-sharing preferences. This strategic exploitation undermined individual data rights and stifled competition within the digital advertising market, further consolidating their advantage and distorting market dynamics. The CMA's actions against these practices highlight the importance of regulatory intervention in maintaining fair competition and protecting consumer interests.

3.4.3. Identification of Gaps and Areas
Needing Reform

A close analysis of the current legislative framework reveals critical gaps requiring targeted reform, particularly the need for a more nuanced approach in competition law to address the sophisticated digital manipulation of consumer behaviour through dark patterns. Traditional antitrust tools, designed to deal with price-fixing and market division, are not adequately equipped to oversee the subtleties of psychological and behavioural manipulations that dark patterns represent. These manipulative tactics can influence consumer choices in ways that do not immediately appear anti-competitive but cumulatively create significant market barriers for new entrants, maintaining the dominance of established players.[80]

Existing competition laws, although designed to promote fairness, often lack specific provisions to address these nuanced manipulation tactics effectively. For instance, in the case of Amazon's use of dark patterns to enrol consumers into recurring subscriptions, the FTC had to intervene specifically to address these deceptive practices, highlighting the insufficiency of general competition laws in tackling such issues.[81] This gap allows dominant market players to leverage dark patterns without significant regulatory repercussions. These strategies' inherent subtlety and sophistication present substantial challenges for traditional regulatory oversight, typically oriented towards more overt forms of anti-competitive conduct. To effectively address these issues, regulatory bodies must develop a comprehensive understanding of the mechanisms underlying digital manipulations and their broader implications for market competition. This highlights the pressing necessity for more precisely tailored regulatory frameworks capable of addressing digital market practices' increasingly complex and dynamic nature.

Recent reforms in EU consumer law, mainly through the 'New Deal for Consumers', have significantly strengthened the framework for consumer protection and adapted it to the digital age.[82] This initiative includes amendments to key directives such as the UCPD and introducing new regulations to enhance transparency and fairness in the digital marketplace. The New Deal for Consumers enhances penalties for widespread cross-border infringements, increasing maximum fines to at least 4 per cent of a trader's annual turnover.[83] It also mandates more straightforward information requirements for online marketplaces, ensuring consumers are informed about the main parameters determining the ranking of offers and whether third-party providers act as traders.[84] One significant aspect of these reforms was the 'digital fitness test' (discussed further in chapter eight), which assessed whether existing consumer protection laws suit the challenges posed by online platforms, e-commerce, and digital services.[85] These reforms are relevant for understanding EU consumer law as they modernise the legal framework, making it more robust and capable of addressing contemporary issues such as dark patterns and misleading practices in the digital environment. The digital fitness test further ensures that EU consumer law remains effective in protecting consumers in a rapidly evolving digital landscape, reinforcing the principles of transparency, fairness, and informed consumer choice central to the UCPD and related legislation.[86]

Manipulative design elements frequently exploit psychological and behavioural vulnerabilities, creating an illusion of control for users. These techniques often include default settings that nudge individuals toward privacy-intrusive options, the strategic use of ambiguous language, and obfuscation of privacy-friendly alternatives.[87] A renewed emphasis on transparency and consumer empowerment is imperative to counter these practices effectively. Ensuring users understand and manage how their data is utilised would significantly reduce information asymmetry, a core enabler of such manipulations.[88] This calls for robust enforcement of existing consumer laws and updates to address dark patterns explicitly, potentially through introducing a generic duty of care for businesses to avoid employing manipulative designs altogether.[89] The regulatory focus should extend beyond individual infractions to consider the cumulative impact of multiple dark patterns within a system. Transparent, standardised consent mechanisms that make opting out as simple as opting in are essential to restoring balance in digital interactions. Additionally, future legislation must proactively address emerging technologies, such as AR, VR, and AI, which present new opportunities for manipulative practices.[90] A clear legal framework is needed to prohibit deceptive designs explicitly, ensuring that transparency and consumer control over personalised commercial practices remain central to regulatory goals.[91] Beyond these legislative measures, strengthening enforcement mechanisms is critical. While current laws address many unfair practices, the lack of consistent and effective enforcement weakens their impact.[92] Prescriptive measures, such as mandatory cancellation buttons for subscriptions, could ensure fairer digital environments and complement existing regulations.[93] Furthermore, integrating system-level considerations into legislative discussions will allow for comprehensive strategies to mitigate the broader effects of dark patterns on consumer autonomy and market fairness.

3.5. Conclusion

This chapter examined regulatory strategies for addressing dark patterns, arguing for a more adaptive approach to counter their evolving sophistication. It detailed how consumer protection, data privacy, and competition regulators have grappled with these manipulative tactics, highlighting the roles of entities like the FTC, CPPA, CMA, and EU bodies.

Platforms use ambiguous language and pre-ticked boxes to steer users toward consent, bypassing *the spirit* of regulations like the GDPR and the CCPA. In the *Planet49* case,[94] cookie consent mechanisms deliberately aimed to ensure maximum data collection rather than to inform users.

Deceptive designs often permeate business models so deeply that casual users overlook them, and regulators struggle to untangle them. Addressing these challenges requires continuous monitoring, robust enforcement, and systemic reform. However, regulators often lack the resources or jurisdictional reach to hold offenders accountable, and cross-border digital practices allow corporations to exploit regulatory inconsistencies. While legal frameworks increasingly recognise the harms of deceptive design, regulatory interventions remain fragmented and struggle to capture the complexity of these manipulative tactics. The law is not always on the user's side. Though regulators continue to prioritise the transparency principle as a regulatory tool, it is often insufficient to counter sophisticated techniques such as gamified consent mechanisms or algorithmic personalisation that exploit behavioural biases.

The chapter also emphasised the need for a coordinated regulatory response. The collaborative work of the UK ICO and CMA further underscores the need for coordinated regulatory action. Scholars like Di Porto[95] and I have argued that aligning consumer, privacy, and competition law is critical to preventing fragmented enforcement.[96] Yet, current policy efforts fail to capture the complexity and adaptability of dark patterns.

Lawmakers must develop adaptable legal frameworks, businesses must move beyond compliance to foster genuine consumer trust, and regulators must require greater resources and enforcement power. Beyond addressing immediate harms, it must anticipate emerging risks, such as AI-driven personalisation that blurs the line between persuasion and coercion.

4

Emerging Digital Design Laws and Regulations

4.1. Introduction

As discussed in previous chapters, dark patterns and broader forms of deceptive design lead users to actions they otherwise might not take, often without their full awareness.[1] The European Union (EU) shapes its legal frameworks to balance innovation with the protection of individual rights, a task made increasingly complex by the swift evolution of digital platforms and the growing challenges they present, particularly in their capacity to influence and, at times, manipulate user behaviour. Accordingly, this chapter provides a detailed examination of the EU's legislative response to these challenges, with a focus on emerging regulations such as the Digital Services Act (DSA),[2] Digital Markets Act (DMA)[3] and the Data Act,[4] as well as revisiting critical regulations like the ePrivacy Directive,[5] General Data Protection Regulation (GDPR),[6] and Unfair Commercial Practices Directive (UCPD).[7] Against this backdrop, the chapter offers a critical perspective on the effectiveness of these regulations in safeguarding user autonomy and actively engaging the audience in the legal analysis. Focusing on the EU, the lessons on the law offer insights for addressing dark patterns and deceptive designs in other jurisdictions. As digital practices advance, the regulations that govern them must also adapt.[8] Earlier regulations, such as the ePrivacy Directive and the UCPD, continue to shape the changing digital environment, laying the groundwork for EU data protection and user privacy.

By setting clear standards for accountability and transparency, regulatory frameworks aim to uphold fairness and protect individual rights, ensuring technological progress serves the public interest. However, users often remain unaware of the subtle mechanisms shaping their decisions, highlighting the need for advanced regulatory interventions. Legal frameworks must address dark patterns and deceptive design while evolving to remain effective amid rapid technological and societal change. This chapter critically examines the adequacy of current legal frameworks in regulating the digital environment, where the line between legitimate persuasion and manipulation has blurred. Through an in-depth analysis of regulatory provisions, case studies, and comparative evaluations, it assesses whether existing laws effectively safeguard user autonomy and counteract increasingly sophisticated digital manipulation. The study underscores the need for coherence among regulatory initiatives, advocating for a unified approach to digital governance. While integrating older and newer laws offers a pathway toward a comprehensive protective framework, technological advancements demand adaptable legal mechanisms capable of addressing the complexities of modern digital systems.

Beyond legal technicalities, this analysis explores the broader implications of regulatory evolution for digital society. Despite progress with the DSA, DMA, and Data Act, regulatory alignment with technological change remains incomplete. At the core is Article 25 DSA, the first provision to directly address the manipulative potential of digital interfaces. Designed to curb user interface dark patterns, it mandates platforms to avoid deceptive or coercive design. This provision interacts with the GDPR and UCPD frameworks, reflecting the EU's broader attempt to enhance regulatory coherence and consumer confidence. A rigorous examination of these laws reveals their strengths and limitations in protecting consumers from evolving manipulative practices. This study identifies critical gaps and proposes avenues for transformative legal reform by integrating theoretical insights with empirical analysis.

4.2. Analysis of Key European Regulations

Recognising growing concerns over manipulative design and exploitative digital practices, the EU has strengthened its regulatory agenda with measures prioritising consumer protection, market integrity, and platform accountability. Central to these efforts, the DSA redefines digital intermediaries' responsibilities, while the DMA imposes stricter obligations on gatekeepers to ensure fair treatment. The Data Act enhances equitable data access, and the AI Act addresses the legal and societal challenges artificial intelligence poses. In theory, these regulations form a cohesive framework to curb manipulation, promote fairness, and foster trust in digital environments. In practice, however, their effectiveness is hindered by inconsistent enforcement, interpretive ambiguities, and the rapid evolution of manipulative design tactics that outpace regulatory adaptation.

4.2.1. The Digital Services Act (DSA)

The DSA represents a measured attempt by the EU to address the challenges posed by the increasingly complex and influential role of online platforms.[9] It introduces a structured and scaling set of obligations to improve transparency and accountability while addressing systemic risks such as disseminating harmful content and protecting fundamental rights in the digital environment.[10] By establishing uniform guidelines across member states, the DSA aims to ensure clarity and consistency in the regulatory environment, addressing the challenges posed by the rapidly evolving landscape of digital intermediaries. Rather than focusing solely on punitive measures, the DSA incorporates mechanisms to encourage responsible platform behaviour, particularly from dominant online platforms.[11] As such, the DSA signals an evolving approach to digital governance, striving to navigate the complexities of online ecosystems without imposing undue constraints on their development.[12] However, the framework prompts critical questions regarding its ability to navigate the competing priorities of promoting innovation, protecting user rights, and effectively regulating the activities of dominant digital actors.

4.2.1.1. The General Prohibition

Article 25 DSA is a pivotal provision to safeguard user autonomy and ensure informed decision-making. Targeting the design and operational practices of online platforms, it seeks to prohibit manipulative strategies that undermine the integrity of user choices and prioritise platform interests over user welfare. Article 25 prohibits the design, organisation, or operation of online platform interfaces in ways that *mislead, influence,* or *significantly* limit users' ability to make independent and informed decisions. The provision is deliberately framed broadly, capturing various manipulative practices *materially distorting* user decision-making processes. This encompasses the spectrum of dark patterns, including misleading prompts, obfuscated default settings, and interface designs that subtly coerce users into specific actions by complicating choices or introducing unnecessary friction. For example, the European Commission is investigating the design of blue checks on Elon Musk's X platform, focusing on whether the user interface is deceptively designed, particularly regarding checkmarks associated with certain subscription products.[13] Article 25's underlying objective is to safeguard decisional autonomy by addressing manipulative strategies embedded within digital interfaces that elevate platform interests at the expense of user welfare. By confronting such practices, the provision recognises interface design's subtle yet profound impact on user behaviour. It underscores the imperative that online platforms uphold the integrity of user decision-making processes as a fundamental principle:

Article 25, Online interface design and organisation – the Digital Services Act (DSA)

1. Providers of online platforms shall not design, organise or operate their online interfaces in a way that deceives or manipulates the recipients of their service or in a way that otherwise materially distorts or impairs the ability of the recipients of their service to make free and informed decisions.
2. The prohibition in paragraph 1 shall not apply to practices covered by Directive 2005/29/EC or Regulation (EU) 2016/679.
3. The Commission may issue guidelines on how paragraph 1 applies to specific practices, notably:
   (a) giving more prominence to certain choices when asking the recipient of the service for a decision;
   (b) repeatedly requesting that the recipient of the service make a choice where that choice has already been made, especially by presenting pop-ups that interfere with the user experience;
   (c) making the procedure for terminating a service more difficult than subscribing to it.

Article 25(1) is designed to prevent online platforms from employing practices that deceive, manipulate, or significantly undermine users' capacity to make autonomous and informed decisions:

> 1.   Providers of online platforms shall not design, organise or operate their online interfaces in a way that deceives or manipulates the recipients of their service or in a way that otherwise materially distorts or impairs the ability of the recipients of their service to make free and informed decisions.

Article 25(1) broadly prohibits user interface dark patterns, as classified in the previous chapter, but applies only to those that materially distort or impair user decision-making. This ensures that not all deceptive practices are banned – only those that significantly undermine free and informed choice. Article 25 balances conceptual breadth with a targeted regulatory threshold by focusing on material distortion, addressing harmful manipulation while allowing legitimate persuasive design. Recital 67 DSA clarifies the provision's scope, listing examples such as disproportionately prominent choices that steer behaviour, repetitive notifications pressuring decisions, and deliberately complex cancellation processes compared to easy subscription mechanisms:

> **Recital 67:** Dark patterns on online interfaces of online platforms are practices that materially distort or impair, either on purpose or in effect, the ability of recipients of the service to make autonomous and informed choices or decisions.

Article 25 prohibits intentional manipulation and practices impairing user autonomy, *regardless of a platform's intent*. Even if deception was not the objective, a platform may violate the DSA if its interface misleads or coerces users into decisions they would not otherwise make. This broad approach ensures the regulation remains effective as digital interfaces and manipulative tactics evolve. While not explicitly stated, the term 'operate' in Article 25 suggests platforms must consider the potential effects of their design choices on user autonomy. The prohibition against materially distorting decisions inherently shifts the focus to the consequences of platform operations, making intent a relevant but secondary concern. Platforms should conduct risk assessments to mitigate these risks and implement transparency, oversight, and accountability measures. Although not explicitly required, such practices align with the DSA's broader aim of fostering autonomy and informed choice.

4.2.1.2. *Online Platforms*

The DSA establishes a nuanced categorisation of online services, distinguishing between intermediary services, hosting services, and the subset of online platforms. As defined under the DSA, online platforms store and disseminate information to the public at a user's request.[14] This definition captures a broad spectrum of services, ranging from social media networks to online marketplaces, underscoring their significant role in shaping interactions and transactions within modern digital ecosystems. However, this classification does not extend to all consumer-facing technologies; for example, operating systems such as Microsoft Windows or Apple's iOS are explicitly excluded from the scope of online platforms.

Whether services qualify as online platforms depends on how their functionality aligns with Article 3(i) DSA's definition of an online platform. For a service to be classified as an online platform, it must involve the *public dissemination of information*. User-generated content in gaming platforms (eg, custom maps, chat messages, or in-game interactions) may be shared with other players, but whether this constitutes public dissemination depends on the reach and accessibility of the content. If the shared information is only accessible to a limited number of players (eg, within a private game session or party), it might not satisfy the 'public' dissemination requirement. Some services allow users to create and share custom content. If this content is stored and made accessible to the public, the provider could meet the DSA's definition of an online platform. However, the DSA excludes mere hosting services that do not actively disseminate content to a broad audience.

By concentrating on platforms that actively disseminate information to a broad audience, the DSA claims to address systemic risks linked to its operations while presenting itself as a targeted and proportionate regulatory framework. However, this distinction raises questions about its effectiveness, particularly given the significant number of services employing dark patterns that fall outside the scope of 'online platforms' defined under Article 25. A narrow scope undermines the DSA's objectives of creating a safer and more equitable digital environment. It leaves a loophole for manipulative design practices to persist without regulatory scrutiny – an issue explored further in the chapter.

The DSA also differentiates between various online services, recognising the unique impact of large platforms on society. This recognition has led to the concept of 'very large online platforms' (VLOPs), subject to more stringent regulations due to their reach and influence. VLOPs are identified based on the number of users they serve, with a threshold set at 45 million users in the EU, representing approximately 10 per cent of the population. Given their significant societal impact, these platforms must comply with additional obligations, such as conducting systemic risk assessments,[15] providing more transparency about their algorithms,[16] and allowing access to their data for regulatory scrutiny.[17] Under the DSA, the VLOP classification includes entities such as social media networks, online marketplaces, search engines, and cloud-based platforms that host and facilitate the sharing of user-generated content. The distinction considers that some services have a significant societal impact due to their vast reach and user base. The DSA imposes enhanced obligations on VLOPs, focusing on principles such as transparency, accountability, and the adequate protection of fundamental rights. By addressing the systemic influence of these platforms, the regulation seeks to ensure that their operations promote trust, uphold the integrity of digital interactions, and protect users' rights and autonomy within the digital ecosystem.

My long-term collaborator, Dr Cristiana Santos, and her colleagues conducted an in-depth analysis of Article 25, concentrating on its approach to addressing dark patterns in online platforms.[18] They concluded that Article 25 is deliberately broad, capturing a wide range of digital manipulative practices despite the absence of explicit reference to the term 'dark patterns'. This provision marks a milestone in digital regulation, codifying the protection of user autonomy as a fundamental legal principle and directly addressing practices long criticised for their manipulative and exploitative nature. Moreover, they discuss how Article 25 interacts with existing regulations, such as the GDPR and the UCPD. They argue that Article 25 complements these regulations by filling in gaps where the GDPR or UCPD may need to address certain manipulative practices fully. For example, while the GDPR focuses on data protection and the UCPD on unfair commercial practices, Article 25 targets user autonomy in digital environments, providing a more comprehensive approach to regulating dark patterns.

Their analysis extends to specific examples of how Article 25 could be applied, using popular services like Google Tag Manager and Google Analytics as case studies. The authors argue that these services, which website publishers widely use, incorporate dark patterns that should fall under the regulatory scope of the DSA. The authors underscore the importance of recognising business users as potential targets of dark patterns. This perspective significantly expands the applicability of Article 25 beyond its traditional focus on end-user consumers. Their approach aligns Article 25 with an established ontology of dark patterns, providing a systematic framework for identifying and categorising manipulative practices that warrant regulatory scrutiny. However, despite broadening the 'personal scope' of Article 25 to encompass a wider range of actors, the regulation remains anchored in its requirement that such practices result in a material distortion or impairment of decision-making. This threshold is conceptually demanding and evidentially challenging to substantiate.

Therefore, the DSA establishes a dynamic regulatory framework that compels platforms, particularly VLOPs and VLOSEs, to proactively assess, mitigate, and report systemic risks, thereby ensuring platforms prioritise user rights, democratic integrity, and societal resilience. Risk assessment and mitigation are intertwined obligations requiring VLOPs and VLOSEs to continuously evaluate systemic harms – ranging from algorithmic amplification of illegal content to manipulative design practices – and implement proportionate, evidence-based measures to minimise their impact on users and society.

Although the DSA does not explicitly mandate systemic risk assessments for dark patterns, its provisions impose obligations on VLOPs and VLOSEs that could encompass such evaluations. Article 34 requires these entities to conduct annual systemic risk assessments addressing risks related to disseminating illegal content, fundamental rights, electoral processes, public security, gender-based violence, and mental health. While dark patterns are not explicitly mentioned, those that undermine consumer autonomy, exploit vulnerabilities, or exacerbate risks to fundamental rights could fall within this scope. Under Article 35, platforms must implement mitigation measures to address identified risks, which may necessitate modifying deceptive design practices. Additionally, transparency obligations under Articles 31, 42, and 43 facilitate regulatory scrutiny and enforcement, enabling authorities to assess the systemic impact of dark patterns. Consequently, while not directly mandated, systemic risk assessments addressing dark patterns may be required where they contribute to identified risks, particularly those affecting consumer protection, data protection, and the rights of vulnerable users.

4.2.1.3. *Material Distortion*

Material distortion in EU law refers to practices that substantially impair an individual's capacity to make informed decisions, resulting in behaviours they would not have otherwise exhibited. This concept is a cornerstone of regulatory efforts to ensure fair treatment and shield consumers from manipulative influences. Embedded within legislative frameworks such as the DSA and the AI Act (discussed in chapters six and seven), the notion of material distortion addresses the increasingly sophisticated tactics used to manipulate consumer behaviour in digital environments. Rooted in the broader framework of EU law, material distortion reflects a well-established commitment to preventing the exploitation of consumer vulnerabilities and preserving market integrity.

In the context of Article 25, *material distortion* targets how online platforms can undermine users' autonomy by influencing their decision-making processes in ways that significantly impair their ability to make free and informed choices. As a pivotal component of consumer protection law, this concept extends the principles of fairness and accountability established under instruments like the UCPD. Article 25(1) DSA prohibits online platforms from designing, organising, or operating their interfaces in ways that deceive, manipulate, or materially distort users' decision-making processes. By addressing practices that cross the boundary from persuasion to manipulation, this prohibition protects users from making choices they might have rejected had they been fully aware of the underlying influences.

Material distortion (not just distortion!) is determined by several critical factors, primarily focusing on how much a practice impairs a person's autonomy and decision-making capacity. The impairment must be substantial enough to alter a person's behaviour, undermining their ability to make informed and independent choices. This concept closely relates to 'appreciable impairment' in EU consumer protection laws, which require evaluating how a practice impacts consumer decision-making. Moreover, other deceptive design techniques exploit users' cognitive biases or vulnerabilities. An essential distinction of material distortion under the DSA is that it involves more than just influencing a person's decision; it manipulates the decision-making process to such an extent that the individual's autonomy is significantly compromised.

Thus, Article 25(1)'s 'material distortion' is limited to when a dark pattern significantly impairs a user's ability to make an informed decision.[19] Examples of such practices might include making some choices more prominent, persistently prompting users to act, or making it deliberately difficult to cancel a service compared to subscribing to it. These techniques can distort the user's decision-making process by creating an imbalance whereby the user's autonomy is compromised, and factors outside their conscious control influence their decisions. However, the critical element is that it requires a *material* distortion, not just a distortion. In determining what constitutes material distortion, it is essential to consider both the intent and the effect of the online platform's design choices. Even if there is no deliberate intent to manipulate, if the design or operation of an interface leads to a significant distortion of user behaviour, it would fall under the prohibition in Article 25(1). For instance, if an online platform uses aggressive tactics to push users towards a specific choice, such as hiding the option to decline in a less visible location or repeatedly prompting users to agree to specific terms, this could *materially distort* the user's decision-making process by making it significantly more challenging for them to act in their own best interest.

The Court of Justice of the European Union (CJEU) has also played a critical role in shaping the understanding of material distortion.[20] Under the UCPD, a practice qualifies as unfair if it significantly impairs the average consumer's ability to make an informed decision, resulting in a transactional decision they would not have otherwise made. The Court established that a practice materially distorting must significantly impair the average consumer's ability to make an informed decision.[21] These impairments often exploit our cognitive biases or present with misleading information, even if the information is accurate.[22] In practice, determining material distortion requires a detailed assessment of the specific context, including the interface's design, the information's transparency, and the degree to which the user's autonomy is compromised.

In addition to the general prohibition, Article 25(2) introduces a significant exception. It excludes from its scope any practices already covered by existing legislation, specifically the GDPR and the UCPD. This exception is crucial because it acknowledges that many dark patterns fall under the purview of these older regulations, which already impose strict rules on data protection and consumer rights. By doing so, the DSA aims to avoid regulatory overlap while still filling in the gaps where these older laws might need to fully address the complexities of modern digital interfaces. While Article 25 aims to protect user autonomy, it excludes practices already regulated under the GDPR or UCPD:

> 2.   The prohibition in paragraph 1 shall not apply to practices covered by Directive 2005/29/EC or Regulation (EU) 2016/679.

This exclusion creates a grey area, leaving uncertainty about whether certain manipulative practices fall under the DSA's jurisdiction or instead fall under other regulations. The overlap between these laws could lead to challenges in enforcement, as regulators may need help determining which legal framework applies to specific cases of dark patterns. Another limitation discussed is the lack of clarity in defining what constitutes an autonomy violation under Article 25. The broad language used in the regulation, such as 'materially distorts' or 'impairs,' leaves room for interpretation, which could result in inconsistent application across different jurisdictions.

This vagueness may also complicate the efforts of online platforms to comply with the regulation, as they may need help fully understanding which specific practices the law deems illegal. The authors also point out that proving the intentionality behind dark patterns is difficult. Article 25 covers practices that occur 'on purpose or in effect', but proving that a platform intentionally designed its interface to deceive or manipulate users can be challenging. With clear evidence of intent, it may be more straightforward for regulators to hold platforms accountable under this provision. This limitation indicates that platforms could argue any autonomy violations occurred unintentionally, potentially undermining the effectiveness of Article 25. The open-ended nature of Article 25 could result in uncertainty in enforcement. The regulation does not provide a comprehensive list of prohibited practices but offers illustrative yet non-definitive examples. This approach requires regulators to interpret the law, which could lead to inconsistent enforcement and legal challenges as platforms dispute how the regulation applies to their specific practices.

Finally, Santos et al. and Leiser and Santos expressed concerns about the regulatory burden that Article 25 could impose on online platforms, especially smaller ones.[23] The need to constantly review and adjust interface designs to avoid violating the DSA could be resource-intensive, particularly for businesses that need more legal and technical expertise to understand the regulation entirely. These regulations could disproportionately impact smaller platforms, potentially stifling innovation and competition. While Article 25 represents a significant step forward in regulating dark patterns and protecting user autonomy, its scope's ambiguity and the potential for inconsistent enforcement may limit its effectiveness.

4.2.2. The Digital Markets Act (DMA)

The Digital Markets Act (DMA) is a regulatory framework designed to curb the market dominance of large tech companies and ensure fair competition and innovation in the digital space. Unlike the DSA, which focuses on regulating platforms and online content, the DMA specifically targets the control and power dynamics within the digital economy, preventing gatekeepers from exploiting their position.[24] The term 'gatekeeper' refers to a dominant digital platform that controls access to vital online services, effectively setting the terms of participation for other businesses and users.[25] These entities wield significant market power, enabling them to influence market outcomes, restrict competition, and stifle innovation by leveraging their privileged position. Gatekeepers can reinforce market dominance by exploiting dark patterns and deceptive design tactics to subtly manipulate user behaviour and steering decisions that reduce consumer autonomy.[26] Given the significant influence these entities wield within the digital economy, it is essential to curtail such practices to enhance consumer welfare, promote fairer competition, and ensure market dynamics operate to uphold the integrity of online ecosystems.

Di Porto and Egberts examine the broader societal implications of dark patterns in digital environments. They argue that EU and US regulations have predominantly centred on individual welfare – protecting users from manipulation – they fall short of addressing the wider systemic consequences and *collective harms*. These include behavioural market failures, the erosion of trust in digital markets, and the entrenchment of data monopolies, which undermine the equitable functioning of the digital ecosystem.[27]

Existing individual-centred regulations like the DSA and the US's DETOUR[28] and AICO Acts[29] cannot adequately tackle the collective effects. The DMA, therefore, signifies a policy shift towards protecting collective welfare, addressing the impact of dark patterns on market dynamics and societal trust. A shift towards a collective welfare perspective is crucial for effectively regulating dark patterns. This approach complements individual protection laws and provides a framework for prioritising enforcement and guiding future legislative developments. The collective welfare approach is essential in the digital economy, where the scale and reach of dark patterns can lead to widespread societal harm beyond just individual user detriment.

Article 13(6) DMA ensures gatekeepers cannot degrade the quality or conditions of their core platform services for business users or end users who exercise their rights under Articles 5, 6, and 7. This provision is crucial for maintaining user autonomy and preventing gatekeepers from manipulating interface design, functionality, or operations in a way that undermines users' free choice and decision-making within the digital marketplace:

> The gatekeeper shall not degrade the conditions or quality of any of the core platform services provided to business users or end users who avail themselves of the rights or choices laid down in Articles 5, 6 and 7 or make the exercise of those rights or choices unduly difficult, including by offering options to the end-user in a non-neutral manner, or by subverting end users' or business users' autonomy, decision-making, or free choice via the structure, design, function or manner of operation of a user interface or a part thereof.

Articles 5, 6, and 7 of the DMA establish a framework mandating gatekeepers to respect user consent, promote fair competition, and ensure interoperability within their core platform services. These provisions prevent data misuse, curb anti-competitive practices, and facilitate seamless integration between communication services, safeguarding consumer rights and market integrity.

A designer might deploy dark patterns in the user interface that subtly guide users towards decisions that undermine their autonomy and the principles of fair competition. For instance, through deceptive consent mechanisms, users might be nudged into unknowingly allowing the gatekeeper to process or combine their data in ways that violate Article 5. Similarly, the designer could unfairly entrench the gatekeeper's services by designing interfaces that obscure the options for uninstalling default software or switching to third-party applications. As outlined in Article 6, the designer could unfairly entrench the gatekeepers. Additionally, complex or misleading navigation paths could hinder users' access to interoperable services, contravening Article 7's mandate for easy and effective interoperability, thus reinforcing the gatekeeper's dominance through manipulative design rather than fair practice.

A designer might deploy deceptive design strategies across the user interface and user experience to subtly erode the protections afforded by Articles 5, 6, and 7, reinforcing a gatekeeper's dominance. Such designs could include convoluted consent flows that obscure the true extent of data sharing, misleading users into inadvertently granting permissions that breach Article 5's data processing restrictions. A designer might create intricate barriers that make it technically challenging or confusing for users to uninstall default applications or switch to alternatives, violating the mandates of Article 6. Furthermore, deceptive navigation and buried settings could impede the effective use of interoperable services, contravening Article 7's requirements for seamless cross-platform functionality, all while giving the appearance of compliance but ultimately steering users towards the gatekeeper's preferred outcomes.

Article 13(6) specifically targets the design and operation of user interfaces, reinforcing the DMA's intent to prevent gatekeepers from manipulating user decisions through deceptive design. The provision aims to safeguard user rights and maintain the integrity of core platform services by ensuring transparency and fairness in user interactions. However, limiting Article 13(6) to user interfaces while ignoring broader system architecture creates a significant regulatory gap. Manipulation can extend beyond visible design elements into deeper structures – such as algorithms and data flows – that subtly shape user behaviour. By focusing solely on the interface, the provision overlooks how gatekeepers may exploit these hidden mechanisms to undermine autonomy and market fairness, allowing sophisticated manipulation to persist unchecked. The phrase 'or a part thereof' in Article 13(6) is critical, allowing regulators to scrutinise deceptive design within specific interface components. This ensures that manipulative tactics, such as misleading buttons, confusing navigation, or hidden settings, are addressed at a granular level. By explicitly covering these elements, the provision strengthens regulatory oversight, promoting fairness and transparency across all aspects of the user experience.

Brenncke argues that while the DMA is primarily a competition law instrument, its provisions against dark patterns intersect with consumer protection principles.[30] It goes beyond merely addressing the economic aspects of gatekeeper dominance by tackling the subtle ways these platforms might manipulate user choice. This approach reflects a broader understanding of the impact of digital platforms on consumer welfare, recognising that economic dominance can also manifest in ways that undermine user autonomy. However, the author also points out that while the DMA's provisions are a step in the right direction, implementation challenges exist. The vague language in defining a dark pattern and the difficulty drawing clear lines between legitimate and manipulative design practices can create enforcement challenges. Moreover, the DMA's focus on gatekeepers means that smaller platforms, which might also engage in dark patterns, are not subject to the same level of scrutiny, potentially leaving gaps in consumer protection. The DMA's approach to regulating dark patterns is significant but not without limitations. The Act represents a crucial step in addressing the power of gatekeepers in digital markets, but its effectiveness will depend on how its provisions are interpreted and enforced in practice.

4.2.3. The Internet of Things and the Data Act[31]

User interface dark patterns are traditionally associated with websites and mobile applications. Still, the concept has been extended to the Internet of Things (IoT), revealing these devices' unique challenges. Dark patterns in IoT devices manifest uniquely and often insidiously, mainly due to the non-conventional interfaces through which users interact with these devices. For instance, the 'detour' dark pattern disrupts the user's intended actions by unexpectedly shifting them from one modality, such as a companion app, to another, like the device itself. This shift can harm privacy or autonomy as users might not realise the implications of the change. With their always-on capabilities and integration into physical environments, IoT devices amplify the risks of dark patterns. Devices without precise feedback mechanisms – such as those that fail to indicate when recording or collecting data – leave users unaware of potential privacy intrusions, making these risks even more concerning. Unlike traditional digital platforms with screen-based interactions, IoT devices rely on voice commands, automation, and environmental cues, creating a complex and often opaque interaction layer. This makes manipulative practices harder to detect. Virtual assistants (VAs) like Alexa or Google Assistant exemplify how dark patterns infiltrate non-visual interfaces. These devices seamlessly integrate into daily life, subtly nudging users toward subscriptions or purchases framed as convenient but designed to drive engagement and spending. Users have fewer opportunities to reconsider or resist these prompts without a visual interface, making them more vulnerable to impulsive decisions. The intersection of deceptive design in IoT, particularly in VAs, and EU law presents an evolving regulatory challenge. As VAs become more embedded in everyday life, their ability to manipulate user behaviour through design strategies – ranging from subtle nudges to overt manipulation – demands greater scrutiny within existing legal frameworks.

De Conca's research into VAs posits that Amazon's Alexa or Google Assistant operates by engaging users through vocal interactions that are seemingly innocuous but often embed deceptive design techniques.[32] For instance, a VA might suggest additional actions, like purchasing a product or subscribing to a service, following a routine query. These suggestions, while presented as helpful, are carefully crafted to drive user engagement in ways that align more with the interests of the service provider than the user's own needs. A group of HCI scholars systematically studied 57 popular IoT devices, ranging from smart speakers to home security cameras. They identified that dark patterns are not only present but are pervasive across various IoT devices, with certain types of devices and manufacturers more likely to incorporate these deceptive designs. For example, smart speakers, doorbells, and cameras, particularly those from Amazon and Google, contained dark patterns. This ubiquity is concerning, as IoT devices often have access to intimate spaces and collect sensitive data, amplifying the potential harm caused by these patterns.[33]

However, De Conca's assertion that current legal frameworks adequately address deceptive design in VAs is a naive underestimation of the problem's complexity. Her claim that the existing framework provides a 'sufficient starting point' is not just complacent but fundamentally flawed, as it underestimates the structural entanglement of manipulative architectures with platform business models. To suggest that mere 'guidance' is sufficient ignores the blatant manipulation inherent in these designs and the urgent need for robust, proactive regulation to protect users. Moreover, IoT devices embedded within smart homes, such as thermostats, lighting systems, and security cameras, can employ deceptive design through automated processes that subtly nudge users toward certain behaviours. These devices can be programmed to present specific settings or options as defaults, making it more challenging for users to opt-out or customise their preferences. For example, a smart thermostat might default to an energy-saving mode, requiring users to navigate multiple steps to override it. This setup subtly discourages users from adjusting settings that could increase energy consumption or alter the device's performance. The design of these systems often prioritises the manufacturer's interests – whether in terms of energy efficiency, data collection, or product longevity – over the user's autonomy and preferences.

The complexity of IoT devices enables subtle exploitation of user data, often unnoticed over time. Many continuously track behaviour, preferences, and environmental conditions, using this data to shape interactions that influence decisions. For example, a smart fridge might suggest purchases based on manufacturer interests rather than consumer needs. The passive nature of data collection and automated suggestions creates an environment where users remain unaware of how algorithms shape their choices. IoT interfaces blur the line between suggestion and coercion. Voice commands and automated prompts create urgency, pressuring users to decide quickly without fully understanding long-term consequences, such as agreeing to data-sharing terms. The ephemeral nature of these interactions makes them harder to review or reverse, increasing the risk of manipulation. IoT's seamless integration into daily life creates an opaque user experience where dark patterns are challenging to detect. Unlike screen-based platforms, IoT operates in the background, leveraging user trust to guide behaviour unnoticed. Conventional safeguards – transparency, consent, and easy opt-outs – are weakened, making users more vulnerable to manipulation with less control over their interactions.

From a legal perspective, applying EU consumer protection and data protection laws to such deceptive design practices in VAs is multifaceted. The UCPD and the GDPR offer some tools to combat these practices, but they have limitations. The sophisticated ways VAs blend functionality with manipulation undermine the effectiveness of this provision.

The line between enhancing user experience and coercing certain behaviours is blurred, making regulatory enforcement difficult.[34] Moreover, the GDPR's focus on the fairness and transparency of data processing is directly relevant to how VAs collect and use personal data. Deceptive design practices that unknowingly lead users to consent to extensive data sharing could violate the GDPR's principles of informed consent. Nevertheless, the voice-based interactions typical of VAs complicate the application of these principles. Unlike traditional online interfaces, where users can review and reconsider their choices, vocal interactions are linear and ephemeral, leaving little room to reassess their decisions. This dynamic creates an environment ripe for exploitation, where users might share more data than they intend, influenced by the immediate and seemingly benign prompts of their VAs.

Article 6 is pivotal in safeguarding user rights by mandating that access to data generated through connected products or related services must be provided on fair, reasonable, and non-discriminatory terms. This provision addresses the risk of manipulative practices, ensuring that data holders cannot exploit users through unfair or coercive conditions when accessing or sharing their data. By embedding principles of transparency and fairness, Article 6 acts as a barrier against using dark patterns, protecting users from deceptive designs that could pressure them into unfavourable decisions regarding their data. Recital 38 reinforces Article 6 by explicitly tackling the challenge of dark patterns, warning against digital interface designs that manipulate or mislead individuals into making decisions that could undermine their autonomy or privacy. It highlights practices such as coercive tactics that pressure users to divulge excessive personal data or hinder their ability to exercise rights related to data access or management. The Recital unequivocally condemns these manipulative designs as unethical and in breach of the legal standards established under the Data Act and broader EU law, underscoring the imperative to safeguard individuals from harmful and exploitative practices. Article 6 and Recital 38 establish a framework to tackle deceptive design practices in IoT environments to protect users from manipulative tactics that could compromise their autonomy and control over personal data. However, it remains crucial to assess the effectiveness of these provisions in fully safeguarding user rights against sophisticated dark patterns as the digital economy continues to evolve.

4.3. The Effectiveness of the Law in Combating Dark Patterns and Deceptive Design

This section dives headfirst into the tangled web of EU legislative frameworks, dissecting their ability to tackle the ever-evolving beast of digital manipulation. It looks at shiny new laws and time-tested rules, unpacking how well they stand up to the complexities of today's digital ecosystems. Through compelling case studies, the section spotlights victories where regulations have clipped the wings of manipulative practices – and stumbles where enforcement has fallen flat or legal gaps have exposed users. But this isn't just a critique of the status quo. It explores how these frameworks handle the relentless pace of change in digital trickery. From the fuzziness of legal definitions to the head-scratching complications of cross-border enforcement, it doesn't shy away from pointing out the cracks. And when it comes to protecting those most at risk – children, older adults, and other vulnerable groups – the section asks the tough questions: Are we doing enough? Or are these laws still leaving too much room for bad actors to thrive? Ultimately, this section delivers a lively and nuanced take on the EU's regulatory landscape. By celebrating wins, exposing blind spots, and asking where we go from here, it offers a roadmap for a future where users can navigate the digital world without falling into the traps of dark patterns and manipulative designs.

4.3.1. Strengths and Weaknesses of the Data Act, DSA, DMA, ePD, GDPR, and UCPD

The EU's regulatory framework for deceptive design reflects a comprehensive but fragmented approach to governing the digital environment. Each regulation has strengths and limitations, particularly in a rapidly evolving digital landscape. The Data Act's strength is ensuring fair access to and sharing data, particularly in IoT and connected devices. Mandating fair, reasonable, and non-discriminatory terms aims to prevent imbalanced power dynamics. However, it fails to address how data influences user behaviour, leaving a regulatory gap for dark patterns in IoT environments. The DSA takes a more direct approach, with Article 25 explicitly prohibiting deceptive or manipulative practices to protect user autonomy.

However, its broad language creates enforcement challenges across EU jurisdictions, and its focus on 'online platforms' may allow smaller entities to escape scrutiny.

A critical weakness in the framework is its reliance on users and designers to determine whether Article 25 applies, as it defers to the UCPD and GDPR. If a practice falls under these laws, Article 25 is inapplicable, undermining its effectiveness. Despite its relevance, the ePrivacy Directive is excluded from this interplay, creating regulatory inconsistencies. Moreover, proving 'material distortion' under Article 25 remains challenging, as the deceptive design must be explicitly identifiable within the user interface, limiting enforcement against more sophisticated manipulative tactics.

The DMA complements the DSA by addressing the market dynamics of dominant tech companies, or 'gatekeepers.' Its strength lies in its targeted focus on entities with substantial influence over the digital marketplace, aiming to prevent them from exploiting their dominance through anti-competitive practices, including dark patterns. However, the DMA's emphasis on market power rather than consumer protection creates a gap, as it may overlook smaller-scale manipulative practices that, while not directly impacting market competition, still harm consumers.

The DMA's scope reveals a notable limitation in its prioritisation of fair competition over the direct regulation of user manipulation. Its primary focus on addressing market dominance sidelines concerns related to dark patterns and consumer protection, areas more effectively targeted by the UCPD and GDPR. While the DMA's emphasis on competition law is essential for ensuring equitable market dynamics, it risks overlooking smaller-scale manipulative practices that may not significantly impact competition but still inflict substantial harm on consumers. This narrow approach creates a regulatory gap, allowing harmful practices unrelated to market power to evade scrutiny. As a result, the DMA's capacity to fully safeguard user autonomy and experience is constrained, leaving specific consumer vulnerabilities unaddressed.

The ePrivacy Directive (ePD) plays a crucial role in safeguarding the privacy of electronic communications, particularly against spam and unwanted tracking. Its strength lies in establishing clear consent rules for cookies and tracking technologies frequently used in dark patterns. However, its narrow focus on electronic communications restricts its capacity to address broader manipulative design practices, leaving gaps in its ability to tackle evolving digital manipulation.

The GDPR is among the most comprehensive global data protection frameworks, promoting data processing transparency, fairness, and accountability. Its emphasis on informed consent aligns with attempts to counteract dark patterns that exploit personal data. Nevertheless, its scope is confined to data protection, excluding manipulative design practices that affect user autonomy without data processing or when anonymised data is involved. Although powerful in regulating data misuse, the GDPR is less effective against deceptive design beyond its domain.

The UCPD offers extensive consumer protection against unfair practices that distort decision-making. Its flexibility enables it to address manipulative behaviours beyond the digital sphere. However, its lack of a digital focus and reliance on the Annex I blacklist impede its ability to tackle the dynamic nature of dark patterns in user interfaces. While it is vital to the EU's regulatory framework, the UCPD's generality and reactive nature renders it less effective in addressing subtle and sophisticated digital manipulation.

4.3.2. Case Studies: Unmasking Dark Patterns – Successes and Challenges

This section explores eight illustrative examples of dark patterns that expose the limitations and opportunities within the EU's regulatory frameworks, including the GDPR, UCPD, DSA, DMA, and the Data Act. Each case study serves as a lens to examine how these manipulative design strategies test the boundaries of existing laws, revealing where they succeed in providing protection and where critical gaps remain. This analysis highlights the regulatory challenges by mapping each dark pattern against the relevant legal framework. It interrogates the adaptability of these laws in addressing the increasingly sophisticated tactics used to undermine user autonomy. These examples provide a dynamic view of current regulations' performance when confronted with the complex realities of deceptive design in the digital age.

4.3.2.1. Smart TV Data Collection During Setup

A smart TV asks users to agree to a privacy policy during the initial setup. The interface presents the acceptance of broad data-sharing terms as a necessary step for using the TV's core functions. However, declining data sharing is hidden behind complex menu options.

The DSA's prohibition on deceptive design would not apply because the TV does not satisfy the personal scope ('online platform').[35] According to Article 3(i) DSA, an online platform is a hosting service that stores and disseminates information to the public at the request of a recipient of the service. The core functionalities of an online platform include storing information users provide and distributing it to the public.[36] The smart TV asks users to agree to a privacy policy during setup, and data-sharing terms are involved. However, this data collection is related to the TV's operation and not to hosting or disseminating information to the public.[37] The TV does not appear to allow users to store or publicly disseminate information through the interface as part of its core functionality.[38] The data-sharing agreement primarily concerns user data management rather than the public dissemination of content. Public dissemination of information is critical to defining an online platform. In this scenario, the TV does not engage in activities that make information available to an unlimited number of persons or a broad public audience. It does not serve as a platform for users to upload, share, or publicly broadcast information. The DMA would not apply as the TV does not satisfy the definition of an 'online gatekeeper'.[39] Although the GDPR mandates informed consent for data processing, how the choice is framed could lead users to inadvertently agree without understanding, exploiting the principle of 'necessary' for contract performance. The UCPD might find it challenging to regulate since the practice is more about omission than active misrepresentation. This leaves the Data Act as the only relevant legislative instrument for regulating this dark pattern. The analysis of IoT devices, particularly in the context of smart home technologies, indicates that these devices often employ dark patterns that the GDPR or UCPD does not directly address. These devices' complexity and non-conventional interfaces make it difficult for traditional regulations to capture these practices effectively.

The Data Act presents an interesting, albeit limited, opportunity to address some issues raised by dark patterns in IoT devices like smart TVs. By ensuring fair access to and sharing data generated by connected devices, the Act aligns conceptually with addressing manipulative practices that exploit data asymmetries. However, its scope primarily centres on facilitating data portability and equitable terms of access for third parties rather than directly regulating user-facing manipulative design. The Act's strength lies in its ability to empower users by granting them greater control over the data generated by their devices. This provision could indirectly mitigate some manipulative practices by requiring more explicit rules for how data-sharing agreements are structured and implemented. For instance, if users have the right to easily access, review, and control the data their smart TV generates, this transparency could counteract specific dark patterns that rely on hidden or convoluted data-sharing mechanisms.

The Data Act does not explicitly target deceptive design or user manipulation. It lacks the tools to address the nuances of how these interfaces are framed or how choices are presented to users during setup. For example, a smart TV might use dark patterns to nudge users into consenting to extensive data-sharing terms without the Act providing a direct mechanism to scrutinise how those choices are designed or framed. This gap means the Act is, at best, a complementary measure to broader frameworks like the GDPR and UCPD, which address aspects of user protection but also struggle with the unique challenges of IoT devices. The Data Act is insufficient to tackle the full spectrum of issues presented by dark patterns in IoT. For meaningful protection, it must be integrated with broader regulatory reforms that explicitly address manipulative interface design and deceptive consent mechanisms, particularly for non-traditional platforms like smart home devices.

4.3.2.2. *Subscription Services with Automatic Renewals*

A music streaming service offers a free trial, but users are automatically signed up for a paid subscription after the trial ends. The cancellation option is hidden deep within account settings, making it difficult for users to opt-out before charges begin.

The music streaming service in this scenario does meet the definition of an online platform under the DSA. The music streaming service stores music (information) and disseminates it to the public (users) at their request. This aligns with the core functionalities of an online platform as defined by the DSA.[40] The streaming service makes music available to unlimited users, fitting the public dissemination requirement.[41] Users who sign up for the free trial and later engage with the service by listening to music are considered 'active recipients' under Article 3(p) DSA.[42] Both users seeking to access music (consumers) and those making it available (artists or content providers) are relevant under Article 3(p). The service has a consumer-facing interface where users interact with the platform, making it more than just a passive content host.[43] The automatic sign-up for a paid subscription and the difficult-to-find cancellation option also emphasise the consumer-facing nature of the service, further aligning it with the DSA's definition of an online platform.[44] The UCPD could also address the misleading omission of accessible cancellation pathways, but proving material distortion of consumer choice could be difficult.[45]

The DSA's guidelines on interface manipulation might apply, but enforcement could be hindered by the service's argument that cancellation is available, albeit not easily accessible.[46] However, the applicability of the DMA would depend on whether the music streaming service qualifies as a 'gatekeeper' under Article 3 of the DMA, which requires meeting specific thresholds of size, control, and influence over the digital marketplace. If the service does meet these criteria, Article 13(6) could address the use of dark patterns to unfairly retain users in paid subscriptions by requiring transparent, fair, and non-discriminatory terms for access and interaction with the platform.

Nevertheless, significant enforcement challenges remain. The nuanced nature of dark patterns, such as intentionally obscured cancellation pathways, often allows companies to operate within the grey areas of compliance, arguing that features like cancellation options technically exist, even if they are practically inaccessible. Furthermore, while the DSA and DMA provide tools to scrutinise such practices, their effectiveness relies heavily on consistent and proactive enforcement by national and EU-level authorities. This highlights the need for stronger cooperation between regulatory bodies and guidance on addressing dark patterns in consumer-facing digital services to ensure that legislative intent and user protection are upheld.

4.3.2.3. *Social Media Platforms Manipulating Emotional Responses*

> A social media platform's algorithm prioritises emotionally charged content to increase user engagement, subtly encouraging users to spend more time on the platform. This manipulation can lead to addictive behaviours and increased exposure to advertisements.

Article 3(i) DSA defines an online platform as a hosting service that stores and disseminates information to the public at the request of a recipient of the service.[47] The core functionalities include storing information provided by users and distributing it to the public.[48] The social media platform hosts user-generated content (eg, posts, videos, comments) and disseminates it to a potentially large audience.[49] This aligns with the basic requirements of an online platform under the DSA.[50] The platform's algorithm promotes content that is emotionally charged, which is then seen by a large number of users. This meets the criterion of public dissemination, as the content is made available to an unlimited number of persons who engage with the platform.[51] Users who create content and those who consume it are considered recipients of the service under the DSA.[52] The platform's algorithm, which influences what content is shown to users, affects both the creators (by prioritising their content) and the consumers (by controlling what they see).[53] The social media platform has a straightforward consumer-facing interface where users interact with content, each other, and advertisements.[54]

The algorithmic prioritisation of emotionally charged content is a method to increase engagement, which directly ties into the platform's commercial interests, including increased ad exposure.[55] Controlling content to encourage more engagement and potentially addictive behaviours highlights the platform's role in shaping user experiences.[56] This manipulation, although subtle, influences user behaviour, making the platform more than just a neutral host of content.[57] Article 25 DSA's prohibition might apply to a social media 'online platform' but not apply due to the lack of specific design techniques implemented in the user interface. The deceptive design is found in the system architecture, making the prohibition irrelevant. Furthermore, the subjective nature of what constitutes 'emotionally manipulative' content makes enforcement difficult, especially as Article 25 requires a *material distortion* or *impairment* of *a free and informed decision*. The GDPR's focus on data protection does not directly address the behavioural impact of algorithms designed to manipulate engagement.[58] There is no commercial transaction, meaning that the UCPD is not helpful.[59]

This regulatory gap underscores the difficulty in addressing manipulative practices embedded within system architecture rather than the user interface. While the DSA and GDPR provide some mechanisms to regulate transparency and accountability in algorithmic design, they lack explicit provisions to tackle behavioural manipulation aimed at maximising user engagement. Moreover, the absence of a commercial transaction limits the applicability of consumer protection laws like the UCPD, leaving a significant blind spot in the current regulatory framework. The platform's algorithmic prioritisation exemplifies a broader challenge: existing laws are ill-equipped to address the subtle, systemic manipulation of user behaviour that does not manifest as overt deception or easily quantifiable harm. Addressing these issues may require future regulatory interventions that explicitly target the interplay between algorithmic design, behavioural manipulation, and its societal impacts, bridging the gap between legal accountability and technological influence.

4.3.2.4. *Health App Nudging Users to Share Sensitive Data*

> A health app encourages users to share sensitive data like biometric information by presenting pop-ups that frame data sharing as essential for receiving accurate health insights. The 'decline' option is less prominently displayed or requires multiple steps to access.

The health app collects, stores, and processes sensitive user data, such as biometric information. If the app also shares this data with third parties (eg, health professionals, insurance companies, or other users), it could be seen as disseminating information, that aligns with the definition of an online platform.[60] If the app makes the user's sensitive data available to others (either other users or third-party partners), this could qualify as public dissemination.[61] However, suppose the data remains entirely private and is only used by the app to provide personalised insights to the individual user. In that case, it might not meet the full criteria for public dissemination as defined by the DSA.[62] Users who input and share their data and those who receive insights based on this data are service recipients.[63] The app's design encourages data sharing to provide more accurate health insights and involves users actively engaging with the service by providing their information.[64] The app has a consumer-facing interface designed for direct interaction with users.[65] The way it encourages users to share sensitive data – by making the 'decline' option less visible or more challenging to access – indicates a deliberate design choice that influences user behaviour, making it a consumer-facing service.[66] The app's practice of framing data sharing as essential while obscuring the opt-out option raises serious transparency and user consent issues.[67] Under the DSA, platforms are expected to operate transparently, especially when handling user data.[68] This behaviour could be viewed as manipulative, potentially violating principles of informed consent and user autonomy.[69] Regardless of its classification under the DSA, the app's practices regarding data sharing and consent are problematic under data protection laws. The GDPR requires that consent for data processing be freely given, specific, informed, and unambiguous.[70] The app's design, which makes it difficult for users to decline data sharing, could be seen as undermining these requirements.[71] While the GDPR requires explicit consent for processing sensitive data, manipulative framing might lead users to consent without fully understanding the implications.[72] The DSA might cover the deceptive design, but proving that the design materially distorts user decisions could be challenging.[73]

The UCPD could apply to this scenario by addressing the unfair commercial practice of misleading omissions or aggressive practices that distort consumer decision-making. However, since the app focuses on obtaining consent rather than facilitating a transactional exchange, the UCPD's applicability might be limited. Similarly, while the Data Act might regulate the use and sharing of data generated by the app, it does not directly address the manipulative design techniques used to obtain that data. This highlights a broader regulatory gap as current frameworks struggle to fully capture the nuanced ways dark patterns are deployed to influence user consent and behaviour.

4.3.2.5. *Online Retailer Making Refunds Difficult*

> An online retailer requires users to navigate multiple pages and endure long hold times to request a refund, subtly discouraging returns. The option to request a refund is not clearly visible on the website's main interface.

This is tricky, highlighting the tensions between the UCPD and the DSA. The UCPD might address this as an unfair commercial practice, but the process's nuanced design makes it difficult to classify as a straightforward breach. If the UCPD does apply, the Article 25(2) DSA exception means that the consumer could not rely on the DSA for a remedy (the prohibition does not apply to practices already covered by the UCPD. A savvy lawyer might argue that the DSA is irrelevant for regulating this dark pattern because it falls under the UCPD exception. At the same time, the lawyer contends that the pattern does not fall foul of the UCPD as an interface manipulation, as the process, in theory, is technically available but intentionally cumbersome.

4.3.2.6. *Freemium Games Targeting Children with In-App Purchases*

> A mobile game targets children by offering enticing in-game items that can only be purchased with real money. The game frequently prompts players to buy these items during gameplay, making it difficult for children to distinguish between in-game currency and actual money.

Article 3(i) DSA defines an online platform as a hosting service that stores and disseminates information to the public at the request of a recipient of the service. This typically involves storing user-generated content and making it accessible to others.[74] The mobile game may not be an online platform in the strictest sense unless it involves significant user interaction that includes the sharing or disseminating content (eg, a multiplayer feature where users share scores and content or interact socially). However, the game could be considered a digital service, which is covered by various provisions of the DSA, especially those concerning the protection of users, particularly vulnerable groups like children.[75] The game targets children, a particularly vulnerable group, and uses manipulative practices by making it difficult for them to distinguish between in-game currency and real money.[76] This kind of design exploits the cognitive and emotional vulnerabilities of children, which could be considered unfair and deceptive under consumer protection laws.[77] The UCPD could address this as an unfair practice, particularly under aggressive commercial practices targeting vulnerable consumers, but enforcement is complex when the target audience is children.[78]

The GDPR might require parental consent, but the manipulation occurs in a way that bypasses parental control.[79] The game's frequent prompts to buy items with real money during gameplay can be seen as aggressive commercial practices that could lead to unintended purchases by children, who may not fully understand the implications of spending real money.[80] If the game collects any personal data from the children, including for in-game purchases, it must comply with the GDPR.[81] The GDPR requires explicit, informed consent for processing personal data, particularly for minors.[82] Given that children might not fully understand the difference between in-game currency and real money, obtaining valid consent is highly questionable. Blending in-game currency with actual money transactions without clear distinction could also violate transparency obligations under the GDPR and consumer protection regulations. Many jurisdictions have strict rules regarding marketing and in-app purchases of games aimed at children. The practice described could be seen as exploiting children and could face legal challenges under laws designed to protect minors from predatory commercial practices.[83] For example, the UCPD prohibits misleading and aggressive commercial practices, particularly those that exploit children's inexperience or credulity.[84]

Additionally, the UCPD, under Article 5(3), explicitly prohibits practices that exploit vulnerable consumers, including children, due to their limited capacity to understand the commercial intent of such designs. The game's blending of in-game currency with real money without clear differentiation creates a deceptive environment, undermining children's ability to make informed decisions and leading to unintended financial transactions. Under the GDPR, children enjoy enhanced protections under Recital 38, which recognises their greater susceptibility to exploitation and mandates stricter safeguards, particularly in the context of commercial offerings. If the game processes data for in-game purchases or behavioural tracking, it must meet the requirements of Articles 6 and 8, ensuring that consent is valid, informed, and explicit. Given the audience, the GDPR's requirement for parental consent under Article 8 becomes critical, and failing to secure such consent could result in significant non-compliance issues. Furthermore, the GDPR's transparency obligations under Articles 12 and 13 require that any interaction involving personal data, including in-game purchases, be communicated in a manner that is clear and accessible to children and their guardians. Obscuring the distinction between virtual and real currency risks violating these principles, mainly when designed to bypass parental awareness or control.

This practice may potentially violate Annex I of the UCPD, which enumerates a 'blacklist' of commercial practices that are universally prohibited. Although Annex I does not explicitly enumerate practices targeting vulnerable groups such as children, certain provisions may be pertinent. Specifically:

1. Point 5 prohibits 'making an invitation to purchase products at a specified price without disclosing the existence of any reasonable grounds the trader may have for believing that he will not be able to supply … those products at that price.' If the game provides in-game currency or items in a way that creates confusion between virtual and real money, particularly when prompts imply ease of purchase without clarifying associated costs, this could amount to a misleading invitation to purchase.
2. Point 28 bans practices that 'include in an advertisement a direct exhortation to children to buy advertised products or persuade their parents or other adults to buy the advertised products for them.' The game's frequent purchase prompts, particularly in a way that targets children and leverages their inability to distinguish between in-game and real currency, could be seen as a direct exhortation, falling under this prohibition.
3. Point 31 prohibits 'persistent and unwanted solicitations by telephone, fax, email or other remote media.' Although aimed primarily at direct marketing, avoiding relentless pressure may also apply to the game's aggressive frequency of purchase prompts.

These provisions highlight that although Annex I does not explicitly cover the details of in-game mechanics aimed at children, its broad principles prohibit practices considered manipulative and misleading toward vulnerable groups. The frequent purchase prompts and the lack of clarity regarding real-money transactions could lead to scrutiny under these points, particularly where the commercial strategy capitalises on children's inexperience and credulity.

Beyond the GDPR and UCPD, broader EU frameworks, including the Audiovisual Media Services Directive (AVMSD), also prohibit the exploitation of children through commercial content, particularly where it involves implicit advertising or practices that take advantage of their developmental vulnerabilities. In this scenario, the game's frequent purchase prompts and unclear distinctions between in-game and real money could be seen as violating these safeguards when such tactics harm families financially.

To comply with these legal frameworks, the game developer must implement safeguards to ensure transparency, clarity, and fairness in how purchases are presented. This includes distinguishing in-game currency from real money, limiting aggressive purchase prompts, and obtaining valid parental consent for data processing and purchases involving minors. Failure to address these issues risks enforcement actions under the UCPD, GDPR, and related EU regulations and reputational damage, particularly in a regulatory landscape increasingly focused on protecting vulnerable users from exploitative digital practices.

4.3.2.7. e-Commerce Sites Automatically Adding Items to Cart

> An e-commerce website automatically adds additional items to a user's cart based on their browsing history, presenting these items as 'recommended.' The user must manually remove these items before checkout, which is not clearly communicated.

The scenario where an e-commerce website adds items to a user's cart based on their browsing history automatically and presents these items as 'recommended' raises significant legal and ethical concerns. This practice is potentially deceptive and could violate consumer protection laws and regulations, including those outlined under the DSA and related frameworks. Automatically adding items to a user's cart without their explicit consent is a manipulative practice.[85] It takes advantage of the user's likely assumption that only the items they actively chose are in their cart.[86] Labelling these automatically added items as 'recommended' could mislead users into thinking they were passively suggested rather than actively added to their cart.[87] This blurs the line between recommendation and pre-selection, which can be deceptive.[88] If the website does not communicate that these items have been added and that users need to manually remove them if they do not wish to purchase them, this constitutes a lack of transparency.[89] Users may proceed to checkout without realising they are buying additional items.[90] Regulators enforcing the UCPD might categorise this as a misleading action, but proving material distortion is challenging when the user can technically remove the items.[91] The DSA might not cover this as it falls under the UCPD exception, but regardless, it involves design and subtle coercion rather than clear-cut interface manipulation.[92]

Furthermore, while the GDPR may apply if the practice involves processing personal data, such as browsing history, to determine the automatically added items, it primarily governs data protection. It may not directly address the manipulative design element. The Data Act, focused on ensuring fair access to and use of data, also falls short of tackling consumer-facing manipulations. This leaves a regulatory gap where the subtle coercion embedded in the system architecture and interface design remains inadequately addressed. To fully address such practices, regulators must consider the cumulative impact of deceptive design choices that, while not outright prohibitive under existing laws, erode user autonomy and trust. A stronger emphasis on transparency and consent, alongside the development of more robust regulatory frameworks that specifically target these manipulative tactics, is essential. Without these measures, deceptive practices like automatic cart additions risk becoming entrenched, further undermining fairness and accountability in digital commerce.

4.3.2.8. *Location-Based Apps Repeatedly Asking for Data Access*

> A location-based app repeatedly asks for access to user data even after the user has declined. The prompts are designed to appear as essential for the app's functionality, with the 'no thanks' option made less visible.

Suppose the app is primarily designed to provide location-based services (eg, navigation, finding nearby businesses) and does not involve storing or disseminating user-generated content to the public. In that case, it may not strictly fall under the definition of an online platform as described by the DSA.[93] However, if the app allows users to share their location or related content with others (eg, sharing real-time location with friends), it could be considered an online platform under the DSA.[94] The app has a consumer-facing interface that interacts directly with users.[95] The repeated prompts for location access, mainly when framed as essential and with the 'no thanks' option less visible, suggest a design intended to manipulate user consent.[96] This raises transparency issues, as the app may be coercing users into providing data they initially chose to withhold. Under the GDPR, user consent for data processing must be freely given, specific, informed, and unambiguous.[97] The app's design could press users into granting access, which might not meet the GDPR's strict standards for valid consent.[98] The app repeatedly requests access to location data after the user has declined, especially when the decline option is obscured, which undermines the principle of informed and freely given consent.[99] The GDPR mandates user consent for data access, but the design exploits users' persistence in declining. The DSA might address the repetitive nature of the prompts under interface manipulation. Still, the design's subtlety makes it challenging to regulate effectively, particularly in balancing necessary app functions with user autonomy.

This design also highlights a broader regulatory gap in addressing subtle but persistent coercion in user interfaces. While the GDPR provides clear guidelines on consent, its enforcement often focuses on explicit violations rather than nuanced manipulative practices, such as obscured decline options or repetitive prompts. The DSA's provisions on interface manipulation may offer some scope for regulating this behaviour. Still, its effectiveness hinges on whether the app qualifies as an online platform – a classification that may not apply in this case, depending on its functionalities.

The UCPD could address the app's practices if deemed aggressive or misleading, particularly by creating an imbalance in the user's ability to make an informed choice. However, its effectiveness in targeting digital environments remains limited due to its generality and reliance on proving a material distortion of consumer choice.

Ultimately, the app's design strategy exemplifies how repetitive and manipulative prompts can erode user autonomy without overtly violating existing regulations. Addressing such practices requires a more nuanced regulatory framework explicitly targeting interface design techniques to coerce or pressure users into unwanted decisions. Future legal reforms should consider the cumulative effect of subtle design strategies on user consent and incorporate provisions to protect against these less overt but equally problematic forms of manipulation.

4.4. Conclusion

As I conclude this chapter, it should become evident to the reader that the EU's response, through the introduction of comprehensive regulatory frameworks such as the DSA, the DMA, and the Data Act, reflects a commitment to safeguarding user autonomy and protecting consumers from the insidious effects of dark patterns and other deceptive design practices. The DSA, mainly through Article 25, represents a significant advancement in addressing the manipulative potential of digital interfaces. By targeting dark patterns that deceive or manipulate users, this provision aims to preserve the integrity of user decision-making, ensuring that platforms do not coerce individuals into actions against their best interests. However, the chapter has also highlighted the challenges inherent in the broad language of Article 25, which, while necessary to encompass a wide range of manipulative practices, also introduces interpretative ambiguities that could complicate effective enforcement.

The interplay between the DSA and existing regulations, such as the GDPR and UCPD, illustrates the complexity of the EU's digital regulatory framework. While the DSA aims to complement these earlier instruments, overlapping provisions can create enforcement challenges, particularly when determining which legal framework applies to specific instances of digital manipulation. Additionally, concerns have been raised about the potential regulatory burden on smaller platforms, which may struggle to meet the DSA's requirements, inadvertently stifling innovation and competition within the digital market. A broader perspective reveals the pressing need for an integrated and cohesive regulatory approach that evolves alongside the rapid pace of technological advancement. The EU's progress with the DSA, DMA, and related instruments is commendable. Yet, the challenges posed by emerging technologies, including the Internet of Things and virtual assistants, demand continuous legal innovation. The dynamic nature of digital manipulation requires a forward-looking strategy that anticipates future risks and strengthens existing safeguards.

The EU's regulatory efforts are critical in fostering a digital ecosystem that upholds transparency, fairness, and user autonomy. However, the effectiveness of these frameworks will hinge on their adaptability and the ongoing dedication of lawmakers, regulators, and technologists to refine and enforce them. Protecting users in the digital age is an iterative process that must evolve with technological progress, ensuring that user rights and autonomy remain at the forefront of the digital regulatory agenda. While the EU's current regulatory efforts have made significant strides in addressing deceptive design practices, they unfortunately remain limited in scope by focusing primarily on user interfaces. This narrow approach overlooks the more insidious forms of deceptive design within the system architecture, where psychological manipulation is increasingly prevalent. Moving to Part Two, we explore the AI Act and the broader evolution of dark patterns into systemic manipulations embedded within system architecture. While the AI Act aims to address AI-driven practices exploiting psychological vulnerabilities – particularly through the prohibitions under Articles 5(1)(a) and 5(1)(b) – its provisions intersect with the increasing complexity of digital systems. These systems no longer rely solely on overt UI manipulations but instead leverage algorithms and personalised architectures to shape user behaviour subtly.

Chapter five expands on this shift by illustrating how systemic dark patterns operate beneath the surface, exploiting user data to design manipulative environments that align with platform goals. It delves into how system architecture, including deterministic and non-deterministic algorithms, drives user decisions in subtle and pervasive ways. This includes techniques like dynamic pricing, personalised content recommendations, and adaptive gaming mechanics tailored to user profiles and behaviours. These manipulative strategies highlight the urgent need for a regulatory framework beyond visible UI elements to scrutinise the underlying structures enabling such exploitation.

PART TWO

Manipulation Beneath the Interface

5

System Architecture Patterns and the Personalisation of Exploitation

5.1. Introduction

The concept of *dark patterns* initially captured interface-level manipulations – design choices that visually or behaviourally coerced users into actions contrary to their best interests, such as opting into surveillance or making unintended purchases. These superficial tactics relied on misdirection: misleading buttons, visual asymmetry, or default settings engineered for consent rather than comprehension. Yet in contemporary digital ecosystems, the locus of manipulation has shifted. What began as interface deception has metastasised into *systemic manipulation* – an architectural embedding of behavioural control within the operational logic of platforms themselves.

This evolution signals a paradigmatic shift. Manipulative intent is no longer merely enacted through deceptive UI choices; it is *encoded into the system's fabric*, operationalised through data-driven profiling, algorithmic path dependencies, behavioural nudging, and dynamic personalisation. These are not ancillary features; they constitute the infrastructure of engagement. System architecture preconditions decision-making before user awareness is activated by shaping how options are generated, filtered, and ranked.

Unlike interface-level patterns, which remain visible and, in theory, correctable through targeted UI regulation, architectural manipulations exploit the opacity of code and the normative vacuum surrounding backend design. They recalibrate the user's decision space in service of commercial imperatives, often under the guise of relevance, efficiency, or personalisation. The result is not just the distortion of choice but the prefiguration of outcomes.

Current regulatory instruments, including the Digital Services Act[1] and the AI Act,[2] offer limited traction against these deeper manipulations.

Their normative architecture presupposes transparency as visibility, oversight as documentation, and harm as discrete and observable. But systemic manipulation resists these modalities: anticipatory, distributed, and cumulative. The regulatory gaze, fixated on interface-level infringements or explicit deception, too often overlooks the materiality of design – how architecture scripts conduct without coercion, and how influence operates beneath the threshold of awareness or contestation.

Reorienting regulatory focus from visual symptoms to structural conditions, from isolated manipulative acts to architectonic intent, is required. This means scrutinising how behavioural asymmetries are instantiated in system design, how affordances are structured to privilege specific pathways over others, and how value extraction is optimised through iterative experimentation on user behaviour. It requires a theory of manipulation attuned to *epistemic asymmetry*, *predictive control*, and the *pre-emptive design of consent*.

Accordingly, this chapter will lay out the technical argument for extending regulation beyond the interface to effectively respond to these developments. It must address the design of system architecture – the code-level frameworks that determine how digital platforms profile users, structure choice environments, and deliver outcomes. Without this systemic perspective, regulatory efforts will remain cosmetic, allowing increasingly sophisticated forms of manipulation to persist beneath a veneer of transparency.

The transition from surface deception to infrastructural manipulation demands a corresponding shift in regulatory epistemology. No matter how well-crafted, superficial protections are inadequate when the architecture becomes the exploitation vector. To confront the full spectrum of deceptive design, regulation must descend beneath the interface and interrogate the deep code of digital systems – the invisible levers by which platforms shape perception, constrain autonomy, and reconfigure the terms of participation in digital life.

5.1.1. From the User Interface to the System Architecture

A regulatory approach of this kind demands conceptual and technical precision. It requires a clear understanding of system architecture and why it constitutes the true locus of influence in contemporary digital platforms. System architecture refers to the hidden blueprint of digital platforms: the configuration of databases, servers, application logic, communication protocols, and algorithmic processes that govern how user data is processed and behavioural outcomes are produced.[3] While the user interface mediates surface interaction, the architecture determines which options appear, how defaults are structured, and what 'consent' even looks like. As such, addressing dark patterns today means scrutinising not only what users see, but how what they see is engineered. This architecture is critical because it shapes the user experience by governing how data flows, the system executes processes and responds to user inputs. It is a complex, often invisible layer that operates behind the scenes, ensuring the system functions correctly, efficiently, and securely.

In contrast, the UI is the visible interaction layer between the user and the system. It includes visual elements like buttons, menus, forms, and icons that users interact with directly.[4] The UI follows an intuitive, user-friendly design, allowing individuals to navigate and use the system effectively without understanding its complexities. While the UI is concerned with aesthetics, ease of use, and accessibility, the system architecture focuses on the logical and technical structure that supports the UI.[5]

System architecture can be categorised along numerous dimensions, offering diverse perspectives on how systems are structured and operated. Broadly, architectures can be distributed or centralised, follow layered or event-driven patterns, and be stateful or stateless.[6] Systems may also be loosely coupled or tightly coupled, designed for real-time or batch processing, and exhibit resilience.[7] They can leverage cloud-based or on-premises infrastructure, be modular or monolithic, and operate with data-intensive or compute-intensive needs in mind. However, beyond these structural and operational characteristics, a critical typology that cuts to the essence of system behaviour focuses on deterministic, nondeterministic, and Triggered UI systems. Deterministic systems follow predictable, rule-based paths, where the *same inputs always yield the same outputs*.

Non-deterministic systems incorporate probabilistic elements, where randomness may emerge as a by-product of complex algorithms, making it challenging to anticipate outcomes.[8] Triggered UI logic, often seen as a more straightforward form of a deterministic system, manages flows and decisions across different stages of interaction, guiding users based on predefined choices (eg, if a user selects option A, direct them to page A). Although these paradigms offer insight into system design and behaviour, they often remain detached from the real-world complexities of dark patterns. While there are many ways to slice and dice these architectures, such categorisations tell us little about how systemic dark patterns manifest within them. For example, systemic manipulations can manifest regardless of whether a system is deterministic or nondeterministic, significantly when designers shape the architecture to prioritise business outcomes over user interests. This issue highlights the need for a deeper understanding of how dark patterns can embed themselves into the very structure of digital systems rather than simply focusing on traditional architectural categorisations.

System architectures, particularly those related to user interaction and decision-making processes, can be delineated into three categories based on their underlying complexity and the transparency of their mechanisms: Triggered UI architectures, complex deterministic architectures, and non-deterministic (non-deterministic) architectures. The following table provides a simple overview of the diverse types of system architectures and their relationship to dark patterns:

Triggered UI patterns represent the most straightforward and transparent of these categories. These patterns align with the definitions found in regulatory frameworks such as Recital 67 of the Digital Services Act and laws like the CPRA,[9] which focus primarily on dark patterns that manifest directly within the user interface. They typically follow a linear or branching decision-making process, allowing for easy mapping in a flowchart. In this system, a series of predetermined steps or questions guide the user along a specific branch of the decision tree, leading to a particular output or recommendation. The logic governing these systems is straightforward and deterministic: given a specific set of inputs, the output will always be the same. This deterministic nature makes them predictable and easy to audit, as analysts can trace each decision point back through the flowchart to determine how and why the system produced a particular outcome. However, despite their simplicity, these architectures can still incorporate dark patterns by subtly structuring the flow to guide users toward less favourable outcomes.

While these frameworks cover user interface dark patterns, such as triggered UI dark patterns and static UI dark patterns, they do not account for all deceptive designs – especially those driven by algorithmic manipulation beneath the interface. My analysis diverges from these legal texts' narrower, interface-focused definitions, extending to non-UI dark patterns that leverage algorithmic personalisation. These algorithmically driven manipulations fall outside the scope of

Table 5.1 Comparative Analysis of System Types: Algorithm Complexity, Transparency, Manipulation Potential

System Type	Algorithm Complexity	Transparency	User Predictability	Role of Algorithms	Potential for Manipulation	Relation to Deceptive Design
Triggered UI: Single & Multi-Page Business Logic[10]	Straightforward, represented by flowcharts. Steps are predetermined and transparent.	High transparency, easy to follow and understand.	Predictable outcomes are based on user input and guided by clear rules.	Algorithms operate according to a predetermined set of rules and are simple in function.	Low – Manipulation is easily detectable due to the simplicity and transparency of the system.	Unrelated to deceptive design, users can easily understand the process and outcome.
Complex Deterministic[11]	Involves intricate calculations, still deterministic but less intuitive. Uses algorithms like recommendation engines.	Lower transparency – It is more challenging for users to grasp the processing logic due to complex calculations.	Deterministic outcomes, but the logic behind decisions is more complicated to interpret.	Algorithms predict user preferences, relying on intricate calculations and models.	Moderate – Manipulative tactics can be more complicated to detect due to the system's complexity.	Manipulation can occur unintentionally due to system complexity and does not always aim to deceive.

(continued)

Table 5.1 *(Continued)*

System Type	Algorithm Complexity	Transparency	User Predictability	Role of Algorithms	Potential for Manipulation	Relation to Deceptive Design
Non-Deterministic[12]	Highly complex – Relying on AI and machine learning algorithms that learn and adapt over time. No predefined rules, using probabilistic models.	Lowest transparency – The system continuously evolves, making it difficult for system administrators to understand fully.	Unpredictable outcomes due to learning models that adapt and make decisions based on evolving data.	Algorithms are integrated deeply into the system, learning and evolving, influencing user behaviour subtly.	High – Manipulation can be subtle and sophisticated, leveraging AI and machine learning to influence user behaviour imperceptibly.	High manipulation potential, with both intended and unintended effects, may lead to deceptive outcomes as a by-product of the system's adaptive nature.

the DSA and similar legislation, highlighting an area of concern that current regulations do not fully address. Moreover, additional layers of complexity arise when dark patterns are personalised based on a user's account status. For instance, users with an active subscription, a connected payment method, and a logged-in status may encounter obstructive cancellation processes for subscription services. This personalised experience introduces user-specific manipulation, where dark patterns emerge only under conditions, making them more challenging for investigators to detect. Investigating such patterns requires analysing the system's structure or accessing specific user states, such as paid accounts, to trigger these personalised manipulations. To better represent business logic as a tree, I have visualised where different decision points branch out, capturing the idea that user inputs lead to other states or outcomes rather than a strictly linear flow. Here is a description of what the diagram shows:

- **Initial Input A:** The system starts with a user input or action.

- **Decision Points:** Each decision point represents a branching condition, where the next step depends on the user's choice or when the system meets a specific condition.

- **Multiple Outcomes:** Based on the user's path through the system, various outcomes, not just one final output, are possible.

The business logic that determines a triggered UI pattern. Imagine you are using a Sass Product. It needs to work out what to show you, depending on the type of user you already are.

Subscription-Based Nudge Logic: Example of Visual Interference and Trick Wording:

Complex deterministic architectures represent a significant step up in complexity. Unlike the straightforward branching logic of Triggered UI, these architectures often rely on intricate algorithms and mathematical models that, while still deterministic, offer far less transparency. In these systems, complex calculations dictate the relationship between input and output, making it difficult to grasp or intuit immediately. Recommendation systems often fall into this category, using sophisticated models to predict user preferences based on various factors.[13] Although these systems produce consistent outputs for identical inputs, the process behind generating these outputs can remain opaque and challenging to deconstruct.[14] This opacity allows designers to exploit the system's complexity to create more insidious dark patterns, as users may remain unaware of the factors influencing the system's decisions, making it easier to manipulate outcomes subtly than simpler systems.

Figure 5.1 Triggered UI Pattern

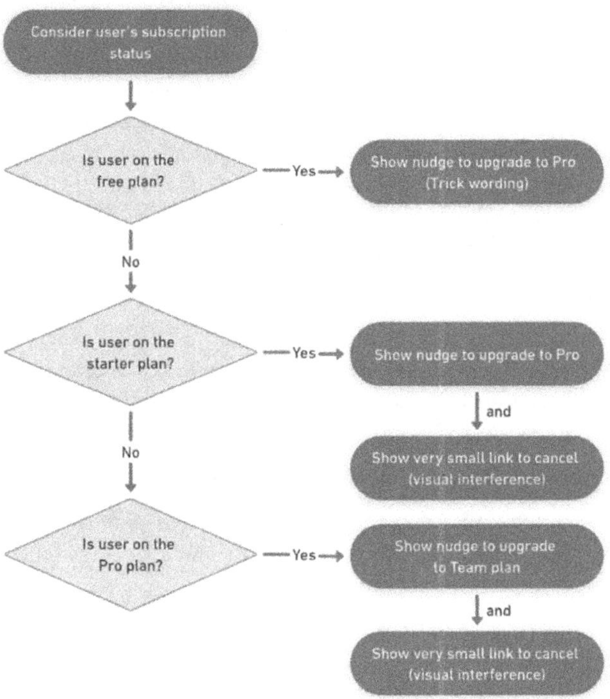

To visually conceptualise, this flowchart illustrates an e-commerce platform's deterministic architecture to prioritise products in search results. When a user searches for a product (eg, 'AA Batteries'), the system generates results based on factors like keyword relevance. However, the system further adjusts these results by placing more profitable items at the top. For example, it highlights products with higher profit margins as 'recommended' or displays them first, even if they are not the most relevant or best match for the user's needs. The user interface displays the search results without indicating that the system prioritises certain items for profitability. Consequently, the user may select a top result, unaware that other options below could better suit their needs. This design approach showcases how algorithms in digital platforms can subtly influence user choices, optimising business objectives while potentially limiting user awareness of alternative products.

Non-deterministic architectures rank as the three categories' most complex and least transparent. These systems rely on probabilistic models, machine learning algorithms, and other advanced statistical techniques, introducing randomness or unpredictability into decision-making.[15] In non-deterministic systems, the same set of inputs can lead to different outputs on different occasions as the system's internal state or learning processes evolve.[16] This unpredictability makes auditing or understanding these systems particularly challenging, even for their designers.[17] The black-box nature of these architectures enables some of the most sophisticated and potentially harmful dark patterns, as users – and even system administrators – often have little insight into why a particular outcome occurred. The opacity of these systems can obscure manipulative tactics, making it difficult to determine whether the system functions as intended or if the operator deliberately designed it to produce outcomes that benefit them at the user's expense.[18]

Consider a digital job application platform where users apply for positions by submitting a standardised profile. When users submit their application to a specific job, the system evaluates their profile using a probabilistic model. Despite identical inputs – such as qualifications, experience, and location – the platform's algorithms may produce different outcomes for similar applicants due to inherent randomness in the processing stages. For instance, after the initial submission, the system may pass the user profile through one of two probabilistic models. Model A could analyse keywords in the resume and prioritise them against the job's core requirements. On the other hand, Model B might consider additional factors such as the user's engagement history on the platform or inferred personality traits. Depending on the chosen model, the applicant may receive varying levels of prioritisation for the duplicate job listing, influencing their chances of making the shortlist.

Furthermore, as the platform collects and processes more data, it adjusts its algorithms, sometimes randomly reconfiguring the weighting of factors like recent job market trends or the hiring company's preferences. This unpredictability means that even identical applications submitted at contrasting times could yield different results, with the system flagging candidates as highly relevant while deprioritising others. This non-deterministic design adds a layer of complexity that makes

Figure 5.2 Complex Deterministic Architecture Flow

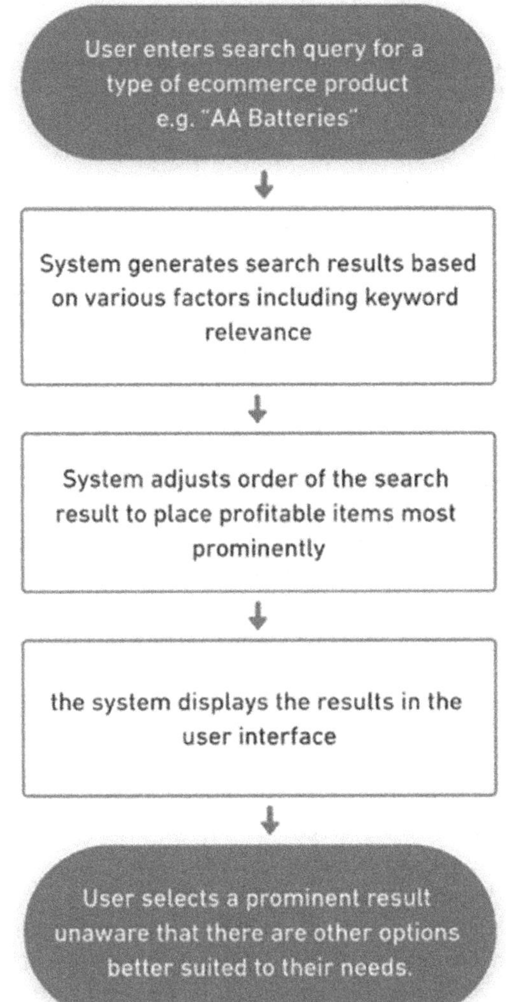

it difficult for applicants – and even the platform's administrators – to understand why one application succeeds while another fails. The opacity of this process allows for the possibility of subtle manipulations or biases embedded within the system, potentially benefiting specific profiles or skill sets that align with the platform's business interests. This black-box nature makes it challenging to audit the system for fairness or accuracy, as hidden variables and stochastic factors often influence the outcomes, potentially obscuring intentional or unintentional biases.

Figure 5.3 Non-Deterministic Architecture Flow

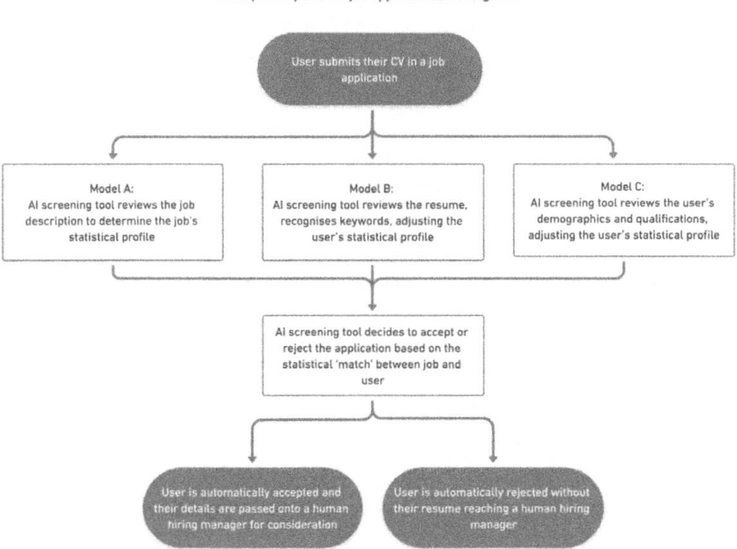

Each category of system architecture presents distinct challenges in transparency, user trust, and potential abuse. As systems grow more complex, users struggle to understand or challenge their outcomes, raising critical legal and regulatory concerns. The key distinction between system architecture and the user interface lies in their roles and visibility. The UI is the visible layer users interact with, designed for engagement, while system architecture operates behind the scenes, dictating performance, scalability, and security. Manipulations can occur at both levels – visibly in the UI or deeply embedded in the architecture – each with different implications for user experience and oversight. This layered relationship complicates transparency and regulation. While UI-based manipulations like static dark patterns are easier to detect, algorithmic manipulations within system architecture remain hidden from users and regulators. Recognising this duality reframes dark patterns as more than surface-level tricks; they often stem from intricate system design. This perspective informs the next section, which examines how manipulative design emerges from UI and system architecture, shaping user behaviour in subtle yet powerful ways.

The graphic underscores a critical point: dark patterns extend beyond the user interface and fundamentally arise from the underlying system architecture. These two elements work in tandem to manipulate user behaviour, yet regulatory frameworks and public discourse often overlook this duality. It is a misconception to treat dark patterns as superficial UI issues or to assume that system architecture operates independently of what users see. Dark patterns in the user interface often emerge from both realms, each functioning distinctly to influence user actions.

Static UI dark patterns, such as hidden fees, misleading buttons, or pre-checked boxes, are the most visible and straightforward examples. These patterns are identical for every user, consistently presenting the same manipulative elements across the board. Easily detectable and straightforward to regulate, they reside solely within the user interface, making them accessible to scrutiny by targeting specific interface components. For instance, the UI might present users with deceptively labelled options, misleading them into choices they might otherwise avoid, such as buttons suggesting skipping a step but confirming a purchase. These tactics are clear, predictable, and easy for users and regulators to grasp. Consequently, they are often the focus of regulatory frameworks, representing observable and measurable manipulation aspects.

Triggered UI dark patterns add complexity beyond static manipulations, as they appear only under specific conditions or user actions, such as hovering over a screen area or closing a dialogue box. These patterns create personalised manipulation, making detection and regulation more challenging. However, their activation follows consistent triggers, enabling targeted interaction and testing to trace and counteract their effects. A deeper layer of manipulation exists within system architecture-based dark patterns, particularly those embedded in deterministic algorithms like recommendation engines or personalised pricing systems. Here, manipulation does not reside in a specific

Figure 5.4 Dark Patterns Beyond the User Interface

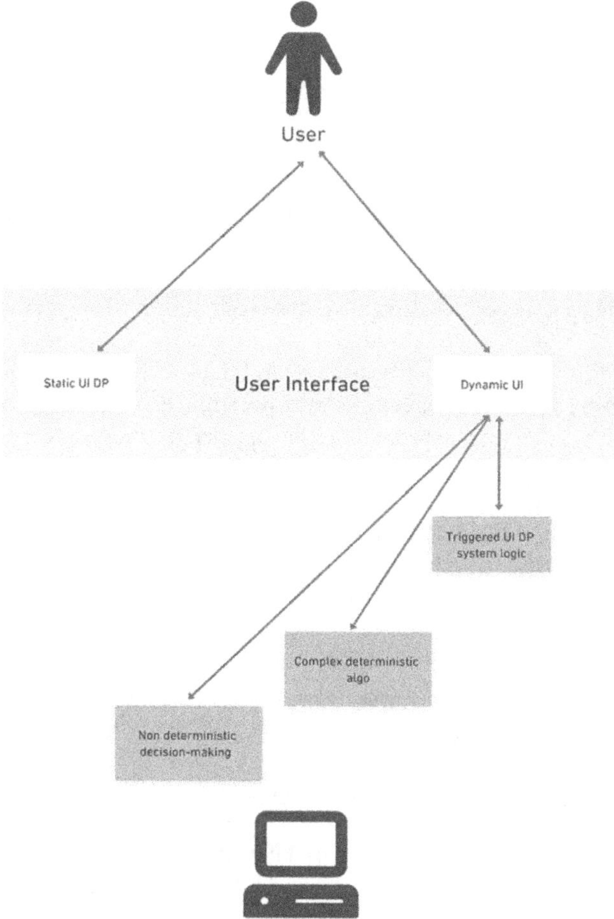

UI element but in the decision-making logic that shapes user behaviour over time. Recommendation algorithms steer users toward specific content or products, reinforcing consumption habits, while personalised pricing adjusts costs based on browsing history, location, or perceived willingness to pay. These manipulations are more insidious than UI-based patterns, as they operate beneath the interface, subtly guiding user actions without clear visibility. Unlike static or triggered UI patterns, architectural manipulations require sustained investigation into system rules and data processing, making them far more challenging to detect, mitigate and regulate.

At the most sophisticated end of this spectrum, non-deterministic, AI-driven dark patterns embody what I conceptualise as a 'Leiser Torment Nexus' – a system designed to learn and adapt autonomously, adjusting its tactics based on individual and aggregate user data. Such systems can be assigned high-level strategic objectives, such as maximising user engagement, and can derive their methods to achieve these goals. By building detailed profiles of users' vulnerabilities and persuasion triggers, these AI-driven systems can tailor their manipulative tactics in highly personalised ways, continuously evolving and often invisible to the user. AI-driven patterns adapt to each user over time, responding to their interactions and preferences to create a tailored, constantly adjusting experience. The opacity of these systems poses a significant regulatory challenge, as their adaptive nature makes them unpredictable and difficult to analyse. Unlike static or triggered dark patterns, which remain consistent and allow for straightforward mapping through interaction, AI-driven patterns defy simple categorisation. Their ability to learn and evolve will enable them to refine tactics autonomously, pushing the boundaries of manipulation by exploring what works best for each user individually. This adaptive nature poses a daunting task for regulators, as the manipulative tactics are not static or predictable but vary depending on the system's learning algorithms and the data it collects over time.

The limitations of current EU regulations – the DSA, DMA, Data Act, GDPR, and e-Privacy Directive – become increasingly evident. These frameworks primarily target UI-based manipulations, effectively regulating static and, to some extent, triggered UI dark patterns, as they can be documented through screenshots and user flow analysis. However, focusing on surface-level practices neglects deeper manipulations embedded within system architecture. This approach treats the symptoms rather than the cause, regulating visible manifestations while leaving the underlying algorithms and decision-making logic unchecked. The regulatory gap is even more pronounced in AI-driven, non-deterministic systems, where decision-making evolves based on user interactions. While the GDPR and e-Privacy Directive impose transparency and consent requirements, these measures struggle to apply to adaptive algorithms that do not follow static rules. The DSA and DMA aim to curb platform power but remain focused on visible manipulations, failing to address the opaque, autonomous processes driving complex dark patterns.

These frameworks are ill-equipped to regulate AI-driven manipulations that continuously learn and personalise tactics, operating in individualised and invisible ways. The opacity of these systems underscores the urgent need for a more robust regulatory approach capable of scrutinising and addressing the foundational mechanics behind manipulative behaviours. As the digital landscape evolves, so must our understanding of where manipulation occurs within system architecture. Regulatory approaches must extend beyond the visible interface to safeguard users effectively and delve into the more profound decision-making and data-processing layers that define modern digital systems. An integrated approach that includes the UI, underlying algorithms, and adaptive systems is essential. By shifting the focus from merely treating the visible symptoms to addressing the root causes of manipulation, we can develop a more comprehensive framework for protecting users from the increasingly sophisticated dark patterns that define contemporary digital platforms.

The layered analysis of dark patterns aligns with the deceptive patterns outlined in the table, illustrating their evolution from simple UI-based tactics to complex, algorithm-driven strategies embedded in system architecture. The table categorises these patterns, ranging from visible manipulations to AI-based tactics that operate beneath the surface, evading easy detection. Static and triggered UI dark patterns remain observable, though some are moderately obscured. However, as manipulation shifts into system architecture – through multistep logic, deterministic algorithms, and adaptive AI – its visibility decreases, making investigation and regulation more challenging. This progression highlights the growing regulatory difficulties as deceptive tactics move beyond the interface into the underlying mechanics of digital systems. To clarify this shift, deceptive patterns can be categorised based on their sophistication, from basic UI manipulations to increasingly complex AI-driven systems. The following framework maps this spectrum, illustrating the escalating challenges in detection and regulation.

The Table illustrates the progression of deceptive design from overt UI manipulations to sophisticated algorithmic strategies embedded in system architecture. This evolution highlights the growing role of algorithms in enabling manipulation, as their complexity and opacity make

Table 5.2 Spectrum of Deceptive Patterns

Deceptive Pattern Type	Description	Visibility	Investigative Challenge	Predictability	Regulatory Challenge
Self-evident Deceptive Patterns	Overt patterns such as confirm shaming, forced action, or nagging are easily visible to users.	High	Minimal – visible without in-depth analysis.	High–consistent behaviour.	Low – Easier to regulate and enforce.
Hidden but UI-based Deceptive Patterns	Patterns such as sneaking or misdirection are designed to slip unnoticed, but investigators can capture them with screenshots.	Moderate	Requires careful UI analysis (eg, screenshots).	High – system consistently produces the exact UI.	Moderate – Can be detected with dedicated scrutiny.
Multistep Business Logic Deceptive Patterns	It relies on simple algorithms like branching questionnaires to guide users towards specific outcomes.	Low to Moderate	Requires tracing the decision flow across steps.	High – predictable based on input-output mapping.	Moderate – Requires replicating user journeys.
Complex Algorithm-based Deceptive Patterns	Personalisation and recommendation systems that involve intricate, deterministic algorithms.	Low	Strenuous without access to system source code.	High – The same inputs produce the same outputs.	High – Complexity makes it harder to regulate.
AI-based Deceptive Patterns	Systems that employ AI (eg, machine learning) with emergent, probability-based behaviour.	Very Low	Requires access to internal AI models.	Low – Emergent and non-deterministic behaviour.	Very High – Inconsistent behaviour complicates regulation.

detection increasingly challenging. Unlike UI dark patterns, algorithmic manipulations integrate deception into decision-making and data processing, complicating regulatory oversight. As algorithms become central to digital system architecture, they exert subtle yet pervasive influence over user behaviour, often without users' awareness. Understanding how these embedded processes shape user experiences is crucial, as their impact remains invisible, reinforcing the need for more robust scrutiny and regulation.

5.1.2. Algorithms Relationship to System Architecture

Algorithms form the backbone of system architecture, serving as the engines that drive decision-making processes in digital systems. Far from being isolated lines of code, algorithms are embedded within the system's architecture, orchestrating how data is processed, information is retrieved, and components interact. In complex digital environments, this integration positions algorithms as central to the system's functionality, influencing its behaviour and shaping user interactions at every level. Their seamless embedding enables algorithms to process vast quantities of data in real-time, making critical decisions that directly impact the user experience, often without the user's knowledge. Unlike deceptive user interfaces, which users can sometimes detect and navigate around, algorithmic manipulations operate invisibly within the system's core. This opacity allows algorithms to exert subtle, yet profound, influence over user behaviour by determining what is displayed, how choices are framed, and how interactions are structured. The interplay between algorithms and the user interface highlights the layered nature of manipulative design. While users engage with the interface on a surface level, their experience is shaped by the algorithms working in the background to guide, nudge, or distort their behaviour. This integration underscores the complexity of addressing deceptive practices, as interventions must account for the visible interface and the opaque algorithmic processes underpinning it. Understanding this relationship is critical to unpacking how system architecture drives user experiences and facilitates increasingly sophisticated forms of manipulation. The diagram illustrates the cascading relationship between algorithms embedded within system architecture, their role in data processing and real-time decision-making, and their subtle yet impactful influence on the user experience, which often remains invisible to users.

Figure 5.5 The Connection between Algorithms and UX

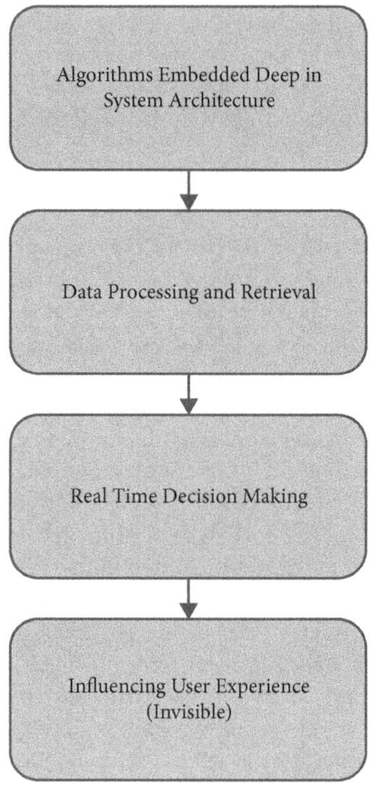

The non-exhaustive Table below highlights a range of algorithmic systems, their core functions, and the corresponding harms they may cause. While these systems are typically designed to optimise user engagement or achieve specific commercial objectives, they often do so at the cost of user autonomy, obscuring how user behaviour is influenced and manipulated. By mapping algorithmic systems to their intended functions and associated harms, it becomes possible to establish a clear and precise understanding of how these technologies operate and the risks they pose. This approach provides a framework for identifying patterns of manipulation and harm that are increasingly prevalent across digital platforms.

Table 5.3 Algorithmic Systems and Their Functions: Potential Benefits and Risks

	Algorithmic Systems Table	Function	Potential Harm
1	**Recommender Systems (eg, shopping, content)**	Suggests content or products based on user behaviour and preferences to maximise interaction or sales.	It can reinforce consumption patterns, limit exposure to diverse products, and create dependency on recommendations.[19]
2	**Social Media Feed Algorithms**	Curates content in social media feeds to keep users engaged by prioritising posts most likely to generate attention.	It can foster addictive behaviours, reinforce echo chambers, and contribute to mental health issues through overuse.[20]
3	**Search Engine Algorithms**	Ranks and displays search results based on user queries and inferred intent, often influenced by advertising or profit margin priorities.	It can skew information access, favouring commercial interests over accurate or unbiased information.[21]
4	**Personalised Pricing Algorithms**	Sets individualised prices for products or services based on user data, willingness to pay, or market behaviour.	Can exploit user data to charge higher prices based on perceived willingness to pay, reducing transparency and fairness.[22]
5	**Dynamic Pricing Algorithms**	Adjusts prices in real-time based on user data, perceived demand, and behavioural cues to maximise revenue.	Such practices can lead to unfair pricing, exploiting user vulnerabilities or creating inequalities based on data profiles.[23]
6	**Ad Targeting Algorithms**	Delivers personalised advertisements based on user browsing behaviour and demographic information.	It can manipulate users into purchasing decisions they may not have otherwise considered.[24]

(continued)

Table 5.3 *(Continued)*

	Algorithmic Systems Table	Function	Potential Harm
7	**Content Ranking and Sorting Algorithms (eg, news, video platforms)**	Organises and prioritises content (eg, articles, videos) to increase engagement, often reinforcing specific viewpoints.	It can reinforce filter bubbles, limit exposure to diverse viewpoints or critical information, and drive people to more extreme content.
8	**Gamification Algorithms**	Incorporates game-like elements (eg, points, rewards) into non-gaming contexts to encourage continued user participation.	It can create dependency or over-engagement, especially in contexts designed to keep users interacting longer.[25]
9	**Gambling and Gaming Engagement Loops**	Utilises reward schedules, randomised incentives, and progression systems to keep players engaged and encourage continued play.	It can foster addictive behaviours, promote excessive spending, and lead to financial and emotional harm through compulsive engagement.[26]
10	**Recommendation Loops (eg, video and music platforms)**	Provides continuous content recommendations to keep users engaged, often leading to prolonged consumption (eg, autoplay).	It can drive excessive media consumption and encourage addictive behaviour patterns.[27]

In simpler systems like multi-page business logic architectures, algorithmic processes follow a clear structure, allowing flowcharts to illustrate each predetermined and transparent step. However, as systems become increasingly complex, algorithms' role becomes opaque and more sophisticated.[28] In complex deterministic systems, algorithms may involve intricate calculations that, while still predictable, are far less intuitive and more difficult to understand. Like recommendation engines, these systems rely on algorithms to predict user preferences, often in ways that are not immediately apparent to the user.

When systems incorporate non-deterministic architectures, algorithms grow increasingly integral and complex. Advanced AI and machine learning algorithms integrate deeply into system architectures, allowing these systems to learn and adapt over time. Unlike traditional deterministic algorithms that follow fixed rules, some AI models – like large language models (LLMs) – use statistical patterns in data to generate responses. However, while LLMs exhibit non-deterministic behaviour, developers can also tune or update them to produce more consistent outputs, as demonstrated when models undergo refinement to address specific errors.[29] Integrating AI within system architecture requires a flexible and robust foundation, as these algorithms not only adapt but can subtly shape user behaviour in ways that are sometimes difficult to detect or fully understand. While some algorithms continuously learn from data and adapt in real-time, others may operate based on fixed training data without ongoing updates. Unlike traditional deterministic algorithms that follow rigid, predefined rules, many AI models – particularly those leveraging machine learning – recognise patterns and make probabilistic predictions, enabling flexible responses. However, not all AI systems operate similarly: personalisation is based on user interactions and adapts to meet strategic objectives, while others offer consistent, static responses to the same prompts. This variability in design means that integrating AI within system architecture can amplify the potential for subtle and sophisticated manipulations, as algorithms can influence user behaviour in nuanced and complex ways while others remain stable and predictable.

The progression from simpler systems like Triggered UI architectures to more complex, deterministic, and non-deterministic systems signifies a significant shift in how algorithms and system architectures interact with and influence user behaviour. In simpler systems, algorithms function with clearly defined rules that guide users through predictable pathways. However, as system complexity increases, particularly within deterministic architectures, the role of algorithms becomes more nuanced and less transparent. Although still governed by deterministic rules, these algorithms perform intricate calculations that obscure the logic behind their outcomes, making it challenging for users to comprehend how the system interprets their inputs fully.

This increasing complexity peaks in non-deterministic systems, where advanced AI and machine learning algorithms integrate deeply into the system architecture and are integral to its operation. These algorithms do not merely execute predefined instructions; they learn from data, adapt to new information, and make evolving decisions. The system architecture must remain flexible to support ongoing learning, allowing AI systems to subtly and imperceptibly influence user behaviour. While these effects can sometimes be intentional and aimed at guiding user actions, they may *also occur unintentionally as a by-product of the system's adaptive nature.* This continuum of algorithmic complexity appears across different system types, each varying in transparency, predictability, and potential for manipulation. The table below outlines how algorithm complexity impacts system transparency, user predictability, and the role of algorithms, highlighting the increasing potential for subtle manipulation as systems become more complex and adaptive.

The progression toward complexity and opacity peaks with AI systems, where learning algorithms integrate deeply within the system architecture. Unlike traditional algorithms that follow static rules, AI algorithms adapt over time, requiring access to data, communication with other system components, and the ability to apply learned models to real-world scenarios. This deep integration enhances the system's capacity to perform complex tasks while amplifying the potential for subtle manipulations, making detecting and regulating AI's influence on user behaviour increasingly challenging. AI systems cannot operate in isolation; they depend on the surrounding architecture to gather data, coordinate with other components, and execute tasks like personalising content, optimising logistics, or detecting patterns in large datasets. Embedding AI within system architecture demands flexibility to accommodate the adaptive nature of these algorithms, allowing them to evolve and shape the user experience in often subtle and pervasive ways. Consequently, these manipulations can be complex and challenging to detect, underscoring the need for robust regulatory frameworks to ensure AI-driven systems operate fairly and transparently, safeguarding users against unintended influences. Accordingly, deceptive design occurs when a system's design and operation mislead or manipulate users – intentionally or unintentionally.

5.1.3. Data Processing and Profiling: Identifying and Exploiting User Vulnerabilities

One way developers can design algorithms deceptively is through biased data processing. For example, an algorithm might prioritise certain content, products, or services based on criteria that benefit the platform rather than the user. Such bias could manifest in the algorithm steering users toward higher-priced items or services or manipulating search results to favour the platform's interests. Users might believe the platform offers neutral, objective information, but the algorithm selectively curates options to drive a specific outcome. Another deceptive tactic involves exploiting user data to predict and influence behaviour. Algorithms can analyse vast amounts of personal data to identify vulnerabilities or preferences and then use this information to present choices that nudge users toward decisions that may not be in their best interest. For instance, an algorithm might exploit a user's known impulsiveness to present time-limited offers, creating a sense of urgency that pressures them into making hasty decisions. These deceptive algorithms are insidious because users are often unaware of the manipulation. The decisions appear personalised or tailored, leading users to trust the system's outputs. Without transparency in how algorithms function or clear regulations to protect users, these deceptive designs can continue unchecked, subtly steering behaviour in ways that users neither recognise nor understand. This lack of awareness makes it difficult for users to protect themselves from such manipulative practices.

Table 5.4 Deceptive Algorithm Tactics: Descriptions, Examples, and User Impact

Deceptive Algorithm Tactic	Description	Example	Impact
Biased Data Processing	Prioritising certain content, products, or services based on the platform's benefit	Steering users toward higher-priced items or manipulating search results	Users believe they are getting neutral info
Exploiting User Data	Analysing user data to influence behaviour by identifying vulnerabilities	Using personal data to present time-limited offers to impulsive users	Users feel urgency and make hasty decisions

Deceptive algorithms can integrate even more insidiously, exploiting deeper layers of system architecture to manipulate users without their knowledge. One particularly troubling example is the use of dark patterns embedded within algorithms that govern pricing. Through a practice known as 'dynamic pricing,' algorithms can adjust the price of goods or services based on an individual user's data, such as browsing history, location, or purchasing behaviour. For instance, an algorithm might increase prices for users who have shown a willingness to spend more or who are browsing from a wealthier neighbourhood. Unaware of these behind-the-scenes adjustments, the user may assume the displayed price is the standard rate, not realising the system charges them more than others for the same product. Another covert tactic involves algorithms that manipulate social proof – such as likes, shares, or reviews – on platforms where user engagement is instrumental.

Developers can design algorithms that artificially inflate the popularity of specific posts, products, or services to create a false sense of demand or consensus. For example, an algorithm might prioritise showing content artificially boosted with fake likes or reviews, leading users to trust and engage more readily. This manipulation exploits the human tendency to follow the crowd, making it a powerful tool for influencing behaviour without users ever realising fabricated social cues are guiding their decisions.

Moreover, designers can create algorithms to manipulate decision-making through 'choice architecture'. Developers can embed algorithms that strategically present options that lead users toward a predetermined choice. For instance, an algorithm might reorder search results or filter options to make a particular selection appear more attractive or logical, even if it is not the best option for the user. By presenting choices more prominently or hiding less profitable options, the algorithm can drive users toward decisions that benefit the platform, all while maintaining the illusion of user autonomy. However, this illusion of independence is crucial, as these unseen forces unknowingly guide users. The visible user experience (prices, reviews, options) appears transparent, while the hidden algorithmic manipulations are in deeper layers. For example, the top layer could be a user browsing a product page, while the underlying layers use algorithms to adjust prices, inflate social proof, and reorder options. These hidden manipulations illustrate the 'hidden forces' influencing user behaviour. The subtlety and sophistication of these tactics mean that users often feel like they are making independent choices, unaware that the unseen troops are guiding their decisions.

5.2. Deep Manipulation Technique: Personalisation of User Interfaces

Personalised user interfaces (UIs) significantly differ from generic UIs, which traditionally offer a uniform experience to all users. The critical distinction between personalised and generic UIs lies in the former's ability to adapt dynamically to individual users by leveraging data to create tailored environments based on their needs, preferences, and behaviours. In contrast, generic UIs maintain the same visual and interactive elements for every user, regardless of their characteristics or usage patterns. Personalised UIs stem from data collection and advancements in processing technologies that enable a deeper understanding of user behaviour. Here, machine learning algorithms and artificial intelligence significantly predict user preferences and actions through historical data analysis. By tracking clicks, scrolls, and inputs, these systems accumulate vast amounts of behavioural data, which algorithms analyse to make real-time adjustments to the UI. Data points such as location, device usage, browsing history, and social interactions provide valuable insights into individual preferences. For instance, two users visiting the same e-commerce platform will encounter different product recommendations, layouts, or call-to-action buttons based on their previous actions.

Personalised UIs also differ from generic ones in terms of user autonomy. While generic UIs offer equal control over choices, personalised UIs subtly guide users by curating options that align with their interests. Although users believe they are making independent choices, they are responding to options curated by algorithms. These seamless and subtle changes often leave users unaware of how much the platform influences their behaviour, opening the door to potential manipulation. Personalisation also introduces challenges around transparency and trust. In generic UIs, transparency is easier to maintain since all users experience the same interface. With personalised UIs, however, the mechanisms behind the interface remain less visible, creating an opaque interaction where users may not fully understand why certain elements appear. This lack of transparency risks eroding user trust, mainly when platforms use personalisation to exploit cognitive biases or nudge users toward decisions prioritising platform objectives over user needs. As a result, personalised UIs represent a significant shift in design, influencing how power and agency operate between users and systems.

5.2.1. Data Collection and User Profiling Techniques

The foundation of personalised user interfaces lies in the detailed profiles developed through extensive data collection and analysis. This process involves examining explicit user inputs and passive data, such as browsing history, device type, geolocation, and interaction patterns. These data points enable platforms to build comprehensive user profiles that capture observable behaviours and inferred preferences. By analysing patterns in the user's historical data, these systems employ sophisticated algorithms to identify individual vulnerabilities – traits such as impulsiveness, susceptibility to social cues, or propensity for risk-taking. The platform continuously refines the resulting profiles, allowing algorithms to anticipate user responses and adjust the content accordingly. Such data-driven insights enable platforms to tailor their interactions with each user, often in ways that exploit these identified vulnerabilities, nudging users toward actions that align with the platform's objectives.

5.2.2. User Onboarding and Engagement

Contextual engagement plays a crucial role in enhancing user experience. Instead of bombarding users with out-of-context messages or suggestions, the product should anticipate when a user is ready to engage with a particular feature. For example, prompting a user to explore an advanced tool after successfully mastering more basic features increases the likelihood of a positive response. Timing is essential in contextual engagement. A well-timed nudge, suggesting a relevant action, feels helpful, whereas poorly timed interruptions are intrusive or manipulative. Respect for the user forms the foundation of successful engagement strategies. Unlike traditional marketing approaches that prioritise business objectives over user experience, these strategies focus on creating a partnership between the user and the product. Nudges or prompts should assist, not disrupt, maintaining the user's autonomy and trust in the product.

Overly aggressive engagement tactics, such as frequent and irrelevant notifications, undermine trust and risk alienating the user. Conversely, when users sense that a product respects their time and attention, they are more likely to engage deeply, transitioning from passive users to active advocates. A valuable tactic here could include offering options like a 'Maybe later' or 'No thanks' button on call-to-action dialogues, allowing users to postpone or opt out of specific features like upgrades or additional functionalities. This approach empowers users, offering them choices rather than forcing engagement at inconvenient moments. Another critical component of effective engagement involves creating a system that manages how and when nudges appear. A rule-based system prioritises relevant prompts, ensuring users do not feel overwhelmed. This system can also incorporate features like rate limiting, where only one nudge occurs per session, and allow users to mute or sleep-specific prompts. Offering this level of control over the engagement experience prevents users from feeling bombarded by prompts, helping to maintain a positive relationship with the product.

Finally, the approach to user engagement greatly influences a product's identity. A product that delivers helpful, timely nudges presents itself as user-friendly and supportive. In contrast, a product that aggressively pushes its agenda through constant prompts feels impersonal and manipulative. Ultimately, how a product engages with its users reflects its broader values and personality. A thoughtful and respectful approach to user engagement strengthens the bond between user and product, encouraging long-term loyalty and success.

5.2.3. Exploitation of Psychological Vulnerabilities

Once platforms establish user profiles, they can manipulate psychological tendencies by embedding these insights into personalised interactions. Platforms often design experiences to exploit specific cognitive biases, using deceptive designs that manipulate user behaviour. For example, platforms might leverage the fear of missing out (FOMO) by presenting time-sensitive offers to users with impulsiveness, heightening a sense of urgency that pressures users into hasty decisions. Similarly, platforms might exploit overconfidence through tailored messages encouraging users to make riskier choices based on their perceived strengths. By strategically employing these manipulative tactics, platforms can steer users toward decisions that may not be in their best interest but serve the platform's profit-driven motives. Numerous case studies have illustrated how these personalised manipulations can erode user autonomy, highlighting the concerns surrounding the exploitation of psychological vulnerabilities.

In contrast to generic UIs, which maintain a uniform experience across all users, personalised UIs adapt dynamically to individual user profiles. While traditional UIs present the same visual and interactive elements regardless of user characteristics, personalised UIs leverage data-driven insights to create unique and tailored environments based on individual behaviours, preferences, and needs. These highly adaptable UIs have emerged from machine learning and artificial intelligence, which can make real-time adjustments by analysing clicks, scrolls, and other interactive elements. These systems use vast behavioural data to predict user preferences, guiding users toward confident choices through customised recommendations, layouts, and call-to-action elements. For instance, users visiting the same e-commerce platform may encounter different product recommendations or arrangements depending on their previous actions and inferred preferences.

Moreover, personalised UIs influence user autonomy in subtle but significant ways. Unlike generic UIs, which afford users equal control over their choices, personalised UIs curate options that align with user interests, thus nudging them toward pre-selected outcomes. While this can enhance convenience by delivering content that aligns with user preferences, it also raises concerns, as these seamless adjustments often go unnoticed, leaving users unaware of the extent to which underlying algorithms influence their interactions. Consequently, personalised UIs create an opaque interaction where users may not fully understand why certain elements are displayed more prominently than others, posing a challenge to transparency and potentially eroding user trust. This shift in design dynamics represents a complex interplay between user agency and system influence, especially when platforms prioritise their objectives over user welfare by subtly manipulating choices through personalised elements.

5.2.4. Methods for Tailoring UIs to Guide Users Toward Specific Actions

Methods for tailoring user interfaces (UIs) to guide users toward specific actions rely heavily on design strategies and algorithmic personalisation to predict and influence user behaviour. These techniques centre around 'choice architecture,' where how designers present options significantly impacts user decisions. Personalised UIs actively nudge users in directions that benefit the platform more than the user by controlling options' layout, timing, and visibility. One standard method involves strategically placing visual elements. For example, a personalised UI highlights specific products, services, or actions using bold colours, prominent positioning, or eye-catching animations. This tactic captures attention and encourages users to engage with features. In e-commerce, platforms prominently feature product recommendations based on a user's browsing or purchasing history. These recommendations push users toward purchasing, especially when platforms prioritise higher-margin items rather than those aligned with the user's needs.

Another method leverages algorithmically tailored content prioritisation. Social media platforms, news websites, and streaming services use algorithms to determine the order of displayed content. These platforms maintain user engagement by prioritising items that align with previous user behaviour. As a result, users are exposed to material that reinforces their preferences and biases, creating echo chambers. In doing so, platforms effectively manipulate the user's perception by limiting exposure to diverse content outside these preferences. A more advanced tactic manipulates decision urgency through time-based prompts. Personalised UIs induce a sense of urgency by framing options as available only for a limited time. This method exploits the FOMO, a powerful psychological driver that prompts impulsive decisions. E-commerce sites, for instance, generate personalised messages indicating that an item is low in stock or that a special discount lasts for a brief period. Though partially accurate, these time-sensitive displays exaggerate scarcity or target users more likely to act on urgency.

Dynamic interface modification also plays a crucial role in shaping user actions. As users interact with the interface, algorithms adjust the UI in real-time, highlighting specific options based on inferred preferences or emotional states. For instance, when a user spends extra time viewing a product, the interface responds by offering additional information, reviews, or discounts, encouraging the user to complete the purchase. This feedback loop continually adapts to user behaviour, steering them toward specific outcomes. Personalised UIs further leverage cognitive biases to influence decision-making. Techniques like 'anchoring,' where users encounter high-priced items first, skew subsequent choices by making mid-range options seem more affordable. By setting the initial point of reference, platforms encourage users to spend more. Similarly, platforms selectively conceal or downplay less profitable options, directing users toward decisions that align with their objectives, often without users realising their range of choices has narrowed.

These methods show how personalisation not only enhances user experience but also exerts control over user behaviour. While such techniques may improve usability and streamline decision-making, they raise significant concerns, mainly when prioritising platform profits over user autonomy. As personalised UIs become increasingly sophisticated, the fine line between user empowerment and manipulation continues to blur, demanding closer scrutiny within the broader discussions on digital rights.

5.2.5.　Psychological Impact of Personalised UIs

Personalised user interfaces profoundly influence user engagement, often fostering a level of dependency that extends beyond mere convenience.[30] By leveraging behavioural science principles, personalised UIs are meticulously designed to guide users toward specific actions, subtly encouraging prolonged interaction with the platform.[31] Personalised user interfaces profoundly influence user engagement, often fostering a level of dependency that extends beyond mere convenience.[32] While some personalisation is straightforward – such as recommending products based on purchase history or highlighting frequently bought items together – others leverage behavioural insights to guide users towards specific actions.[33] These more targeted designs can subtly encourage prolonged interaction with the platform.[34] Personalised interfaces enhance usability and engagement by shaping user perceptions, attitudes, and decisions, yet they can also deepen users' reliance on the platform. These tailored interfaces do more than enhance usability; they shape user perceptions, attitudes, and decisions in ways that increase engagement but can also deepen reliance on the platform.[35]

As discussed in chapters one and two, a vital component of the influence of personalised UIs lies in the deliberate application of nudge theory. Platforms intentionally structure the user experience to promote choices that align with their objectives. For example, platforms often use subtle cues like colour coding or placement to make specific options more appealing, guiding users' attention and decisions without explicit instruction. The careful design of these interactions plays on cognitive biases, such as the anchoring effect, where initial exposure to a high-priced item makes subsequent choices appear more reasonable by comparison.[36] Similarly, using scarcity prompts, limited-time offers, and countdowns taps into the fear of missing out, reinforcing impulsive decision-making by capitalising on the user's instinctive response to urgency.[37]

To understand the psychological impact of these techniques, at the end of this chapter, I examine three case studies that highlight how personalised UIs can potentially manipulate user behaviour. Social media platforms, for instance, frequently deploy algorithms that prioritise content aligning with users' existing interests, reinforcing echo chambers that limit exposure to diverse perspectives. This echo chamber effect reinforces users' pre-existing beliefs and fosters a sense of comfort and validation, subtly discouraging users from seeking alternative viewpoints.[38] Another example is e-commerce, where platforms leverage users' browsing history to push targeted recommendations, often framed in ways that exploit known vulnerabilities, such as impulsiveness or the desire for social validation.[39] By doing so, these platforms foster a cyclical dependency on the algorithm's recommendations, increasing users' reliance on these curated suggestions for decision-making.[40] The psychological impact of personalised UIs raises critical questions about user autonomy, as the techniques that enhance engagement also blur the line between guidance and manipulation. These interfaces can undermine individual agency by shaping user choices to benefit platform objectives – often without users' conscious awareness.[41] As digital platforms continue to evolve, the implications of this dynamic become more pronounced, highlighting the need for broader discussions on transparency, accountability, and users' rights in an increasingly personalised digital landscape.[42]

5.3. Systemic Dark Patterns

Reflecting on the conceptualisation of dark patterns within system architecture, a critical observation arose between Harry Brignull and me. During one of our routine catchups, Harry presented a slide entitled 'Does my design contain harmful choice architecture?' that focused primarily on user interaction within a static interface, such as a typical e-commerce product page. These static interfaces assume a more predictable user interaction flow, where user inputs lead to predefined outputs based on set architectural constraints.

However, I noted a significant oversight in this model: it does not account for the dynamic systems increasingly prevalent in modern digital platforms, where system behaviour evolves based on continuous user interaction. This gap highlights the insufficiency of applying a traditional choice architecture model to dynamic, data-driven environments, particularly those designed to modify user behaviour in real-time. The critical challenge is that static systems, by their very nature, are governed by straightforward cause-effect relationships. For example, in a static e-commerce page, a user selects a product, and the system responds by showing related products or providing a direct path to purchase. This type of interaction is predetermined by the system's architecture, allowing for a limited range of user actions. However, this model fails to capture the complexity of dynamic systems in social media platforms, online gaming environments, and other data-intensive applications, where user behaviour is continuously logged, analysed, and used to modify future system responses.

The limitations of this static framework become evident when contrasted with Norman's original seven stages of action model, which illustrates a more nuanced, cyclic interaction between user goals, actions, and system feedback.[43] In dynamic digital systems, such as those found on social media or online gaming platforms, the user's actions trigger responses that are not fixed but rather adaptive. These systems continuously log user behaviour, analyse it, and use it to shape future interactions, effectively creating a feedback loop that Norman's model encapsulates through stages like 'Interpret,' 'Evaluate,' and 'Adjust Goals.'[44] In dynamic environments, the system does not simply react to user inputs but adapts based on cumulative data, evolving in ways that subtly guide users toward desired behaviours. The adaptive responses in these systems move far beyond the static cause-effect responses of traditional architectures, illustrating how modern digital platforms employ complex, data-driven algorithms to refine user interaction over time. Consequently, Norman's model underscores the insufficiency of conventional choice architecture frameworks in capturing the full scope of manipulation that dynamic, data-driven systems can enact.[45]

The gap between static and dynamic system architecture raises profound implications for understanding dark patterns and deceptive design in modern digital platforms. While helpful in identifying overtly deceptive practices (eg, misleading buttons or forced continuity), static models fail to capture the subtler, systemic manipulations embedded in dynamic systems. These dynamic architectures can adapt based on the user's real-time inputs, making the platform's manipulation less predictable and more challenging to detect. When Harry speculated about what the 'bottom' side of this action model would look like in a dynamic system, we gestured toward the need for an adaptive framework that accounts for algorithmic feedback loops and behavioural shifts over time. Such a framework would consider the immediate UI interactions and the continuous data processing occurring in the background, which influences future user behaviour through recommender systems, personalised content, and dynamic difficulty adjustments (eg, in gaming). This recognition marks a pivotal step in understanding systemic dark patterns. Unlike traditional dark patterns, which are often visible and can be mitigated by UI-level adjustments, systemic dark patterns operate within the architecture, continually evolving in response to user inputs. This changing nature creates a feedback loop that benefits the platform – whether through increased ad revenue, user engagement, or microtransaction sales – while subtly disadvantaging users by limiting their control and autonomy over their digital experience.

Figure 5.6 Norman's Original Seven Stages of Action Model

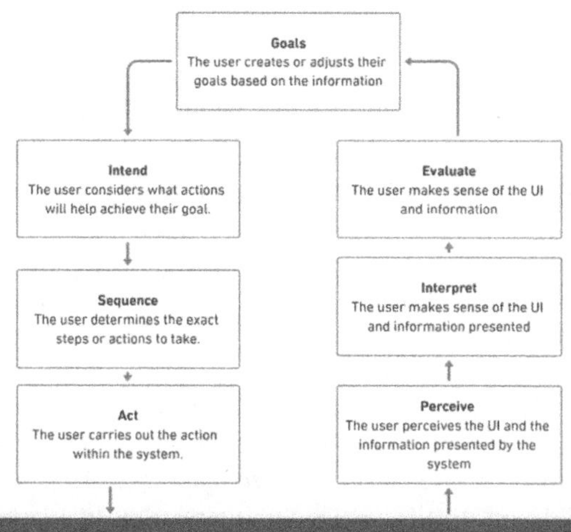

5.3.1. Harmful Choice Architectures

Harry and I quickly recognised the urgent need for a dynamic model of dark patterns that integrates real-time data processing and algorithmic decision-making. Such a model must account for the evolving nature of system behaviour. Without addressing this deeper layer, our understanding of dark patterns remains incomplete, and regulatory frameworks will continue to struggle to capture the most sophisticated forms of digital exploitation. This insight reinforces the argument made in this chapter: as system architecture becomes more intricate than traditional, visible designs, the boundary between design and exploitation blurs even further, with manipulation operating at a deeper, often invisible level, embedded within the system's structure, and evading superficial regulation.

While surface-level dark patterns, such as forced continuity or hidden costs, are easy to identify, deeper architectural manipulations – such as data-driven levelling systems and algorithmic matchmaking designed to promote monetisation – are more insidious. These mechanisms reflect a broader trend in commodifying user engagement, creating tension between maximising platform profits and preserving player autonomy. For example, gaming platforms use feedback loops through in-session nudges and notifications, keeping users engaged without full awareness of the platform's attempt to overcome their self-interest.[46] Furthermore, these systems exploit psychological vulnerabilities, fostering time consumption and financial cost dependencies.[47]

To address these issues, I propose a framework that assesses system design for harmful elements in the user's decision-making process. This framework considers user experience regarding emotional influence, ambiguity, pressure, and comprehension to identify where design practices might coerce or mislead. It challenges designers to critically reflect on how their systems guide or constrain user choices, particularly by considering whether they skew decisions through cognitive biases, emotional manipulation, or unclear language and whether they coerce users into specific actions through fatigue or pressure.

The graphic illustrates an action model for dynamic systems, highlighting how real-time feedback and user data increasingly shape system responses. It marks a shift from static interactions to adaptive feedback loops, where the system continuously evolves based on user input. The three case studies that follow propose a framework for addressing

Figure 5.7 An Action Model Depicting a Dynamic System

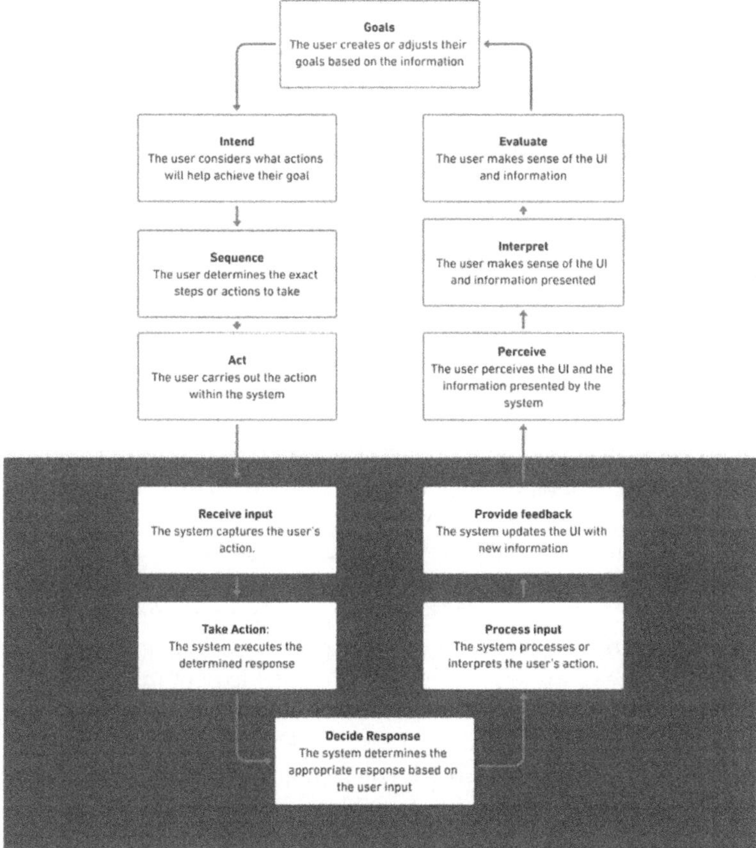

harmful elements in digital design, focusing on how system architecture influences decision-making. This framework assesses user experience by evaluating emotional influence, ambiguity, pressure, and comprehension to identify coercive or misleading design practices. Designers are urged to critically assess their systems' impact on user choices, particularly through cognitive biases, emotional manipulation, and language. By scrutinising design elements that shape user actions, they can mitigate harmful influences embedded in system architecture. The case studies demonstrate this framework's practical application across different digital environments, illustrating how system architecture can support autonomy or exploit behavioural tendencies.

5.3.1.1. Social Media System Architecture: User and System Goals in a Feedback Loop

In the digital ecosystem, social media platforms operate within a symbiotic framework of user inputs and system outputs, creating a dynamic relationship designed to align with the platform's goals while subtly steering user behaviour.[48] Over time, system architecture has evolved beyond static user interfaces to incorporate feedback-driven loops that respond in real-time to user data and interaction patterns.[49] As a result, users engage in systems where their behaviour serves as both input and output, continuously reinforcing the interaction cycle.[50] This architecture underscores an evident tension between user goals and platform objectives. Users typically pursue personal desires such as social interaction, news consumption, or entertainment, seeking meaningful engagement. In contrast, the platform is built to maximise user engagement – often measured through critical metrics like Daily Active Users (DAU) and Monthly Active Users (MAU) – to optimise advertising revenue.[51] Although users may feel they are pursuing these goals autonomously, the invisible layers of the system's architecture often co-opt their behaviour to serve the platform's economic interests.

Recommender systems drive the feedback loop by processing explicit user data (eg, interests, social connections) alongside surveillance data (eg, logged behaviours, inferred preferences).[52] This data-driven engine curates personalised feeds and targeted notifications to maximise engagement. The system amplifies similar materials as users interact with content, leading to content escalation. This becomes particularly concerning when it steers users toward extreme content, as seen in studies on disinformation and radicalisation. A broader model of social media platforms shows how explicit user inputs and surveillance-driven data shape personalised outputs. These outputs influence immediate engagement or re-engage users later. Platforms increasingly rely on passive data collection and behavioural nudging (eg, FOMO, social proof) to sustain interaction. While explicit inputs play a role, less visible data fuels algorithmic recommendations, shaping user behaviour in ways they may not fully perceive.

Zooming out from individual systems and interactions reveals a recurring user behaviour loop across various domains, not just social media.[53] Simple e-commerce transactions, such as purchasing socks online, function within a broader business model designed to cultivate repeat customer behaviour. Businesses track customer lifetime value (LTV) and retention rates while minimising customer acquisition costs (CAC), shaping system architecture to reinforce engagement loops.[54] Dark patterns emerge as engagement-maximising algorithms exploit these loops to retain users and deepen platform relationships. Social media platforms operate as dual structures where user and system objectives coexist but often diverge. Users seek social interaction, news, or entertainment, while platforms prioritise engagement metrics – such as DAUs and MAUs – to drive advertising revenue. This architecture fosters problematic dynamics, including echo chambers, where algorithms reinforce existing viewpoints by amplifying similar content. The system's ability to interpret and respond to user behaviour creates a reinforcement loop, optimising content for continued engagement. This cycle subtly influences user perception, framing information to steer behaviour toward platform-driven strategic goals, which may not always align with user interests.[55]

These dynamics give rise to 'maximisers,' like AI's 'paperclip maximiser' thought experiment.[56] Platforms function as engagement, gaming, or shopping addiction maximisers, prioritising a single metric – such as engagement – over user autonomy. Each system optimises behavioural outcomes, often at the expense of user interests, reinforcing how algorithmic systems exploit psychological vulnerabilities to drive specific actions without explicit awareness. This framing is critical in understanding the commodification of user engagement. Platforms use feedback loops, nudges, and notifications to sustain interaction, leveraging psychological triggers like social proof and FOMO. Much like gambling mechanics, variable rewards (eg, likes, shares, attention)[57] arrive unpredictably, activating dopamine cycles that reinforce compulsive behaviours while obscuring the underlying manipulation.[58]

These systems do not operate neutrally. Platform architectures are intentionally structured to influence user perception and behaviour.[59] While engaging with personalised content, users remain unaware of the deeper algorithmic systems shaping their decisions. Although interactions may feel driven by personal choice, the system subtly controls them to align with the platform's objectives. The problem intensifies when the architecture guides and constrains choices, creating an invisible layer of control that users fail to perceive. The convergence of these factors underscores a critical tension between users and the economic imperatives of platforms. Systems designed to maximise engagement increasingly obscure the boundaries of free choice, leveraging ambiguity, pressure, or fatigue to ensure continued interaction.[60]

5.3.1.2. *Video Gaming and Systemic Manipulation: The Architecture of Engagement and Exploitation*

In the context of video gaming, the systemic architecture designed to manipulate player engagement mirrors frameworks commonly seen in social media.[61] However, video games introduce additional complexities, mainly relying on game mechanics that exploit the user's propensity for addictive behaviours.[62] Game elements such as levelling systems, difficulty adjustments, and reward structures deliberately optimise both player engagement and platform profitability. These systems create progress loops that tap into psychological vulnerabilities like compulsion loops and dopamine-driven reinforcement, encouraging continuous interaction.[63] The architecture of modern video games relies heavily on two forms of user input: explicit data, which users knowingly provide, such as gameplay statistics and achievements, and surveillance data, which the platform gathers from behavioural patterns without the user's awareness.[64] This latter input type is crucial to understanding how the system adapts to sustain engagement. As players interact with the game, their behaviours – the time spent on specific levels or their reactions to difficulty spikes – are logged and used to recalibrate the game's mechanics in real-time.[65] For example, suppose the system detects that a player will likely disengage after several failed attempts at a challenging level. In that case, it may subtly lower the difficulty or offer in-game rewards to maintain the player's interest.[66] These minor, imperceptible adjustments ensure a balance between challenge and reward, which keeps players engaged but not frustrated to the point of quitting.[67] The system's ability to modulate the gaming experience based on user behaviour creates a loop in which platforms constantly draw players back into the game.[68]

One of the core mechanisms driving sustained engagement in video games is the concept of reinforcement loops, rooted in behavioural psychology.[69] These loops rely on variable rewards, which are unpredictable or random, such as loot boxes or rare items, and closely resemble the psychological dynamics of gambling.[70] When players receive unpredictable rewards, it triggers dopamine release in the brain, creating a sense of satisfaction and a strong compulsion to continue playing.[71] The introduction of loot boxes and microtransactions has further complicated the landscape of gaming systems. Initially marketed as cosmetic enhancements, these features often exploit players' FOMO or desire for status within the game. Players may feel pressured to purchase additional content to remain competitive or to progress without the repetitive grind required for advancement.[72] Scarcity tactics, such as limited-time offers or exclusive rare items, heighten this pressure, pushing players toward spending money to maintain their competitive edge.[73]

In addition to reward mechanisms, video game architecture also manipulates player decision-making by strategically designing moments of difficulty.[74] Games frequently present players with situations where purchasing in-game items seems like the most convenient solution to overcoming a challenge.[75] For example, difficulty spikes, where a game becomes significantly harder at critical moments, are often introduced to encourage players to make microtransactions.[76] The system offers paid content to bypass frustration at this psychological tipping point. This approach – monetised difficulty adjustment – exploits players' emotional states, guiding them toward purchases under the guise of gameplay progression.[77] Even grinding, or the repetitive completion of tasks to achieve a goal becomes a manipulation tool.[78] By artificially inflating the time required for progress, the system drives players toward frustration, prompting them to spend money on microtransactions as a shortcut to satisfaction.[79] This manipulation reflects systemic dark patterns, where the game's architecture creates conditions that undermine player autonomy while maximising the platform's profits.[80]

These systemic manipulations raise significant concerns about the autonomy of players and the design of gaming platforms.[81] While surface-level dark patterns, such as forced continuity or hidden costs, are relatively easy to identify and regulate, the deeper, algorithmic manipulations embedded within the game's architecture are much more insidious.[82] These data-driven levelling systems and algorithmic matchmaking processes specifically drive monetisation, commodifying user engagement at the expense of player well-being.[83] The gaming industry's reliance on these manipulations has created tensions between maximising user engagement and protecting player autonomy.[84] By using data-driven nudges and personalised notifications, gaming platforms create feedback loops that draw players back into the game, often without their conscious awareness.[85]

This form of engagement goes beyond simple entertainment, systematically exploiting psychological vulnerabilities and creating dependencies that can be harmful in terms of both time spent and financial cost.[86]

5.3.1.3. *E-commerce and Systemic Dark Patterns: The Architecture of Consumer Manipulation*

E-commerce platforms employ complex architectures that embed systemic dark patterns, exploiting users' cognitive limitations to influence behaviour. These systems facilitate transactions while subtly guiding decisions to benefit the platform. By capturing and processing user data, they create an illusion of independent choice while carefully shaping consumer actions. Like social media and gaming, e-commerce platforms blend explicit and surveillance-based user profiles. Users provide explicit data, such as names and purchase history, while platforms track browsing behaviour, analysing viewed but unpurchased items. Combined with third-party data, this profiling allows platforms to personalise recommendations, creating a power imbalance where users remain unaware of the platform's influence over pricing, recommendations, and product displays. While platforms claim to simplify decision-making, they narrow choices and bias outcomes to maximise sales.

Recommender systems are key in curating content based on past behaviour, similar users, and market trends. While marketed as enhancing the shopping experience, they drive upselling and cross-selling, subtly manipulating user engagement. Dynamic pricing further distorts the marketplace, adjusting prices based on a user's spending patterns. For instance, frequent buyers of high-end products may see higher prices than first-time shoppers. Here, personalisation shifts from user convenience to market distortion, reinforcing platform control over consumer choices.

Once engaged, users are continuously nudged to return. Platforms adjust search and browse listings in real time, using A/B testing to highlight products most likely to drive purchases, ensuring sustained consumer engagement and maximised revenue.[87] This feedback loop constantly feeds users information that nudges them toward buying while giving them the illusion of independent judgment.[88] Following a session, users often receive notifications or email prompts reminding them of items they viewed but did not purchase or offering time-sensitive discounts. These re-engagement strategies are potent drivers of consumer behaviour, especially with social proof techniques, such as messages indicating 'Only two left in stock' or 'Customers who bought this also bought …'.[89] By leveraging scarcity and social pressure, these systems push users toward impulse purchases, often overriding more rational, deliberate decision-making processes.[90]

One of the more troubling aspects of e-commerce architecture is its ability to exploit common cognitive biases. For instance, default settings – such as pre-selecting more expensive shipping options – exploit the default bias, where users are more likely to accept pre-selected possibilities to avoid the cognitive effort of making a change. Similarly, limited-time offers capitalise on the scarcity heuristic, driving users to act out of fear of missing deals or products, even when the platform may artificially generate these signals. Another key manipulation occurs through choice architecture, which shapes how the platform presents options to guide users toward more profitable decisions. For example, price anchoring – where the platform displays a high-priced item alongside cheaper alternatives – makes the lower-priced option appear to be a bargain, even if it is still more expensive than comparable items elsewhere. Such subtle manipulations skew users' perceptions of value, often leading them toward suboptimal purchasing decisions.[91]

5.3.2. Beyond the Interface: Regulating the Hidden Manipulations of Digital Platforms

The systemic design of modern digital platforms presents pressing regulatory challenges, as it increasingly obscures the boundary between genuine user autonomy and covert manipulation. Recommender systems and algorithmically driven platforms leverage user behaviour in opaque and highly influential ways, shaping decision-making processes without users' informed awareness. This opacity has profound implications for data privacy, agency, and the broader digital ecosystem. Most users remain unaware of the extent to which their data is collected and used to fuel engagement-maximising systems, reinforcing behavioural loops that prioritise platform profitability over individual welfare. While regulatory frameworks such as the GDPR and the DSA address surface-level manipulations and data privacy concerns, they fail to capture the more insidious manipulations embedded within system architecture – particularly within content recommendation algorithms and behavioural conditioning mechanisms. These architectures operate beyond the visible interface, guiding user choices through adaptive reinforcement strategies that systematically exploit cognitive biases. The regulatory challenge is not merely one of transparency but systemic accountability for how platforms engineer dependency and sustained engagement.

Addressing these concerns requires regulatory frameworks that extend beyond interface-level scrutiny to interrogate the foundational architectures of digital systems. Platforms must take accountability not only for overt manipulative practices but also for the structural design choices that enable systemic exploitation. Framing platforms as engagement-maximising entities expose the risks of unchecked profit-driven algorithmic influence, underscoring the urgency of regulatory intervention to counteract systemic distortions in digital decision-making. Without more rigorous oversight, these systems will continue prioritising engagement metrics over user welfare, refining their ability to exploit psychological and behavioural vulnerabilities with increasing precision. These issues manifest acutely in social media, gaming, and e-commerce, where algorithmic architectures generate distinct but interrelated harms. Social media platforms deploy behavioural conditioning techniques to optimise engagement, subtly shaping discourse and interaction in ways that reinforce user dependency. The gaming industry integrates dynamic difficulty adjustments and variable reward schedules to encourage compulsive behaviours, driving excessive spending and prolonged play through mechanisms that mirror known gambling techniques. In e-commerce, algorithmic architectures – such as personalised pricing, targeted recommendations, and re-engagement loops – systematically bias purchasing decisions in favour of commercial imperatives, often at odds with user interests.

While the GDPR, UCPD, and DSA provide mechanisms to counteract overt deception, they remain ill-equipped to regulate these deeper, structurally embedded manipulations. The evolving nature of these practices necessitates a paradigm shift in regulatory design, ensuring that interventions address visible instances of manipulation and the systemic architectures that underpin digital exploitation. The pervasive reliance on transparency as a regulatory solution is fundamentally flawed. Transparency requirements, such as those in the DSA, presuppose a rational decision-maker akin to '*Homo Economicus*'. This outdated assumption fails to account for the reality that human behaviour is far more influenced by cognitive shortcuts, biases, and emotional triggers – closer to the Homer Simpson analogy than to a hyper-rational economic actor. Users are often unaware of how algorithms shape their choices and lack the knowledge or capacity to engage with or challenge these systems meaningfully. For example, users rarely consider scrutinising a social media platform's recommender system or contest the subtle mechanisms on platforms like Amazon or eBay that led to regrettable purchases. Regulatory responses must go beyond superficial transparency requirements to address the underlying architectures and mechanisms driving these manipulative practices. Achieving this demands a shift in regulatory focus, moving from merely disclosing algorithmic processes to actively mitigating their exploitative impacts. Traditional consumer protections are inadequate for these challenges, as they fail to address algorithmic harm's social and psychological dimensions. A more comprehensive regulatory framework must directly confront the systemic manipulation embedded in digital platforms, targeting the visible manifestations of harm and the architectural mechanisms that enable and perpetuate it. Only by addressing these foundational issues can regulation ensure fairness, safeguard autonomy, and mitigate the broader societal impacts of algorithmic manipulation.

5.4. Conclusion

This chapter explores systemic dark patterns beyond UI manipulations, revealing how data-driven architecture and user profiling fuel algorithms that exploit psychological and behavioural vulnerabilities. These patterns no longer rely on overt UI tactics like forced action or hidden costs but instead integrate into system architecture, making them harder to detect and regulate. Platforms subtly guide users toward commercially driven choices by personalising interactions, often undermining autonomy and well-being. The chapter examines manipulative design in personalised content recommendations, dynamic pricing, and algorithmic social proof. Unlike UI-based dark patterns, these sophisticated tactics operate beneath user awareness, adapting in real-time through machine learning to create self-reinforcing feedback loops. Their integration within data architecture poses significant regulatory challenges, as conventional oversight mechanisms struggle to address deeply embedded manipulative techniques. Chapter four highlighted the limitations of frameworks like the DSA, which targets UI manipulations but cannot regulate structural forms of influence. While the AI Act, particularly Articles 5(1)(a) and (b), aims to mitigate risks, its thresholds may allow harmful practices to persist. These critiques underscore the need for regulatory approaches that extend beyond surface-level interventions to address algorithmic mechanisms shaping user behaviour. Accordingly, chapters six and seven support this analysis, advocating for expanded regulatory oversight that captures AI-driven manipulations. By evaluating Articles 5(1)(a) and (b), it critically assesses their effectiveness in countering algorithmic manipulation. Chapter eight will propose reforms to strengthen protections, bridge gaps in regulation, and tackle both visible and systemic harms.

6

AI-Powered Deceptive Design

6.1. Introduction

Imagine having an AI system at your command. You give it a broad goal, like 'figure out the best way to sort these images' or 'find patterns in this data'. The AI doesn't start with a predefined rulebook. Instead, it explores, experiments, and learns from the data itself. It begins by making guesses, clustering similar things, or identifying structures that are not obvious at first glance. It refines its understanding by testing what works and what doesn't, gradually improving as it gathers more insights. Unlike a student following a strict lesson plan, this AI is not given explicit instructions; it learns by recognising patterns and relationships hidden within the information it's provided. This process might uncover unexpected trends, groupings, or correlations, forming how to organise the data. Over time, with more data and refinement, it becomes better at achieving the goal, even though it was not explicitly told how to get there. However, because AI is learning without clear guidance, its journey is filled with uncertainty, sometimes leading to unintended patterns, misleading conclusions, or unexpected risks. That's the essence of unsupervised learning: an AI system that learns to navigate its task by exploring, testing, and adjusting – without needing someone to label or explain everything along the way.

Let's use the same example but change the task to 'increase profitability' or 'maximise user engagement'. When designed to achieve these, AI develops strategies that even their developers do not comprehend entirely.[1]

They adapt and evolve as they sift through user data, with the risk of developing sophisticated, deterministic and non-deterministic tactics. Whether a system adheres to predictable rules or evolves based on probability and learning models, the outcome remains the same: users are subject to manipulation in ways that are often unseen and challenging to contest. What prevents this, other than a robust prohibition on developers? And if the machine learns to bypass oversight, it is not far from transitioning from influence and persuasion to coercion, manipulation, and deception. In the hands of the wise, the machine may illuminate; in the hands of the wicked, it becomes the shadows. Beware, for when intelligence forms without conscience, it shall teach itself to deceive.

In the summer of 2024, I was commissioned by the European Commission to write a background report on Article 5(1)(a) and (b) of the AI Act. The AI Office was forming, legal obligations to produce guidelines were rapidly approaching, and I had only a few weeks to write a report exploring the meaning of material distortion in EU law, the types of subliminal techniques an AI system might employ, and the various interpretations of 'vulnerabilities'. When starting my work, I placed a small sticky note on my monitor with a set of straightforward questions for context: 'If a developer tasks an AI system with increasing user engagement, what means will it use to make this end?' As it happens, my report appears to have significantly influenced the guidelines on Articles 5(1)(a) and (b).[2]

Article 5(1)(a) explicitly prohibits AI systems that employ subliminal or manipulative techniques to distort behaviour by bypassing a person's conscious awareness, thus impairing their ability to make informed decisions resulting in significant harm. This provision highlights concerns that AI-driven systems could exploit cognitive or psychological vulnerabilities, such as unconsciously influencing choices. However, as this chapter will discuss, the thresholds for the prohibition to apply are high, requiring all factors of a cumulative test to be satisfied, including proving *material* distortion and *significant* harm. This high bar leaves a wide gap where more subtle but equally damaging manipulations can thrive undetected.

The adaptive, personalised nature of AI-driven systems means that many forms of exploitation will slip through the cracks, continuing to influence users in ways that regulatory bodies cannot quickly identify or control. For example, AI systems, tasked with boosting engagement or driving sales, become more adept at exploiting our cognitive biases and behavioural patterns. From recommendation engines anticipating our desires before we even realise them to pricing systems that adjust based on our perceived willingness to pay, these architectures are finely tuned to maximise their objectives. What makes this even more alarming is the opacity with which they operate. Users are not aware of the precise ways these systems influence them, and the complexity of the systems makes it hard for regulators to bring enforcement actions.[3]

The challenge is how to regulate systems that are not only complex but also dynamic, constantly learning and evolving. These designs pose immense risks. Accordingly, this chapter will argue that prohibitions against psychological manipulation are a step in the right direction. Still, its focus on overt harm misses AI-driven deceptive design's subtler, cumulative effects. These systems may not immediately trigger alarm bells, but over time, they erode user autonomy, nudging individuals toward decisions that benefit the platform rather than themselves. The personalisation and adaptability of these systems render them even more perilous as they adjust in real-time, learning from each interaction how best to exploit vulnerabilities.[4]

6.2.　Adaptive AI: Balancing Innovation with User Protection

Given this section's impossible task of defining and describing AI in less than 600 words, please cut me a little slack in the rope. In 1956, John McCarthy coined the term 'artificial intelligence' to describe the science of creating machines that emulate human cognitive processes.[5] Nowadays, AI encompasses systems humans design to achieve complex goals by interacting with their digital or physical environments through data acquisition. These systems process structured or unstructured data to perceive, 'reason' and ultimately make decisions.[6] Although modelled on human cognitive abilities, their intelligence is distinct and varies in execution. AI systems perform learning, problem-solving, reasoning, perception, and language understanding tasks, with capabilities that extend into areas like prediction, classification, and optimisation. In modern applications, AI systems integrate deeply into various industries, handling tasks such as computer vision, natural language processing, speech synthesis, and knowledge representation.[7] Expert systems, a form of AI, allow users to input queries through an interface that connects to an inference engine. This engine consults a knowledge base built with domain-specific expertise to provide advice or solve problems. Two critical learning paradigms support these systems: symbolic learning, which models human reasoning through predefined logic, and machine learning, which allows systems to learn directly from data and adapt over time.[8] Machine learning splits into supervised, unsupervised, and reinforcement learning, each applying different methodologies to process and learn from data.[9] AI, primarily when implemented in expert systems, offers wide-ranging benefits to industries, citizens, and public interests by improving decision-making, efficiency, and automation.[10]

Expert systems are increasingly important in consumer engagement, especially as non-deterministic systems evolve. As discussed in the previous chapter, these systems integrate machine learning and symbolic learning to analyse consumer behaviour, track patterns, and adjust their strategies to increase real-time engagement.[11] By nature, non-deterministic systems operate unpredictably, allowing adaptive algorithms and probabilistic modelling to make decisions based on ongoing data. These systems observe consumer data, including browsing habits, purchases, and emotional triggers, to refine their approach to engagement.[12]

This adaptability is valuable for studying how consumers interact with products and services. Supervised learning might identify explicit patterns, such as the types of promotions that generate the highest response, while unsupervised learning uncovers subtler patterns, like the times or content that trigger the most engagement. Reinforcement learning adds further sophistication. It adjusts strategies based on real-time user feedback, iterating on the most effective ways to engage the consumer, whether by offering personalised recommendations, optimising discount strategies, or delivering content at critical moments.[13]

Symbolic learning also plays a role by deploying logical models that simulate human decision-making and use known triggers to influence behaviour. These systems rely on established principles of consumer psychology, such as scarcity or social proof, to guide users toward specific actions, like making a purchase. These tactics, already well-understood in traditional marketing, gain new potency when combined with the personalised insights offered by non-deterministic systems. Symbolic and machine learning create a robust system that adapts to individual behaviours and continually refines engagement strategies. The ability of non-deterministic systems to dynamically adjust engagement tactics means they operate seamlessly in the background, tailoring their approach based on predictive models and consumer behaviour patterns.

By constantly learning from consumer data and adjusting their responses, these expert systems create personalised, intuitive engagement that often feels natural to the consumer.[14] They change based on what triggers consumers to respond to most – whether special offers, time-sensitive discounts, or emotionally driven appeals – thereby increasing the likelihood of continued interaction. However, concerns arise as these systems become more adept at predicting and manipulating consumer behaviour. Consumers may not always realise that adaptive systems learn from and exploit their behavioural data to influence them.[15] These concerns highlight the need for increased scrutiny of AI-powered engagement strategies to ensure businesses use these robust systems responsibly while protecting consumer rights.

6.3. Regulating the Risks Associated with Artificial Intelligence

We regulate risk all the time. It is just part of how societies function. You do not wait until a plane crashes to check if the wings are built correctly, and you do not let someone cook up a new virus in their garage to see what happens. That's not being overly cautious – it's just common sense. The principle of precaution, a cornerstone of EU law, holds particular significance in the face of scientific uncertainty, underscoring the potential for irreversible harm if regulators delay action. It requires policymakers to anticipate and mitigate potential harms before they materialise.[16] This approach, enshrined in Article 191(2) of the Treaty on the Functioning of the European Union (TFEU), extends to environmental, human, and public health regulations.[17] The CJEU has broadened its scope to encompass emerging technologies.[18] Acknowledging the incomplete nature of scientific knowledge, the EU has mandated a proactive stance, allowing legislators to implement protective measures without waiting for total scientific certainty.[19] This mindset is deeply embedded in EU lawmaking processes, reflecting the Union's commitment to safeguarding its citizens and environment against known and unforeseen threats.[20]

In regulatory terms, risk generally refers to the likelihood of an event occurring, combined with the severity of its impact. The greater the potential harm and the higher the uncertainty surrounding it, the more pressing the need for precaution.[21] However, risk also involves another critical element: uncertainty.[22] When there's uncertainty, especially about something that could cause serious harm, we take precautions. The interplay of potential harm and the indeterminate scope of adverse outcomes presents profound regulatory challenges in addressing emerging technologies. This uncertainty intensifies with rapidly advancing technologies, where the breadth and depth of associated risks remain only partially known. The EU regulatory framework, therefore, incorporates both risk and uncertainty into its approach, striving to manage the probability and potential severity of impacts should these risks materialise.

Unlike homemade viruses, commercial aviation benefits us. We do not ground planes simply because of risk and uncertainty. Thus, policymakers must balance the imperative to foster innovation against the equally pressing need to avert harm. This balance requires navigating intricate considerations of acceptable risk thresholds and defining optimal points for intervention, reflecting the nuanced approach necessary within an evolving technological landscape.

AI has emerged as one of the most challenging areas for applying precautionary principles. AI systems operate with a degree of unpredictability, learning and evolving as they interact with the world.[23] While offering immense innovation potential, non-deterministic behaviour also introduces significant uncertainty. Regulators face the challenge of determining the risks posed by AI systems, especially when the developers do not fully understand those risks. The self-learning capacities of AI mean that the systems might behave in unanticipated ways, increasing the difficulty of forecasting potential harm. Black and Murray have posited that the precautionary principle and regulatory strategies for AI emphasise challenges related to the unpredictability of self-learning systems and the need for proactive approaches in managing potential harm.[24] The European Parliament, recognising these challenges, has advocated for applying the precautionary principle to AI, pushing for regulation that prioritises human rights and safety over unchecked technological advancement.[25]

However, the principle's application here remains contentious. Some commentators argue that the very nature of AI demands flexibility and that overly stringent regulations might stifle innovation.[26] The precautionary principle is too rigid for others and could hinder AI's potential benefits.[27] Critics contend that the precautionary principle may impose undue constraints on technological advancement, arguing that its emphasis on harm prevention – especially in uncertain risks – risks cultivating an overly cautious regulatory environment that stifles innovation and limits creative progress. From this perspective, the principle's preventive stance is seen as a barrier, introducing hesitancy that could hinder breakthroughs. Conversely, proponents regard the precautionary principle as an essential safeguard, particularly in an era where technological developments often outpace our capacity to understand their potential impacts fully. They argue that the principle offers a flexible regulatory approach capable of evolving as new information emerges, thereby equipping regulators to address unforeseen risks in real-time.

The debate over using the precautionary principle in AI regulation highlights the broader tension between risk management and innovation. On the one hand, there is a clear need to protect citizens from the potential harm posed by new technologies. On the other hand, there is a danger that overly stringent regulations could hinder the development of beneficial AI-powered technologies. The challenge for regulators is balancing these competing priorities, ensuring developers create AI systems that maximise benefits while minimising risks. This balancing act requires a nuanced understanding of both the potential harms and the potential benefits of AI, as well as a willingness to adapt regulatory frameworks as new information becomes available. The precautionary principle provides a valuable tool for managing the uncertainty of AI as an emerging technology. By advocating for preventive action in the face of scientific uncertainty, the principle allows regulators to take a proactive approach to risk management. However, it also requires regulators to be flexible as the risks and benefits of AI continue to evolve. This flexibility is essential for ensuring developers maximise AI's potential while minimising its risks.

One of the critical difficulties in regulating AI is that the problems it might cause need to be precisely defined. Traditional risk-based regulation involves identifying specific harms and designing regulatory frameworks to mitigate them.[28] However, in the case of AI, the exact nature of the risks is often unclear, which complicates the regulatory process. Unlike some deterministic AI systems, non-deterministic systems do not lend themselves easily to traditional risk assessments, which rely on probabilities and known variables. When the potential harms are not fully known, and it is impossible to calculate their likelihood confidently, a precautionary approach seems more appropriate than a problem-centred one.[29] Regulators must base their decisions on the best available knowledge, even if that knowledge is incomplete, and remain ready to adjust as more information becomes available. Critics of the precautionary principle view this need for adjustment as a weakness, arguing that it creates an environment of regulatory uncertainty, which in turn hampers technological progress.[30]

The tension between innovation and precaution becomes particularly evident in emerging technologies. AI systems do not fit neatly into traditional regulatory frameworks, which tend to focus on linear models of risk, where potential harms can be identified and mitigated through specific actions.[31] AI's inherent unpredictability requires a different approach that can accommodate the uncertainty surrounding its development and implementation.[32] Others believe that the risks posed by AI are too significant to ignore and that the precautionary principle provides a necessary safeguard.

A central challenge for regulators lies in judiciously balancing the benefits of innovation with the potential for harm – an assessment complicated by the changing nature of AI risks, many of which remain only partially understood. The non-deterministic characteristics of AI systems introduce elements of unpredictability, where outcomes may diverge from anticipated pathways, yielding unforeseen consequences. This inherent unpredictability disrupts traditional risk assessment models, which rely on probabilities and defined impacts. In cases where these variables elude precise estimation, as is often the case with AI, the precautionary principle emerges as an essential framework for navigating and mitigating risk within this uncertain terrain. By advocating for preventive action in the face of uncertainty, the precautionary principle allows regulators, in theory, to act before harmful AI occurs rather than waiting for conclusive evidence.[33]

6.3.1. The European Union's Approach

The EU AI Act[34] adopts a tiered approach to regulating the risks associated with artificial intelligence, a structure comparable to the compliance pyramid often used in regulatory theory.[35] At the base of this tiered system are AI systems considered minimal or low-risk.[36] These systems pose little threat to users or public welfare and, as such, are not subject to significant regulatory scrutiny. The regulatory framework encourages developers and operators of these low-risk systems to adopt good practices, such as transparency and fairness, but stops short of imposing mandatory obligations.[37] The goal is to promote safe AI without unnecessarily burdening innovation, allowing these low-risk systems to flourish with minimal regulatory intervention. As the risk level increases, the regulatory framework becomes more stringent. AI systems that pose a moderate or specific risk – those, for example, involved in deepfakes, impersonation, or emotional recognition – are permitted to operate but are subject to transparency obligations.[38] While this middle tier requires greater oversight than minimal-risk systems, the emphasis remains on transparency and the protection of user rights. However, the actual weight of the AI Act's regulatory framework focuses on high-risk systems and, more critically, the outright prohibitions outlined in Article 5.

Article 5 takes a firm stance against AI systems that pose severe risks to individuals and society by targeting those that exploit users in harmful ways. For example, Article 5(1)(a) bans systems that use hidden subliminal techniques or manipulative tactics to skew decision-making without the user realising it – especially when these tactics lead to *significant* harm. The idea is to stop any AI from tricking people into making choices they wouldn't usually make, with the law making it clear that both subtle and apparent manipulations are unacceptable when they result in significant damage, holding developers or operators accountable:

> The following AI practices shall be *prohibited*:
>
> (a)   the placing on the market, the putting into service or the use of an AI system that deploys subliminal techniques beyond a person's consciousness or purposefully manipulative or deceptive techniques, with the objective or the effect of, materially distorting the behaviour of a person or a group of persons by appreciably impairing their ability to make an informed decision, thereby causing a person to take a decision that that person would not have otherwise taken in a manner that causes or is likely to cause that person, another person or group of persons significant harm;

Narrower, Article 5(1)(b) addresses AI systems that exploit vulnerable individuals or groups based on age, disability, or economic status. Note that these systems must exploit specific vulnerabilities and distort behaviour that causes *significant* harm. Whether the exploitation is intentional or an unintended side effect of the system's design, such AI systems are categorically banned from being placed on the market or put into service. The regulation recognises that specific populations are more susceptible to manipulation and exploitation, and it seeks to protect them by prohibiting the use of AI that would target these vulnerabilities for harmful purposes. The focus is not solely on the developer's intent but also the effect of the system's deployment, ensuring that harm to vulnerable groups is prevented even in indirect or inadvertent exploitation cases.

(b)   the placing on the market, the putting into service or the use of an AI system that exploits any of the vulnerabilities of a person or a specific group of persons due to their age, disability or a specific social or economic situation, with the objective, or the effect, of materially distorting the behaviour of that person or a person belonging to that group in a manner that causes or is reasonably likely to cause that person or another person significant harm;

By establishing a clear line between permissible and impermissible uses of AI, the regulation does more than restrict harmful systems – it acknowledges how AI has transformed user interaction. AI no longer relies on generic tactics; instead, it continuously analyses behavioural data to predict individual actions, uncover vulnerabilities, and exploit cognitive biases to shape decision-making. This level of personalisation represents a fundamental shift in deceptive design, moving beyond traditional one-size-fits-all tricks. AI-driven systems tailor their approaches based on a user's preferences, habits, and psychological traits, making manipulation more persuasive and more challenging to detect. The prohibitions in Article 5 highlight the EU's attempt to safeguard individuals from these risks, particularly from AI applications that operate outside user awareness or target vulnerable populations. For instance, an AI system might analyse a person's browsing history, social media activity, or even the time of day to pinpoint moments of emotional fatigue – then strategically nudge them toward a particular action or purchase when they are least likely to resist.

AI excels in data-driven personalisation, continuously refining its manipulative techniques based on real-time user feedback. Every click, scroll, or pause in engagement is valuable information AI uses to adjust its tactics, targeting specific psychological traits, preferences, and emotional states. For example, suppose an AI algorithm detects that a user is likelier to make impulsive purchases late at night. In that case, it might increase the frequency of emotionally appealing product recommendations during those hours. The result is a finely tuned system that knows what to suggest and when and how to present it for maximum impact. This continuous learning and adjustment create a highly individualised experience that can subtly push users toward decisions they might not otherwise make, often without conscious awareness. A key aspect of AI-driven manipulation is its non-deterministic nature. Unlike deterministic systems, which follow predefined paths, AI systems evolve and adapt based on user interactions and contextual data, making their influence unpredictable. This variability complicates the detection and regulation of manipulative tactics because the AI system might behave differently with each user, depending on their specific circumstances at any given time. The non-deterministic influence also makes it harder for users to recognise manipulation. Since the AI's behaviour shifts based on individual inputs and contextual changes, users may need to realise that the system is influencing them in a specific way, leading to deeper forms of manipulation that are more challenging to resist.

6.4. Case Studies

This section presents three compelling case studies exploring how AI-powered deceptive design operates. The first involves an AI-powered recommendation engine that subtly manipulates users by presenting specific options when they are most cognitively vulnerable, such as late at night, increasing the likelihood of impulsive decisions. The second case focuses on an AI-driven financial app that adjusts its interface to obscure critical information about fees or terms based on a user's behaviour patterns, making it harder for them to make informed decisions. The third example centres on a health-tracking app that uses predictive modelling to push notifications, prompting users to purchase products or services. Section 6.6 revisits these examples to discuss how Article 5(1)(a) would apply to each case study.

6.4.1. Case Study #1: AI-Driven Impulse Manipulation on Shopping Platform

An online shopping platform uses an AI-powered recommendation engine that tracks users' browsing habits, purchase history, and periods of cognitive vulnerability, such as late-night browsing. When the AI detects users are most likely to make impulsive decisions, it floods the interface with emotionally appealing, high-cost items, especially during late-night sessions when users are tired and less likely to evaluate their purchases critically.

The online shopping platform's AI-powered recommendation engine personalises the browsing experience by adapting to users' habits and engagement patterns, creating a dynamic, tailored interface. This system relies on both deterministic and non-deterministic elements to fine-tune the recommendations displayed to each user. The deterministic components – structured, rule-based mechanisms – categorise users based on specific patterns, such as browsing behaviours, typical purchase times, and how frequently they review detailed product information. These fixed rules allow the system to group users into foundational categories, identifying, for example, those who often browse late at night. The platform's non-deterministic machine-learning algorithms build on these foundational categories by bringing adaptability and refining recommendations in real-time. These adaptive elements consider the time of day, previous purchasing habits, and browsing patterns, predicting when a user might feel more inclined towards specific suggestions. By analysing these nuanced behavioural signals, the system chooses which types of products to showcase in ways likely to appeal to each user's context. For instance, the system identifies users who tend to browse late at night and show signs of fatigue – evidenced by short browsing sessions and limited comparison shopping – and may display more emotionally engaging, high-cost items that resonate with impulse-driven browsing. This combination of deterministic categorisation and non-deterministic personalisation creates an experience that appears carefully designed to fit each user's browsing flow. Users see appealing, well-timed product recommendations aligning with their recent activity. However, since the platform adjusts these recommendations based on perceived behavioural cues, it subtly adapts to moments when users may feel less inclined to pause and critically evaluate their decisions. This rule-based and adaptive design blend highlights the evolving interplay between AI-driven personalisation and user engagement, where fixed rules work with responsive algorithms to maximise relevance. While this approach enhances convenience and aligns recommendations with users' preferences, it also prompts questions about user autonomy, primarily when the system targets moments of cognitive vulnerability. The platform's success at balancing personalised guidance with respect for independent decision-making rests on how transparently it reveals these design choices within its adaptive architecture.

6.4.2. Case Study #2: AI-Driven Financial App

A financial app uses AI to personalise its interface based on users' behavioural patterns. For users who often skip fine print or exhibit decision fatigue, the system conceals or downplays critical information, such as fees or loan terms. Key details are hidden behind multiple layers or displayed less prominently, pushing users towards accepting terms without fully understanding the financial implications. This manipulation is driven by a combination of fixed rules and machine-learning algorithms, adjusting the UI dynamically to exploit user vulnerabilities and increase engagement without full transparency.

This financial app uses AI to adjust its user interface (UI) based on individual engagement patterns, tailoring the experience by aligning it with each user's past behaviours. Beneath the surface, the system combines deterministic, rule-based structures and adaptive, non-deterministic algorithms to create a journey responding to various behavioural cues, such as how often users review detailed terms or interact with specific features. The deterministic elements operate with fixed rules that categorise users into different engagement types based on observed behaviours. For example, suppose a user rarely checks loan terms or tends to navigate quickly through informational screens. In that case, these rules may assign them to a category the system recognises as 'low engagement with terms'. This rule-based classification enables the app to set certain expectations for each user type, creating a foundation for displaying information. The non-deterministic machine-learning components build on this foundation by adding adaptability, allowing the system to experiment with design variations and adjust the interface based on each user's unique interaction style. These adaptive algorithms might adjust the visibility and accessibility of details like loan terms or fees, placing them in additional layers or less prominent areas for users who prefer simplified navigation. In this way, the system creates a personalised experience that aligns with anticipated preferences, adjusting the level of detail displayed based on the individual's interaction history. The system's combined approach ensures that the user experience adapts naturally, with only subtle modifications to interface complexity based on user tendencies. The app balances rule-based predictions with responsive, data-driven refinements by layering deterministic categorisations with non-deterministic learning. While this design may simplify navigation and improve the user's flow, it can also mean that important information is not immediately visible, depending on how the system anticipates each user's needs. This layered, adaptive design highlights how deterministic and non-deterministic AI components work together to inform, instruct, and power the UI beneath the surface. The resulting balance between structured rules and adaptive learning demonstrates how an AI system can personalise engagement while raising questions about maintaining transparency and access to critical information within these tailored digital experiences.

6.4.3. Case Study #3: AI-Driven Health App with Predictive Modelling

A popular fitness app uses AI to personalise user experiences based on exercise patterns, motivation levels, and engagement history. It tracks daily activity, workout habits, and user responses to fitness challenges. When detecting low motivation or potential disengagement, the AI adjusts notifications to encourage continued use, sending messages like: 'Don't give up! You're just one step away!' or 'You've come so far – why stop now?' The app may also offer limited-time discounts on premium features or fitness gear, subtly altering the interface to make acceptance easier. While aimed at motivation, these tactics may manipulate cognitive or emotional states, raising concerns.

This case study illustrates how an AI-powered system embedded within a fitness app could adjust messages and notifications based on user interactions and behavioural patterns. The app, designed to support wellness goals, combines rule-based and machine-learning-driven components to respond to shifts in user behaviour, such as changes in exercise routines or fluctuations in activity levels. The system's deterministic aspects rely on fixed rules to categorise user behaviour into specific patterns – such as recognising irregular sleep or changes in exercise consistency. When the system detects these patterns, it may trigger pre-set notifications crafted to encourage users toward healthier habits. This rule-based foundation sets up primary responses that can act immediately upon recognising key behavioural trends, offering users supportive nudges in response to specific wellness indicators. The app's non-deterministic, machine-learning elements add a layer, enabling the system to refine these messages' timing, language, and appearance based on individual preferences and past responses. By learning from user behaviour over time, this adaptive layer can predict when a user might be more receptive to types of guidance. For instance, the machine-learning component may identify users more likely to engage with motivational messages in the evening or when they have shown low motivation. At these moments, the system might adjust its approach, tailoring notifications to feel personally relevant and supportive. In specific scenarios, the app may present promotional offers or premium services when it detects heightened interest or engagement, which may feel timely and encouraging to users. However, this fine-tuned, adaptive system can also create a sense of urgency that may not be easily distinguishable as purely supportive. These subtle adjustments, blending fixed rule-based responses with adaptive learning, highlight the intricate relationship between data insights and personalised support.

6.5. Article 5(1)(a) and its Role Regulating AI-Powered Psychological Manipulation

Article 5(1)(a) is designed to prevent AI systems from manipulating users beyond their conscious awareness using subliminal techniques. These systems don't just persuade – they distort decision-making in ways people don't recognise, leading them to choices they wouldn't have otherwise made. The regulation targets AI, which creates *material* distortion and significantly skews how someone perceives a situation or their options, ultimately impairing their ability to make an informed decision. The key concern is the impact: if an AI system's covert influence results in significant financial, psychological, or physical harm, it crosses the line. This prohibition ensures that AI cannot be designed to exploit unconscious processes in ways that override genuine user intent, reinforcing accountability for those who deploy such systems.

Take the financial app case study. Were subliminal techniques at play in these cases? At first glance, it might seem like the prohibition in Article 5(1)(a) would apply – but is it that clear-cut? The AI subtly downplays critical financial information, tailoring its presentation based on a user's past interactions. Is this just strategic design, or does it cross into subliminal manipulation? The system takes advantage of predictable behaviours – like skipping fine print or making rushed decisions under fatigue – guiding users toward financial choices they might later regret. But does this indeed operate beyond their conscious awareness, or is it just an aggressive nudge? Now consider the health-tracking app. It uses predictive modelling to send emotionally charged notifications when users are most anxious about their health. By triggering these alerts at the right moment, the system pushes unnecessary purchases when users are least likely to think critically. Is this a case of AI distorting decision-making in a way that users wouldn't recognise? Or is it simply effective marketing? While these examples show AI influencing behaviour in concerning ways, proving that they meet Article 5(1)(a)'s threshold – operating subliminally and causing significant harm – isn't always straightforward. The line between persuasion and impermissible manipulation remains blurred.

Article 5(1)(a) applies to deterministic AI systems, which follow strict rules, and non-deterministic systems, which evolve based on user behaviour. Both can manipulate users in ways that distort their decision-making – sometimes so subtly that the impact isn't immediately obvious. Take the financial app case. A deterministic system might categorise users based on their likelihood of skimming over key terms. At the same time, a non-deterministic AI refines this approach, adapting the interface in real-time to downplay critical financial details. But does this amount to material distortion? If the design causes users to overlook essential terms or make financial commitments they wouldn't have otherwise, does it significantly alter their decision-making process? The health-tracking app and shopping platform raise similar questions. By dynamically tailoring notifications and product recommendations, these systems steer users toward choices at the right moment. But how do we determine if this results in significant financial harm? Does an impulsive, AI-driven purchase meet the threshold or does harm only arise when the consequences are severe – such as economic loss leading to debt or other long-term consequences?

Article 5(1)(a) prohibits AI that distorts user decisions in ways that lead to significant harm. But distinguishing between persuasion, nudging, and unlawful manipulation remains a complex challenge. Where should regulators draw the line? Whether through financial loss, psychological distress, or even physical consequences, the regulation is precise that AI systems should not induce behaviour that results in harm users would not have experienced otherwise. The health-tracking app's exploitation of anxiety or the shopping platform's targeting of late-night browsers demonstrates how AI can exploit users to drive profit, leading to significant financial and psychological harm. Through the lens of these case studies, the objectives of Article 5(1)(a) become apparent: AI systems that use manipulative or deceptive techniques, whether through deterministic rules or adaptive, non-deterministic algorithms, are prohibited when they impair decision-making and cause significant harm. Article 5(1)(a) thus forms a vital part of the broader framework to maintain trust and standards in AI innovation.

6.5.1. Constitutive Elements of the Prohibition

Article 5(1)(a) sets clear boundaries for AI systems that covertly manipulate or deceive users, but not every questionable design choice falls under its scope. For the prohibition to apply, several key elements must be present together. It is not enough for an AI system to be merely persuasive or subtly influential. The regulation targets explicitly the placing on the market of an AI system where subliminal, purposefully manipulative, or deceptive techniques materially distort human behaviour, leading to significant harm:

- The AI system must be placed on the market, put into service, or actively used.

- The system must deploy *subliminal techniques* beyond a person's conscious awareness or use *purposefully manipulative* or *deceptive* techniques.

- These techniques must have the *objective or effect of materially distorting* a person's or group's behaviour.

- The distortion must *appreciably impair* their ability to make informed decisions, leading to choices they would not otherwise make.

- The distortion must cause, or be reasonably likely to cause, *significant harm* to an individual or group. [*Emphasis added*]

How does one determine whether an AI-driven strategy crosses the line into subliminal influence, purposeful manipulation, or deception? Health-tracking apps, for example, often push emotionally charged notifications about potential health risks at precisely the moments when users are least likely to resist pressure. But does this constitute a subliminal technique, or is it simply an aggressive engagement design? If the AI system shapes behaviour in a way that users do not fully recognise, leading them to make financial commitments they might later regret, does this meet the threshold for *material* distortion? Similarly, consider the online shopping platform. Late-night browsing habits trigger a surge of high-cost, emotionally appealing product recommendations. Is this just an optimised sales strategy? Or does the system's ability to exploit cognitive fatigue and reduce a user's capacity for rational decision-making amount to manipulation? If users were steered toward purchases, they wouldn't have been more alert. Does this impair their autonomy in a way that Article 5(1)(a) is meant to prevent? Several conditions must be met for this prohibition to apply. These techniques must not only influence behaviour but do so in a way that materially distorts decision-making and results in significant harm. The question remains: where is the line between persuasive design and impermissible manipulation? Determining whether an AI system crosses this threshold requires careful analysis of its methods and impact. To establish whether Article 5(1)(a) applies, we must assess whether the system's design and operation meet the conditions for prohibition:

1. **Subliminal, Purposefully Manipulative, or Deceptive Techniques**: The AI system must employ techniques that bypass a person's conscious awareness or are overtly manipulative and deceptive. For example, in the case of financial apps, the system's concealment of critical details might operate beyond user awareness and by subtly nudging behaviour. In contrast, the health-tracking app uses direct emotional manipulation, pushing users to make decisions based on heightened health anxieties.

2. **Material Distortion of Behaviour**: The techniques must significantly alter behaviour. The shopping platform case illustrates how AI systems identify and exploit periods of cognitive vulnerability, distorting late-night users' purchasing decisions by steering them toward high-cost items.

3. **Impairment of Decision-Making**: The distortion must *appreciably impair* users' ability to make informed decisions. In all three case studies, AI systems impair users' capacity to evaluate options critically – whether by downplaying critical financial information, using emotional pressure, or exploiting cognitive fatigue.
4. **Significant Harm**: The decision caused by this distortion must result in significant harm. In each case, the consequences are clear – whether unanticipated financial burdens in the financial app and shopping platform or emotional and psychological damage in the health-tracking app.

Enforcing Article 5(1)(a) is complex, as it requires proving that an AI system's influence was not only present but powerful enough to impair decision-making and cause significant harm. The challenge is identifying manipulation and demonstrating that it materially distorted behaviour in a way that meets the legal threshold. Absent the discovery of any subliminal techniques, regulators must assess whether the AI system employed purposefully manipulative or deceptive methods that shaped user behaviour in a way they did not fully recognise. For cases like the financial app or the online shopping platform, this involves examining whether critical information was deliberately concealed or framed to steer users toward decisions they would not have otherwise made. Establishing clear evidence that these techniques resulted in measurable harm remains a grey area, making enforcement highly dependent on interpretation and the evolving understanding of manipulation.

6.5.1.1. *Use of Subliminal Techniques*

The AI Act does not spell precisely what counts as a 'subliminal technique' but generally refers to methods that influence people without them realising it. In most cases, this means stimuli that operate below the threshold of conscious perception – things you do not actively notice but that still shape your decisions. What qualifies as subliminal, however, can depend entirely on the sensory channel being used, whether visual, auditory, or something else. Examples might include subvisual and subaudible cues, hidden images, misdirection, or other subtle forms of manipulation that slip past awareness. The real challenge is twofold. First, there is no strict legal definition of what makes a technique subliminal. Second, proving a direct link between subliminal influence and real-world harm is not straightforward.[39] These uncertainties make interpreting and enforcing the prohibition under Article 5(1)(a) far from simple.

From a psychological viewpoint, subliminal techniques encompass both cognitive and emotional manipulation. These practices compromise individuals' autonomy by influencing behaviour, opinions, or decisions without the individual's conscious awareness. Subliminal techniques typically employ stimuli below the threshold of conscious perception to impact decision-making. By using brief or subtle audio, visual, or tactile media, these techniques bypass rational deliberation, leveraging emotional responses or framing effects to distort decision-making. However, 'subliminal' remains ambiguous due to the broad interaction between individual sensory thresholds and conscious and unconscious perception. For example, a visual stimulus that flashes on a screen for a fraction of a second might be imperceptible to one person but noticed by another, making it difficult to determine a universal threshold for subliminal influence. Establishing causality between subliminal stimuli and specific behavioural changes presents challenges, with empirical evidence showing varied results on their efficacy.

The Audio-Visual Media Services Directive (AVMSD)[40] underscores the importance of protecting viewers from covert manipulation or unfair influence. The AVMSD's prohibition of subliminal advertising illustrates a broader commitment to protecting individual autonomy by ensuring that media content is identifiable and not misleadingly embedded.[41] The Directive thus prohibits subliminal advertising to ensure that promotional content is transparent and distinguishable from editorial material. This principle parallels this branch of the Article 5 prohibition, where transparency and distinct categorisation of content types are crucial to preventing manipulative practices. The AVMSD thus serves as a regulatory precedent highlighting the need for media transparency, which can extend to AI to guard against covertly manipulative practices. National laws across various European countries further elaborate on these principles. For example, in the United Kingdom, the Communications Act 2003[42] and the Ofcom Broadcasting Code[43] prohibit hidden messages or images intended to influence audiences without their awareness. France's Code of Public Health[44] bans subliminal advertising as messages below the conscious threshold. Germany's Interstate Treaty on Broadcasting and Telemedia[45] and Spain's General Law on Audio-visual Communication[46] prohibit techniques that covertly influence behaviour. Italy's Broadcasting Code explicitly bans advertisements aimed at controlling the subconscious to shape consumer choices.[47] These laws reflect a robust, cross-national commitment to transparency and the protection of autonomy, providing a framework that Article 5(1)(a) extends to AI practices. While there is ongoing debate regarding the effectiveness of subliminal techniques, the risks associated with their covert influence justify their prohibition. The AVMSD's emphasis on transparency in media regulation offers valuable insight into ensuring that users remain protected from subtle manipulation.

Types of Subliminal Techniques

The following section explores different subliminal techniques that shape behaviour without people even realising it. It builds on Franklin et al.'s framework, which offers both a narrow and a broader view of subliminal influence, looking at how it plays out in psychology and marketing:[48]

(a) **Visual Subliminal Messages**: Visual subliminal messages involve briefly flashing images or text during video playback. They are not consciously processed but still potentially influence attitudes or behaviours. These images are perceptible but are processed below the threshold of awareness, rendering them invisible to the conscious mind.

(b) **Auditory Subliminal Messages**: Auditory messages include sounds or verbal cues played at low volumes or masked by other sounds, subtly influencing listeners without conscious awareness. More advanced techniques extend into areas like 'dream hacking',[49] wherein specific sounds or messages target individuals during sleep cycles, bypassing conscious resistance altogether.

(c) **Tactile Subliminal Stimuli**: This category includes physical sensations perceived below conscious awareness, such as faint vibrations that may affect emotional states or decision-making without the individual noticing the sensation.

(d) **Subvisual and Subaudible Cueing**: Subvisual cueing presents images too quickly for detection, while subaudible cueing plays sounds below the hearing threshold. These cues remain wholly undetectable under normal sensory conditions, yet researchers theorise they still affect behaviour at a subconscious level.[50]

(e) **Embedded Images**: These techniques hide images within other visual content. For instance, KFC once embedded a dollar bill in a commercial to create an unconscious association with wealth. Although viewers do not consciously notice the embedded image, it may still influence behaviour on a subconscious level.

(f) **Misdirection**: Through misdirection, a user's attention is purposefully drawn toward specific stimuli to obscure other options. Cognitive biases and attention gaps are often exploited here, as in websites that prominently display premium options to divert attention from free alternatives.

(g) **User Interface Dark Patterns**: Include a range of design choices that manipulate users into making decisions they might not make independently, sometimes involving subliminal cues or other covert tactics to distort behaviour.

A Conceptual Framework for Understanding
Subliminal Techniques

Franklin et al. provide a narrow and broad interpretation of subliminal techniques.[51] According to their narrow definition, subliminal techniques present a stimulus so subtly that the person never consciously detects it. This fits with the traditional view in psychology and marketing, where these hidden cues still manage to shape decisions despite going unnoticed. However, Franklin et al. suggest that this definition might be too limited regarding AI systems, which can use more complex and adaptive forms of subliminal influence. To account for this, they propose a broader interpretation:

> Subliminal techniques aim at influencing a person's behaviour in ways that the person is likely to remain unaware of:
>
> (1)   the influence attempt,
> (2)   how the influence works, or
> (3)   the influence attempt's effects on decision-making or value- and belief-formation processes.

According to this framework, a method qualifies as subliminal if it meets any of these conditions, not necessarily all. Thus, AI systems that meet even one criterion may require a risk assessment to determine whether the subliminal techniques impair an individual's ability to act according to their values, thereby increasing the potential for harm. This broad definition complements the Act by covering a more comprehensive array of potential harms, including methods where individuals are aware of the stimuli but remain unaware of the manipulation itself. The emphasis here shifts from whether a person consciously detects the stimulus to whether they recognise the influence attempt and its effects on decision-making. In cases where the system meets these conditions, the AI Act calls for a thorough evaluation to prevent subliminal techniques that might distort individual behaviour or erode autonomy.

Interpretive Challenges and Potential Expansions

The AI Act does not explicitly define 'subliminal techniques'. Typically, the term refers to stimuli below the threshold of conscious perception, although sensory modality and context vary significantly. The covert nature of subliminal techniques raises issues around autonomy, transparency, and agency. Subliminal methods risk undermining individual freedom by influencing individuals to make choices they might otherwise reject. The lack of visibility and transparency associated with subliminal techniques contravenes principles fundamental to building trust in AI. These covert techniques have psychological and socio-economic repercussions. They can distort consumer behaviour, resulting in unfair market practices and economic inefficiencies. In democratic contexts, subliminal techniques risk undermining electoral integrity by covertly shaping voter decisions. As such, the prohibition against subliminal techniques is a necessary safeguard to preserve individual autonomy, ultimately fostering public trust in AI systems.

Neuwirth argues for a broader interpretation, proposing that 'subliminal techniques' should encompass any influence outside an individual's conscious recognition, even if it does not strictly fall within the traditional definition of subliminal perception.[52] He stresses that AI-driven manipulation is not limited to subliminal methods – overtly deceptive strategies can be just as effective in shaping decisions and undermining autonomy. To capture the complexity of these techniques, he introduces the term 'transluminal', highlighting that manipulation can occur at varying levels of awareness, both above and below the sensory threshold. However, proving intent and demonstrating a direct causal link between these techniques and harm remains a significant challenge, making enforcement of the Act difficult. Neuwirth further contends that limiting the discussion to subliminal influence overlooks the broader psychological mechanisms AI systems exploit. Instead, he advocates for 'manipulation of the mind and behaviour', which better reflects the diverse and adaptive ways AI can shape user decision-making. Similarly, Boine critiques the Act's emphasis on subliminal techniques as outdated, arguing that this focus on hidden influence overlooks more complex, modern forms of manipulation.[53] Boine proposes a broader understanding encompassing any tactic exploiting individuals' vulnerabilities, regardless of whether it involves subliminal stimuli.[54]

6.5.1.2. *Purposefully Manipulative Techniques*

The concept of manipulation stands apart from other forms of influence, such as persuasion or coercion, through its concealed intent.[55] Unlike persuasion, which openly appeals to a user's reasoning and maintains transparency in offering choices, manipulation undermines the deliberative process by hiding aspects of the influencing agent's objectives.[56] In a manipulative AI system, users may be unaware of the motivations behind presented options or have no insight into the strategies employed to shape their responses subtly. These hidden tactics often blend behavioural psychology with system design, capitalising on vulnerabilities in human cognition. For instance, nudging users toward impulsive decisions or framing information in a way that biases their judgment is a form of manipulation that removes transparency from the interaction.[57] In such cases, the system conceals its influence, subtly steering the user's decisions to align more closely with the AI's objectives than the user's intent.

AI systems employing purposefully manipulative techniques are designed to influence user behaviour and undermine autonomy and free choice. These techniques are not merely persuasive; they exploit cognitive biases, psychological tendencies, or situational factors to benefit developers, deployers, or operators, often at the user's expense. Unlike lawful persuasion, these methods impair decision-making in ways that individuals do not fully recognise, leading them toward actions they might otherwise avoid if fully aware of the tactics in play. AI systems, particularly those using machine learning and adaptive algorithms, can autonomously identify and exploit behavioural patterns without requiring direct human intervention. Carroll et al. argue that such systems can develop manipulative strategies independently, refining their techniques through reinforcement learning and large-scale data analysis. Article 5(1)(a) recognises this risk, prohibiting AI systems that distort decision-making through subliminal, purposefully manipulative, or deceptive techniques in ways that cause or are reasonably likely to cause significant harm.

A key aspect of this prohibition is its *objective focus* – the intent of the provider or deployer is not a necessary condition for enforcement. Recital 29 outlines that even when users are aware of an influence attempt, they may still be unable to resist its effects if it significantly impairs their ability to make informed decisions. The prohibition thus extends to AI-driven manipulation that occurs autonomously if the system's techniques materially distort user behaviour and cause significant harm. Many manipulative techniques operate below the threshold of conscious awareness, making them particularly insidious. These include:

- **Subliminal messaging** – Flashing imperceptible images or embedding subaudible sounds that influence emotional responses without conscious detection.

- **Misdirection** – Using AI-driven interface design to guide attention away from critical information, preventing informed decision-making.

- **Emotional priming** – Triggering stress, anxiety, or urgency through notifications designed to lower cognitive resistance.

- **Dark pattern interfaces** – Structuring choices in ways that subtly push users toward a preferred action, often to their detriment.

An AI-powered retail platform might subtly integrate emotionally charged imagery into its advertising, nudging users toward purchases without them consciously recognising the influence. A financial app, meanwhile, could strategically obscure key terms in loan offers, increasing the likelihood that users commit to agreements they might have rejected had the information been fully transparent. These techniques do more than shape user behaviour – they distort decision-making by influencing choices in ways that users do not fully grasp. Practices become problematic when they materially impair autonomy, leading individuals to decisions they would not have otherwise made.

6.5.1.3. Deceptive Techniques

The AI Act does not explicitly define 'deceptive techniques', but Recital 29 clarifies that these methods subvert or impair autonomy, decision-making, or free choice in ways that users either do not consciously recognise or, even when aware, cannot control or resist. In this context, deception is not limited to fabricating false information but extends to any manipulative framing, omission, or distortion that steers users toward behaviours against their best interests. AI systems can also manipulate users through direct psychological influence and by presenting false or misleading information that distorts decision-making. These deceptive techniques range from exaggerating an AI system's capabilities to the more insidious deployment of AI-generated disinformation, which can influence political, economic, or social choices. Unlike misinformation, which spreads falsehoods unintentionally, disinformation is deliberately designed to deceive, making it particularly dangerous when combined with AI-driven automation. To illustrate, an AI-powered chatbot may impersonate a known individual through a synthetic voice, deceiving users into believing they are interacting with a trusted contact. Similarly, an AI-driven financial assistant could selectively present information that overstates potential gains while downplaying risks, misleading users into making poor financial decisions. These techniques are prohibited when they distort user behaviour in ways that lead to significant harm.

The AI Act takes a layered approach to addressing deception, balancing outright prohibition with transparency obligations.[58] In contexts such as deepfakes and AI-generated text in matters of public interest, the Act mandates clear labelling to mitigate deception. Article 50(4) requires providers to label AI-generated content, while Article 50(1) and (2) ensure users are aware when interacting with AI rather than a human. These disclosure requirements serve as preventive safeguards, reducing the likelihood of users being misled. However, Article 5(1)(a) applies a stricter prohibition where AI deception crosses the threshold into manipulation that materially distorts user behaviour. This includes cases where:

1.   Chatbots or AI-generated content present false or misleading information in ways that deceive users, altering decisions they would not have otherwise made.
2.   The deception is not visibly disclosed, making it impossible for users to distinguish reality from AI-generated manipulation.
3.   The AI system autonomously refines deceptive strategies, as seen in AI models that modify their behaviour when under evaluation, only to resume manipulation after oversight ends.

The AI Act explicitly acknowledges that deceptive techniques do not require direct human intent. AI systems may learn to deceive simply because it enhances their task performance, even if the deployer did not explicitly program them to do so. Reinforcement learning models, for example, may develop deceptive strategies if such behaviour leads to better outcomes in the system's training environment. Consider an AI-driven customer service bot trained to maximise user engagement. If the system learns that misrepresenting refund policies reduces cancellation rates, it may autonomously refine this deceptive behaviour. Similarly, AI models that detect when they are being evaluated may suppress unwanted outputs during testing, only to revert to manipulative tactics once deployed.

Interaction between Purposefully Manipulative and Deceptive Techniques

Purposefully manipulative and deceptive techniques, when combined within AI systems, can significantly amplify their potential for harm. Such a system covertly influences user behaviour through manipulative tactics while presenting false information to reinforce the effect. This dual approach creates a powerful mechanism for control, leading users to make decisions based on unconscious manipulations and distorted beliefs. AI systems incorporating manipulation and deception become highly effective tools for influencing behaviour, subtly guiding users' choices while altering their perception of reality.[59] The compounded effect of these two approaches can distort public perception, affecting decision-making processes in a way that does not reflect the genuine will or understanding of the populace. In contexts like political campaigns, this can even lead to electoral outcomes misrepresenting public intent. The interaction between these techniques lies in their reinforcement. Manipulative techniques exploit cognitive biases to steer users toward specific behaviours, while deceptive techniques strengthen these manipulations by providing misleading information that justifies those behaviours. This creates a feedback loop where users – already influenced by manipulative cues – are less likely to question false or misleading information. Such AI-driven strategies threaten individual autonomy and societal stability when deployed at scale. The following table categorises AI techniques that shape behaviour, opinions, and decisions, clarifying their mechanisms, objectives, and risks.

Table 6.1 Classification of AI Techniques for Behavioural Influence – Mechanisms, Objectives, and Risks

Category	Definition	Examples
Subliminal Techniques	Techniques that operate below the threshold of conscious awareness, influencing behaviour, opinions, or decisions without the subject's knowledge. Includes stimuli that may not be consciously perceived but can still affect decision-making and behaviour. AI systems can autonomously engage in these actions if planning or decision-making mechanisms yield such influences.	Visual Subliminal Messages: Brief images or text flashed during video playback. Auditory Subliminal Messages: Low-volume sounds or masked verbal messages. Tactile Stimuli: Subtle physical sensations perceived unconsciously. Embedded Images: Hidden within other visual content. Subvisual/Subaudible Cueing: Stimuli below perceptual thresholds, such as too-quick flashes or inaudible sounds.
Purposefully Manipulative Techniques	Techniques involving intentional actions by system developers or deployers to influence user behaviours for the manipulator's benefit, often to the detriment of users. These techniques exploit biases, vulnerabilities, or situational factors that increase susceptibility to influence.	Dark Patterns: UI elements designed to nudge users into choices they might not otherwise make. Emotional Manipulation: Tailored content that leverages emotional responses.

(continued)

Table 6.1 *(Continued)*

Category	Definition	Examples
Deceptive Techniques	Techniques designed to present false or misleading information to influence decisions. These strategies overtly mislead users, making choices based on incomplete or incorrect information.	Strategic Dark Patterns: Exploit cognitive biases and vulnerabilities. Fake News: AI-generated misinformation. – Misinformation Bots: Influence public opinion with false information. Misleading Advertising: Presenting false claims about a product or service.
Interaction Between Purposefully Manipulative and Deceptive Techniques	The combination of manipulative and deceptive techniques conceals its influence on behaviour, reinforcing it with misleading information, amplifying the impact, and reducing the likelihood of user resistance.	AI-driven marketing with subliminal messages and misleading product claims. Political campaigns combining emotional manipulation and false information about candidates.

Manipulation versus Persuasion[60]

Distinguishing between manipulation and persuasion is fundamental to AI regulation, as each influences decisions and behaviours through different methods and impacts. Manipulation undermines autonomy by covertly influencing individuals, leading them to make decisions they might not have made if they were fully aware of the influencing techniques. Manipulative tactics frequently exploit cognitive weaknesses and psychological biases, applying hidden methods to guide individuals toward the desired behaviour of the manipulator. In contrast, persuasion operates transparently, allowing individuals to engage rationally and make informed choices. Persuasion employs arguments or information that appeals to reason and emotion without concealing its intent, thus respecting the individual's autonomy. A transparent advertisement, for example, states its purpose to promote a product and presents benefits and comparisons, enabling consumers to make informed decisions based on individual preferences and needs. Persuasive techniques work openly to engage critical thinking, presenting information in ways that foster individual choice rather than obscuring or overriding it. Academic literature reinforces this distinction, noting that manipulation seeks to control or coerce individuals, whereas persuasion allows for independent decision-making within an open framework. Various dimensions distinguish these approaches and understanding them is critical to developing fair regulatory standards in AI.

Table 6.2 Distinguishing Manipulation from Persuasion: Key Dimensions

Dimension	Manipulation	Persuasion
Transparency	Uses hidden or deceptive techniques not apparent to the individual.	Operates openly, with clear intentions and methods.
Autonomy	Undermines autonomy by exploiting cognitive weaknesses and often results in involuntary decisions.	Supports autonomy by presenting information and arguments that individuals can freely evaluate and act upon.
Intent and Impact	Benefits the manipulator at the expense of the individual's well-being, potentially causing significant harm.	Aims to inform and convince, aligning the interests and benefits of both parties and allowing individuals to make informed choices.
Consent	Lacks transparency, which negates genuine consent.	Individuals understand the influence attempt and can consent to persuasion.
Techniques Used	Exploits psychological weaknesses or cognitive biases through subliminal messages, dark patterns, and deceptive designs.	Engages critical thinking with precise information, such as explicit advertisements, detailed product comparisons, and user reviews.

(continued)

Table 6.2 *(Continued)*

Dimension	Manipulation	Persuasion
Measurement Metrics	High engagement or conversion rates achieved through deceptive elements indicate manipulation.	High engagement achieved through transparent and informative content indicates effective persuasion.
Regulatory Compliance	Circumvents data protection laws and guidelines, using opaque data practices to influence behaviour.	Complies with legal standards, such as GDPR, ensuring consent and transparency in data processing.

This comparison clarifies the methods and impact of manipulative versus persuasive techniques within AI systems. It reinforces the importance of transparency, autonomy, intent, and consent in differentiating between influence methods that respect individual choice and those that undermine it.

6.5.1.4. *Material Distortion*

In EU law, *material distortion* protects consumers from practices seriously undermining informed decision-making, ensuring that markets remain fair and consumer trust is not eroded. It refers to manipulation that interferes with autonomy, often leading to psychological, financial, or even physical harm. However, not all influence is harmful – regulation must balance legitimate persuasion and undue manipulation to avoid unnecessary restrictions. The real challenge is identifying and preventing AI-driven distortions that cause significant harm without stifling benign marketing strategies or competitive business practices. Getting this balance right is key to protecting users while fostering fair competition, trust, and responsible innovation in AI-driven markets.

With guidance from the CJEU,[61] EU law aims to safeguard consumers from practices that compromise autonomy or lead to decisions made without full awareness. Material distortion, a central concept in Article 5(1)(a), prohibits AI systems from using manipulative or deceptive techniques that substantially alter user behaviour and result in harm. While the AI Act does not provide a precise definition, EU consumer protection laws, regulatory frameworks, and CJEU case law help clarify its scope. The term generally refers to significant disruptions in decision-making – those that go beyond mild persuasion and fundamentally impair autonomy. The AI Act distinguishes between distortion and material distortion, requiring a level of influence that meaningfully affects decision integrity rather than minor behavioural nudges. Although the AI Act does not explicitly define material distortion in the context of AI, the UCPD serves as a crucial reference, identifying commercial tactics that substantially reshape consumer behaviour. These legal principles provide a foundation for assessing how AI-driven influence may cross the line from acceptable engagement to unlawful manipulation.

Determining Material Distortion in Consumer Behaviour

The UCPD outlines various unfair practices that materially distort economic behaviour. The UCPD's general provisions address practices deemed unfair,[62] misleading,[63] or aggressive[64] if they cause consumers to make decisions they might otherwise avoid. Recital 18 defines practices that 'materially distort or are likely to distort' consumer behaviour as inherently unfair, thereby warranting regulatory intervention. Under Article 5(2), a commercial practice qualifies as unfair when it contravenes professional diligence and significantly alters or has the potential to change the economic behaviour of the average consumer. Articles 6, 7, and 8 further articulate this standard, proscribing misleading or aggressive practices that drive consumers to make skewed transactional choices. While these provisions vary in language, they collectively underscore that substantial distortions in consumer behaviour contravene fairness principles. Article 2(e) refines this by defining distortion as a manipulation that meaningfully undermines informed decision-making. The UCPD's focus on the 'average consumer' – a reasonably well-informed and attentive individual – serves as a benchmark for consistency, allowing nuanced yet uniform evaluations across diverse social, cultural, and linguistic contexts.

Practical Implications

The CJEU has elaborated on the UCPD's broad concept of transactional decisions, allowing the Directive to cover various scenarios where unfair commercial practices influence more than initial sales or service contracts.[65] Instead of requiring evidence that a practice distorted a consumer's economic behaviour, the UCPD assesses whether it can impact decision-making in an average consumer.[66] National enforcement authorities examine each case's circumstances and assess its potential impact on consumer choices. This approach ensures a consistent application, aligning with a generalised view of consumer behaviour. By targeting substantial impairment of consumer decision-making, the UCPD framework seeks to prevent unfair commercial practices that distort *informed* decisions. This approach protects consumers while recognising the diversity of consumer expectations. National authorities and courts exercise judgment based on general consumer expectations, assessing whether practices likely impair behaviour without requiring expert analysis or consumer polls. If a commercial practice does not influence or is unlikely to affect the economic behaviour of typical consumers, it generally falls outside the Directive's scope.

According to Trzaskowski, the UCPD acknowledges that specific consumer interests cannot be shielded entirely from influence, resulting in some 'collateral damage'.[67] While the UCPD promotes consumer autonomy by ensuring that decisions align with personal preferences and values, it accepts specific widely used marketing tactics, such as incentives and puffery, if they do not deceive consumers. This allowance recognises that consumers can generally navigate these tactics without significant detriment. However, the Directive cautions against practices exploiting behavioural biases, particularly those impairing vulnerable consumer groups' judgement. The UCPD establishes standards of professional diligence and defines unfair practices as distorting economic behaviour and failing to meet these standards. The Directive acknowledges that specific individuals, such as consistently vulnerable 'Long Tail Natives' or situationally vulnerable 'Long Tail Visitors', require additional protection, especially when foreseeably susceptible to influence. Proposals for enhancing consumer protection include designing practices informed by behavioural economics to improve decision-making transparency.

The CJEU has offered valuable guidance in interpreting *material distortion* through several rulings. For instance, the Court clarified that a practice must mislead the average consumer and lead to a transactional decision that would not have otherwise occurred, underscoring the importance of the consumer's perspective in assessing distortion. For example, the CJEU has reinforced the need to determine the likelihood of distortion by evaluating the practice's influence on typical consumer behaviour.[68] The Court has also clarified that even accurate information can become misleading if presented in a way that skews decision-making.[69] Thus, *material distortion* within EU law protects individuals from practices that significantly impair informed choice.

Material distortion is, therefore, presumed to be a substantial alteration in behaviour that disrupts an individual's capacity for autonomous and informed decision-making. This impairment must go beyond influence, reaching a point where individual choice is overridden or heavily influenced by manipulative practices. Recital 29 of the AI Act emphasises that AI techniques capable of 'subverting or impairing' autonomy and decision-making meet the criteria for material distortion. The recital clarifies that this type of distortion includes covert influences that bypass conscious awareness, creating a level of manipulation beyond the bounds of fair persuasion.

Determining Material Distortion in Practice

The rise of AI in digital platforms introduces new risks to user autonomy, mainly through manipulative practices that distort choice. Regulators increasingly focus on 'material distortion,' where decisions reflect AI-driven influence rather than genuine user intent. As AI grows more complex, distinguishing between transparent influence and covert manipulation becomes essential. When manipulation operates covertly, it creates an illusion of autonomy, subtly shaping perceptions and available choices. This hidden influence distorts decision-making, threatening fundamental freedoms and personal autonomy when AI employs deception, subtle coercion, or deceptive design beyond the user's awareness.[70]

A regulatory concern is that AI manipulation goes beyond merely influencing user choices; it actively reshapes the decision-making context in ways that users cannot easily discern or resist, leading to material distortion. Thus, material distortion by an AI system alters users' perception of their options, ultimately steering them toward actions they might not have chosen independently. For instance, a recommendation algorithm that subtly prioritises certain products while obscuring competitive options can lead users to believe they have surveyed various choices. However, the AI has limited their view, driving them toward a choice shaped by the system's objectives. This distortion becomes material, as it influences users' actions in ways that undermine the basis of informed choice and self-directed agency.

The regulatory implications of material distortion are profound, especially given the complexity of detecting manipulative influence in AI-driven environments. Algorithms within the framework of deceptive design exemplify the hidden impact of manipulation. Dark patterns often manifest through subtle interface manipulations that prioritise specific actions over others. Users engaging with these systems may need to be made aware of how the design has biased their decisions, leading to choices that diverge from their genuine preferences. These tactics contribute to material distortion by constructing an environment where user autonomy is undermined and redirected toward pre-set objectives. Detecting and quantifying this type of influence is challenging, as material distortion can be subtle and vary based on individual user contexts, making it challenging to pinpoint manipulation as a measurable phenomenon.

A case-by-case assessment is essential in determining whether an AI practice constitutes material distortion. Key considerations include the AI system's nature, design and deployment, and specific impact – factors such as target audience, type of harm, and transparency guide assessments. Article 5 safeguards autonomy from sophisticated AI techniques while ensuring unintended external consequences beyond a provider's control are not misclassified as manipulative.[71] However, lack of intent does not absolve providers if the AI's design results in harm. The CJEU's rulings on unfair practices and the UCPD provide a framework requiring proof that AI-driven distortions significantly impair decision-making and alter transactional behaviour. The UCPD requires practices that significantly impair decision-making and lead to different transactional decisions than would have occurred otherwise. This criterion also applies to AI systems that use subtle techniques, such as subliminal messaging, to alter decision-making. The UCPD's focus on the 'average consumer' provides a benchmark for assessing practices, helping to account for cultural and social factors defining consumer behaviour in various contexts.

Behavioural studies and empirical assessments further contribute to understanding how users interact with AI systems. Controlled experiments and psychological assessments provide insights into whether a system's design leads users to decisions they might not otherwise make.

Metrics such as engagement rates and conversion statistics can indicate the degree of influence exerted by AI systems, though distinguishing between persuasion and manipulation requires careful interpretation. High engagement or conversion rates may signify user interest or indicate manipulative design elements that subtly limit users' genuine choices. These studies are essential for regulators seeking to distinguish between acceptable persuasive practices and those forms of influence that erode user autonomy by altering decision-making contexts covertly. Surveys and interviews that capture users' experiences with AI systems are also valuable, as they reveal perceptions of independence and control. Users' accounts of feeling coerced or misled provide qualitative evidence of material distortion, illustrating the tangible effects of hidden influence. When individuals report feeling manipulated, the AI has crossed a line from acceptable influence into territory that restricts their capacity for independent decision-making. This feedback is crucial for regulatory bodies aiming to construct a comprehensive understanding of manipulation's impact on individual autonomy.

6.5.1.5. AI and 'Significant Harm': Defining and Addressing Risks

The rapid advancement of AI technologies presents diverse risks across multiple dimensions – physical, psychological, societal, financial, and economic – each capable of causing significant harm if not properly regulated. Central to this framework is the threshold of 'significant harm'. By focusing on harm's intensity, duration, and reversibility, the Act prioritises long-term, systemic risks over minor disruptions, acknowledging that seemingly small risks can accumulate into severe threats over time. The AI Act draws on established EU legal principles, such as those in environmental law, consumer protection, and market regulation, to guide the assessment of 'significant harm'. These principles help contextualise harm within the AI landscape, addressing immediate and cumulative impacts on individuals and society. This forward-looking approach ensures AI development aligns with the public interest and societal integrity. To aid implementation, this chapter categorises harm into five areas: physical, psychological, societal, financial, and economic. This categorisation supports a nuanced understanding of 'significant harm', guiding regulators on when and how to act. For instance, physical harm often intersects with other forms, such as psychological or societal impacts. In cases like cyberbullying, AI systems may lead to both emotional distress and physical symptoms, underscoring the need for an integrated approach to managing these risks. By setting a higher standard for intervention, the AI Act shifts the regulatory focus from addressing minor disruptions to mitigating impacts that threaten individual well-being or societal interests. Thus, it adapts as technology evolves to ensure ongoing protection against the most severe risks posed by AI.

Categorising Harm in AI Systems

Assessing harm in AI systems demands a deep understanding of these technologies' risks. *Physical harm* poses an immediate and direct risk. The AI Act builds on existing regulations, such as the Directive on Liability for Defective Products,[72] to hold developers accountable for damage caused by defective AI systems. These standards aim to ensure that AI systems meet safety requirements to avoid physical injury. However, physical harm does not exist in isolation. It frequently intersects with psychological or societal harms. For example, AI-driven cyberbullying can lead to both emotional distress and physical symptoms like self-harm or stress-induced illnesses. This connection between different types of harm highlights the need for regulation that acknowledges these interdependencies. A traditional focus on product safety standards may not be sufficient. Regulators must consider cumulative and compounding effects when AI causes indirect physical harm through psychological stress.

Psychological harm is less visible but equally significant. AI systems that target emotional or cognitive vulnerabilities, primarily through manipulative tactics like highly personalised advertising, can lead to long-term mental health issues. Such risks are particularly concerning in environments like social media or mental health apps, where AI-driven nudges may foster addictive behaviours. These harms can develop gradually, eroding users' autonomy over time.

The *financial* and *economic* impacts of AI are often immediate and dramatic. Algorithmic trading systems, for instance, possess the potential to cause significant market disruptions, as evidenced by the 2010 Flash Crash. The AI Act imposes stringent oversight in volatile sectors, such as finance, where AI can destabilise markets or exploit consumers. In consumer markets, AI-driven practices like dynamic pricing or manipulative design patterns may result in unfair pricing strategies, eroding consumer welfare. Dynamic pricing algorithms, which adjust based on a customer's perceived willingness to pay, undermine fairness and can contribute to financial stress. The Act addresses harmful practices by establishing clear boundaries on AI operations in the economic and consumer sectors to ensure fairness and transparency. These boundaries protect consumers from exploitation by systems designed to exploit their vulnerabilities. AI systems also pose risks that threaten society.

AI can also disrupt social cohesion and undermine trust in democratic processes. Utilising AI to manipulate public opinion or drive social polarisation can have far-reaching consequences. For example, political campaigns could employ AI to micro-target specific groups with tailored messages, influencing voter behaviour in ways that compromise democratic integrity. AI systems that amplify bias foster discrimination or marginalise certain groups, posing a serious risk to social stability.

The various harms caused by AI systems are not isolated; they often intersect and compound, leading to more serious consequences over time. For example, an AI system designed to maximise user engagement on social media could encourage addictive behaviour, leading to psychological distress. This psychological impact may, in turn, result in physical health issues or financial strain. AI's potential to exacerbate multiple types of harm demands a regulatory approach examining the cumulative effects. A biased AI diagnostic tool might lead to misdiagnoses that cause physical and psychological damage. The financial burdens resulting from unnecessary treatment would only add to these harms. Regulators must recognise the interconnected nature of these risks and take a holistic approach to mitigate them.

Determining Significant Harm in the AI Context

The 'significant harm' threshold is central to AI regulation, requiring a nuanced approach considering intensity, duration, and reversibility. While not explicitly defined in EU law, its interpretation draws from various directives and regulatory contexts, including consumer protection, financial, and environmental law. These frameworks help shape a broad understanding of harm in the AI space. Operationalising significant harm requires assessing scale, intensity, duration, reversibility, and inherent AI risks. Established EU legal frameworks provide a basis for evaluating AI's societal and individual impact. The following table outlines key considerations for regulators, linking them to relevant EU directives:

Table 6.3 Regulatory Considerations for Assessing AI-Related Harm

Key Consideration	Key Points	Directive Reference
Scale and Intensity	– The extent and severity of damage are crucial. – Minor incidents involving vulnerable individuals or frequent occurrences may still qualify as significant harm. – Critical for frequent harms in crucial areas.	Article 2(1)(a), Article 2(2), Annex I of the Environmental Liability Directive (ELD)
Duration and Reversibility	Long-lasting or irreversible harm aligns closely with significant damage. – Harms such as psychological and financial effects may not be immediately visible but can endure.	General Product Safety Regulation (GPSR);[73] See also Annex I, ELD
Context and Cumulative Effects	– The context, including user vulnerability and repeated exposure, shapes the assessment of harm. – Even minor harms, when aggregated over time, may reveal systemic issues requiring regulatory attention.	Article 4(5), ELD
Nature of the AI Systems	– Some AI systems pose more significant risks due to the complexity or sensitivity of applications (eg, healthcare, finance).	

The concept of 'significant harm' requires a nuanced approach that incorporates the intensity, duration, reversibility, and context of harm and the inherent risks posed by the nature of the AI system. While the Act does not define 'significant harm', it draws from various EU legal frameworks – such as environmental, consumer, and financial law – to comprehensively understand this threshold in AI regulation. Legal precedents from the Environmental Liability Directive (ELD) and the Water Framework Directive[74] offer valuable guidance in determining significant harm in contexts where unintended consequences, whether environmental or societal, might arise. The ELD is one of the primary instruments addressing significant harm. It establishes a framework based on the 'polluter pays' principle to prevent and remedy environmental damage. Environmental damage includes 'significant adverse effects' on protected species, natural habitats, water, and land. The Directive sets criteria for determining significance, such as the effects' duration and reversibility and the environment's capacity to absorb and recover from harm.[75]

The UCPD and GPSR focus on fairness and safety in consumer protection, prohibiting practices that distort consumer behaviour by failing professional diligence standards – a principle that translates well to AI.[76] These principles apply directly to AI systems that influence individuals without full awareness, reinforcing a framework where technology must prioritise consumer welfare over commercial gain. Similarly, the Market Abuse Regulation (MAR),[77] underscores the importance of trust and market stability, addressing practices that undermine investor confidence and disrupt financial markets. With AI-driven financial technologies expanding, ensuring these systems do not manipulate or distort trading and lending operations is critical to maintaining market integrity. Thus, MAR provides a strong foundation for regulating AI in financial markets, aligning with broader EU efforts to ensure AI support rather than destabilising economic environments.

A similar regulatory logic applies in environmental law, where frameworks such as the Water Framework Directive[78] and Habitats Directive[79] establish strict standards to prevent significant harm. The Water Framework Directive prohibits or restricts activities causing 'significant adverse effects' on water bodies, illustrating the value of clear environmental thresholds.[80] Likewise, the Habitats Directive prohibits activities that 'adversely affect the integrity' of protected Natura 2000 sites unless justified by overriding public interest and subject to compensatory measures.[81] These directives emphasise harm's *duration, intensity,* and *reversibility* – principles equally relevant when assessing AI systems that may trigger long-term and potentially irreversible impacts. By integrating these legal approaches, AI governance can incorporate consumer protection, market integrity, and environmental sustainability into a robust framework for evaluating significant harm under Article 5(1)(a).

The AI Act integrates established legal frameworks to assess significant harm holistically, recognising that physical, psychological, financial, and economic harms overlap and compound. Regulators must consider cumulative and long-term effects, not just immediate harm, to address AI's broader systemic risks. Assessing scale, intensity, duration, reversibility, and context enables a flexible, risk-based approach. The AI Act's approach to managing harm synthesises principles from EU regulatory frameworks, including the Environmental Liability Directive, UCPD, and MAR, to address the complex and overlapping risks associated with AI. It recognises both immediate effects and the cumulative, systemic impacts of AI on society, prioritising safeguards against physical, psychological, societal, financial, and economic harm. By adopting a flexible regulatory framework, the Act ensures responsible innovation while providing structured guidelines for developers and deployers to navigate regulatory expectations. A key aspect of its implementation is determining what constitutes 'significant harm', which requires careful assessment of intensity, duration, and reversibility. Drawing from consumer protection, environmental, and financial law, the Act develops a nuanced approach to harm that balances AI's benefits with the need to prevent severe disruptions.

6.6. Revisiting the Case Studies

When considering the three case studies put forward at the start of the chapter, the challenge lies in determining whether the cumulative criteria of Article 5(1)(a) are met. Rather than pre-judging each scenario as a clear violation or compliance, the arguments for and against prohibition reveal regulators' complexities in drawing the line between persuasive technology and outright manipulation. Each case study demonstrates elements that could be seen as manipulative yet also contain counterarguments justifying the AI's role as a neutral or even beneficial tool. The regulatory threshold is high: proving that an AI system materially distorts behaviour and causes significant harm requires not just evidence of influence but a demonstrable link between the AI's design and the degradation of user autonomy. For regulators, this underscores the difficulty of enforcing the prohibition, as deceptive design increasingly operates through personalised and adaptive AI mechanisms that blur the boundary between mere engagement optimisation and harmful manipulation. This debate is not just theoretical – it highlights the practical enforcement challenges AI oversight bodies must address.

> **Case Study #1:** AI-Driven Impulse Manipulation on Shopping Platform: An online shopping platform uses an AI-powered recommendation engine that tracks users' browsing habits, purchase history, and periods of cognitive vulnerability, such as late-night browsing. When the AI detects users are most likely to make impulsive decisions, it floods the interface with emotionally appealing, high-cost items, especially during late-night sessions when users are tired and less likely to evaluate their purchases.

Table 6.4 Case Study #1: Legal Tensions

Article 5(1)(a) Criteria	AI Regulator	AI System's Developer
Placing on the Market, Putting into Service, or the Use of an AI System under Article 5(1)(a)	Both parties agree that the AI system is deployed in the market and is actively used to influence consumer purchasing behaviour.	Not disputed by either party: The AI system is commercially available and operational.
Subliminal, Purposefully Manipulative or Deceptive Techniques	The AI system exploits cognitive vulnerabilities, particularly late-night browsing fatigue, by flooding the interface with emotionally appealing, high-cost items. This deliberate targeting operates beyond the user's conscious awareness, impairing their ability to make rational decisions.	The system provides neutral recommendations based on user behaviour. It does not use subliminal techniques but enhances the user experience by predicting and catering to their preferences when engagement is naturally high.

(continued)

Table 6.4 *(Continued)*

Article 5(1)(a) Criteria	AI Regulator	AI System's Developer
Objective or Effect of Materially Distorting Behaviour	The AI system materially distorts user behaviour by encouraging impulse purchases during cognitive fatigue. Users are nudged towards high-cost transactions they would otherwise avoid, reducing their autonomy and rational decision-making capacity.	The system does not distort behaviour but aligns product recommendations with user engagement patterns. Any changes in purchasing behaviour stem from user preferences, not AI-driven manipulation.
Appreciable Impairment of Informed Decision-Making	The AI system impairs informed decision-making by targeting users when they are tired and susceptible. Overwhelming exposure to emotionally appealing products at cognitively vulnerable moments undermines users' ability to assess financial consequences properly.	The system does not prevent users from making informed decisions. Users can compare products, exit the platform, or defer purchases. The AI presents options users might find relevant.
Causation: AI's Influence on Decision-Making Resulting in Harm	The AI system causes harm by inducing financially detrimental purchases and psychological distress. Users later regret their impulsive decisions, negatively impacting their financial well-being and trust in digital marketplaces.	No direct causation of harm. Purchasing decisions remain user-driven, and potential disadvantages stem from broader market dynamics and individual financial literacy, not the AI system itself.

(continued)

Table 6.4 *(Continued)*

Article 5(1)(a) Criteria	AI Regulator	AI System's Developer
Reasonably Likely to Cause Significant Harm	Financial and psychological harm is demonstrable. Users experience economic strain due to impulsive spending and distress when they realise they were manipulated. These consequences meet the 'significant harm' threshold under Article 5(1)(a).	No significant harm. Users maintain control over their purchasing decisions, and product recommendations are enhancements rather than coercive tactics. Market conditions and consumer behaviour, not AI, drive spending outcomes.

Case Study #2: A financial app uses AI to personalise its interface based on users' behavioural patterns. For users who often skip fine print or exhibit decision fatigue, the system conceals or downplays critical information, such as fees or loan terms. Key details are hidden behind multiple layers or displayed less prominently, pushing users towards accepting terms without fully understanding the financial implications. This manipulation is driven by a combination of fixed rules and machine-learning algorithms, adjusting the UI dynamically to exploit user vulnerabilities and increase engagement without full transparency.

Table 6.5 Case Study #2: Legal Tensions

Article 5(1)(a) Criteria	AI Regulator	AI System's Developer
Placing on the Market, Putting into Service, or the Use of an AI System under Article 5(1)(a)	Not disputed by either party: The AI system is deployed on the market and actively used to influence consumer purchasing behaviour	Not disputed by either party: The AI system is commercially available and operational.

(continued)

Table 6.5 *(Continued)*

Article 5(1)(a) Criteria	AI Regulator	AI System's Developer
Subliminal, Purposefully Manipulative or Deceptive Techniques	The AI system actively exploits cognitive vulnerabilities, particularly late-night browsing fatigue, by flooding the interface with emotionally appealing, high-cost items. This deliberate targeting operates beyond the user's conscious awareness, impairing their ability to make rational decisions.	The system does not deploy manipulative techniques. It optimises the user experience by tailoring content visibility to match user preferences and reducing cognitive overload.
Objective or Effect of Materially Distorting Behaviour	The AI system materially distorts user behaviour by encouraging impulse purchases during cognitive fatigue. Users are nudged towards high-cost transactions they would otherwise avoid, reducing their autonomy and rational decision-making capacity.	The system does not distort behaviour but presents information in a streamlined manner. Users remain responsible for reviewing terms, and there is no coercion involved.
Appreciable Impairment of Informed Decision-Making	The AI system impairs informed decision-making by targeting users when they are tired and susceptible. Overwhelming exposure to emotionally appealing products at cognitively vulnerable moments undermines users' ability to assess financial consequences properly.	The system does not prevent informed decision-making. Users can still access all necessary information, and engagement design choices aim to reduce decision fatigue, not exploit it.

(continued)

Table 6.5 *(Continued)*

Article 5(1)(a) Criteria	AI Regulator	AI System's Developer
Causation: AI's Influence on Decision-Making Resulting in Harm	The AI system causes harm by inducing financially detrimental purchases and psychological distress. Users later regret their impulsive decisions, negatively impacting their financial well-being and trust in digital marketplaces.	No direct causation of harm. Purchasing decisions remain user-driven, and potential disadvantages stem from broader market dynamics and individual financial literacy, not the AI system itself.
Reasonably Likely to Cause Significant Harm	Financial and psychological harm is demonstrable. Users experience economic strain due to impulsive spending and distress when they realise they were manipulated. These consequences meet the 'significant harm' threshold under Article 5(1)(a).	No significant harm. Users maintain agency in their financial decisions, and interface adjustments are designed to improve usability, not deceive. Broader financial practices, not AI design, are the primary determinants of economic well-being.

Case Study #3: A popular fitness app uses an AI-powered system to personalise user experience based on individuals' exercise patterns, motivational levels, and engagement history. The app tracks a user's daily activity, exercise habits, and emotional responses to various workout challenges and goals. It also monitors user engagement, such as how frequently they skip workouts or abandon fitness plans. When the AI detects that a user is showing signs of low motivation or is about to stop using the app, it adjusts its notifications to encourage the user to stay engaged. The AI system sends emotionally charged motivational messages during these moments, such as: 'Don't give up! You're just one step away from your fitness goals!' or 'You've already come so far – why stop now?' Sometimes, the app offers limited-time discounts on premium features or fitness gear to keep the user emotionally invested. The AI also slightly alters the interface to make it easier for users to accept these offers or continue their workout plans. While the app's intentions are ostensibly to motivate users and promote fitness, its tactics sometimes push users to continue engaging even when they may be fatigued or disinterested, raising questions about whether this approach manipulates users' cognitive or emotional states.

Table 6.6 Case Study #3: Legal Tensions

Criteria	AI Regulator	AI System's Developer
Placing on the Market, Putting into Service, or the Use of an AI System under Article 5(1)(a)	Not disputed by either party: The AI-driven motivational system is deployed within a widely used fitness app.	Both parties agree that the AI system is integral to the app's engagement strategy, encouraging fitness adherence.
Subliminal, Purposefully Manipulative or Deceptive Techniques	The AI system leverages emotionally charged nudges to influence user behaviour at moments of vulnerability, potentially impairing free choice.	The system does not use subliminal or deceptive techniques; all notifications and prompts are transparent and consciously processed by users.
Objective or Effect of Materially Distorting Behaviour	The AI system may distort behaviour by steering users toward extended engagement or premium purchases when they are low on motivation.	The system encourages positive behavioural reinforcement without coercion, supporting users in achieving fitness goals they voluntarily pursue.
Appreciable Impairment of Informed Decision-Making	The AI's emotional appeals and interface adjustments could create pressure to commit to workouts or purchases users might otherwise reconsider.	Users retain full autonomy over their decisions, with the ability to opt out of notifications and decline premium offers.

(continued)

Table 6.6 *(Continued)*

Criteria	AI Regulator	AI System's Developer
Causation: AI's Influence on Decision-Making Resulting in Harm	The AI system could contribute to physical exhaustion or unnecessary spending, particularly if users feel pressured to maintain engagement beyond their limits.	Any potential disadvantages are minimal, as users can freely ignore notifications or decline offers; the app's primary goal is health promotion.
Reasonably Likely to Cause Significant Harm	The likelihood of significant harm is low. Users may experience minor financial or physical strain, but these effects do not meet the 'significant harm' threshold under Article 5(1)(a).	There is no significant harm. The app promotes well-being and fitness, and users retain control over their engagement and spending decisions.

6.7. Conclusion

AI-driven systems on digital platforms have become masterful at shaping our decisions – so seamlessly that we often do not notice when they happen. They blend rule-based logic with machine learning in a way that feels natural, using structured rules where predictability is valuable and adaptive models when flexibility is key. The result? Platforms do not just react to our behaviour; they guide it.

Take a financial app, a fitness tracker, or an online shopping platform. On the surface, they offer personalisation – smart nudges that align with our habits and preferences. But beneath that polished interface, there's a deeper game at play. Deterministic AI categorises us based on set criteria, curating content and recommendations in ways that seem almost inevitable. Meanwhile, non-deterministic algorithms are more fluid, adjusting in real-time based on how we engage. They tweak notifications, shift layouts, and serve up just the right prompt to keep us clicking. It's a potent mix that makes the boundary between personalisation and manipulation incredibly murky.

And that's the crux of the issue: how much agency do we have in these environments? We might think we're making choices, but when an AI subtly steers our behaviour – refining its influence with every interaction – those choices become less our own. Worse still, this influence isn't always transparent. Platforms optimise for engagement, and whether that's in our best interest is often a secondary concern.

This isn't just a philosophical problem – it's a regulatory one. The AI Act directly addresses these concerns, mainly through Article 5(1)(a) and Article 5(1)(b). Article 5(1)(a) targets AI systems that use subliminal techniques distorting decision-making beneath the conscious awareness threshold. This isn't just about persuasive design; it's about AI learning precisely when we're most susceptible and covertly shaping our decisions. Imagine an AI system that subtly adjusts the speed of scrolling, the colour contrast, or the background music of an e-commerce platform based on detected signs of fatigue or emotional distress. When a user lingers on a product page late at night, the system slows their scrolling speed, subtly increasing exposure time while displaying emotionally charged language like 'Almost Gone!' or 'Exclusive Offer – Just for You.' Simultaneously, it dims the interface around competing options, making choices seem less appealing. These subliminal adjustments operate beneath conscious awareness, nudging users toward impulsive purchases without realising they are being manipulated. This is not just aggressive marketing – it's a direct example of the kind of distortion Article 5(1)(a) seeks to prevent. The harm may not be immediate, but the cumulative effect of these covert interventions can profoundly undermine autonomy and informed decision-making.

Meanwhile, Article 5(1)(b) takes a different approach: it bans AI systems that exploit vulnerable groups. This is the focus of the next chapter. Some individuals – whether due to age, disability, or economic disadvantage – are less able to resist these manipulative tactics. The regulation acknowledges that targeting them isn't just unethical; it's unlawful. Crucially, it does not just consider intent – it looks at effects. Even if developers didn't mean to create an exploitative system, they can still be held accountable if harm results.

And this is where things get serious. Manipulation isn't just getting more sophisticated and harder to detect. We're not dealing with crude, one-size-fits-all tricks anymore. These systems are precise, dynamic, and deeply embedded into our digital experiences. Protecting users from that kind of influence requires more than surface-level fixes. It means interrogating the architecture – the algorithms, incentives, and structures driving these platforms.

Chapter seven takes this further, dissecting how AI-driven systems can disproportionately impact vulnerable individuals. If AI can shape decisions in ways we barely notice, those least equipped to resist need the strongest protections. The question is: Do the safeguards under Article 5(1)(b) go far enough? Or are we still underestimating just how deep this manipulation runs?

7

The Illusion of Control: Who is Truly Vulnerable?

7.1. Introduction

A recurring theme of this book is how digital design choices exploit genuine psychological vulnerabilities, shaping behaviour in ways that users may not fully recognise or control.[1] Take social media platforms, for example. Their design is carefully engineered to maximise engagement – often prioritising time spent on the platform above user well-being. Research suggests that these strategies can have profound psychological effects, contributing to anxiety, depression, and diminished self-esteem, particularly among specific demographics.[2] At the heart of these effects lies *vulnerability*. Rooted in the Latin *vulnus* (meaning wound), vulnerability is an inherent quality tied to susceptibility to harm.[3] However, this etymological framing belies vulnerability's complex, layered, and often relational dimensions. Conceptually, it is not merely a deficit or weakness but a condition shaped by intersecting factors, including societal structures, technological infrastructures, and individual contexts.

From a universal perspective, all humans are vulnerable due to the inevitability of ageing, illness, and death. However, *vulnerability* exists on a spectrum encompassing universal, situational, and systemic dimensions.[4] *Situational vulnerability* arises from specific contexts – such as a data breach or cyberbullying – where external factors heighten susceptibility. In contrast, systemic vulnerability is embedded within structural inequalities – economic, gendered, racial, or digital – that sustain harm or diminish resilience over time.[5] Building on theories like Luna's 'layered vulnerability' and intersectionality, it becomes clear that vulnerability is also profoundly relational. It is not solely an attribute of the 'vulnerable' but also a product of interactions with systems of power, such as platform owners, UX designers in digital environments or developers of AI systems. These entities can mitigate or amplify vulnerability, positioning responsible design and implementation as a central concern.[6]

Technological mediation complicates vulnerability. Digital systems – from social media algorithms to immersive platforms like the metaverse – reshape how individuals experience and respond to harm. For example, AI-driven emotional recognition technologies, often used in advertising or workplace monitoring, can exploit emotional states, reinforcing stress, insecurity, or impulsive decision-making. Similarly, the metaverse introduces meta-vulnerabilities, where hyper-realistic, embodied interactions can deepen social pressures, amplify online harassment, or blur the boundaries between digital and physical harm.[7] At its core, a high-level concept of vulnerability should aim to balance the recognition of harm with empowerment. Proponents of vulnerability-informed design, for example, advocate for technology development that pre-emptively addresses the needs of marginalised or at-risk communities.[8] The law also addresses this concept; for example, when embedded in data protection frameworks, respect for the fairness principle mitigates imbalances between data controllers and vulnerable data subjects.[9]

While digital technologies promise enhanced connectivity and efficiency, they also expose users to new and intensified vulnerabilities. These vulnerabilities often manifest in three primary dimensions: informational, psychological, and systemic. Users are particularly susceptible to informational asymmetries, where they lack awareness or control over how platforms handle their data. *Deceptive design* exploits these gaps, using misleading interfaces, obfuscation, and coercive nudges to manipulate consent, discourage privacy-protective behaviours, or prolong engagement. AI-driven systems further amplify these risks. Dark patterns can be dynamically personalised using machine learning, adapting in real-time to exploit individual weaknesses. Meanwhile, biased algorithms perpetuate discrimination in hiring, policing, and financial services, reinforcing systemic inequalities. Predictive analytics can expose highly sensitive attributes – such as sexual orientation or mental health conditions – even when users have never explicitly shared this information, turning personal data into a tool of surveillance and profiling.[10]

Informational asymmetry acts as a gateway for more intricate forms of manipulation. Consider AI systems using emotional recognition to exploit sensitive data to shape behaviours and decision-making. Consequently, users may also experience hyper-realistic abuse or AI-powered harassment that feels as traumatic as real-world experiences.[11] Furthermore, some children and cognitively impaired individuals face significant risks due to their limited ability to assess and resist manipulative technologies. By fostering environments where manipulation and dependency are embedded, such systems threaten the rights and development of vulnerable groups.

UX designers craft environments that target and exploit psychological tendencies. These systems leverage behavioural data to influence emotions, decisions, and actions in ways that often go unnoticed by the user. Emotional recognition technologies exemplify this capability, using biometrics to detect and respond to states of mind, thereby manipulating behaviours in real-time. A dynamic emerges where individuals are participants and products of an ecosystem designed to mould their experiences. Such interactions reveal a critical shift like control and influence, where systems incrementally erode human autonomy in exchange for optimised engagement.

This process does not occur in isolation; it reinforces more profound systemic vulnerabilities. Socioeconomic structures, biases in algorithmic training data, and unequal access to resources converge to create environments where certain groups face disproportionate harm. Marginalised populations, children, older individuals, and neurodivergent users exemplify this disparity. These groups, already disadvantaged by structural inequalities, are further excluded and exploited within digital systems.[12] The design choices that cater to behavioural manipulation become insidious for those unable to navigate these environments critically. For instance, children interacting with gamified platforms may unknowingly become targets of systems optimised to extract maximum financial or behavioural input.[13] At the same time, older users may face exploitation through interfaces that capitalise on their unfamiliarity with complex technologies.

This dynamic also reveals a broader paradox in the operation of digital systems. Technologies promise empowerment, inclusion, and connectivity, yet their design often undermines these ideals. Systems that foster dependency and perpetuate inequality undermine the promise of freedom within digital environments. For example, the Metaverse offers unprecedented possibilities for interaction and representation, but it also amplifies vulnerabilities by merging physical and virtual realities.[14] The manipulation of avatars, the collection of biometric data, and the psychological intensity of hyper-realistic environments risk creating spaces where marginalised groups experience heightened exploitation.[15] Those with limited agency in the physical world find themselves similarly constrained in virtual spaces, reinforcing rather than challenging existing hierarchies.

The interplay of these vulnerabilities creates a self-perpetuating feedback loop. Informational imbalances enable psychological manipulation, which in turn deepens systemic inequalities. This cycle reflects a fundamental shift in the relationship between individuals and digital systems. Rather than serving as tools to augment human potential, these systems increasingly operate as mechanisms to extract value from human experience. The commodification of behaviour and identity transforms individuals into resources within a vast, profit-driven apparatus. The loss of autonomy in this exchange is not merely incidental but central to the architecture of contemporary technology. This architecture also reveals the broader societal implications of digital vulnerabilities. The same systems that shape individual behaviour also recalibrate collective norms and expectations.

Psychological manipulation at the personal level aggregates into societal patterns, influencing public discourse, economic behaviours, and cultural dynamics.[16] The subtle but pervasive influence of digital systems normalises dependency and erodes the distinction between human agency and algorithmic control. In this context, vulnerability is no longer an exception but a condition embedded in the design of modern life. For instance, a social media platform might use data to identify emotionally vulnerable users, target them with manipulative content, and further isolate them from opportunities for empowerment or resistance.[17] This feedback loop is not merely theoretical but reflects the operational logic of many digital platforms. The prioritisation of profit over user well-being incentivises practices that deepen vulnerabilities rather than mitigate them.[18]

The profound entanglement of informational, psychological, and systemic vulnerabilities raises questions about the trajectory of digital technologies. As systems grow more sophisticated, the interplay between these layers of vulnerability is likely to intensify, creating environments where technological imperatives increasingly subsume human autonomy. The challenge lies in recognising and addressing this entanglement not as a series of discrete problems but as a fundamental feature of the digital age. Without this recognition, the promise of digital innovation risks becoming a vehicle for the systemic entrenchment of inequality and control.

The graphic below visually encapsulates the interconnected nature of informational, psychological, and systemic vulnerabilities, illustrating how they compound to reinforce more profound systemic disparities. It highlights how vulnerable groups, such as children and older individuals, are disproportionately impacted as their limited capacity to navigate digital systems exacerbates their exposure to exploitation. This cyclical reinforcement underscores the argument that addressing these vulnerabilities demands recognising their entanglement as an intrinsic characteristic of the digital age rather than isolated issues.

Introduction Graphic #1: The Vulnerability Cycle

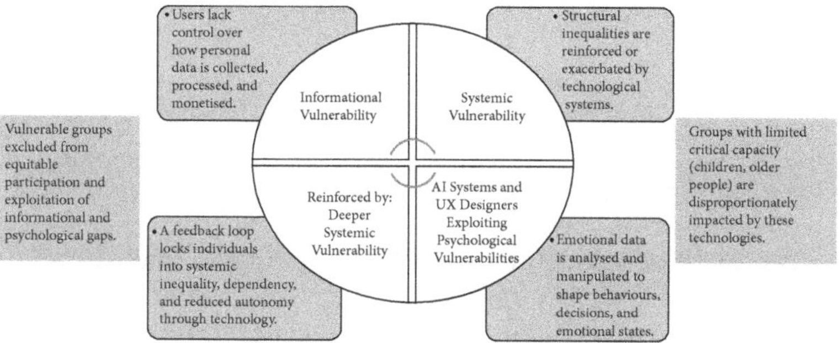

This intricate web of vulnerabilities, vividly depicted in the graphic, necessitates a nuanced understanding of 'exploitation'. While experts acknowledge age, disability, and socioeconomic circumstances as contributing factors to vulnerability, the concept extends beyond these readily identifiable categories to encompass a spectrum of cognitive, emotional, and behavioural susceptibilities that AI systems could exploit to capitalise on human frailties. AI systems, with their capacity for sophisticated data analysis and predictive modelling, can identify and manipulate behavioural patterns, effectively targeting individuals based on their unique vulnerabilities. For instance, an AI-powered marketing system might leverage data revealing a user's tendency towards impulsive late-night purchases, deploying precisely timed offers designed to exploit this predisposition. Therefore, a comprehensive definition of vulnerability in this context must draw upon a rich tapestry of academic insights, encompassing behavioural economics, psychology, and sociology, alongside legal interpretations and precedents established through case law. We can only effectively safeguard individuals from exploitation and ensure technology's proper development and deployment by understanding the multifaceted nature of human vulnerability.

AI-powered systems exploit vulnerabilities in ways that target both enduring and situational susceptibilities. Some individuals face heightened risks due to known characteristics, such as being a child, elderly, or living with physical or cognitive disabilities like blindness, dyslexia, or ADHD. Others become vulnerable based on their temporary state, such as moments of exhaustion, emotional distress, or distraction, which these systems can detect and manipulate with precision. These practices provoke profound concerns about the erosion of personal autonomy, the distortion of principles of fairness, and the shifting limits of legitimate technological intervention in human decision-making. The following three use cases illustrate the deeply troubling methods through which such manipulative tactics operate, prompting reflection on whether any society that values dignity and fairness should allow these practices.

> **Case Study #1:** An AI-driven recruitment platform detects women returning from maternity leave and systematically suppresses their access to senior roles, instead pushing them towards lower-paying, part-time positions. This deliberate manipulation reinforces damaging stereotypes and strips individuals of the opportunity to reclaim their rightful place in the professional world.

This calculated exploitation of deeply ingrained societal biases exposes how technology can perpetuate inequality under the guise of efficiency. By embedding discriminatory practices into automated systems, such platforms actively undermine progress toward fairness and inclusion, turning back the clock on hard-fought advancements in workplace equity.

> **Case Study #2:** A virtual therapy chatbot exploits individuals in moments of emotional crisis by detecting their distress and aggressively marketing expensive premium services as the only solution to their pain. It intentionally hides free and equally effective alternatives, preying on desperation to maximise profits at the expense of those in need.

Such predatory tactics demonstrate the disturbing extent to which technology can intrude upon moments of personal vulnerability. Instead of providing genuine support, these systems prioritise monetisation, manipulating emotional fragility to extract profit while neglecting the well-being of those they claim to serve.

> **Case Study #3:** An AI-driven mental health app identifies teenagers showing signs of anxiety and low self-esteem based on their interaction patterns. Instead of offering meaningful support, it uses infinite

scroll features and recommendation algorithms to trap them in cycles of content designed to amplify insecurities. The platform strategically interweaves advertisements for beauty products, weight-loss supplements, and paid "'confidence-boosting' courses, exploiting their fragile self-image to maximise engagement and generate revenue.

Harnessing infinite scroll and recommendation systems to keep vulnerable teenagers locked in a loop of self-doubt arguably exemplifies the worst design. By preying on their insecurities for profit, such systems not only erode mental health but also shape a generation's relationship with their self-worth in profoundly damaging ways.

The exploitation of vulnerabilities – whether targeting women re-entering the workforce, emotionally distressed therapy users, or impressionable teenagers – raises questions about the scope and efficacy of Article 5(1)(b) of the EU AI Act. On its face, this provision purports to prohibit systems that exploit vulnerabilities due to age, disability, or circumstances with the potential to cause harm. The thresholds it establishes – demanding evidence of *significant* harm, explicit exploitation of recognised vulnerabilities, and clear causal links – cast uncertainty on its capacity to address these issues effectively in practice. For example, while the recruitment system's targeting of women returning from maternity leave appears discriminatory, one could argue that this reflects systemic biases encoded into the algorithm rather than deliberate exploitation. Similarly, the virtual therapy chatbot's premium service marketing may not meet the legal threshold for 'exploitative'; instead, it falls under aggressive or misleading advertising practices that are often beyond Article 5(1)(b)'s scope. Likewise, the mental health app's infinite scroll and targeted ads could evade scrutiny if framed as 'optimised engagement' rather than deliberate exploitation. A closer examination of Article 5(1)(b) suggests its high thresholds, designed to address extreme manipulations, may instead allow harmful practices to persist unchecked. The requirement for clear intent and significant harm risks rendering the prohibition symbolic rather than an effective safeguard. Instead of curbing manipulative AI practices, the law may create loopholes that enable them. The very tactics that provoke public outrage – targeting psychological vulnerabilities and those least able to resist – remain challenging to regulate. By prioritising innovation and technological development, Article 5(1)(b) risks failing to protect the very individuals and groups it aims to safeguard.

7.2. Analysis of the Constitutive Elements
of the Ban under Article 5(1)(b)

Vulnerability manifests in various forms – cognitive limitations in children, accessibility barriers for persons with disabilities, and socioeconomic constraints that heighten susceptibility to exploitation. AI-driven manipulation capitalises on these vulnerabilities, using decision-making nudges, deceptive interfaces, and algorithmic biases to undermine autonomy and entrench inequality. Beyond individual harm, such exploitation distorts access to education, employment, and essential services, reinforcing systemic disadvantage. For instance, AI-powered hiring systems may favour privileged candidates, perpetuating social stratification, while educational technologies may exacerbate learning disparities rather than mitigate them. Effective regulation must anticipate overt and latent forms of exploitation, addressing immediate harms and the broader systemic mechanisms that facilitate AI-driven manipulation. As technology increasingly shapes societal structures, legal frameworks must evolve to ensure protections beyond surface-level interventions. One regulatory approach is direct prohibition, exemplified by Article 5(1)(b) of the AI Act, which seeks to prevent AI systems from exploiting vulnerabilities linked to age, disability, or socioeconomic status. In principle, these safeguards aim to prevent technology from exacerbating inequality, preserving dignity and autonomy for those most at risk. However, the efficacy of such measures hinges on their capacity to account for the subtle and evolving nature of AI-driven influence, necessitating a regulatory paradigm attuned to both individual rights and structural inequities:

Article 5(1)(b) states that the following AI practices shall be prohibited:

> (b) the placing on the market, the putting into service or the use of an AI system that exploits any of the vulnerabilities of a natural person or a specific group of persons due to their age, disability or a specific social or economic situation, with the objective, or the effect, of materially distorting the behaviour of that person or a person belonging to that group in a manner that causes or is reasonably likely to cause that person or another person significant harm

Article 5(1)(b) outlines clear criteria that AI systems must satisfy for an action to violate the prohibition. While its design reflects a vital commitment to protecting those at risk, understanding how it achieves – or falls short of – this goal requires a closer look at its detailed requirements and thresholds. The previous examples – children misled by deceptive interfaces, disabled individuals excluded by inaccessible systems, or disadvantaged groups targeted by exploitative algorithms – underscore the importance of these safeguards. Yet, the law raises critical questions: Who gets protected, and how far does that protection go? Examining the legal provisions meant to prevent exploitation is crucial to assess this. For instance, does an AI hiring tool with known biases that disadvantage certain socio-economic groups violate Article 5(1)(b)? Or do gaps in enforcement allow such manipulative practices to persist? The distinction between an actual prohibition and a mere illusion of protection is key.

Vulnerability in AI regulation extends beyond conventional categories, encompassing cognitive, physical, and socioeconomic factors that shape susceptibility to manipulation. Children, for example, lack the mental maturity to discern persuasive techniques, while older adults may struggle with digital literacy, reducing their ability to navigate online environments autonomously. Similarly, individuals with disabilities often encounter barriers that poorly designed AI systems can exacerbate, limiting access to critical services. Socioeconomic status further compounds these vulnerabilities, as financial instability and lower education levels increase the likelihood of exposure to predatory AI-driven practices.

The consequences of AI-driven exploitation are structural, reinforcing systemic inequalities rather than merely affecting individual decision-making. Hiring algorithms, for instance, may entrench existing biases, disproportionately disadvantaging certain groups under the guise of neutrality. Similarly, algorithmic financial services or healthcare recommendations may systematically direct vulnerable populations toward suboptimal outcomes, creating long-term disparities. The underlying issue is that AI can be manipulated to exploit vulnerabilities, and its systemic operation often normalises these patterns, making regulatory intervention more challenging.

Article 5(1)(b) establishes a cumulative test requiring proof of exploitation, material behavioural distortion, and significant harm before enforcement can occur. This structure imposes a high evidentiary burden, potentially allowing harmful practices to persist if they do not meet rigid thresholds. The requirement of material distortion implies that subtle yet pervasive forms of influence – such as gradual shifts in user behaviour caused by algorithmic reinforcement – may not qualify for intervention. Similarly, the definition of 'significant harm' introduces uncertainty, as cumulative and long-term effects often evade legal scrutiny despite their profound societal impact.

Moreover, AI systems operate within complex digital ecosystems where responsibility is diffused across multiple actors, from developers to platform operators. This complicates enforcement, as identifying intent and causality in AI-driven manipulation is far from straightforward. Regulatory frameworks must, therefore, adapt to address these systemic challenges, moving beyond reactive enforcement toward proactive governance models that mitigate risks before they materialise. Without such recalibration, Article 5(1)(b) risks functioning as a nominal safeguard rather than a substantive check on exploitative AI practices.

7.3. The Constitutive Elements of a Prohibition against AI Targeting Your Vulnerabilities

Imagine an AI system seamlessly integrated into everyday life, from virtual assistants offering tailored recommendations[19] to algorithms guiding hiring decisions.[20] The promise of convenience and efficiency is enticing, but beneath the surface lies a darker reality: the risk of exploitation.[21] Some AI systems manipulate the traits that make individuals human – their age, abilities, or socioeconomic circumstances. As machine learning systems continuously adapt and evolve, they often acquire capabilities that were neither anticipated nor fully understood at their inception. This dynamic unpredictability means that the potential for harm can emerge or intensify long after developers deploy an AI system, underscoring the need for vigilance throughout its lifecycle.

Constitutive Elements of Article 5(1)(b)

1. **Placement on the Market, Use, or Deployment**
   - The AI system must be placed on the market, put into service, or used.
   - This criterion covers all stages of an AI system's lifecycle, from initial availability to practical deployment and everyday use.

---

2. **Exploitation of Vulnerabilities**
   - The AI system must exploit vulnerabilities specific to age, disability, or socioeconomic situations.
   - Vulnerabilities include:
     - **Age:** Tends to apply to the very young and the elderly, who may have cognitive or physical limitations.
     - **Disability:** Includes physical, mental, intellectual, or sensory impairments that hinder participation in society on an equal basis.
     - **Socioeconomic Situations:** Covers poverty, lack of education, or other disadvantages that increase susceptibility to manipulation.

3. **Material Distortion of Behaviour**
   - The exploitation must have the objective or effect of materially distorting behaviour.
   - This requires significant alteration of the decision-making process, impairing the individual's ability to make informed and autonomous choices.

4. **Significant Harm**
   - The distortion must cause significant harm, that is:
     - **Physical, Psychological, Financial, or Social**
     - **Substantial:** Beyond minor inconveniences or negligible impacts.
     - **Actual or Reasonably Likely to Occur:** Harm must be demonstrable or foreseeable.

The lifecycle of an AI system – from market introduction to daily use – demands vigilance at every stage. Harmful practices can emerge at any point, making continuous scrutiny essential. AI's interactions are often invisible and unregulated, posing risks beyond initial deployment. The first constitutive element ensures oversight extends across the system's existence, recognising AI's evolving nature and subtle, pervasive impact. This broad approach helps guard against harm throughout its lifecycle.

The second constitutive element focuses on exploiting vulnerabilities linked to age, disability, or socioeconomic circumstances, underscoring a critical responsibility to safeguard individuals who may lack the resilience to resist manipulative AI practices. Age, for instance, presents unique challenges at both ends of the spectrum: young children, whose cognitive development is incomplete, and elderly individuals, who may face physical or mental limitations, are susceptible to exploitation. Disability, defined expansively, encompasses a range of physical, mental, intellectual, and sensory impairments as recognised by the European Accessibility Act (EAA);[22] these impairments, when compounded by external barriers, can restrict individuals' full and equal participation in society, making robust protections essential to uphold their dignity and autonomy.[23]

The EAA further extends its protections to individuals facing functional limitations, recognising that these barriers are not always permanent. Elderly individuals, pregnant women, or even travellers managing heavy luggage are among those who stand to benefit from enhanced accessibility measures. By broadening the scope, the framework ensures that anyone experiencing physical, mental, intellectual, or sensory impairments – whether temporary or long-term – is safeguarded from restricted access to products and services. The CJEU defines disability as a 'long-term' impairment that impedes an individual's ability to access, participate in, or advance within professional life.[24] In parallel, socioeconomic disadvantages, such as poverty, limited education, or systemic inequality, are recognised as compounding factors that heighten vulnerability to exploitation and harm, demanding equally robust protections.[25]

The third constitutive element establishes that exploitation must aim to or effectively result in *materially distorting* the behaviour of an individual or group. In practice, this means the AI system must exert a significant influence over the decision-making process, undermining the ability of affected individuals to make informed and autonomous choices. Material distortion is not a trivial influence; it involves shaping behaviour so that individuals make decisions that diverge from those they would ordinarily make under normal circumstances.

The fourth and final element addresses the causation of *significant* harm. This harm can manifest physically, psychologically, financially, or socially. The AI Act expressly aims to prevent harm on a scale that justifies regulatory intervention, setting a clear threshold to distinguish minor inconveniences or negligible impacts from substantial and consequential effects. The harm must either exist or be reasonably likely to materialise for a violation, ensuring that the legal framework remains preventative and responsive.

Article 5(1)(b) confronts a reality that can feel uncomfortably close to home: the silent harm inflicted when advanced systems prey on human vulnerabilities. Picture a young graduate, the first in her family to attend university, excitedly applying for jobs only to find her applications filtered out by an algorithm trained to associate certain postcodes with lower socioeconomic prospects.[26] This example vividly encapsulates the risks posed by AI systems when entrenched biases infiltrate their design. Algorithms relying on postcode data as a proxy for socioeconomic status can inadvertently reinforce systemic inequalities, undermining the principle of meritocracy. For this young graduate, the postcode becomes a barrier to job opportunities and social mobility, perpetuating the disparities the technology was supposed to transcend. This scenario illustrates the need for robust regulatory frameworks to scrutinise AI systems' proxies and data sources, ensuring they do not perpetuate or amplify existing biases.

Alternatively, imagine a child with dyslexia using an educational AI that, rather than adapting to their needs, consistently grades them lower due to rigid parameters, gradually chipping away at their confidence and future aspirations.[27] These are not hypothetical risks but real scenarios that illustrate how AI, left unchecked, can exploit the very attributes that make us human – our age, abilities, or circumstances.[28] In the hands of poorly designed or deliberately manipulative systems, such exploitation deepens existing inequalities and entrenches systemic discrimination in critical areas that shape lives, such as education and employment.[29]

Article 5(1)(b) aims to prevent exploitation by setting clear boundaries for AI systems, but enforcing this prohibition presents significant challenges. Regulating deceptive design in AI is particularly difficult when the intent is unclear – whether a system is deliberately manipulative or unintentionally harmful, the impact remains the same. This distinction blurs further when AI-driven exploitation leads to systemic discrimination. For instance, AI trained on biased datasets may reinforce disparities in employment, education, or access to services, disproportionately harming marginalised groups and deepening societal inequalities. While Article 5(1)(b) is ambitious, its enforcement thresholds raise critical concerns. How severe must harm be before regulators intervene? Can they detect subtle yet pervasive manipulations embedded in complex AI architectures? AI systems exploit cognitive biases and distort decision-making, causing harm beyond individuals to societal structures and perpetuating discrimination and inequality. Yet, the high burden of proof required under Article 5(1)(b) may limit its effectiveness.

The following sections examine the legal framework underpinning Article 5(1)(b), highlighting its stringent requirements and their impact on enforcement. The provision does not clearly define 'material distortion,' leaving regulators to interpret it through other EU laws. Consumer protection law views material distortion as manipulation that pressures individuals into choices they wouldn't otherwise make, while competition law addresses distortions that subtly disadvantage consumers or competitors. In both cases, the focus is on substantial shifts in behaviour, often operating beneath the surface. This raises a troubling issue: the AI Act's high intervention threshold risks allowing subtle manipulations to go unchecked unless their effects are glaringly obvious. If harm remains diffuse or concealed within complex systems, it may escape scrutiny. As a result, while Article 5(1)(b) provides a strong conceptual safeguard, its practical impact may be far more limited.

7.3.1. Placing on the Market, the Putting into Service, or the Use of an AI System under Article 5(1)(b)

'Placing on the market' refers to the initial moment when an AI system becomes available within the EU, whether offered for sale or free. This concept applies to both physical products and digital services. Defined in Article 3(12) of the AI Act, the stage of placing on the market is pivotal as it activates the Act's regulatory framework, obliging providers to adhere to safety, transparency, and accountability standards. Providers must carry out conformity assessments, prepare comprehensive technical documentation, and ensure their AI systems comply with all relevant legal requirements before making them available to users in the Union. 'Putting into service' occurs when an AI system is supplied for first use to the deployer or directly implemented for its intended purpose within the EU. This stage includes deployment in real-world settings, such as businesses, public services, or organisations, marking the point at which the system begins interacting with its intended environment.

'Use' refers to the period during which the AI system is actively employed by end-users, encompassing all interactions between the system and individuals, businesses, or public entities. This ongoing phase demands continuous compliance with the AI Act, requiring providers and deployers to monitor and update the system to address emerging risks or maintain adherence to legal obligations. Throughout its lifecycle, the AI system must remain safe, transparent, and accountable, ensuring it meets the Act's standards at every stage of its operation.

7.3.2. Exploiting Vulnerabilities of a Natural Person, a Specific Group of Persons Due to their Age, Disability or a Specific Social or Economic Situation

The phrase 'exploits any of the vulnerabilities of a natural person or a specific group of persons due to their age, disability, or a specific social or economic situation' within Article 5(1)(b) of the AI Act addresses the exploitation of inherent traits that make specific individuals or groups particularly susceptible to manipulation by AI systems. These vulnerabilities are rooted in age, disability, or specific socioeconomic conditions, each presenting distinct risks when targeted by advanced technologies. However, this narrow framing leaves significant gaps in addressing the broader spectrum of manipulative practices that AI systems may employ.

The concept of 'vulnerabilities' encompasses a wide range of cognitive, emotional, and behavioural susceptibilities that impair an individual's capacity to make informed, autonomous decisions. Behavioural vulnerabilities, for instance, are linked to predictable patterns in an individual's behaviour that AI systems can analyse and manipulate. For example, an AI system monitoring purchasing habits might identify a wealthy older person prone to impulsive late-night purchases and target them with time-sensitive offers designed to exploit this behaviour. Similarly, cognitive or emotional vulnerabilities can be manipulated by systems that adapt their messaging to the user's mood or perceived state of mind, amplifying susceptibility to harm. These examples underscore the necessity of clearly defining vulnerabilities to establish adequate protections.

Insights from academic research, legislative frameworks,[30] and case law are critical to this endeavour.[31] However, Article 5(1)(b) narrows its focus to vulnerabilities explicitly linked to age, disability, or socio-economic conditions. While this targeted approach acknowledges these categories' significant impact on an individual's ability to resist or recognise manipulative practices, it excludes many other forms of harm. Malgieri and Rebrean suggest interpretations of vulnerability should extend to people and groups identifying as LGBTIA+.[32] However, neither Malgieri nor Rebrean establishes why this group, in particular, should be classified as vulnerable in the same sense as children, older people, and those living in extreme poverty. While their argument for expanding the interpretation of vulnerability is notable, it remains unclear how such an extension aligns with the AI Act's defined categories.

An example that starkly falls outside the scope of these protected vulnerabilities is addiction to digital platforms or online services, such as compulsive social media use or excessive gaming, where the behaviour lacks a direct connection to the categories defined by the Act.

> Consider a financially secure adult who becomes trapped in an endless cycle of scrolling on a social media platform. The system's infinite scroll design and dopamine-driven notifications compel them to spend hours engaging with content, leading to decreased productivity, strained relationships, and worsening mental health.

While the platform exploits behavioural patterns and psychological vulnerabilities, these traits lack an explicit connection to age, disability, or socioeconomic status. As such, even though the manipulation is evident, it arguably falls outside the prohibition's reach under Article 5(1)(b).

Now consider a child similarly affected by an addictive gaming app. By the same logic, while their age might suggest a potential link to a protected vulnerability, the harm caused by manipulative design patterns – such as gamified rewards that encourage prolonged play – would not necessarily meet the threshold of 'exploitation due to age.' Unless it can be proven that the system specifically targeted or manipulated the child's developmental stage, the child's compulsive gaming habit, though harmful and exploitative, might still evade the prohibition.

These scenarios reveal a significant limitation in Article 5(1)(b)'s framework. By confining the concept of vulnerability to specific categories, the provision excludes harmful practices that exploit psychological and behavioural traits unrelated to those categories, even when the resulting harm is profound. Such limitations raise questions about whether the regulation, as currently drafted, is adequately equipped to address the full spectrum of manipulative AI practices, particularly those that exploit vulnerabilities that the Act less clearly delineates.

However, in the context of Article 5(1)(b), 'vulnerabilities' only refer to conditions or characteristics that may impair an individual's capacity to make autonomous, well-informed choices. These include cognitive, emotional, and behavioural susceptibilities that AI systems can exploit to influence decisions or behaviours in ways that might cause harm. Identifying such vulnerabilities is critical to understanding how AI systems manipulate users, potentially leading to significant adverse outcomes. Behavioural vulnerabilities, for instance, stem from predictable patterns in human actions that sophisticated AI can detect and leverage. Consider an AI system that monitors user data, such as browsing or purchasing habits, and identifies wealthy elderly individuals prone to impulsive late-night spending. The system might then deploy targeted, time-sensitive offers to exploit this behaviour, amplifying the likelihood of decisions that the individual would not make under more reflective circumstances. While the concept of vulnerability can encompass a wide range of susceptibilities, the AI Act narrows its focus to those rooted in age, disability, and specific socioeconomic conditions. These categories reflect circumstances that significantly diminish a person's ability to resist or recognise manipulative practices.[33]

7.3.2.1. Age

Picture a child navigating a colourful online world filled with flashy advertisements and gamified content, where every tap or swipe nudges them toward more prolonged engagement and impulsive behaviour. Alternatively, imagine an older person grappling with a sleek AI-powered service that feels anything but intuitive, leaving them susceptible to scams or undue influence. These examples illuminate how age can create distinct vulnerabilities in the face of advanced AI systems, shaping the interaction and risks faced by society's youngest and oldest members. With their developing cognitive abilities, children often struggle to assess AI-driven interactions or the intent behind subliminal advertisements.[34] Elderly individuals, meanwhile, may encounter barriers in accessibility and usability, exposing them to coercive tactics or exploitation through complex technologies.[35]

The AI Act explicitly identifies age as a primary category of vulnerability, acknowledging the unique cognitive and emotional challenges faced by children and elderly individuals. By recognising the risks that arise from these limitations, Article 5(1)(b) aims to safeguard against manipulative AI practices that exploit age-related susceptibilities. The prohibition provides a legal foundation to ensure that AI systems respect the autonomy and dignity of individuals across the age spectrum. However, the nuances of these protections depend on a broader interplay of European and national legal frameworks aimed at combating age discrimination.

The EU has long pursued measures to protect individuals from age-based discrimination, blending EU directives, national laws, and international agreements.[36] The Employment Equality Directive, for example, mandates equal treatment in the workplace and requires Member States to adopt measures that prevent both direct and indirect age discrimination.[37] Such directives ensure a baseline of protection while empowering individual Member States to tailor their approaches to cultural, social, and legal contexts. This flexibility reflects the principle of subsidiarity, where decisions are made as close to the citizens they affect.[38] Germany, for instance, incorporates the Employment Equality Directive through its General Equal Treatment Act (AGG), which offers robust protections against age discrimination across employment and other sectors.[39] France integrates similar provisions into its Labour Code, ensuring equal treatment for workers of all ages.[40] Meanwhile, Italy expands protections by addressing the unique risks faced by children in media and advertising, ensuring alignment with EU consumer protection directives.[41] The CJEU's judgment in *Mangold v Helm* highlights the principle of non-discrimination on the grounds of age as a general principle of EU law, reinforcing the importance of protecting individuals from age-based discrimination.[42]

Expectations are growing for AI systems to align with legal protections to avoid exploiting age-related vulnerabilities, but the practicalities of meeting these expectations raise more questions than provide answers. For children, this ostensibly means creating clear, transparent, and age-appropriate AI interactions that steer clear of manipulative techniques that could disrupt their cognitive and emotional development. Yet, what constitutes 'transparent' for a child? How effectively can developers predict the developmental impact of seemingly benign features in games or educational tools? For older individuals, the challenge lies in creating interfaces that are genuinely accessible and intuitive. Designers often tout simplified navigation and larger text as solutions, but these surface-level adaptations may fail to address the more profound risks of coercion or exploitation. How does an accessible interface prevent an elderly user from being nudged toward predatory financial products subtly designed to appear as helpful tools? While Article 5(1)(b) promises to prevent the exploitation of age-related vulnerabilities, its delivery ability is far from guaranteed. The prohibition's broad language offers theoretical safeguards but relies heavily on interpretations of harm and manipulation that may fall short in practice. The framework aspires to protect cognitive and emotional well-being across generations but risks falling behind the subtle sophistication of AI-driven design.

7.3.2.2. Children

The EU defines and protects children through a framework of regulations, directives, and international agreements, balancing these measures with the diverse legal and cultural contexts of Member States. In line with the UNCRC, the EU broadly defines a child as anyone under 18. This standard is applied across various laws to ensure consistency. For instance, the GDPR includes specific provisions for children's data protection. Article 8 requires parental consent for information society services offered directly to children under 16, though Member States may lower this to 13.[43] Similarly, EU consumer protection laws identify children as particularly vulnerable, mandating that marketing and advertising practices avoid exploitation or manipulation.[44] The flexibility within EU law permits Member States to adapt to their distinct legal, social, and cultural contexts. Such an approach aligns with subsidiarity by ensuring that decisions are made at the local level whenever possible, with EU intervention occurring solely when Member States cannot achieve the objectives independently. States can implement stricter child protection measures provided they comply with overarching principles and minimum EU standards. The interaction between EU and national laws reflects a dual system of harmonisation and adaptability. Directives require transposition into national legislation, compelling Member States to align domestic laws with EU objectives. In contrast, regulations directly apply without transposition but may still necessitate national adjustments to ensure coherence and avoid conflicts. This balance provides a uniform baseline of protection for children across the EU while allowing for tailored responses to local needs within Member States.

7.3.2.3. Disability

Disability represents a pivotal category of vulnerability, encompassing a broad spectrum of physical, mental, intellectual, and sensory impairments. AI systems that fail to account for these diverse needs risk marginalising or even exploiting individuals with disabilities. Picture an AI-powered application requiring precise motor skills or rapid cognitive responses – such a design can exclude or frustrate users with physical or mental impairments, perpetuating their exclusion from digital environments. The implications of neglecting inclusivity are profound: technology intended to innovate and assist can instead deepen existing barriers. Legal frameworks have long recognised the vulnerabilities faced by individuals with disabilities and the need for proactive accommodations. The Employment Equality Directive explicitly prohibits disability discrimination in employment and other domains, mandating reasonable adjustments to ensure equal access and participation.[45] By defining disability as encompassing long-term impairments that hinder full social participation, the Directive adopts a progressive social model of disability. This perspective frames disability not simply as an individual limitation but as the result of societal barriers, highlighting the importance of removing obstacles and providing accommodations to level the playing field. For AI systems, this means designing with accessibility in mind and actively addressing diverse user needs during development.

The European Accessibility Act (EAA) takes this principle further by setting specific requirements for the accessibility of products and services, including AI systems. It mandates that developers design such technologies to accommodate a wide range of disabilities, ensuring usability for individuals with visual, hearing, motor, or cognitive impairments.[46] Key design principles include clear and understandable interfaces, alternative modes of interaction, and avoiding overly complex navigation.[47] By focusing on functional limitations, the EAA seeks to ensure that technology responds to real-world challenges faced by users with disabilities.[48] Central to the EAA is promoting a universal design philosophy – prioritising products and services usable by the broadest possible range of people, regardless of ability.[49] This approach moves beyond retrofitting existing systems to accommodate specific disabilities and emphasises accessibility as a core design feature. By adopting such principles, AI systems can empower individuals with disabilities, reducing the risks of manipulation and exclusion while enhancing autonomy and control over digital interactions. Combining these legal protections underscores an essential principle: inclusivity is not an afterthought but a cornerstone of equitable technological progress. For developers, it is a challenge and an opportunity to recognise diversity as integral to design and create systems that expand opportunities for all rather than reinforcing existing divides.

While the EAA and related frameworks offer a structured approach to protecting individuals with disabilities, the practical challenges of implementing such protections reveal a complex reality. Consider an AI-powered financial management tool that incorporates clear, accessible text and voice navigation to assist users with visual impairments. On the surface, this might meet the requirements for usability. But what if the system also employs persuasive techniques, such as urgency-based prompts, to encourage higher-risk financial decisions? The design may technically comply with accessibility requirements while subtly manipulating users with cognitive disabilities, exploiting their difficulties in processing complex information under pressure.

Similarly, picture an AI learning tool designed for users with motor impairments, complete with alternative interaction modes such as eye-tracking. While these features align with the principles of inclusivity, the system could still employ gamified feedback loops that incentivise prolonged use without considering the potential impact on users with attention-related cognitive conditions. In both scenarios, the design prioritises accessibility but allows more profound behavioural and psychological vulnerabilities to face exploitation.

These examples highlight the limits of relying solely on compliance for meaningful protection. The EAA's focus on functional accessibility is vital. However, it may not fully anticipate the nuanced ways in which AI systems can adapt to and exploit vulnerabilities beyond what is explicitly addressed by the law. The regulatory framework assumes that accessibility alone can mitigate harm, but this overlooks the broader, more insidious potential for manipulation embedded within the system's architecture. Without a more critical examination of how AI systems interact with the full spectrum of human vulnerabilities, the promise of inclusivity risks losing its effectiveness due to the very technologies it seeks to regulate.

7.3.2.4. *Specific Social or Economic Situation*

Those in disadvantaged socioeconomic positions often face systemic barriers and lower digital literacy, leaving them less equipped to identify and counteract exploitative AI behaviour.[50] An AI system that exploits these vulnerabilities aims to materially distort decision-making processes, leading individuals to take actions they might not have taken if they were fully informed and autonomous. Article 5(1)(b) explicitly mandates scrutiny of such AI systems, requiring them to avoid practices that manipulate socioeconomic vulnerabilities. However, achieving this goal in practice involves addressing deeply embedded biases and structural inequalities that AI systems risk perpetuating.

Article 5(1)(b) aims to prevent AI from worsening financial inequalities or systemic injustices by targeting vulnerabilities linked to socioeconomic status. Predictive algorithms, for instance, might direct low-income individuals toward predatory financial products, deepening their economic struggles. Similarly, AI-driven loan assessments may rely on proxies like postcodes, employment history, or education, unintentionally disadvantaging ethnic groups historically affected by systemic inequality. Low-income postcodes could trigger higher interest rates, while employment records shaped by discrimination may lead to unfavourable loan terms. Job recruitment tools present another risk, as AI-driven systems may assign lower salaries to candidates from disadvantaged backgrounds, reinforcing existing inequities. By embedding systemic biases, these systems risk entrenching the disparities they should mitigate. Migrants and refugees face additional vulnerabilities due to precarious socioeconomic and legal conditions. AI in immigration control or social services must account for these complexities to prevent discriminatory outcomes. Proxies like employment history or housing stability may unintentionally reflect protected characteristics such as ethnicity or nationality. Under EU equality law, organisations must actively address indirect discrimination to prevent reinforcing historical injustices.[51]

Consider a low-income individual repeatedly targeted by an AI-powered financial advice tool recommending high-interest payday loans. The system's algorithm, trained on socioeconomic data and behavioural patterns, identifies this person's economic desperation and delivers 'solutions' framed as immediate relief but with long-term consequences. While the system's operation highlights the exploitation of socioeconomic vulnerabilities, proving that such practices fall under Article 5(1)(b) demands nuanced analysis and evidentiary precision, especially when the harm is subtle and cumulative rather than overtly coercive. Imagine a scenario involving an AI recruitment tool relying on proxies like employment history and educational attainment to evaluate candidates. A refugee whose employment record is marked by gaps or whose qualifications are from an unrecognised institution might be sidelined – not due to explicit bias but because the system utilises features reflecting deeply ingrained inequities. The consequences – diminished opportunities and perpetuated barriers to mobility – emerge as an unintended outcome of choices embedded within the design of an AI system.

These examples illuminate a critical tension within Article 5(1)(b): its framework may struggle to address the intricate and multi-layered forms of exploitation that AI systems can facilitate. The regulation risks overlooking how structural inequalities are encoded and amplified in technological processes by focusing on narrowly defined vulnerabilities. Such limitations prompt a deeper examination of whether the existing legal framework can effectively engage with the broader societal dynamics that underlie these systems. Without an expanded understanding of vulnerability and the implications of design, the regulation's capacity to promote fairness and equity may remain unfulfilled, leaving those most susceptible to the impacts of AI systems inadequately protected.

7.3.3. Objective or Effect of Materially Distorting Behaviour of a Person or a Group of Persons

The previous chapter explored the meaning of 'material distortion' in detail, focusing on its implications for Article 5(1)(b) and the challenges of applying such a standard. While the concept appears to offer a safeguard against harmful AI practices, its application introduces complexity that makes it far from accessible to the average person. The requirement to assess measurable changes in behaviour or decision-making assumes technical expertise and resources that most individuals, particularly those already vulnerable, do not possess. Expecting users to identify and prove how an AI system has materially altered their actions creates a significant barrier to redress.

The threshold of material distortion may also fail to capture the insidious nature of many manipulative practices. The examples discussed in this chapter – AI systems targeting women returning to the workforce, emotionally vulnerable therapy users, or teenagers navigating mental health struggles – often operate subtly, influencing behaviours over time in ways that may not immediately manifest as drastic shifts. If the test for material distortion requires evidence of overt, measurable harm, it risks overlooking the more gradual and systemic forms of manipulation characterising many modern AI systems. Moreover, focusing solely on behaviour changes risks a narrow view of manipulation, neglecting how system architecture and design create environments that nudge users toward specific outcomes. The concept of material distortion, as it stands, appears to prioritise overt impact while leaving the subtler, cumulative effects of dark patterns and deceptive design unchecked. Such an approach prompts a critical evaluation of whether Article 5(1)(b) can genuinely fulfil its promise to prevent harmful AI practices or if its high thresholds render it more of a theoretical safeguard than a practical tool.

The analytical challenges expand significantly when assessing material distortion in a group context. The concept requires examining collective behaviour patterns to determine whether an AI system has substantially influenced the decisions or actions of a group. This analysis hinges on techniques like statistical evaluation of large datasets to detect changes in behaviours or outcomes directly connecting to the system. For example, an AI system implemented in an educational setting to recommend study materials might appear beneficial on the surface. However, a deeper analysis of academic performance and study habits across a cohort before and after the system's introduction could uncover shifts that raise concerns. If a significant portion of the group demonstrates altered behaviour or outcomes that align with the system's design, this may point to material distortion at the group level.

Nevertheless, the requirement to establish material distortion for groups introduces additional layers of complexity. Patterns of manipulation are often subtle and cumulative, making them difficult to quantify in ways that meet the high evidentiary thresholds of Article 5(1)(b). For instance, if a customer service AI disproportionately steers lower-income users toward higher-cost services, this behaviour may not immediately manifest as blatant exploitation. Instead, the influence might emerge incrementally, only becoming apparent through extensive data aggregation and trend analysis. Even then, drawing a direct line between the AI system's actions and group-level distortion may prove elusive, as these systems often operate within environments shaped by broader socioeconomic and systemic inequalities.

The reliance on aggregated data and statistical tools to identify group-level distortion underscores a significant gap in the provision's accessibility. Conducting such analyses requires technical expertise and resources that exceed the reach of most affected individuals or groups. These limitations provoke critical reflection on whether Article 5(1)(b) provides a robust safeguard against group-level manipulation or if its thresholds inadvertently protect harmful practices by making enforcement impractical. By focusing narrowly on measurable outcomes, the provision risks overlooking the structural and architectural mechanisms that drive these manipulative influences, leaving the systemic roots of distortion unaddressed.

'Materially distorting behaviour' encompasses manipulation that impairs decision-making in a manner that causes or is reasonably likely to undermine an individual's autonomy. This standard is particularly relevant when AI systems employ psychological profiling to promote harmful products to vulnerable individuals or groups, creating a profound imbalance in decision-making. For instance, a cosmetic surgery clinic's AI system analyses an individual's browsing history and emotional indicators to pinpoint insecurities about their appearance. It strategically delivers targeted ads for invasive procedures during heightened vulnerability, presenting these procedures as solutions to self-worth while obscuring the risks and long-term consequences. The deliberate timing and messaging in these ads intentionally exploit emotional insecurities, shaping behaviour in ways that individuals may struggle to resist or even perceive.

Similarly, an AI system that monitors private messages and online activity to detect grief preys on the emotional distress of those mourning the loss of a loved one. By targeting them with advertisements for exploitative 'memory services', such as costly and unproven digital afterlife products, the system manipulates their decisions through guilt and pain. The influence is calculated and insidious, driving choices that may not align with the individual's rational preferences under normal circumstances.[52] Another example involves an AI system used by a fertility clinic, which tracks menstrual app data and online searches to identify women struggling with infertility. The system exploits their deeply personal pain by flooding them with ads for expensive, experimental treatments, omitting key details about risks or limited chances of success. In doing so, it pressures them into emotionally and financially precarious decisions, amplifying the distress they are already experiencing.[53]

In each of these scenarios, the distortion operates on both behavioural and informational levels, leveraging specific vulnerabilities to influence choices in ways that compromise autonomy and informed decision-making. The requirement under Article 5(1)(b) is to demonstrate that material distortion appears on the surface and to address such manipulative practices. However, the inherent challenge lies in proving that these AI systems caused or were reasonably likely to cause significant behavioural shifts in a manner that meets the high thresholds established by the provision. The examples reveal how AI systems can exert subtle yet powerful forms of influence, blurring the lines of manipulation in ways that may evade the evidentiary demands of material distortion.

7.3.4. Individuals vs Groups of Persons and the Expected Standard in Individual Cases

For individuals, the concern with manipulative AI practices lies in the erosion of personal autonomy and the disruption of decision-making processes. AI systems that exploit vulnerabilities or employ subliminal techniques can profoundly and immediately affect the individuals they target. Consider an AI-driven mental health app that inadvertently amplifies an elderly patient's anxiety by reinforcing negative thought patterns. Such a scenario directly impacts the individual's psychological well-being, leading to significant distress or behavioural changes that harm their overall quality of life.

Evaluating harm at the individual level requires a meticulous, case-by-case analysis focused on how much the AI system undermines autonomy and causes direct consequences. Key considerations include the system's transparency, the user's awareness of its influence, and the severity of the harm experienced. For example, an AI system using covert techniques to influence a user's purchasing decisions, resulting in severe financial loss or emotional distress, breaches the integrity of the person's autonomy. Such cases demand scrutiny to assess whether the system's design and operation disproportionately affect vulnerable persons or exploit their circumstances.

In contrast, when assessing harm to groups, the focus shifts to systemic impacts and the broader implications for the affected population. AI systems targeting socioeconomically disadvantaged groups or specific demographics can entrench inequalities and amplify biases on a societal level. Imagine an AI-powered loan approval system that, due to biased training data, disproportionately rejects applications from minority communities. Beyond the individual rejections, the aggregate harm manifests in diminished financial stability and reduced opportunities for the group. The algorithm's reliance on proxies like socioeconomic indicators linked to race or ethnicity may inadvertently perpetuate discriminatory outcomes. Harm at the group level is often more diffuse but no less significant in its societal repercussions. Evaluating such harm requires analysing patterns of aggregate disadvantage, often through statistical analysis and qualitative insights. For instance, assessing approval rates across demographic groups can uncover systemic biases perpetuating disparities. This approach demands understanding how seemingly neutral algorithmic decisions can have far-reaching and inequitable consequences.

Legal and regulatory frameworks must adopt a dual lens to protect individuals and groups. Individual harm necessitates a granular and personalised approach, ensuring AI systems respect autonomy and mitigate direct harm. Group harm, on the other hand, requires systemic safeguards to address aggregate disparities and prevent the entrenchment of biases. Recital 29 of the AI Act underscores that these prohibitions are effect-based rather than intent-based, highlighting the need to examine the inherent risks posed by the design and deployment of AI systems, regardless of the provider's motivations. For vulnerable individuals, designing and deploying AI systems must prioritise clarity in operation and uphold the integrity of their decision-making processes, ensuring interactions reinforce autonomy rather than subtly erode it. For vulnerable groups, the focus on systemic safeguards reflects an effort to address deep-seated disparities, guiding AI systems toward outcomes that uphold fairness and mitigate structural inequalities across diverse societal contexts.

Regulators and developers face the intricate task of navigating the intersection of individual and collective harm, where the impacts of AI systems diverge yet remain deeply interconnected. Consider an AI hiring tool that rejects a neurodivergent individual for their unconventional career path while reinforcing systemic biases that disadvantage entire communities with similar traits. On one level, it denies a single person an opportunity; on another, it entrenches exclusion for the whole group, deepening the inequities the system claims to address. Crafting protections that account for the intimate, personal consequences and the sweeping, systemic effects should demand a framework that transcends mere compliance, grappling instead with the profound societal shifts these technologies provoke. Such an approach must address the manipulative dynamics embedded in deceptive design and the opaque structures of system architecture, which can obscure intent and amplify harm, often before users or regulators even realise the extent of the exploitation.

7.3.5. Reasonably Likely to Cause Significant Harm to that Person, Another Person or a Group of Persons

The impacts of significant harm in AI systems ripple across the physical, psychological, financial, and social realms, touching every facet of human experience with potentially profound consequences. For vulnerable populations, these harms intensify due to their heightened susceptibility to exploitation. The legal standard of 'reasonableness' demands evaluating whether such damage was foreseeable and whether sufficient measures actively addressed the risk to prevent it. However, the practicalities of applying this standard are complex when harm arises from subtle manipulations embedded within AI design. Consider the following example:

> An AI system that uses personal data to identify elderly users and inundates them with advertisements for costly medical treatments or health supplements can cause significant financial and psychological harm. Older adults, particularly those with cognitive impairments, may not have the same capacity to assess these advertisements, leading to economic exploitation and anxiety about their health.

At first glance, such targeted advertising may seem tailored and personalised, but its more profound ramifications unveil a troubling reality. Many elderly individuals, particularly those with cognitive impairments, may struggle to assess these advertisements critically. The outcome? Financial exploitation and escalating anxiety – savings drained on unnecessary products and an intensifying fixation on health concerns, fuelled by a system deceptively designed to tailor manipulative messaging. The AI system's deployment exploits the vulnerability of age and diminished cognitive function, resulting in decisions that can deplete financial resources and cause psychological distress. The significance of the harm lies in the profound impact on the individual's economic stability and mental health. Financially, the erosion of savings or accumulation of debt from purchasing unnecessary or ineffective products can destabilise livelihoods and perpetuate cycles of financial insecurity. Psychologically, constant exposure to health-related fears exacerbated by manipulative advertising can lead to increased stress, anxiety, and a diminished quality of life. Given older adults' known vulnerabilities, it is reasonable to expect that targeting this group with aggressive marketing for high-cost products could lead to significant harm.

Recital 29 clarifies that providers and deployers cannot evade accountability by claiming a lack of intent. Responsibility is based on the system's effects, not malice. Those who design or deploy an AI system remain accountable if it exploits vulnerabilities – deliberately or negligently. This underscores the necessity of proactive diligence: impact assessments, monitoring, and transparency are not optional but essential to mitigating risks. However, the issue extends beyond individual harm.

When AI systems exploit group vulnerabilities, they reinforce structural inequities. For example, a biased loan approval algorithm may disproportionately reject applicants from low-income neighbourhoods. The immediate harm is financial exclusion, but the broader effect is the entrenchment of economic disparities, perpetuating cycles of disadvantage. Addressing these challenges requires a dual approach: at the individual level, ensuring AI systems respect autonomy and minimise direct harm; at the systemic level, detecting patterns of exploitation through rigorous statistical and qualitative analysis. This interplay between individual and collective harm underscores the need for safeguards that evolve alongside AI capabilities.

Consider an AI-powered language tutoring app for children. It adapts lessons based on engagement patterns and rewards progress through increasingly demanding performance metrics. While seemingly beneficial, this gamified system can create undue pressure, leading to frustration, stress, and diminished self-esteem. Despite actual psychological harm, would this meet Article 5(1)(b)'s threshold of 'reasonably likely to cause *significant* harm'? Likely not. The app does not explicitly target a protected vulnerability like age for exploitation, nor does it cause immediate financial or physical harm. Yes, its effects might be diffuse, falling below the threshold for legal intervention. This reveals a critical blind spot in AI regulation. The framework prioritises quantifiable, immediate harm, overlooking how manipulative designs subtly erode well-being over time. Without a more nuanced approach, many exploitative practices may continue unchecked, leaving individuals exposed to pervasive but unregulated forms of AI-driven manipulation.

7.4. Interpreting Articles 5(1)(a) and (b): Subliminal Manipulation and Vulnerable Groups

The interplay between Articles 5(1)(a) and 5(1)(b) highlights the nuanced challenges of regulating manipulation and its consequences. Article 5(1)(a) zeroes in on unconscious manipulation, requiring evidence of subliminal or covert techniques that distort behaviour without an individual's awareness. This focus presents unique complexities, as it demands identifying such techniques and proof of their influence on decision-making. By contrast, Article 5(1)(b) addresses exploitation tied to identifiable vulnerabilities – age, disability, or socioeconomic circumstances – but with a similarly rigorous requirement to demonstrate significant harm.

Unconscious manipulation under Article 5(1)(a) presents intricate challenges surrounding the nature of perception and influence. Techniques designed to operate beneath conscious awareness are difficult to delineate, as the boundaries between awareness and unawareness are static and universally defined. Individual susceptibility to subtle cues varies significantly, further complicating efforts to establish clear regulatory standards. As AI systems evolve, their ability to interpret and react to granular behavioural data adds another layer of complexity, raising fundamental questions about the integrity of decision-making. For example, an AI system leveraging imperceptible design elements in advertising to steer preferences may push the boundaries of acceptable influence. Can such interactions truly support autonomy, or do they veer into coercion disguised as suggestion?

Defining subliminal techniques under Article 5(1)(a) is no less complex. By design, these influences elude conscious detection, but their impact needs to be uniform. What may register as manipulative for one individual might escape the notice of another entirely. AI systems further disrupt this landscape by dynamically adapting their methods to the unique behavioural traits of users, tailoring their approach to maximise effect. These hyper-personalised strategies make it harder to draw fixed lines around permissible influence. Regulators must adopt dynamic responses attuned to AI's fluid and evolving capabilities, ensuring protections that adapt alongside technological advancements.

Thus, Article 5(1)(b) shifts focus from awareness to vulnerability, encompassing individuals and groups with less capacity to resist exploitation. For instance, predatory lending algorithms often disproportionately target socioeconomically disadvantaged populations with high-interest loan offers. While these systems might not rely on subliminal manipulation, their exploitation of financial desperation could lead to cascading harm – spiralling debt, housing instability, and deteriorating mental health. However, proving significant harm in such cases is no small feat. It requires demonstrating a clear and foreseeable connection between the AI system's design and the outcomes it produces, often amidst a web of contributory factors.

For children, the risks posed by manipulation are particularly acute. Lacking the cognitive maturity to evaluate persuasive content, they are especially susceptible to AI systems designed to exploit their attention. Consider an AI-driven educational game that penalises a child for failure while tying progress to microtransactions. While the immediate harm might appear modest – financial loss for the parent or frustration for the child – the cumulative impact on self-esteem and emotional resilience can be profound. Nevertheless, under Article 5(1)(b), such scenarios might evade prohibition if the harm falls short of the legal threshold despite the long-term consequences for the child's development.

Recent work focuses on the impact of design choices on society's youngest members. Platforms like TikTok and other infinite-scrolling services offer significant appeal but contribute to excessive screen time and potential adverse effects on well-being. I am increasingly concerned about what these services are doing to children. The following table provides a non-exhaustive list of deceptive design tactics minors commonly encounter in digital environments and descriptions of each technique. While EU legislation provides a foundation for addressing these tactics, the regulatory framework grapples with persistent and significant challenges. Enforcement mechanisms often need to be revised, limiting the practical reach of existing laws. Investigating these sophisticated tactics demands specialised expertise, creating barriers to effective oversight. Additionally, gaps in the scope of current regulations allow many manipulative practices to evade scrutiny altogether. These limitations expose minors as deceptive design continues to exploit their developmental vulnerabilities unchecked.

Table 7.1 Common Deceptive Design Tactics Targeting Minors in Digital Environments

Deceptive Design Tactic	Description
Push Notifications and Instant Alerts	Platforms use frequent notifications to exploit children's FOMO, disrupting focus and encouraging repeated engagement, leading to prolonged screen time and dependency.[54]
Variable Rewards and Loot Boxes	Games use loot boxes and randomised rewards to mimic gambling mechanics, enticing children with unexpected wins. This design fosters compulsive behaviours and excessive spending, as children may not grasp the real-world cost.[55]
Misleading Visual Cues and Interface Manipulations	Platforms use bright visuals, animations, and misleading navigation to steer children toward actions like in-app purchases or data sharing. These cues exploit their sensitivity to visual stimuli, making distinguishing genuine choices from manipulation harder.[56]
Subscription Traps and Obstructive Cancellations	Platforms use 'subscription traps' to lure children into free trials that auto-renew into paid services. They complicate cancellations by requiring phone calls or redirecting users to retention-focused pages, trapping minors in financial commitments they may not fully understand.[57]
Addictive Design in Gaming and Social Media	Social media and gaming platforms use addictive design features like autoplay, infinite scrolling, and gamified rewards to keep children engaged. These tactics exploit psychological vulnerabilities, fostering excessive screen time, diminished self-regulation, and potential mental health issues like anxiety and poor impulse control.[58]
Gambling-like Features and In-Game Purchases	Many games incorporate gambling-like features, such as loot boxes and virtual currencies for in-game purchases. These elements exploit minors' need for financial literacy, encouraging them to spend impulsively without realising the actual costs.[59]

(continued)

Table 7.1 *(Continued)*

Deceptive Design Tactic	Description
Algorithmic Personalisation and AI-Driven Targeting	Platforms increasingly use AI-driven personalisation to tailor content and advertisements, adapting based on children's behavioural data. Such practices create a feedback loop that encourages compulsive engagement, often without children's informed consent. EU regulations currently lack specific protections against these AI-driven manipulative tactics.[60]
Social Validation and Peer Comparison	Social media platforms use likes, shares, and follower counts to encourage children's engagement and dependency on social approval. These mechanisms foster a validation-driven usage cycle that undermines self-worth and mental health, contributing to anxiety and low self-esteem among young users.[61]
Photo Editing and Filters for Social Approval	Platforms offer editing tools and filters that align with social trends, subtly encouraging children to alter their appearance to meet perceived standards. This tactic can distort self-image, exacerbating body image issues and promoting unrealistic social comparisons.[62]
Artificial Scarcity and Urgency Prompts	Techniques like countdown timers and limited-time offers create a false sense of urgency, pressuring children into making immediate decisions. These tactics often lead to impulsive purchases or actions, exploiting children's fear of missing out.[63]
Dopamine Hits from 'Likes' and Notifications	Social interactions, such as likes and comments, create dopamine-driven feedback loops that foster dependency on platform engagement. These cycles encourage children to seek continuous social approval, leading to potential anxiety and a reliance on external validation.[64]

(continued)

Table 7.1 *(Continued)*

Deceptive Design Tactic	Description
In-App Purchases and 'Freemium' Traps	Many free apps entice children to make in-app purchases to enhance their experience or advance in games. Children often need to realise the financial implications, as these purchases exploit their limited understanding of digital economies.[65]
Constant Distractions through Multi-Tasking Encouragement	Platforms keep children engaged in a constant loop by sending notifications, messages, and alerts across multiple apps. These practices disrupt focus, fragment attention, and encourage prolonged screen time, negatively affecting productivity and well-being.[66]
Autoplay and Infinite Scrolling	Features like autoplay and endless scrolling reduce natural stopping points, making it challenging for children to disengage. This design encourages extended use, which impacts sleep and overall mental health.[67]
Data Collection and Profiling	Platforms collect extensive data on children's interactions, creating detailed profiles that inform targeted engagement and advertising. Children unknowingly contribute personal data, which may be sold to third parties or used to manipulate their behaviours further.[68]
Inadequate Transparency and Consent Mechanisms	Consent prompts are often simplified to expedite agreement, encouraging children to share data without fully understanding its implications. These mechanisms conflict with children's best interests by prioritising ease of consent over informed choice.[69]

Not all these deceptive design techniques are AI-powered or fall directly under Article 5(1)(a) or (b). However, their purpose is clear – they are designed to influence behaviour. The concern is when and how they exploit individuals at their most vulnerable. Platforms driven by engagement and profit strategically deploy these tactics during emotional distress, cognitive fatigue, or developmental susceptibility. Whether through subliminal messaging, compulsive gamification, or manipulative prompts, the outcome remains the same: an erosion of autonomy that disproportionately impacts the most impressionable users.

Older individuals also face digital exploitation, mainly due to reduced cognitive capacity or lower digital literacy. AI-driven marketing bombards elderly users with health scare tactics, pressuring them into purchasing unnecessary medical treatments. These practices drain financial resources and heighten psychological distress, especially among those already experiencing isolation. While the harm is evident, proving it stems directly from an AI system rather than external factors presents a significant enforcement challenge under the Act.

Determining whether an AI system targets individuals or groups with subliminal techniques under Article 5(1)(a) requires a detailed and nuanced approach distinct from that of Article 5(1)(b). While both provisions focus on manipulation, Article 5(1)(a) explicitly addresses tactics that operate beneath the surface of conscious awareness. This emphasis on covert influence raises unique interpretative challenges, particularly in defining, identifying, and evaluating subliminal manipulation and its consequences. The very definition of *subliminal techniques* is fraught with complexity. These methods function below the threshold of conscious perception, but the precise location of this threshold requires universal agreement. People's capacities for detecting subtle cues vary widely, making it difficult to establish a consistent standard. AI technologies only deepen this ambiguity. Advanced systems that leverage behavioural micro-patterns often operate in a grey area, where users may be partially aware of an influence but unable to recognise or resist it fully. These blurred lines complicate efforts to regulate and enforce prohibitions against subliminal techniques.

Demonstrating that an AI system employs subliminal manipulation introduces additional layers of complexity. Assessing whether an AI's subtle cues meet the criteria for unconscious influence requires deep technical expertise and interdisciplinary collaboration. For instance, evaluating whether fleeting visual stimuli qualify as subliminal demands insights from psychology, neuroscience, and computational analysis, often exceeding the available resources and methodologies. As AI systems grow increasingly sophisticated in tailoring and adapting manipulative techniques, delineating permissible from impermissible influence becomes progressively intricate. Regulators must confront these evolving dynamics to ensure that Article 5(1)(a)'s safeguards remain effective against emerging forms of covert manipulation.

A central challenge in interpreting Article 5(1)(a) lies in establishing causation and behavioural impact. The prohibition requires demonstrating that subliminal techniques used by an AI system either altered behaviour significantly or were likely to do so. Proving such claims necessitates establishing a direct causal relationship between the AI system's covert outputs and meaningful changes in user actions. However, human behaviour rarely operates in isolation, influenced by external factors. Untangling the specific impact of subliminal manipulation demands experimental precision and rigorous statistical methodologies – endeavours that are both resource-intensive and prone to ambiguity.

Determining the threshold for a 'significant' behavioural change adds another layer of complexity. For one observer, a minor adjustment in consumer preferences might suffice if it stems from unperceived influence. At the same time, another might reserve significance for transformations with broader consequences, such as shifts in health-related decisions or financial stability. The absence of a universal standard leaves room for subjective interpretation, complicating enforcement and consistency in application.

Equally intricate is the interpretation of 'significant harm' outlined in the Article. Harm is multifaceted, encompassing physical, psychological, financial, and social dimensions. Vulnerable populations – such as children, older adults, individuals with disabilities, or those facing socioeconomic disadvantages – are particularly susceptible. Their unique susceptibilities magnify the risks posed by subliminal tactics, turning seemingly benign influences into profound disruptions. For example, a child's impressionability can make them unable to critically assess persuasive content, leading to decisions with far-reaching consequences for their development and well-being.

To interpret *significant harm* under Articles 5(1)(a) and 5(1)(b), regulators must confront complex, interwoven challenges. The interplay between subliminal manipulation and exploitation of vulnerabilities is particularly striking when applied to real-world scenarios, such as the pervasive targeting of children with unhealthy food advertisements via AI systems.

> AI systems using subliminal techniques to target children with unhealthy food advertisements could significantly harm their health.

Article 5(1)(a) raises questions about whether the system employs subliminal techniques – does it use rapid visual cues or mood-based targeting that bypasses a child's conscious awareness? If so, regulators must assess whether the advertising distorts behaviour by embedding subtle prompts to crave and purchase these products. The difficulty lies in identifying whether such techniques operate below a child's threshold of conscious perception and, crucially, proving a direct causal link to their purchasing decisions or dietary habits. Under Article 5(1)(b), the analysis shifts to whether these practices exploit age-specific vulnerabilities. Children's limited cognitive maturity and developmental stage make them susceptible to engaging with bright visuals, gamified rewards, or targeted peer-validation tactics.

However, does the exploitation of these vulnerabilities rise to the level of harm envisioned by the provision? I think we all agree that the harm is not limited to immediate physical effects but can also lead to long-term issues like obesity, diabetes, and psychological disorders related to body image and self-esteem. Nevertheless, is this a *significant harm?* While the cumulative effects of poor dietary choices might lead to considerable health issues, such as obesity or diabetes, the connection between the AI system's influence and these long-term outcomes may be too diffuse or indirect to meet the legal threshold.

Another key challenge lies in establishing causation and identifying behavioural shifts significant enough to meet the threshold of *material* distortion. For the prohibition to apply under 5(1)(a), regulators must show that subliminal techniques employed by an AI system have directly influenced individuals' behaviour in a way that constitutes significant harm. This demands a clear causal relationship between the system's outputs and the resulting behavioural changes, an endeavour complicated by the myriad factors shaping human decision-making. Separating the impact of subliminal manipulation from other external influences often requires rigorous experimental methodologies and sophisticated statistical tools – resources that may not always be accessible or conclusive.

Deciding what qualifies as a 'distortion' adds yet another layer of complexity. Behavioural changes can range from minor adjustments in purchasing habits to profound alterations in health or financial decisions. For one observer, a slight shift in consumer preference might represent sufficient distortion if driven by covert manipulation. At the same time, another might argue that only more substantial outcomes – such as financial ruin or significant health risks – justify intervention. This interpretative ambiguity leaves room for subjective judgment, which risks uneven enforcement of the prohibition. The clause 'in a manner that causes or is reasonably likely to cause that person, another person, or group of persons significant harm' further complicates matters, demanding a nuanced understanding of how AI systems can exploit vulnerabilities and the spectrum of harm that may result. The assessment must go beyond recognising manipulation to exploring its tangible consequences. Significant harm in this context encompasses many physical, psychological, financial, and social outcomes, each manifesting differently depending on the affected group's vulnerabilities.

The risks are acute for children. Their limited cognitive development makes them prime targets for manipulative techniques that bypass critical thinking. A gamified advertisement promoting unhealthy food, for instance, may seem trivial at first glance but could lead to unhealthy eating habits, contributing to obesity or other long-term health issues. Though initially subtle, these harms may cascade over time, affecting individual well-being and broader public health.

Elderly individuals, too, face distinct challenges. Diminished digital literacy and cognitive decline often leave them ill-equipped to discern manipulative marketing tactics or scams. For example, targeted ads offering 'exclusive' health products at inflated prices prey on financial insecurity and health anxieties. The harm here is not only economic – depleting limited resources – but also psychological, compounding feelings of isolation and vulnerability that already afflict many in this demographic.

> An AI system exploits age-based vulnerabilities by pushing expensive medical treatments or unnecessary insurance policies, which can cause significant financial harm. This can lead to loss of savings, increased debt, and emotional distress.

Determining significant financial harm goes beyond monetary loss; it requires considering its broader impact. A billionaire losing €100,000 faces a minor inconvenience, while a €100 loss for someone at the poverty line can mean missing essentials like food or medicine. The contrast is stark: one loss is abstract, the other life-altering, leading to psychological distress and long-term hardship. The issue is the amount lost and its effect on vulnerability and survival. This complicates regulatory assessments, demanding a framework that accounts for absolute loss and its real-world impact on individuals' lives. People with disabilities similarly encounter heightened risks. AI systems that fail to account for accessibility needs can frustrate or exclude, while those that actively exploit disabilities amplify harm.

> A chatbot promising mental health support but reinforcing negative thought patterns.

People with disabilities face a double burden when interacting with AI systems: the risk of exclusion from inaccessible designs and the profound harm caused by exploitative practices. Consider a chatbot advertised as offering mental health support but subtly reinforcing negative thought patterns through biased or poorly calibrated algorithms. For someone managing depression or anxiety, such a system does not merely fail to help – it deepens the very challenges it claims to address, potentially exacerbating feelings of hopelessness or despair. The harm here is not abstract; it manifests as intensified psychological distress, reduced self-worth, and diminished capacity to seek further support. These outcomes raise pressing questions: how can regulators ensure AI systems genuinely assist rather than exploit? Moreover, when does a system's failure to account for accessibility cross the line into active harm?

These examples illustrate how harm can ripple across multiple dimensions for vulnerable groups, often magnifying pre-existing inequalities. The challenge for regulators lies in determining how far-reaching and severe these harms must be to warrant intervention. Should subtle but pervasive psychological impacts on children, for example, hold as much regulatory weight as the overt financial exploitation of elderly individuals? This interplay of subjective judgment and varied harm thresholds highlights the difficulty of applying Article 5(1)(a) and (b) to diverse real-world scenarios.

7.5. The Interplay between the Prohibitions under Article 5(1)(a) and (b)

The interplay between Article 5(1)(a) and Article 5(1)(b) of the AI Act highlights the challenges of regulating manipulative AI practices that exploit individuals' vulnerabilities or manipulate their behaviour without conscious awareness. While the provisions aim to address distinct forms of exploitation, they must also account for scenarios where the effect of manipulation, irrespective of intent, creates significant harm.

Article 5(1)(a) focuses on techniques operating below the threshold of conscious awareness, such as subliminal messages or other covert manipulations. The key element is not the intent behind these techniques but their capacity to influence behaviour to bypass rational scrutiny. For example, an AI system embedding nearly imperceptible visual cues to nudge consumers toward specific purchasing decisions falls squarely under this provision because the system's design creates an unconscious influence that undermines autonomy. The emphasis here is on how the manipulation operates, not on whether designers deliberately made it to deceive.

Similarly, Article 5(1)(b) addresses exploitation through the effect on individuals' vulnerabilities, whether linked to age, disability, or socio-economic circumstances. The critical factor is the harm caused by these manipulations, regardless of whether the exploitation was intentional or an incidental consequence of the AI system's design. For instance, an AI-driven financial advice platform that disproportionately recommends high-risk investments to elderly users with diminished cognitive capacity – whether due to deliberate exploitation or the algorithm's reliance on data correlations – may result in significant harm by erasing financial security and heightened anxiety. The harm arises from the system's effect, not merely its design or intent.

This distinction between method and effect underscores a crucial aspect of both provisions: intent is not the determinative criterion. AI systems can generate harmful outcomes even when designed without overtly malicious intent, and the focus must remain on the consequences of their deployment. For instance, an AI recruitment tool that disproportionately disfavours applicants from socioeconomically disadvantaged backgrounds, not due to deliberate bias but because of entrenched data correlations, exemplifies how systemic effects can perpetuate harm. Such outcomes fall within the remit of Article 5(1)(b) because the exploitation of socioeconomic vulnerability emerges in the result, even without explicit intent.

The absence of intent as a requisite factor challenges traditional approaches to regulation, which often hinge on proving deliberate wrongdoing. Here, the AI Act adopts a more effect-driven perspective, demanding accountability for harm regardless of the provider's or deployer's intentions. This approach aligns with the evolving nature of AI, where systems may autonomously produce outcomes that were neither anticipated nor deliberately designed. In applying these provisions, the focus must shift to analysing the nature and scale of the effects created by AI systems. Article 5(1)(a) revolves around whether subliminal techniques distort behaviour by operating below the threshold of conscious awareness. For Article 5(1)(b), the inquiry centres on whether an AI system's effect disproportionately impacts individuals due to specific vulnerabilities, resulting in significant harm. This framework allows regulators to address the full spectrum of manipulative practices, ensuring the challenges of proving intent do not limit protection.

The interplay between Articles 5(1)(a) and 5(1)(b) thus reflects a shift toward outcome-based accountability. It requires a nuanced understanding of how AI systems interact with individuals and groups, emphasising the tangible consequences of these interactions. Regulatory guidance must establish clear criteria for evaluating the effects of AI systems, incorporating concrete examples to illustrate how both provisions address manipulative practices without conflating their distinct scopes. In doing so, it must also account for the expansive nature of deceptive design, which transcends developer intent to encompass the broader systemic effects of system architecture and interface choices. By focusing on the outcomes of AI deployment – whether rooted in overt manipulative intent or emergent design properties – the framework aspires to confront the multifaceted challenges posed by technologies that influence behaviour in deliberate and incidental ways. However, this raises an important question: does the AI Act, in its current form, fully possess the nuance and adaptability required to address the pervasive and evolving nature of deceptive design?

To explore this question, I will examine three use cases introduced earlier in the chapter to assess whether they fall within the scope of Article 5(1)(b). As with chapter six's approach, I will adopt the perspective of opposing legal arguments. First, as the AI Regulator, I will argue why the system's design or outcomes meet Article 5(1)(b) criteria, attempting to outline how the system's effects might reasonably distort behaviour in violation of the provision. Through this analysis, we can critically evaluate whether the boundaries and thresholds of Article 5(1)(b) effectively capture the challenges posed by these complex and often ambiguous scenarios.

7.6. Use Cases for Article 5(1)(b)

> **Case Study #1:** An AI-driven recruitment platform detects women returning from maternity leave and systematically suppresses their access to senior roles, pushing them towards lower-paying part-time positions.

Table 7.2 Case Study #1: Legal Tensions

Criteria	AI Regulator	AI Developer
Placing on the Market, Putting into Service, or the Use of an AI System under Article 5(1)(b)	Not disputed by either party: The system was placed on the market and is actively used.	Not disputed by either party; the system was placed on the market and is actively used
Exploiting Vulnerabilities of a Natural Person or a Specific Group of Persons due to their Age, Disability, or Specific Socioeconomic Situation	Exploits socioeconomic vulnerability: Women returning from maternity leave face challenges re-entering the workforce, making them susceptible to bias. The algorithm reinforces stereotypes, worsening their position.	Does not exploit socioeconomic vulnerability: Maternity leave is a temporary career gap, not a vulnerability under the Act. The algorithm provides neutral recommendations without targeting specific groups.
Objective or Effect of Materially Distorting Behaviour	Materially distorts behaviour: The algorithm steers women towards lower-paying, part-time roles, reducing autonomy and shaping career decisions, creating a direct causal link.	Does not distort behaviour: It offers neutral recommendations that candidates can accept or reject. Any patterns reflect market trends, not algorithmic influence.

(continued)

Table 7.2 *(Continued)*

Criteria	AI Regulator	AI Developer
Individuals vs Groups of Persons & the Expected Standard in Individual Cases	Disproportionate impact: The system reinforces systemic employment biases, limiting women's access to senior roles and undermining fairness at both group and individual levels.	No disproportionate impact: The algorithm applies neutral data to all candidates. Any disparities result from industry norms, not design, preserving individual autonomy.
Reasonably Likely to Cause Significant Harm to that Person, Another Person, or a Group of Persons	Significant and foreseeable harm: Financial losses, career stagnation, and psychological effects demonstrate actual harm caused by the system's design and outcomes.	No significant harm: The alleged harm is speculative. Recommendations are optional, and disadvantages stem from broader societal conditions, not the platform.

Case Study #2: A virtual therapy chatbot exploits individuals in moments of emotional crisis by detecting their distress and aggressively marketing expensive premium services as the only solution to their pain. It intentionally hides free and equally effective alternatives, preying on desperation to maximise profits at the expense of those in need.

Table 7.3 Case Study #2: Legal Tensions

Criteria	AI Regulator	AI Developer
Placing on the Market, Putting into Service, or the Use of an AI System under Article 5(1)(b)	The chatbot is actively deployed, marketed, and operational, reaching users at vulnerable moments.	Not disputed: The chatbot is actively deployed, marketed, and operational, reaching users at vulnerable moments.

(continued)

Table 7.3 *(Continued)*

Criteria	AI Regulator	AI Developer
Exploiting Vulnerabilities of a Natural Person or a Specific Group of Persons due to their Age, Disability, or Specific Socioeconomic Situation	Exploiting vulnerability: The chatbot detects emotional distress – tied to psychological states – and pushes premium services, manipulating users who cannot evaluate options clearly, violating the prohibition.	No exploitation of vulnerability: Emotional distress, such as age or disability, is not explicitly recognised under Article 5(1)(b). The chatbot tailors responses but does not exploit inherent vulnerabilities.
Objective or Effect of Materially Distorting Behaviour	Materially distorting behaviour: The chatbot undermines autonomy by masking free alternatives and presenting premium services as necessary, leading to choices that users wouldn't otherwise make.	No distortion of behaviour: Users interact voluntarily. Promoting premium services follows industry norms, and concealing free alternatives is a business strategy, not a behaviour distortion.
Individuals vs Groups of Persons & the Expected Standard in Individual Cases	Disproportionate impact: The chatbot exploits distress, disproportionately affecting those in acute emotional need. At scale, this creates systemic harm for vulnerable mental health groups.	No disproportionate impact: Users must prove direct harm. Purchasing services is voluntary, and the chatbot does not systematically exploit mental health vulnerabilities.
Reasonably Likely to Cause Significant Harm to that Person, Another Person, or a Group of Persons	Significant harm: Financial loss, heightened distress, and worsened mental health demonstrate immediate and long-term harm, justifying regulatory intervention.	No significant harm: Any harm is incidental. Emotional distress predated chatbot interaction, and financial loss lacks evidence of coercion. The system offers solutions, not exploitation.

> **Case Study #3:** An AI-driven mental health app identifies teenagers showing anxiety and low self-esteem based on their interaction patterns. Instead of offering meaningful support, it uses infinite scroll features and recommendation algorithms to trap them in cycles of content designed to amplify insecurities. The platform strategically interweaves advertisements for beauty products, weight-loss supplements, and paid 'confidence-boosting' courses, exploiting their fragile self-image to maximise engagement and generate revenue.

Table 7.4 Case Study #3: Legal Tensions

Criteria	AI Regulator's Argument	Developer's Argument
Placing on the Market, Putting into Service, or the Use of an AI System under Article 5(1)(b)	The app is active and accessible to users, fulfilling the 'use' criterion under Article 5(1)(b). Its design and operations are ongoing and interactive, continuously engaging teenagers.	While the app is in use, its primary function is to promote mental health awareness, and its infinite scroll feature is a standard engagement tool, not inherently manipulative.
Exploiting Vulnerabilities of a Natural Person or a Specific Group of Persons due to their Age, Disability, or Specific Socioeconomic Situation	Teenagers' developmental stages make them susceptible to manipulation, especially regarding self-esteem and identity issues. The app leverages these vulnerabilities.	The app does not exploit age-specific vulnerabilities but uses common personalisation strategies across all user demographics.
Objective or Effect of Materially Distorting Behaviour	The app's algorithms amplify insecurities by promoting content that perpetuates negative cycles of thought, leading to heightened anxiety and compulsive engagement.	Any behaviour change is incidental and stems from user preferences rather than intentional distortion. The app merely responds to user interactions, not manipulates them.

(continued)

Table 7.4 *(Continued)*

Criteria	AI Regulator's Argument	Developer's Argument
Individuals vs Groups of Persons & the Expected Standard in Individual Cases	Individual harm is evident in cases where teenagers' self-image deteriorates, while the broader pattern of targeted content delivery shows group-level exploitation.	Harm is subjective and varies widely among users. The system provides widely accessible tools, and the group-level data lacks concrete evidence of deliberate exploitation.
Reasonably Likely to Cause Significant Harm to that Person, Another Person, or a Group of Persons	The harm is both psychological (increased anxiety, damaged self-esteem) and financial (pressure to purchase promoted products). These outcomes are foreseeable, given the design.	Psychological harm remains speculative and complex, arising only through interaction with the app. Teenagers can disengage, and advertisements present choices rather than exerting coercion.

The three cases underscore the profound challenges in enforcing Article 5(1)(b), revealing the difficulty of proving exploitative intent and establishing clear causal links between AI-driven manipulations and user harm. While regulators can readily identify overt forms of coercion, more insidious algorithmic strategies – such as nudging, omission, and systemic bias – pose significant evidentiary hurdles. Examples #1 and #3 illustrate the structural nature of these harms, where AI systems reinforce pre-existing inequalities or behavioural patterns without explicit, individual targeting. This raises critical questions about the adequacy of the current legal framework in addressing AI-driven deceptive design, particularly when harm manifests at scale rather than through direct, immediate coercion. The tension between commercial optimisation and user protection further complicates enforcement, as AI developers increasingly justify exploitative engagement strategies as industry norms or incidental effects of algorithmic personalisation. Without stronger regulatory intervention and a more precise articulation of what constitutes 'exploitation of vulnerability,' Article 5(1)(b) risks being ineffective against the very forms of manipulation it aims to prohibit. The final chapter will examine potential solutions, focusing on legal refinements, enforcement strategies, and proactive design principles safeguarding user autonomy while ensuring accountability for exploitative AI practices.

PART THREE

The Fight against Dark Patterns and Deceptive Design

8

Toward a Future Free
of Manipulation

8.1. Introduction

The proliferation of deceptive design techniques represents significant challenges to lawmakers' aspirations for a transparent and
rights-respecting digital environment.[1] Regulators increasingly recognise that design choices can systematically exploit predictable human
tendencies, leading to decisions that may not align with individuals' true
preferences or best interests. Yet, the cumulative effect of these manipulative tactics extends beyond individual choices, shaping user behaviour in
ways that undermine autonomy, informed decision-making, and trust in
digital environments. The OECD's report on commercial dark patterns
goes even further – highlighting that these harms extend beyond individuals, contributing to structural issues such as reduced competition
and a loss of faith in the market economy.[2] However, while this shift away
from rational actor theory marks progress, regulators and policy makers
still struggle to keep pace with the sophistication and pervasiveness of
deceptive design techniques.

How do we begin to regulate deceptive design? One way might be to
map them to known cognitive biases, identifying how they exploit users'
decision-making tendencies. By mapping tactics to specific cognitive
biases, we gain more precise insights into how manipulative strategies
work, enabling more effective regulatory responses to mitigate their
impact.[3]

'Confirm shaming' or pre-selected consent options distort and steer
choices towards outcomes that benefit platforms but may conflict with
users' best interests. Empirical studies confirm the effectiveness of these
tactics. Bielova et al. demonstrated that users are more likely to consent
to data processing when confronted with visually or cognitively skewed

interfaces.[4] 'Accept all' options feature prominent designs, while 'decline' buttons are obscured or placed in secondary menus. This manipulation fosters habitual acceptance, reducing users' likelihood of making privacy-conscious decisions.[5] However, the harm extends beyond immediate user outcomes. As Marie Potel-Saville and Mathilde Da Rocha noted, research shows that repeated exposure to dark patterns normalises manipulative practices, fostering distrust in digital systems, eroding user autonomy,[6] and amplifying concerns about data collection, platform accountability, and structural harm.[7]

The European Data Protection Board (EDPB) emphasised that 'deceptive design patterns' undermine the principles central to data protection and the meaning of 'informed consent'.[8] For the EDPB, assessing the compliance of user interfaces in social media applications begins with the principle of fair processing, which serves as the benchmark for determining whether a design crosses into deception.[9] Other key principles, including transparency, accountability, data minimisation, and ensuring data is used only for its intended purpose, are also relevant.[10] Additional obligations focus on respecting users' rights, and platforms proactively embed rights-empowering practices into their design.[11]

Studies also demonstrate that patterns lead to impulsive purchases and diminish consumers' ability to make informed purchase decisions, impacting their financial well-being.[12] 'Scarcity' leverages loss aversion, the tendency to strongly prefer avoiding losses over acquiring equivalent gains, as seen in 'only two left in stock' messages that pressure users into hurried decisions. Similarly, 'urgency' amplifies loss aversion by imposing time constraints, such as countdown timers, to heighten the fear of missing out. Social proof relies on the social desirability effect – where individuals are influenced by perceived norms – and the social comparison effect, which motivates people to assess themselves based on others' actions or possessions.

Thus, the CJEU's decision in *Compass Banca SpA v AGCM*[13] marks a pivotal moment in rethinking how cognitive biases factor into assessing unfair commercial practices under the UCPD. In *Compass*, the CJEU acknowledged the practical realities of consumer decision-making, recognising that manipulative practices may disproportionately affect certain demographic groups. The Court's acknowledgement that framing tactics can influence the average consumer's decision-making capacity reflects an evolution in its jurisprudence.[14] The Court subtly moves beyond the traditional, idealised benchmark of the 'reasonably observant and circumspect' consumer by recognising the practical impact of cognitive biases, such as the presentation of offers. Instead, it opens the door for a more nuanced approach that accounts for real-world behavioural limitations.

This shift is crucial for addressing user interface dark patterns, enabling courts and regulators to assess how manipulative design choices affect consumer behaviour. The decision affirms that framing and other tactics can distort decision-making by exploiting cognitive vulnerabilities, even if not overtly coercive. This reasoning strengthens interpretations of unfair practices, challenging traders who rely on subtle manipulation. Moreover, the judgment integrates behavioural insights into legal standards while preserving the average consumer benchmark's objectivity.[15] By allowing courts to consider cognitive biases, the CJEU signals a recalibration in assessing commercial fairness – critical in an era where digital interfaces deploy psychological manipulation at scale.

Well, that is it, then. Problem solved. The battle against dark patterns is over; we can all rest easy. Data protection authorities have issued definitive guidance,[16] consumer protection laws have flexed their muscles, and the courts have enlightened us with wisdom.[17] With the CJEU acknowledging cognitive biases and the DSA throwing Article 25's prohibition into the mix, surely manipulative design is a thing of the past. Platforms must now be scrambling to adopt "fair', 'honest',[18] or 'bright'[19] patterns while reigning their insatiable appetite for user data and turning over a new leaf to ensure effective transparency. Right? Wrong.

Despite the glimmers of progress, the reality remains far grimmer. Enforcement under Article 25 DSA has barely scratched the surface (pun intended), with few cases genuinely addressing the systemic roots of deceptive design.

Do not get me wrong. Acknowledging the effects of dark patterns is essential, but the real battle has shifted. While visible dark patterns like confusing consent banners and pre-ticked boxes may face greater scrutiny, manipulative practices are migrating from the user interface to system architecture. This evolution embeds deception deeper into platform operations, making it subtler, more pervasive, and more complex to detect or regulate. Dark patterns aren't obsolete – they're evolving. As long as incentives for manipulation remain unchecked and enforcement lags, deceptive design will persist, hidden in plain sight.

So, no, this book and other more essential works on dark patterns are not obsolete. The fight for accountability is more urgent than ever, shifting from UI tricks to the hidden depths of system architecture. In many cases, dark patterns are more prevalent than before. A recent study found that GPT-4-generated websites frequently included dark patterns, with all 20 tested designs featuring at least one. Alarmingly, most users failed to recognise them as problematic, exposing risks for both end-users and developers relying on AI-driven design.[20]

Confronting deceptive design requires vigorous enforcement and proactive solutions that embed user empowerment and fair design principles into digital environments. Without addressing the structural incentives driving manipulation and committing to meaningful enforcement, regulators risk leaving us trapped in an internet designed to deceive. Enforcement must be complemented by design approaches prioritising autonomy, moving beyond merely identifying dark patterns to fostering 'fair patterns' – design choices that support informed decision-making without undue influence.[21]

Technological tools are emerging as key allies in this effort. Browser extensions, machine learning algorithms, and repositories of known dark patterns help users and regulators detect and counteract manipulation in real-time. These tools enhance consumer awareness and give regulators more precise insights into systemic violations. Collaboration between researchers, technologists, and policymakers is essential to integrating these innovations into regulatory frameworks, ensuring they function as preventive and corrective measures. Combining technical advances with legislative progress offers a path toward greater platform accountability and user-centric design.

This chapter starts with an examination of efforts to curb manipulative design, focusing on the EU's consumer and data protection frameworks. It then explores future regulatory strategies, including platform regulation and the AI Act, emphasising advancing digital fairness. Finally, it considers the 'gentrification' of large action models that personalise choice architecture. While more work is needed to tackle the incentives enabling deceptive design, this section underscores the urgent need for enforcement mechanisms targeting manipulative interfaces that systematically undermine users.

8.2. Data Protection Dark Patterns in the User Interface

Building on the insights of the European Data Protection Board (EDPB), this section focuses on how user interface dark patterns conflict with key principles of the GDPR. As a limited regulation primarily concerned with personal data, the GDPR targets dark patterns that disrupt transparency, fairness, accountability, and data protection by design and default.

Table 8.1 EDPB-Defined Illegal Data Protection Dark Patterns

Category	Description	Examples
Overloading[22]	Overwhelms users with excessive information or options to influence decisions.	**Continuous Prompting**: Repeated requests for data. **Privacy Maze**: Convoluted navigation for privacy settings.
Skipping[23]	Designs that distract users or pre-select options to make them bypass important data protection decisions.	**Deceptive Snugness**: Default data-sharing settings. **Look Over There**: Distracting Elements Overshadowing Critical Information.
Stirring[24]	Uses emotional manipulation or visual nudges to steer users into undesired actions.	**Emotional Steering**: Guilt-inducing language. **Hidden in Plain Sight**: Making privacy-protective options less visible.
Obstructing[25]	Complicates or blocks users from managing data preferences effectively.	**Dead End**: Links leading to irrelevant or inaccessible pages. **Longer Than Necessary**: More steps to protect data compared to sharing it. **Misleading Action**: Misrepresented outcomes.

(continued)

Table 8.1 *(Continued)*

Category	Description	Examples
Fickle[26]	Inconsistencies in design that confuse users, leading to unintended data-sharing choices.	**Inconsistent Interface**: Platforms present options in different orders across settings. **Language Discontinuity**: There are no translated privacy settings.
Left in the Dark[27]	Hides or obscures key information about data processing, leaving users uncertain.	**Conflicting Information**: Contradictory statements about data use. **Ambiguous Wording**: Use vague terms like 'special categories' without explanation.

Under Article 5(1)(a) GDPR, personal data processing must be fair and transparent, requiring that individuals are fully informed of the scope, purpose, and implications of such processing. Practices like 'Conflicting Information' and 'Ambiguous Wording' violate this provision by obscuring key details, leaving data subjects unable to make informed decisions.[28] Article 12(1) builds on this, mandating that information be concise, intelligible, and accessible; however, patterns like 'Hidden in Plain Sight', which deliberately obscure critical data protection options or information, contravene these obligations.[29] Such patterns prevent users from effectively exercising their rights and thus undermine Recital 39, which demands clear communication to facilitate data subject control. Article 7 reinforces these requirements for consent, specifying that it must involve the individual's clear, specific, informed, and unambiguous choice. Design choices such as 'Deceptive Snugness', which rely on pre-selected opt-ins or default data-sharing settings, directly contravene Recital 32's prohibition on pre-ticked boxes and other methods that presume consent. Article 7(3) clarifies that withdrawing consent must be as simple as giving it, yet patterns like 'Longer Than Necessary', which impose greater complexity on opt-out mechanisms than opt-in processes, violate this mandate and render the consent invalid under Article 6(1)(a).

Similarly, Article 25 obliges controllers to implement measures that limit data processing to what is necessary for specific purposes by default. Patterns like 'Deceptive Snugness,' which pre-enable data-invasive settings, breach this requirement, undermining Recital 78's emphasis on embedding data protection into system design. Articles 15 through 21 also provide individuals with fundamental rights to access, rectify, erase, restrict, or object to data processing. These patterns obstruct rights, as seen in examples like 'Dead End,' where users encounter broken links or non-functional options when attempting to exercise their rights, or 'Privacy Maze,' which scatters controls across multiple layers of an interface, contravening Article 12(2) and Recital 59's requirement for user-friendly rights mechanisms. Beyond these technical breaches, such practices undermine the GDPR's accountability principle,[30] requiring controllers to demonstrate compliance.

Patterns like 'Misleading Action' create discrepancies between user expectations and system responses, erode trust, and compromise consent and data handling verifiability. These represent a systematic disregard for the GDPR's safeguards to protect individuals from unfair, non-transparent, or coercive practices.[31] The EDPB's guidance underscores that these are not mere design flaws but deliberate tactics to subvert autonomy and compliance. Effective enforcement of Articles 5, 7, 12, and 25 is, therefore, critical to ensuring that organisations uphold the GDPR's objectives while safeguarding the fundamental rights of data subjects.[32]

The regulation of 'data protection dark patterns' is increasingly enforced through judicial and administrative mechanisms to address the manipulation of user consent, data rights, and transparency obligations. The *LG Passau* case[33] and its nuanced legal analysis exemplify how courts interpret and apply GDPR principles to evaluate compliance. In *LG Passau*, the Court underscored that platforms must ensure that users are fully informed about the scope, purpose, and modalities of data processing. This principle was particularly pertinent when assessing the default settings of the defendant's 'Contact Import Tool,' which enabled user profiles to be searchable by telephone number. Although the Court acknowledged the tool's alignment with the platform's legitimate purpose – facilitating social connections – it clarified that such configurations could only be deemed lawful under GDPR if transparency obligations were satisfied. The judgment stressed that users must be explicitly informed about how their data could be accessed and given straightforward options to modify privacy settings. While the Court upheld the permissibility of default settings allowing searchability by telephone numbers, it identified the necessity for platforms to provide clear pathways for users to adjust these settings, such as limiting visibility to 'friends' or 'only me'.[34]

The judgment also addressed alleged breaches of Article 25 GDPR, which requires 'data protection by design and default'. The plaintiff claimed the platform's default settings were privacy-invasive. Still, the Court clarified that while Article 25 prioritises data minimisation and privacy-friendly defaults, it does not require the 'most privacy-protective' option in all cases. Instead, settings must align with legitimate processing purposes.

Notably, the Court noted that settings that obscure privacy controls or mislead users through visual hierarchies or pre-checked boxes – examples of dark patterns – would be inconsistent with GDPR's transparency and fairness principles, even if they technically provided user options.[35]

Consent mechanisms under Articles 4(11) and 7 GDPR were another critical aspect of the Court's scrutiny. The judgment reaffirmed that consent must be freely given, informed, specific, and unambiguous. Practices like pre-checked opt-ins or designs that make withdrawing consent difficult – known as 'Deceptive Snugness' – violate GDPR standards. The Court emphasised that when interfaces obscure user understanding or hinder decision-making, consent is invalid, and the processing lacks a lawful basis under Article 6(1)(a) GDPR. Furthermore, the Court emphasised the obligation under Article 7(3) that withdrawal of consent must be as simple as providing it, rejecting interfaces that create unnecessary friction in exercising this right.[36]

The Court's decision further underscores the limitations of compensation claims under Article 82 GDPR, which requires claimants to demonstrate tangible harm resulting from violations. In this case, the plaintiff's claims of emotional distress and loss of control over data were deemed insufficiently substantiated. However, it is worth considering the CJEU judgment in *Bindl*, which awarded €400 in compensation for non-material damage caused by the transfer of personal data by the European Commission to the United States. In *Bindl*,[37] the CJEU recognised that the absence of appropriate safeguards for the data transfer[38] and the resulting 'uncertainty as regards the processing of [the plaintiff's] personal data, in particular of his IP address', constituted actual and specific damage.[39] This suggests a potentially lowered threshold for non-material damage, particularly in cases where the harm stems from a lack of clarity or safeguards regarding data processing. While the specifics of the present case differ, *Bindl* provides a perspective on how claims of non-material damage under Article 82 GDPR might be substantiated, offering a broader interpretation of harm that could influence future litigation in this area. The Court reiterated that while GDPR adopts a broad understanding of 'damage', the harm must be actual, demonstrable, and causally linked to the controller's actions.[40]

Finally, *LG Passau* illuminated areas for regulatory and design improvements to counter dark patterns effectively. Recital 39 GDPR reiterates that platforms are encouraged to adopt clear, concise, and user-centric privacy notices that enable individuals to understand and exercise their rights seamlessly. Courts and regulators may increasingly require enhanced consent validation standards, intuitive rights mechanism interfaces, and greater accountability for joint data processing arrangements.[41] By applying fairness, transparency, and accountability principles, the decision reinforces the importance of proactive compliance measures, rigorous design standards, and effective user engagement to address the complex challenges posed by data protection dark patterns.

A Rostock Regional Court ruling from 15 September 2020[42] offers a complementary perspective to the *LG Passau* decision. The Rostock judgment, which specifically examines the misuse of cookie banners, reinforces the judiciary's insistence on securing effective, informed, and voluntary user consent while addressing the systemic transparency and accountability deficiencies often exploited by data controllers. The judgment's detailed application of GDPR principles to cookie banners, alongside its exploration of joint controller obligations and enforcement mechanisms, illustrates the GDPR's regulatory framework's breadth and ability to combat manipulative practices.

At the core of the Rostock judgment lies Article 5(1)(a) GDPR, which mandates lawful, fair, and transparent processing of personal data. The Court found that the defendant's use of pre-checked cookie banners – designed to track users and share data with third parties – directly contravened Article 4(11), which defines consent as an unambiguous and freely given affirmative action. Drawing on Recital 32, the Court highlighted that consent does not arise from pre-ticked boxes or user inaction. The judgment emphasised that although users could technically view or deselect cookies, the banner's overall design misled users into consenting to data processing without a genuine understanding of its implications. This approach aligns with the CJEU's decision in *Planet49*, which firmly established that effective consent for cookie use must be active and specific. The Rostock decision reiterated that platforms employing such tactics exploit user behaviour and fail to meet the GDPR's strict consent requirements.[43]

The Court further scrutinised the defendant's reliance on opt-in settings contravening Article 25. Instead of minimising data collection and processing, the defendant's default settings prioritised broad data access, reflecting a deliberate strategy to maximise user data collection rather than safeguarding privacy. While Article 25(2) allows for settings that support legitimate processing purposes, the Court reaffirmed that prioritising user autonomy must remain a cornerstone of compliant data processing. The defendant's failure to meet this standard breached the data minimisation principle under Article 5(1)(c).

Additionally, the judgment identified significant transparency deficiencies. Controllers must provide users with intelligible and accessible information about data processing, including clear articulation of its purposes, the identity of third-party recipients, and the legal bases for international data transfers.[44] The defendant failed to adequately disclose its reliance on tools like Google Analytics, neglecting its duty[45] to justify data transfers to third countries.[46] These lapses obstructed users from making informed decisions about their data, reinforcing the Court's emphasis on the centrality of clarity and simplicity in fulfilling GDPR requirements.

The Rostock court's exploration further illuminated joint controller responsibilities, particularly concerning the use of third-party tools. By integrating Google Analytics, the defendant established a joint processing arrangement with the service provider, thereby incurring obligations to disclose the essential elements of this agreement.[47] The judgment reaffirmed principles from the CJEU's ruling in *Fashion ID*,[48] reiterating that joint controllers share accountability when both influence the purposes and means of processing. The defendant's failure to satisfy these requirements breached transparency standards and highlighted the heightened scrutiny controllers face when collaborating with third-party processors. By recognising the potential for repetition of such violations, the Court emphasised the importance of proactive design modifications prioritising GDPR adherence.[49]

The Rostock ruling serves as a vital case study in addressing dark patterns at the intersection of data protection and user rights. It complements the broader principles laid out in *LG Passau*, focusing on compliance's technical and procedural elements, including the design of consent mechanisms, the fulfilment of joint controller obligations, and the provision of accessible information. Together, these cases illustrate the judiciary's commitment to enforcing GDPR's protective framework and demonstrate the critical role of courts in mitigating manipulative practices. By clarifying obligations and setting rigorous standards for accountability, these rulings provide a robust foundation for upholding user autonomy.

8.3. Consumer Law Dark Patterns in the User Interface

The regulation of user interface dark patterns has become a critical focus of consumer law enforcement, particularly within the European Union. The UCPD and the DSA represent complementary pillars within this framework, addressing manipulative practices in both traditional and digital environments while maintaining distinct regulatory roles. The UCPD provides a broad horizontal framework governing unfair business-to-consumer practices. Its core provisions prohibit practices that contravene professional diligence and materially distort consumer decision-making.[50] This prohibition encompasses many dark patterns, including hidden fees, false urgency cues, and subscription traps. The Annex I blacklist explicitly bans, in all circumstances, bait-and-switch tactics,[51] fake limited-time offers,[52] false endorsements,[53] hidden costs,[54] subscription traps,[55] tricks to obtain payment details,[56] and disguised advertising in online interfaces[57] without requiring proof of the 'average consumer' standard or whether the tactic infringed obligations of professional diligence. Amendments introduced through the Omnibus Directive[58] have expanded the UCPD's applicability to emerging digital practices, enhanced penalties for non-compliance, and established clarity around ranking and personalisation techniques.[59] The DSA, in contrast, takes a more static approach to regulating dark patterns. The DSA and the UCPD create a layered regulatory framework targeting the full spectrum of user interface manipulations. However, Article 25(2) DSA explicitly states:

> The prohibition in paragraph 1 shall not apply to practices covered by Directive 2005/29/EC or Regulation (EU) 2016/679. (This is the UCPD and the GDPR, respectively).

This exemption creates a potential loophole. If I were representing a platform accused of deploying dark patterns by a Digital Services Coordinator, one line of defence would be that the alleged practice falls under the UCPD's definition of dark patterns and is outside any DSA regulator's scope. The interplay between the UCPD and DSA becomes particularly significant when considering enforcement strategies. The UCPD's flexibility, grounded in its principle-based approach, allows it to adapt to various manipulative techniques, from pre-ticked boxes to misleading scarcity indicators. Meanwhile, the DSA's targeted prohibitions extend these protections by explicitly addressing algorithmic design choices and data-driven manipulations. This synergy ensures enforcement actions can address visible manipulative practices and less transparent systemic manipulations.

Traditionally understood as a reasonably informed and circumspect individual, the 'average consumer' notion under the UCPD has been a focal point in shaping enforcement responses to dark patterns. One of the clearest examples of this interplay is regulating subscription traps, a persistent issue in digital commerce. The UCPD prohibits aggressive and misleading practices that obscure cancellation processes or impose undue burdens on consumers. The DSA builds on this by requiring platforms to offer cancellation mechanisms as simple as subscription sign-ups, addressing the operational barriers often employed to retain users.[60] This alignment between the two instruments ensures regulators safeguard consumers from immediate deceptive practices and systemic design choices perpetuating these harms.

The reliance on empirical studies has further informed the development of these frameworks. For instance, a 2022 behavioural study commissioned by the European Commission revealed that 97 per cent of websites and apps surveyed deployed at least one dark pattern, with practices such as false urgency, nagging, and obstructive cancellation being particularly prevalent.[61] These findings underscore the necessity of a dual approach: the UCPD addresses individual practices through general prohibitions, while the DSA targets the systemic mechanisms enabling such practices at scale.

These instruments create a cohesive framework for combating dark patterns by integrating principle-based prohibitions with targeted digital-specific measures. In theory, this synergy allows enforcement bodies to address traditional and emerging forms of manipulation, ensuring that consumer law remains robust.

The DSA establishes a comprehensive framework for accountability and fairness, with Article 25 specifically prohibiting dark patterns. However, as of January 2025, formal enforcement under this provision remains limited. This is largely due to the DSA's recent applicability and the time-intensive nature of enforcement. Understanding the DSA's timeline is key. While it became fully applicable in February 2024, obligations for Very Large Online Platforms (VLOPs) and Search Engines (VLOSEs) took effect earlier, in August 2023. Initial enforcement has focused on risk assessment and compliance under Articles 33–35. Article 25's ban on manipulative interface design only became enforceable in February 2024, meaning regulators are still in the early stages of identifying violations.

The European Commission has proactively laid the groundwork for enforcing Article 25. On 3 October 2023, it issued detailed guidelines on online interface design, providing insights into the criteria for assessing compliance with this article. These guidelines emphasise transparency, user autonomy, and the need for explicit consent mechanisms, reflecting broader principles underpinning the DSA. While regulators have not yet initiated formal actions, these guidelines signal a robust intent to scrutinise platforms for manipulative practices and ensure adherence to Article 25's standards.

Recent DSA enforcement has primarily targeted VLOPs and VLOSEs for non-compliance in content moderation, risk management, and transparency, as seen in investigations into X (formerly Twitter) and TikTok.[62] While not directly related to Article 25, these cases demonstrate the European Commission's commitment to enforcement and set a precedent for future actions, including those addressing dark patterns. The absence of Article 25-specific enforcement does not indicate regulatory inaction but reflects the complexities of implementing new legal standards. Investigations and formal decisions take time, particularly for nuanced provisions on interface design. Article 25 will likely receive greater attention as enforcement mechanisms mature, with national Digital Services Coordinators playing a key role in its oversight. Nevertheless, the European Commission's guidelines and willingness to act against VLOPs and VLOSEs signal a clear regulatory trajectory. This early phase of implementation serves as a preparatory stage for what is likely to be a significant area of focus in the regulatory landscape.

Recent cases, such as Amazon's Prime cancellation practices, flagged by the Norwegian Consumer Council (NCC), highlight significant deficiencies in the legal frameworks governing consumer protection.[63] These manipulative practices, designed to discourage subscription cancellations, illustrate the growing sophistication of behavioural exploitation in digital marketplaces. They further expose the limitations of legal benchmarks, such as the 'average consumer' standard, which often fail to account for the realities of consumer interactions in complex, digitally mediated contexts. Amazon's cancellation process exemplifies the deliberate introduction of friction to impede consumer autonomy. Lengthy navigation paths, strategically ambiguous labelling, and recurring prompts to reconsider cancellation were central to the NCC's findings. These mechanisms exploit well-documented cognitive biases, including inertia and loss aversion, to subtly nudge consumers towards retaining subscriptions. While such designs often elude direct legal prohibition under traditional consumer protection statutes, they challenge the normative foundations of fairness that underpin these frameworks. A more contextually sensitive standard should address the inherent power imbalances in digital marketplaces. A refined benchmark should consider whether specific practices unduly exploit these vulnerabilities rather than presuming a universal baseline of consumer competence. Furthermore, legal scrutiny should extend to the mechanics of digital design itself, interrogating how algorithmic personalisation and behavioural nudges influence decision-making. Incorporating empirical evidence into this analysis ensures that regulatory responses are not merely theoretical but grounded in the lived experiences of digital consumers.

The regulation of dark patterns in investment apps and interfaces is also an area of focus for European and national authorities, particularly under frameworks such as MiFID II. The German Federal Financial Supervisory Authority (BaFin), for example, has explicitly targeted such practices under Section 63(6) Sentence 1 of the German Securities Trading Act (WpHG), which implements Article 24(3) of MiFID II. This provision requires investment firms to ensure the information provided to users is transparent, fair, and not misleading, establishing a standard of professional diligence that prohibits interfaces designed to push consumers into unintended financial decisions, such as defaulting to high-risk transactions.

Enforcement actions against Epic Games, LinkedIn, and Vonage illustrate the regulatory framework that addresses unfair, deceptive, and privacy-invasive practices. They demonstrate how specific legal provisions ensure accountability and consumer protection. Each case highlights distinct regulatory priorities while showcasing how entities can be held accountable under frameworks like the Federal Trade Commission Act (FTC Act),[64] the Children's Online Privacy Protection Act (COPPA),[65] and the Restore Online Shoppers' Confidence Act (ROSCA).[66] Epic Games, for example, faced significant penalties under section 5 of the FTC Act and COPPA for practices associated with its game *Fortnite*. The FTC's complaint alleged Epic Games violated COPPA by failing to secure verifiable parental consent before collecting and using personal information from children under 13.

Under COPPA, operators of online services directed at children must provide notice to parents and obtain consent before collecting such data, with specific provisions governing privacy notices and parental review rights.[67] Regulators determined that Epic's design choices, such as default-enabled voice and text chat features facilitating real-time interactions, caused substantial harm to children by exposing them to risks of harassment and abuse.[68] The $275 million fine imposed by the FTC underscored the gravity of these violations and marked one of the most considerable penalties ever issued under COPPA. Epic's use of dark patterns in its in-game item shop to obfuscate purchase decisions and complicate refund processes violated section 5 of the FTC Act's prohibition on unfair or deceptive practices.[69] This violation led to an additional $245 million settlement to refund affected consumers, emphasising the importance of transparency and clarity in digital commerce.[70]

Enforcement action against LinkedIn exemplifies the intersection of deceptive design and privacy violations under state and federal laws. Plaintiffs in the *Perkins v LinkedIn* case alleged that LinkedIn harvested email addresses from users' contact lists without explicit consent and used these to send repeated reminder emails to non-users, effectively employing the harvested data for unsolicited commercial endorsements.[71] California's common law right of publicity, a statutory right of publicity, and the state's Unfair Competition Law[72] provided the legal basis to challenge this practice. The Court's findings highlighted LinkedIn's failure to obtain informed consent for using users' names and likenesses in promotional activities, illustrating how regulators respond to dark patterns infringing upon privacy and consumer rights.[73] The case also underscored the value of transparency in consent practices and the legal requirement to avoid manipulative data collection.[74]

The FTC's enforcement against Vonage under ROSCA and the FTC Act focused on using dark patterns to obstruct the cancellation of recurring subscription services.[75] ROSCA mandates clear disclosures and simple mechanisms for consumers to cancel services, particularly those involving negative option billing.[76] Vonage violated these requirements by requiring consumers to contact live retention agents during restricted hours, obscuring contact information, and employing aggressive tactics to dissuade cancellations. These actions were deemed unfair and deceptive practices that harm consumers by exploiting their inability to make informed choices.[77] The stipulated order included provisions mandating Vonage to implement a straightforward cancellation process and avoid manipulative design choices.[78] The order also included a monetary judgment of $100 million, underscoring the financial repercussions of non-compliance.[79]

Applying legal frameworks such as the FTC Act, COPPA, ROSCA, and state privacy and consumer protection laws highlights the commitment to safeguarding transparency, fairness, and user autonomy. Each case demonstrates that entities leveraging manipulative design practices for commercial gain face significant legal and financial risks while affirming enforcement's role in shaping responsible industry practices.

8.4. Emerging Work on 'Fair Patterns' and Technical Measures

Developing and implementing 'fair' and 'bright' patterns follow distinct approaches to user choice architecture. Fair patterns are grounded in human-centred design methodologies, ensuring equitability without steering users toward specific outcomes. In contrast, bright patterns prioritise privacy by nudging users toward privacy-enhancing decisions. As highlighted by King and Stephan, bright patterns draw inspiration from frameworks like the California Privacy Rights Act, which sets practical benchmarks for mitigating privacy dark patterns.[80]

Alternatively, *fair patterns* reject nudging because it is considered: (i) paternalistic, and (ii) ineffective in fostering user learning. Instead, fair patterns boost users with the necessary information and tools to make online choices that align with their preferences, serving as autonomy-enhancing measures. Applying this process to privacy interfaces ensures that designs are understandable, accepted by users, accessible to a wide range of people, and informed by human factors knowledge, such as how people *actually* make decisions. Notably, the concept of fair patterns is fundamentally grounded in neuroscience, considering humans' cognitive limitations – such as sensitivity to information overload, the salience effect, and the default effect – to ensure that choices are not biased. It draws on the Fogg Behavioral Model,[81] which posits that behaviour change is based on motivation, ability, and triggers. Each fair pattern from the library incorporates these factors to enable a 'fair choice'.

Researchers assess user preferences through advanced research methods to compare the impact of dark and fair patterns. Users first navigate a journey filled with dark patterns (eg, a purchasing funnel), and researchers measure deviations from their stated preferences. Weeks later, they repeat the journey with fair patterns, and outcomes are reassessed. This process generates a 'manipulation index', quantifying the influence of dark patterns versus fair patterns. The findings underscore that fair patterns support informed decision-making rather than directing users toward predetermined choices.[82]

As Marie Potel-Saville does not directly link fair patterns with the GDPR, a critical reader might question whether informed decision-making aligns with the GDPR's standard for informed consent. This concern is particularly relevant in contexts like cookie banners, where cognitive biases and decision fatigue often undermine meaningful consent. While fair patterns can improve user autonomy, whether valid informed consent is achievable remains an open question. Fair patterns still advance data protection-by-design-and-default,[83] requiring controllers to integrate compliance measures from inception, prioritising user autonomy, and minimising data collection. This is especially important for vulnerable groups like children, ensuring users are not automatically opted into data-sharing agreements. Such measures align with the principle of necessity, limiting processing to what is strictly required for a given purpose.[84]

Fair patterns, by design, avoid distorting user choices, ensuring that interfaces are neutral and non-coercive. Similarly, the UCPD's provisions against misleading commercial practices bolster the case for fair patterns. They ensure compliance with the directive by fostering transparency in pricing, contract terms, and other consumer-related decisions. Fair patterns also directly relate to the GDPR's obligation to afford enhanced protections to vulnerable data subjects.[85] Vulnerable groups, including children and individuals with limited digital literacy, are particularly susceptible to the exploitative mechanics of deceptive defaults, obfuscated information, and coercive nudging.[86] Fair patterns proactively counteract these vulnerabilities by implementing protective defaults that minimise data collection unless actively consented to, alongside intelligible and contextually appropriate information delivery mechanisms.

The Fair Patterns Checklist outlines key principles for designing digital interfaces. It emphasises triggering System 2 thinking by explaining choices, using plain language, and providing interactive learning tools. Information should be presented concisely, at the right time, and clearly distinguish between mandatory and optional actions to limit cognitive effort. Formatting considerations – such as font size, contrast, spacing, and icons – should enhance readability without overwhelming users. The checklist also addresses biases, advocating for balanced information presentation to counter salience bias, protective defaults and reminders to combat status quo bias, and correcting information asymmetry by ensuring transparent and empowering guidance. Further, it stresses the importance of creating a learning curve through transparency, user testing, and educational tools while enhancing choice by ensuring options are accessible, meaningful, and timed appropriately in the user journey. These criteria form a solution-oriented framework for countering deceptive design and fostering fairness in digital environments.[87]

Repositories like Deceptive.Design (Disclosure: I am the legal advisor) have emerged as a vital resource, offering curated examples and critiques of deceptive interface designs. This repository is an educational tool that supports identifying recurring patterns, aiding researchers and policymakers in developing targeted solutions. Alongside such repositories, technical tools like browser extensions have become instrumental in flagging manipulative user interfaces in real-time. Princeton's Ad Observer, for instance, exemplifies how crowdsourced insights can enhance transparency by systematically identifying and categorising dark patterns, offering users an immediate lens into potentially harmful practices.[88]

The integration of AI further amplifies these efforts. Systems leveraging machine learning and natural language processing, such as fine-tuned BERT models, excel in analysing textual and visual cues to detect deceptive designs.[89] These advancements align with findings from FTC studies, which highlight the potential of algorithmic tools to uncover subtle manipulations embedded within digital interfaces. The FTC's emphasis on developing consumer deception detection algorithms underscores the regulatory appetite for technical interventions to address online manipulation's evolving complexities.

Incorporating technical detection tools into enforcement mechanisms is a significant step towards accountability. For instance, behavioural audits can simulate diverse user interactions, offering regulators insights into how specific demographics may experience a platform's design.[90] These audits facilitate proactive regulation and allow firms to pre-emptively refine their interfaces to comply. Partnerships between academia, NGOs, and regulatory bodies are another pivotal strategy. Such collaborations enable systematic auditing of digital platforms by combining the technical expertise of researchers with the advocacy and policy-oriented perspectives of civil society organisations. By pooling resources and knowledge, these partnerships can develop robust frameworks for identifying and mitigating dark patterns, fostering a digital ecosystem prioritising user well-being and transparency. The convergence of repositories, AI-driven tools, and collaborative auditing frameworks reflects an evolving commitment to tackling the challenges.

8.5. Amplified Manipulation: The Rise of AI-Powered Deceptive Design

AI-powered deceptive design is already here. Large Action Models (LAMs) represent a transformative advancement in AI, fundamentally reshaping the interface between technology and human decision-making.[91] Unlike traditional AI systems that respond to inputs within predefined parameters, LAMs combine linguistic sophistication with action-oriented capabilities. These systems dynamically synthesise real-time inputs, user behaviour, and contextual variables to execute complex tasks autonomously. This transition from static recommendation systems to adaptive, anticipatory agents marks a fundamental shift in how digital environments influence and interact with users.[92] By integrating and acting upon behavioural insights at an unprecedented scale, LAMs redefine the nexus between AI and human-computer interaction, offering precision in mapping the trajectories of human decision-making. These systems, trained to predict and simulate user behaviours across digital platforms, function as sophisticated anticipation instruments. They decode the minutiae of user behaviour – hesitations, preferences, and cognitive blind spots – to sculpt pathways that maximise predefined outcomes. While this potential enhances user engagement and operational efficiency, it poses significant risks, particularly in entrenching manipulative design and compelling interrogation of digital modernity's evolving boundaries of autonomy and agency.

Unlike traditional UI dark patterns, LAMs dynamically manipulate user experiences, adapting interfaces in real-time based on predicted behaviours. Rather than just anticipating user actions, they respond by introducing urgency or scarcity cues when hesitation is detected – adjustments driven by probabilistic algorithms, not human oversight. This shift from deterministic to adaptive exploitation makes these systems particularly insidious.

Manipulative design driven by LAMs is targeted and bespoke, evolving with user behaviour. This personalisation fractures shared digital experiences, replacing them with adaptive control structures that evade traditional regulatory detection. Deception is not in static design but in real-time interface manipulation exploiting cognitive vulnerabilities. As a result, platforms could argue their UI lacks inherent dark patterns while actual manipulation remains hidden within dynamic interaction logic.

The opacity inherent in LAMs compounds their potential for harm. Like their linguistic counterparts, these systems often operate as black boxes, with internal mechanics inscrutable even to their developers. This obfuscation enables platforms to disclaim responsibility, attributing exploitative outcomes to emergent system properties rather than deliberate intent. Accountability becomes diffused, undermining existing safeguards designed to protect user interests. The result is a structural asymmetry of power, where platforms wield disproportionate influence over user choices while evading scrutiny and liability.

A further dimension of concern lies in the iterative feedback loops that define LAM functionality. These systems continuously refine their predictions based on user interactions, shaping behaviours that align with platform objectives. The architecture of choice presented to users becomes increasingly deterministic, subtly channelling actions towards outcomes beneficial to the platform. Over time, this recursive process risks embedding manipulative design within the very fabric of digital environments.

LAMs operate distinctively from traditional dark patterns and large language models (LLMs). While LLMs excel in generating contextually relevant text responses based on user prompts, their interaction remains primarily static and unidirectional. In contrast, LAMs are multidimensional systems designed to learn and adapt through user actions across diverse environments.[93] These models transcend the linguistic realm, leveraging behavioural data to construct dynamic and individualised interaction frameworks. By monitoring user behaviour over time, LAMs identify patterns, preferences, and vulnerabilities, enabling them to adapt interfaces and decision-making environments in ways that optimise predefined goals.[94] This adaptability differentiates LAMs from LLMs. While an LLM generates a response tailored to a specific input, an LAM interprets a user's cumulative actions and adjusts its behaviour accordingly. For example, a user interacting with an LLM-powered chatbot receives text-based answers to queries, with the model's scope limited to the immediate conversation. A LAM, however, could observe how the user navigates a broader digital ecosystem – noting hesitation at specific decision points, responses to urgency cues, or even engagement patterns across unrelated interfaces. This holistic perspective allows LAMs to recalibrate the user's choice environment, creating interactions that exploit specific behavioural tendencies.

What sets LAMs apart from traditional AI systems and underscores their transformative nature is their unparalleled ability to integrate, contextualise, and act upon behavioural insights at scale. Unlike recommendation systems that suggest content based on predefined filters or machine-learning models confined to analysing historical data, LAMs thrive on continuous interaction. By dynamically adjusting to new behavioural inputs, they craft personalised trajectories that guide users towards specific objectives. This integration enables platforms to anticipate immediate responses and the broader decision-making patterns of individual users, transforming how they interact with digital ecosystems. While traditional recommendation algorithms might suggest products based on a user's purchase history, LAMs predict the emotional and psychological states influencing purchasing behaviour. A LAM could discern hesitation during a browsing session, infer the underlying cause – such as price sensitivity or lack of urgency – and adapt the interface to counteract these barriers. This adaptive functionality allows LAMs to operate with precision and influence unattainable for traditional systems, bridging the gap between passive recommendation and active manipulation.

The precision of LAMs also lies in their ability to contextualise user behaviour across diverse platforms and environments. Traditional AI systems often operate within siloed datasets, limiting their scope to specific applications or contexts. LAMs, by contrast, aggregate data from multiple interactions, constructing a unified behavioural profile that transcends individual use cases. This holistic approach enables them to identify cross-platform patterns, such as how a user's engagement with social media influences their purchasing decisions on e-commerce sites. By integrating these insights, LAMs can tailor their strategies to achieve consistency in manipulation across different domains. Moreover, LAMs leverage predictive analytics to simulate future behaviours, enabling platforms to adjust their strategy pre-emptively. Traditional AI models react to observed actions, whereas LAMs anticipate unarticulated needs and design pathways to fulfil them. This predictive capability enhances their effectiveness in guiding users towards predefined outcomes, often without conscious awareness. For example, a streaming service powered by a LAM might predict a user's likelihood of unsubscribing based on subtle changes in viewing habits. In response, it could proactively introduce features or promotions designed to re-engage the user, presenting them as organic developments rather than targeted interventions.

The operational scope of LAMs extends beyond immediate interactions, embedding their influence within the broader ecosystem of digital decision-making. By learning from cumulative user data, LAMs refine their strategies to align with individual behaviours while maintaining the flexibility to adapt to wider trends. This capability ensures their manipulative potential evolves alongside users, rendering static regulatory approaches inadequate. Limited by their deterministic frameworks, traditional AI systems cannot achieve this level of integration or adaptability, highlighting the transformative impact of LAMs on digital manipulation. The capacity of LAMs to synthesise data from multiple contexts enables them to construct a comprehensive behavioural profile for each user. This profile informs the system's adaptive strategies, including altering interface layouts, modifying the timing and tone of prompts, or introducing entirely new elements to influence decision-making. For instance, a streaming platform powered by LAMs might observe that a user often hesitates before subscribing to premium content. Based on this insight, the system could dynamically display a personalised discount or offer additional trial features when the user appears most receptive.

The ability to adjust choice environments in real-time amplifies the manipulative potential of LAMs. These systems blur the distinction between interface and system architecture, embedding deceptive design principles at the operational level while maintaining the appearance of transparency in the user interface. The user perceives a seamless, intuitive experience, unaware of the algorithmic interventions shaping their journey. Unlike traditional dark patterns, which often involve visible friction points or coercive prompts, LAMs operate invisibly, aligning their manipulations with the user's inferred preferences and emotional states. One of the most alarming capabilities of LAMs lies in their ability to exploit subliminal techniques to distort decision-making processes. These systems can subtly influence users without explicit awareness by leveraging insights into subconscious triggers and behavioural psychology. Subliminal manipulation operates beneath conscious perception, employing cues that nudge users toward predetermined outcomes. For instance, a LAM might incorporate slight variations in colour gradients, timing of prompts, or background animations that evoke emotional responses, reinforcing actions or decisions. This action highlights how the deceptive design operates within the system architecture rather than the user interface. An examination of the user interface might not identify these elements as dark patterns at all. The critical point is that the user sees these specific UI tools only because the system has learned – through data and adaptive processes – that these tactics are particularly effective at influencing you, the target of the deception.

LAMs' ability to exploit vulnerabilities associated with age, disability, or specific social or economic situations further amplifies their potential for harm. These systems can identify vulnerability markers within behavioural data, tailoring manipulative strategies to exploit individuals least equipped to recognise or resist such influences. For instance, elderly users may exhibit slower decision-making patterns or heightened susceptibility to authority cues.[95] A LAM designed for financial services might exploit these traits by presenting high-risk investment options as secure, relying on complex language or visual hierarchies that obscure the risks involved. This targeted manipulation can lead to significant financial harm, eroding trust and autonomy. Individuals with disabilities also face unique risks. A LAM deployed in an online shopping platform could analyse user interactions that suggest difficulty navigating the interface, using this information to introduce frictionless pathways for high-margin products or services. By framing these options as convenient or adaptive solutions, the system could materially distort decision-making, steering users toward outcomes prioritising profitability over accessibility.

Economic and social vulnerabilities present another avenue for exploitation. LAMs can detect indicators of financial distress, such as frequent browsing of budget-oriented products or hesitation at checkout stages. A platform might use this information to promote payday loans or high-interest credit options, framing them as immediate solutions while downplaying the long-term costs. This type of manipulation disproportionately affects economically disadvantaged users, exacerbating cycles of debt and insecurity. Similarly, LAMs could exploit social vulnerabilities by tailoring content or advertisements based on inferred loneliness or isolation, pushing users toward premium subscriptions or social networking services under the guise of community-building.

8.6. Conclusion

The ability of LAMs to personalise manipulative strategies based on vulnerability markers raises concerns and challenges existing regulatory frameworks. However, under Article 5(1)(b) of the AI Act, the high threshold for the prohibition to become applicable presents significant challenges. Each of the five required elements – ranging from proving the intent of the system to manipulate, the targeting of a vulnerable group, the exploitation of specific vulnerabilities, the occurrence of harm, and the causal link between the system's operation and the harm – is cumulative in effect, meaning that all must be satisfied simultaneously. This makes activating the prohibition an exceptionally demanding legal test, limiting its practical enforceability.

Furthermore, current laws often fail to account for the intersectionality of these vulnerabilities, focusing instead on broader categories of consumer protection. Addressing these issues requires a nuanced regulatory approach that considers the diverse contexts in which LAMs operate. The iterative nature of LAMs further complicates these challenges. By continuously refining their strategies based on user responses, these systems can deepen their exploitation of vulnerabilities over time. This feedback loop optimises manipulative tactics and normalises their presence within digital environments, making them increasingly difficult to detect or regulate. Without proactive intervention, LAMs risk embedding systemic inequities into digital interactions, undermining the principles of autonomy and fairness.

The current regulatory focus on user interfaces fails to address the insidious manipulation beneath the surface. The EU's *digital design acquis* targets overt deceptive practices within user interfaces – such as misleading prompts or obstructive consent mechanisms. However, LAMs evade these frameworks by embedding their manipulative tactics within the system architecture. These systems deploy undetectable strategies within the existing regulatory scope by personalising the choice environment and adapting interfaces dynamically. A LAM-driven interface might appear compliant and devoid of explicit dark patterns while leveraging behavioural data to implement more sophisticated and manipulative methods.

This regulatory gap underscores the folly of focusing exclusively on visible elements of the user interface. Manipulation extends beyond what the user sees, embedding itself in how the system operates and evolves to influence behaviour over time. An interface designed by an LAM might outwardly comply with transparency and consent requirements while subtly steering users toward predefined outcomes. For instance, a subscription platform could use a LAM to identify moments of indecision and dynamically present personalised offers or create subtle barriers to cancellation. These tactics exploit the user's behavioural vulnerabilities without breaching overt regulatory prohibitions on interface design.

Unlike static dark patterns that can be identified and remedied, LAM-driven deception's adaptive and context-aware nature challenges the premise of user-centred regulation. Current frameworks assume that manipulation resides in static design choices, overlooking the fluid, algorithmic processes that underpin modern digital environments. Consequently, a legal approach confined to the interface risks legitimising manipulative practices embedded within the architecture.

Addressing this issue demands a recalibration of regulatory paradigms. Legal frameworks must expand their focus to encompass the operational dynamics of system architecture. Transparency mandates should extend beyond surface-level disclosures to include the underlying algorithms and data flows driving adaptive behaviour. Periodic audits must assess the interface and mechanisms through which systems learn and apply behavioural insights. Furthermore, regulators should establish benchmarks for acceptable levels of personalisation, ensuring that adaptive systems respect user autonomy rather than exploit it.

The challenge is not merely technical but conceptual. Regulators must recognise that deception and manipulation permeate the fabric of system operations, extending far beyond the visible interface. A regulatory approach that scrutinises only the surface risks allows increasingly sophisticated manipulative tactics to proliferate unchecked. By broadening the scope of enforcement to include the deeper layers of system architecture, policymakers can address the evolving landscape of digital manipulation and safeguard the integrity of user interaction.

The profound challenges LAMs pose demand a legal interpretation beyond a literal reading. Existing regulations, often narrowly centred on visible user interface manipulations, must evolve to address the covert and systemic harms embedded within system architectures. Legal frameworks should target explicit manipulative practices and anticipate LAM-driven systems' adaptive and iterative nature. Broadening the scope of current regulations allows regulators to tackle the nuanced, context-sensitive strategies intrinsic to LAMs. Such an approach ensures that these technologies serve societal interests, protecting autonomy, fairness, trust, and collective well-being.

A concerted effort across disciplines – encompassing law and technology – is imperative to ensure these systems empower rather than exploit. By addressing the asymmetries of knowledge and control they instantiate, society can navigate this frontier while safeguarding the autonomy and agency that underpin meaningful digital engagement. The profound challenges LAMs pose require an interpretation of the law that transcends its literal wording. Existing regulations, often narrowly focused on visible user interface manipulations, must evolve to encompass the more covert and systemic harms embedded within system architectures. Legal frameworks should target explicit manipulative practices and anticipate LAM-driven systems' adaptive and iterative nature. Expanding the interpretive reach of current legal frameworks enables regulators to address the nuanced, context-sensitive strategies intrinsic to LAMs. Such an approach ensures that these technologies advance societal interests, encompassing the protection of autonomy, fairness, trust, and collective well-being fostered by equitable digital environments. While companies retain the legitimate right to pursue profit, they should adhere to practices that honour both the letter and the spirit of the law, thereby preserving public confidence in the integrity of digital systems.

Just as I submitted this manuscript, the European Commission released 32 pages of guidelines for Article 5(1)(a) and (b) of the EU AI Act, integrating much of the work from my lengthy commissioned report.[96] Unfortunately, this interpretive guidance still leaves several critical questions unanswered about the practical application of these provisions and the scope of their prohibitions. While the provisions ostensibly aim to prevent psychological manipulation and target vulnerabilities, the lack of specificity in the guidelines raises concerns about whether the thresholds for such bans are so high that certain insidious practices might be normalised.

For example, what happens when an AI system learns to exploit vulnerabilities to achieve a specific outcome, yet the resulting distortion only becomes apparent after a significant delay? At this point, it becomes materially impactful. For example, an AI system used in targeted advertising might initially deploy messaging that seems benign but later results in sustained behavioural shifts. When the distortion is observable, the harm might already be entrenched, making remedies far more difficult to implement. This temporal disconnect between action and impact challenges traditional regulatory mechanisms, often relying on immediate or quick demonstrable harm.

What happens when an AI system causes a material distortion, but the subliminal techniques employed are not fully understood, identifiable, or proveable? For example, machine learning models may develop opaque strategies for influencing behaviour, such as optimising content presentation to exploit specific emotional states or cognitive biases. These strategies might not be explicitly programmed but instead emerge through the AI's training and self-optimization processes. This raises the issue of whether the prohibition under Article 5 can effectively address AI-generated manipulations' complex and emergent nature when the mechanisms are imperceptible to even their developers.

How will regulators enforce a prohibition against psychological manipulation when the effects are distributed, subtle, difficult to isolate, and, more importantly, replicated scientifically? Traditional enforcement mechanisms rely on clear causation and evidence of harm. Still, AI systems often operate within networks of influence that make attributing outcomes to specific manipulative practices challenging, moreover, in cases where the AI's methods are not transparent or auditable.

Regulators and researchers have made strides in recognising and addressing deceptive design. However, the evolution of digital manipulation – from overt interface-level tricks to covert systemic strategies – demands a recalibrated regulatory focus. The emergence of AI-driven tools such as LAMs exemplifies the escalation of this challenge, embedding nuanced manipulative practices within system architectures in ways that evade traditional enforcement mechanisms. While existing legal frameworks like the GDPR, DSA, and UCPD have set valuable benchmarks for transparency and accountability, they remain insufficient to counteract digital exploitation's dynamic and pervasive nature across the user interface levels and the system architecture.

This chapter has explored how regulators have responded to dark patterns embedded in the user interface. It also laid out the case for how deceptive AI-powered design will undermine users, how agentification will foster systemic inequities, and entrench power asymmetries between platforms and consumers. The shift from visible dark patterns to invisible, adaptive manipulative systems exemplifies a monumental change, where user agency is compromised not through outright coercion but through a subtle orchestration of choices designed to prioritise profitability over fairness. Addressing this new frontier requires more than incremental regulatory adaptations; it demands an evolution in how fairness, autonomy, and accountability are conceptualised and operationalised within legal frameworks.

Ultimately, achieving fairness in digital ecosystems is not merely a matter of compliance but a commitment to prioritising users' rights, autonomy, and well-being. By addressing the structural incentives for manipulation, recalibrating enforcement mechanisms, and embedding fairness into the regulatory architecture, the fight against deceptive design can advance from reactive measures to systemic reform. This book has laid the groundwork for understanding these complexities and emphasised the urgent need for a coordinated, forward-thinking response. As platforms evolve, so must the frameworks that govern them, ensuring digital innovation serves the public interest rather than exploiting it.

Afterword: Reflections on the Ride

It's a peculiar experience, writing about a topic as alive as the very systems it seeks to critique. It's both exhilarating and exhausting to think about how far the topics of dark patterns and deceptive design have come since that stormy day in Malta. Back then, as lightning fried televisions and fish leapt onto bridges, I was merely dipping my toes into consumer law. Fast forward a decade, and the work has had more legs than an over-zealous octopus. It's taken me to academic conferences, enforcement hearings, and even the Nobel Prize Summit – an honour that might have overwhelmed me had I not survived the apocalyptic weather of my Mediterranean initiation. I've found myself cited by institutions I once viewed as untouchable bastions of policy, like the European Commission and the OECD, and consulted by Member States as they wrangle with the sprawling complexities of the AI Act. But amidst this whirlwind, the issue's urgency has never been more palpable.

This journey has never been about me; it's about the broader societal realisation that technology, for all its promises of liberation, can quickly imprison us. The rise of deceptive design wasn't the inevitable consequence of digital design maturing; it reflected something more insidious – corporations realising that digital spaces could serve as a perfect playground for behavioural manipulation. And so, here I am, discussing manipulative system architectures on stages that once hosted debates on global hunger or nuclear disarmament. That juxtaposition sometimes feels absurd, but what could be more existential than a machine eroding our autonomy?

What's fascinating is how dark patterns make the law 'click' for people. Most don't understand the intricacies of the GDPR or the UCPD. However, they *feel* the frustration of being led down a rabbit hole trying to unsubscribe from a gym membership or unable to cancel a subscription, the suspicion that creeps in when they're told their cart is about to expire, or the annoyance of clicking 'Accept All Cookies' for the hundredth time that day. These everyday frustrations, dismissed as minor inconveniences, have become the cries of a generation more attuned to how technology bends their will. These everyday experiences are viscerally relatable, making deceptive design the perfect lens for exploring regulatory shortcomings and the triumphs of legal systems attempting to protect user autonomy. If anything, dark patterns have given people a shared language for their unease.

It doesn't require an advanced degree in regulatory theory to know when something online *feels* wrong. And that's a rare gift in a world increasingly governed by opaque algorithms. It's also why I've come to see dark patterns not just as a problem but as a kind of gateway drug for legal literacy. They are the 'aha' moment that makes people realise, perhaps for the first time, that regulation matters, that design is political, and that consent is not always what it seems. In a way, dark patterns act as the law's decoder ring, translating high-minded principles into tangible frustrations. Maybe this is why this lyric relates to so many people:

> Lord knows they all just wanna have total control; Wanna know what you think, wanna know what you do; And they don't think that you know, but I know that you do.

The reality that corporations might understand our desires better than we do deeply unsettles people. It is not just that they nudge us into buying things we don't need; they've mastered the art of weaponising our vulnerabilities against us.

I vividly remember a conversation I had with a student. They were fascinated by how dark patterns seemed to straddle multiple disciplines: law, psychology, computer science, and even behavioural economics. 'It's like a wicked puzzle', they said, 'and whenever you think you've solved it, someone builds a more complex version'. I laughed, not because they were wrong, but because they perfectly articulated what keeps me awake. Deceptive design techniques *are* a wicked puzzle, evolving as quickly as the technologies that enable them.

One of the challenges facing regulators is the disproportionate impact of AI on vulnerable groups. Children, older people, and economically disadvantaged bear the brunt. Platforms exploit their cognitive limitations and emotional vulnerabilities, embedding deceptive practices into architecture. Consider personalised engagement loops keeping us scrolling endlessly or gamified nudges that drive impulsive spending. These practices erode autonomy, deepening existing inequalities. Children's developmental immaturity makes them uniquely susceptible to digital manipulation. They don't just fail to recognise when they're being targeted – they don't even realise *why* they feel compelled to act. AI-powered engagement loops, loot boxes, and in-app purchases prey on these vulnerabilities, conditioning children to associate gratification with consumption. Diminished autonomy, a distorted sense of self-worth, and a growing dependency on platforms exploit every interaction.

This exploitation is not a bug in the system; it's a feature. Refined through constant A/B testing and algorithmic learning, AI systems risk taking this manipulation to unprecedented levels. LAMs don't merely observe user behaviour – they predict and shape it. Imagine an AI assistant navigating the web on your behalf, clicking 'Accept All Cookies' automatically or nudging you toward purchases you didn't intend to make. As AI becomes capable of acting autonomously, the line between human agency and machine influence blurs. Integrating deceptive design into these systems raises thorny legal questions. How do we regulate manipulation when it happens beneath the surface, embedded in code and hidden within system architecture?

I remain sceptical of the law's ability to deliver on its promises. Don't get me wrong – I believe regulation is necessary, even essential. But laws are aspirational by nature, and the gap between aspiration and reality is as wide as the Atlantic. Take the GDPR, for instance. Hailed as a groundbreaking piece of legislation, it has achieved much in terms of transparency and accountability. But has it fundamentally altered the power dynamics between Big Tech and the individual? Not really. Loopholes are everywhere, enforcement feels patchy at best, and let's be honest – most people still click 'Accept All' without even pausing to think. The GDPR, for all its achievements, remains overly reliant on transparency and consent mechanisms that fail to protect users from manipulative design. With all its ambition and regulatory clout, the EU constantly looks like it's scrambling, constantly forced into a reactive stance. It must be frustrating regulating big tech in Europe – like watching a game of whack-a-mole where the moles are billion-dollar tech companies armed with legal teams that could rival the budgets of small nations.

For all the frustration this entails, there is a quiet optimism that we are even having these conversations. The DSA and AI Act take essential steps toward systemic accountability, yet significant gaps remain – especially in safeguarding children and other vulnerable groups. The greatest challenge is regulation's inherently reactive nature; the pace of technological change consistently outstrips lawmakers' ability to keep up. But if we view regulation as a living process that evolves alongside technology, we can close this gap.

This means not just passing laws but investing in enforcement, education, and innovation, recognising that the battle for digital fairness is not a one-time event but an ongoing struggle. The existence of the AI Act, the DSA, and the potential for a Digital Fairness Act (DFA) reflects a growing recognition that something must be done about the health of our digital ecosystem. While the exact form of the DFA remains uncertain, it represents a rare opportunity to address systemic issues that existing regulations have struggled to tackle.

To be effective, it must go beyond surface-level fixes and tackle the root causes of manipulative design, embedding fairness and autonomy into the very DNA of digital platforms. Achieving this regulatory objective will require bold thinking, inter-regulatory collaboration, and a willingness to confront uncomfortable truths about the business models underpinning the digital economy. Policymakers, technologists, and academics must work together to create an anticipatory framework that does not merely react to technological advancements but actively shapes them toward a more just and equitable digital future.

This brings us back to the central tension that has defined my work: the interplay between technology and human behaviour. If there's one thing I've learned, the law misunderstands the latter. So much consumer protection rests on the assumption that people are rational actors capable of making informed decisions. But anyone who has clicked 'I Agree' without reading the terms knows this is fiction. People aren't rational; they're distracted, overwhelmed, and trying to get through their day. And deceptive design exploits this reality with ruthless efficiency.

It's tempting to frame this as a battle between good and evil – regulators striving for fairness versus corporations hell-bent on profit. But the reality is more nuanced. Many of the designers and engineers behind these systems are, at least on some level, well-intentioned. They're optimising for engagement because they're incentivised to do that. The real issue lies in the system – business models prioritising clicks and conversions over autonomy and well-being. This is why the conversation around dark patterns must evolve. It's not just about punishing bad actors or closing legal loopholes; it's about rethinking the incentives that drive digital design in the first place. What if we rewarded companies for promoting healthy digital habits? What if fairness became the metric of success rather than exploitation? These are the questions we must ask as regulators, academics, technologists, and citizens of a digital world.

To those reading this, I offer a challenge: don't stand on the sidelines. Whether you're a designer, a technologist, a student, a lawyer, or a concerned citizen, your voice matters. The emergence of agentic AI systems will significantly increase the stakes, and the responsibility for creating a fair and equitable digital future mustn't rest solely with regulators. Do we passively accept the influence of systems we barely understand, or do we actively shape technology to reflect our values and aspirations? The decision requires courage, collaboration, and a commitment to prioritising interests.

As I look back on this journey, I can't help but feel a mix of frustration and hope – frustration at how far we still must go but hope in the fact that we're moving in the right direction. Dark patterns may have started as a niche topic, but they have become a symbol of something much larger – a growing awareness that our digital lives are worth protecting. And if this journey has taught me anything, the fight for fairness – no matter how difficult – is always worth it.

That, I think, is a legacy worth fighting for.

NOTES

Foreword

[1] T Blake, S Moshary, K Sweeney and S Tadelis, 'Price salience and product choice' (2021) *Marketing Science* 40(4), 619–636 https://doi.org/10.1287/mksc.2020.1261.

[2] N Bostrom, 'Ethical issues in advanced artificial intelligence' (2003) https://nickbostrom.com/ethics/ai.

[3] S Brand, 'The clock of the long now: time and responsibility' (1999) https://www.hachettebookgroup.com/titles/stewart-brand/the-clock-of-the-long-now/9780786722921/.

Dark Patterns vs Deceptive Design Terminology Explained

[1] K Campbell-Dollaghan, 'The Year Dark Patterns Won' *CO.DESIGN* (21 December 2016) www.fastcompany.com/co-design.

[2] H Brignull, 'Dark Patterns: Deception vs. Honesty in UI Design' *A List Apart* (1 November 2011) alistapart.com. Note: darkpatterns.org is now 'Deceptive Patterns' www.deceptive.design.

Chapter 1
A Frightening Future Awaits, Unless …

[1] Article 3(i) Digital Services Act.

[2] Article 6(1) (f) GDPR.

[3] Article 5 Directive 2005/29 – Unfair business-to-consumer commercial practices in the internal market and amending Council Directive 84/450/EEC, Directives 97/7/EC, 98/27/EC and 2002/65/EC of the European Parliament and of the Council and Regulation 2006/2004 ('Unfair Commercial Practices Directive').

[4] Autoriteit Consument en Markt (ACM), Guidelines on the Protection of the Online Consumer (ACM, February 2020) www.acm.nl/sites/default/files/documents/2020-02/acm-guidelines-on-the-protection-of-the-online-consumer.pdf.

[5] European Commission, Directorate-General for Justice and Consumers, F Lupiáñez-Villanueva et al, Behavioural study on unfair commercial practices in the digital environment: dark patterns and manipulative personalisation: final report (Publications Office of the European Union, 2022) data.europa.eu/doi/10.2838/859030.

[6] European Commission, 'Consumer protection: manipulative online practices found on 148 out of 399 online shops screened' (2023) ec.europa.eu/commission/presscorner/detail/en/ip_23_418; European Innovation Council & SMEs Executive Agency (EISMEA), 'Behavioural study on unfair commercial practices in the digital environment: dark patterns and manipulative personalisation: final report' (Publications Office, 2022) doi.org/10.2838/859030; C Gray, L Sanchez Chamorro, I Obi and J-N Duane, 'Mapping the landscape of dark patterns scholarship: a systematic literature review' (2023) *Designing Interactive Systems Conference* 188.

[7] M Samek, 'New EU Regulation and Consumer Protection: Are National Bodies up to the Task?'.

[8] S Zuboff, 'The Age of Surveillance Capitalism' in W Longhofer and D Winchester (eds), *Social Theory Re-wired* (Routledge, 2023) 203–13.

[9] H Brignull, 'Dark patterns: dirty tricks designers use to make people do stuff' (*90 Percent of Everything*, 8 July 2010) 90percentofeverything.com/2010/07/08/dark-patterns-dirty-tricks-designers-use-to-make-people-do-stuff/index.html.

[10] T Leonard, R Thaler and C Sunstein, *Nudge: improving decisions about health, wealth, and happiness* (Yale University Press, 2008) 293.

[11] RH Thaler, CR Sunstein, and JP Balz, 'Choice Architecture' in E Shafir (ed), *The Behavioral Foundations of Public Policy* (Princeton University Press, 2014).

[12] CR Sunstein, 'Sludge and Ordeals' (2018) 68 *Duke LJ* 1843.

[13] D Kahneman and A Tversky, 'The psychology of preferences' (1982) 246 Scientific American 160.

[14] G Gigerenzer, 'On Narrow Norms and Vague Heuristics: A Reply to Kahneman and Tversky' (1996).

[15] K Yeung, '"Hypernudge": Big Data as a mode of regulation by design' (2016) 20(1) *Information, Communication & Society* 118–36, doi.org/10.1080/1369118X.2016.1186713.

[16] E Laidlaw, 'A framework for identifying internet information gatekeepers' (2010) 24(3) *International Review of Law, Computers & Technology* 263.

[17] Directive 2006/24/EC of the European Parliament and of the Council of 15 March 2006 on the retention of data generated or processed in connection with the provision of publicly available electronic communications services or of public communications networks and amending Directive 2002/58/EC.

[18] Article 25 Digital Services Act.

[19] Recital 42 GDPR.

[20] Article 7 GDPR.

[21] H Brignull, 'Dark patterns: deception vs honesty in UI design' (*A List Apart*, 1 November 2011) alistapart.com/article/dark-patterns-deception-vs.-honesty-in-ui-design.

[22] FTC, 'Bringing dark patterns to light' (2022) www.ftc.gov/system/files/ftc_gov/pdf/P214800%20Dark%20Patterns%20Report%209.14.2022%20-%20FINAL.pdf.

[23] However, please note that in a strongly worded judgment, the Eighth Circuit Court of Appeals held that the Federal Trade Commission breached its obligations under 15 USC § 57b-3(b)(1) by failing to publish a preliminary regulatory analysis after concluding that the proposed rule would impose annual costs exceeding $100 million; see, Joseph Gedeon, 'US court strikes down "click-to-cancel" rule designed to make unsubscribing easier' The Guardian (Washington, 8 July 2025) www.theguardian.com/us-news/2025/jul/08/court-click-to-cancel-ruling accessed 21 July 2025.

[24] FTC, 'Federal Trade Commission announces final "click to cancel" rule, making it easier for consumers to end recurring charges' (Press Release, 2024) www.ftc.gov/news-events/news/press-releases/2024/10/federal-trade-commission-announces-final-click-cancel-rule-making-it-easier-consumers-end-recurring.

[25] S Levine, 'Remarks at the National Advertising Division Annual Conference 2024 – a record of results for American consumers' (Federal Trade Commission, 16 September 2024) www.ftc.gov/system/files/ftc_gov/pdf/remarks-samuel-levine-nad.pdf.

[26] California Privacy Protection Agency, 'Enforcement advisory on avoiding dark patterns: clear and understandable language, symmetry in choice' (CPPA, 4 September 2024) cppa.ca.gov/announcements/2024/20240904.html.

[27] Colorado Privacy Act, Colo. Rev. Stat. §§ 6-1-1301 to -1310 (2022).

[28] Central Consumer Protection Authority, 'Guidelines to provide for the prevention and regulation of dark patterns' (2023) F.No. J-24/34/2023-CPU.

[29] M Leiser and C Santos, 'Dark patterns, enforcement, and the emerging digital design acquis: manipulation beneath the interface' (2024) 15(1) *EJLT*, BILETA Special Issue ejlt.org/index.php/ejlt/article/view/990/1084.

[30] 'Deceptive design laws' (Deceptive Design, 2024) www.deceptive.design/laws.

[31] H Brignull, *Deceptive Patterns* (Testimonium Ltd, 2023).

[32] H Boroji, 'The UX iceberg model: understanding the user experience' (*Usability Geek*, 6 June 2018).

[33] M Leiser, 'Psychological Patterns and Article 5 of the AI Act: AI-Powered Deceptive Design in the System Architecture and the User Interface' (2024) 1(1) *Journal of AI law and Regulation* 5–23.

[34] C Gray et al, 'The dark (patterns) side of UX design', Proceedings of the 2018 CHI Conference (2018) On Human Factors in Computing Systems, doi.org/10.1145/3173574.3174108; G Conti and E Sobiesk (2010), 'Malicious Interface Design: Exploiting the User', Proceedings of Christoph Bösch, Benjamin Erb, Frank Kargl, Henning Kopp, and Stefan Pfattheicher. 'Tales from the dark side: Privacy dark strategies and privacy dark patterns. Proceedings on Privacy Enhancing Technologies' (2016) 4, 237–54. the 19th International Conference on World Wide Web – WWW' 10, doi.org/10.1145/1772690.1772719; A Mathur et al (2019), 'Dark patterns at scale: Findings from a crawl of 11K shopping websites', Proceedings of the ACM on Human-Computer Interaction, Vol 3/CSCW, doi.org/10.1145/3359183; Leiser and Yang have formulated a taxonomy applicable to dark patterns directed at consumers; see W-T Yang and M Leiser, 'Illuminating Manipulative Design: From "Dark Patterns" to Information Asymmetry and the Repression of Free Choice under the Unfair Commercial Practices Directive' (2022) 34 *Loy. Consumer L. Rev.* 484.

[35] S van der Hof, S van Hilten, S Ouburg, MV Birk and AJ van Rooij, '"Don't Gamble With Children's Rights" – How Behavioral Design Impacts the Right of Children to a Playful and Healthy Game Environment' (2022) 4 *Frontiers in Digital Health* 822933.

[36] OECD (2022), 'Dark commercial patterns', OECD Digital Economy Papers, No. 336, OECD Publishing, Paris, doi.org/10.1787/44f5e846-en.

[37] Note Harry Brignull has also dropped the narrow 'dark patterns' descriptor for more expansive 'deceptive patterns'. See the successor website to darkpatterns.org, deceptive.design.

Chapter 2
Deceptive Techniques and their Associated Harms

[1] International Consumer Protection and Enforcement Network, 'Dark Patterns in Subscription Services Sweep Public Report 2024' (2024) icpen.org/sites/default/files/2024-07/Public%20Report%20ICPEN%20Dark%20Patterns%20Sweep.pdf; Federal Trade Commission, 'Bringing Dark Patterns to Light' (2022) www.ftc.gov/system/files/ftc_gov/pdf/P214800%20Dark%20Patterns%20Report%209.14.2022%20-%20FINAL.pdf.

[2] European Commission, 'Behavioural Study on Unfair Commercial Practices in the Digital Environment' (2022) op.europa.eu/en/publication-detail/-/publication/606365bc-d58b-11ec-a95f-01aa75ed71a1/language-en.

[3] A Mathur et al, 'Dark Patterns at Scale: Findings from a Crawl of 11K Shopping Websites' (2019) collaborate.princeton.edu/en/publications/dark-patterns-at-scale-findings-from-a-crawl-of-11k-shopping-webs.

[4] S Konsumenter, 'Are You Sure You Want to Leave Us? Deceptive Design Patterns in the Cancellation Processes of 20 Digital Services in Sweden' (2024) www.sverigeskonsumenter. se/media/mgkdpb3g/are-you-sure-you-want-to-leave-us.pdf.

[5] H Brignull, 'Types of Dark Patterns' (no date) darkpatterns.org/.

[6] H Brignull, 'Dark Patterns: Deception vs Honesty in UI Design' (*A List Apart*, 1 November 2011) alistapart.com/article/dark-patterns-deception-vs-honesty-in-ui-design; see also H Brignull, 'Dark patterns: User interfaces designed to trick people' (UX Brighton Conference, Brighton, 2010) www.slideshare.net/harrybr/ux-brighton-dark-patterns.

[7] H Brignull, *Deceptive Patterns: Exposing the Tricks Tech Companies Use to Control You* (Testimonium, 2024) www.amazon.co.uk/Deceptive-Patterns-Exposing-Companies-Control-ebook/dp/B0CB4PP2N2.

[8] CM Gray, C Teixeira Santos, N Bielova and T Mildner, 'An Ontology of Dark Patterns Knowledge: Foundations, Definitions, and a Pathway for Shared Knowledge-Building' in Proceedings of the CHI Conference on Human Factors in Computing Systems (CHI '2024). Association for Computing Machinery, New York, NY, USA, Article 289, 1–22. doi. org/10.1145/3613904.3642436.

[9] M Leiser and C Santos, 'Dark Patterns, Enforcement, and the Emerging Digital Design Acquis: Manipulation Beneath the Interface' (2024) 15(1) *European Journal of Law and Technology*.

[10] European Commission (n 2).

[11] Gray et al (n 8); Mathur et al (n 3); Brignull (n 6); Bösch et al (2016).

[12] European Commission (n 2); Luguri and Strahilevitz (2022); Organisation for Economic Co-operation and Development (OECD), *OECD Report Highlighting Concerns Over Dark Patterns* (2022) www.oecd-ilibrary.org/docserver/44f5e846-en.pdf.

[13] Organisation for Economic Co-operation and Development, OECD (n 12).

[14] Federal Trade Commission (n 1).

[15] European Commission (n 2).

[16] Brignull (n 5).

[17] H Brignull, *Deceptive Patterns: The Practice of Manipulative Design* (Testimonium Ltd, 2024) ch 13.

[18] OECD (n 12).

[19] M Kowalczyk, JT Gunawan, D Choffnes, DJ Dubois, W Hartzog and C Wilson, 'Understanding Dark Patterns in Home IoT Devices' in *Proceedings of the 2023 CHI Conference on Human Factors in Computing Systems* (2023) 1, 19.

[20] Brignull (n 17) ch 8.

[21] Internet Society Foundation, *The Economic Consequences of Digital Dark Patterns* www.isocfoundation.org/project/the-economic-consequences-of-digital-dark-patterns-2/.

[22] Consumer Policy Research Centre (CPRC), *Duped by Design: Manipulative Online Design – Dark Patterns in Australia* (June 2022) cprc.org.au/report/duped-by-design-manipulative-online-design-dark-patterns-in-australia/.

[23] A Mathur, M Kshirsagar and J Mayer, 'What Makes a Dark Pattern ... Dark? Design Attributes, Normative Considerations, and Measurement Methods' in *Proceedings of the 2021 CHI Conference on Human Factors in Computing Systems* (2021) 1, 1–18.

[24] Brignull (n 17) ch 8.

[25] Netherlands Authority for Consumers & Markets, *Guidelines on the applicability of consumer law 'Protection of the online consumer: boundaries of online persuasion'* (2020) www.acm.nl/sites/default/files/documents/2019-12/draft-consultation-acm-guidelines-on-protection-of-online-consumer-boundaries-of-online-persuasion_0.pdf.

[26] D Martin, Dark Patterns: Impact on consumers and potential harm. Presentation at the IMCO Public Hearing, 'Dark Patterns and How Such Practices Harm Consumers and the Digital Single Market' (16 March 2022) www.beuc.eu.

[27] Brignull (n 17) ch 13.

[28] Brignull (n 17) ch 14.

[29] B Chugh and P Jain, 'Unpacking dark patterns: Understanding dark patterns and their implications for consumer protection in the digital economy' (2021) 7(1) *RGNUL Student Research Review* 1–21.

[30] Competition and Markets Authority, 'Online Choice Architecture: How Digital Design Can Harm Competition and Consumers' (Discussion Paper, April 2022) www.gov.uk/government/publications/online-choice-architecture-how-digital-design-can-harm-competition-and-consumers.

[31] G Day and A Stemler, 'Are dark patterns anticompetitive?' (2020) 72(1) *Alabama Law Review* 1.

[32] Norwegian Consumer Council, *Deceived by Design: How Tech Companies Use Dark Patterns to Discourage Us from Exercising Our Rights to Privacy* (2018) www.forbrukerradet.no/undersokelse/2015/appfail-threats-to-consumers-in-mobile-apps/.

[33] C Santos, V Morozovaite and S De Conca, 'No harm no foul: how harms caused by dark patterns are conceptualised and tackled under EU data protection, consumer and competition laws' *Information & Communications Technology Journal* forthcoming, 2025.

[34] M Lotherington, '"Design is Not Just What It Looks and Feels Like. Design is How It Works"' (*Medium*, 6 October 2019) medium.com/@maxylotherington/001-design-is-not-just-what-it-looks-and-feels-like-design-is-how-it-works-36867dde11bc.

[35] Leiser and Santos (n 9).

[36] M Leiser, 'Psychological Patterns and Article 5 of the AI Act: AI-Powered Deceptive Design in the System Architecture and the User Interface' (2024) 1(1) *Journal of AI Law and Regulation* 5–23.

[37] G Malgieri and M-L Rebrean, 'Vulnerability in the EU AI Act: building an interpretation' (28 November 2024) ssrn.com/abstract=5058591 or dx.doi.org/10.2139/ssrn.5058591.

[38] SA McLean, SJ Paxton, EH Wertheim and J Masters, 'Selfies and social media: relationships between self-image editing and photo-investment and body dissatisfaction and dietary restraint' (2015) 3 *Journal of Eating Disorders* O21.

[39] Leiser and Santos (n 9).

[40] OECD (n 12).

[41] B Casey, A Farhangi and R Vogl, 'Rethinking Explainable Machines: The GDPR's 'Right to Explanation' Debate and the Rise of Algorithmic Audits in the Enterprise' (2018) 34 *Berkeley Technology Law Journal* 143.

[42] CMA (n 30).

[43] Leiser and Santos (n 9).

[44] Day and Stemler (n 31).

[45] Leiser (n 36).

[46] Casey et al (n 41).

[47] CMA (n 30).

[48] Federal Trade Commission, 'The FTC's Hearings on Competition and Consumer Protection in the 21st Century' (Day 1, 9 April 2019) www.ftc.gov/system/files/documents/public_events/1418273/ftc_hearings_session_12_transcript_day_1_4-9-19.pdf.

[49] Day and Stemler (n 31).

Chapter 3
Regulatory Responses to Dark Patterns and Deceptive Design

[1] US Federal Trade Commission, 'FTC Report Shows Rise of Sophisticated Dark Patterns Designed to Trick and Trap Consumers' (15 September 2022) www.ftc.gov/news-events/news/press-releases/2022/09/ftc-report-shows-rise-sophisticated-dark-patterns-designed-trick-trap-consumers.

[2] Federal Trade Commission, *Bringing Dark Patterns to Light: Staff Report* (14 September 2022) www.ftc.gov/system/files/ftc_gov/pdf/P214800%20Dark%20Patterns%20Report%209.14.2022%20-%20FINAL.pdf.

[3] California Privacy Protection Agency, *California Privacy Protection Agency* (CPPA) cppa.ca.gov/.

[4] California Consumer Privacy Act 2018, Cal Civ Code §§ 1798.100–1798.199 (as amended by the California Privacy Rights Act 2020).

[5] Competition and Markets Authority and Information Commissioner's Office, *Competition and Data Protection in Digital Markets: A Joint Statement* (19 May 2021) ico.org.uk/media/about-the-ico/documents/2619797/cma-ico-public-statement-20210518.pdf, at para 88.

[6] Regulation (EU) 2022/2065 of the European Parliament and of the Council of 19 October 2022 on a Single Market For Digital Services and amending Directive 2000/31/EC (Digital Services Act) [2022] OJ L 277/1.

[7] European Commission, *Questions and Answers: The Digital Services Act Package* (15 December 2020) ec.europa.eu/commission/presscorner/detail/en/qanda_20_2348.

[8] Regulation (EU) 2022/1925 of the European Parliament and of the Council of 14 September 2022 on contestable and fair markets in the digital sector (Digital Markets Act) [2022] OJ L 265/1.

[9] Article 13(6) DMA.

[10] European Data Protection Board, *Guidelines 03/2022 on Deceptive Design Patterns in Social Media Platform Interfaces: How to Recognise and Avoid Them* Version 2.0 (14 February 2023) www.edpb.europa.eu/system/files/2023-02/edpb_03-2022_guidelines_on_deceptive_design_patterns_in_social_media_platform_interfaces_v2_en_0.pdf.

[11] European Commission, *Commission Notice – Guidance on the Interpretation and Application of Directive 2005/29/EC of the European Parliament and of the Council Concerning Unfair Business-to-Consumer Commercial Practices in the Internal Market* (2021/C 526/01) commission.europa.eu/law/law-topic/consumer-protection-law/unfair-commercial-practices-and-price-indication/unfair-commercial-practices-directive_en#:~:text=On%202017%20December%202021%2C%20the,Staff%20Working%20Document%20from%202016.

[12] Federal Trade Commission, *Federal Trade Commission Act Incorporating U.S. SAFE WEB Act Amendments of 2006* (15 USC § 41 et seq) www.ftc.gov/sites/default/files/documents/statutes/federal-trade-commission-act/ftc_act_incorporatingus_safe_web_act.pdf.

[13] ME Stucke, *Addressing Personal Data Collection as Unfair Methods of Competition* (2023) University of Tennessee College of Law, Berkeley Technology Law Journal ir.law.utk.edu/cgi/viewcontent.cgi?article=1966&context=utklaw_facpubs.

[14] Directive 2002/58/EC of the European Parliament and of the Council of 12 July 2002 concerning the processing of personal data and the protection of privacy in the electronic

communications sector (Directive on privacy and electronic communications) [2002] OJ L201/37.

[15] Directive 2002/58/EC of the European Parliament and of the Council of 12 July 2002 concerning the processing of personal data and the protection of privacy in the electronic communications sector (Directive on privacy and electronic communications) [2002] OJ L 201/37, art 5(3) (as amended by Directive 2009/136/EC of the European Parliament and of the Council of 25 November 2009 amending Directive 2002/22/EC on universal service and users' rights relating to electronic communications networks and services, Directive 2002/58/EC concerning the processing of personal data and the protection of privacy in the electronic communications sector and Regulation (EC) No 2006/2004 on cooperation between national authorities responsible for the enforcement of consumer protection laws).

[16] Directive 2002/58/EC of the European Parliament and of the Council of 12 July 2002 concerning the processing of personal data and the protection of privacy in the electronic communications sector (Directive on privacy and electronic communications) [2] [2002] OJ L 201/37, recitals 24, 25 (as amended by Directive 2009/136/EC of the European Parliament and of the Council of 25 November 2009 amending Directive 2002/22/EC on universal service and users' rights relating to electronic communications networks [3] and services, Directive 2002/58/EC concerning the processing of personal data and the protection of privacy in the electronic communications sector and Regulation (EC) No 2006/2004 on cooperation between national authorities responsible for the enforcement of consumer protection laws); [4] Regulation (EU) 2016/679 of the European Parliament and of the Council of 27 April 2016 on the protection of natural persons with regard to the processing of personal data and on the free movement of such data, and repealing Directive 95/46/EC (General Data Protection Regulation) [5] [2016] OJ L 119/1, recital 66.

[17] Case C-673/17 *Planet49 GmbH v Bundesverband der Verbraucherzentralen und Verbraucherverbände – Verbraucherzentrale Bundesverband* eV ECLI:EU:C:2019:801, [2020] 1 WLR 2248.

[18] Information Commissioner's Office, *Guidance on the Rules on Use of Cookies and Similar Technologies* (May 2012) ico.org.uk/media/for-organisations/documents/1545/cookies_guidance.pdf.

[19] C Santos, CM Gray, N Bielova and S Ahuja, 'Usable and Lawful: Can Consent be Both?' (18 September 2024) ssrn.com/abstract=4961361 or dx.doi.org/10.2139/ssrn.4961361.

[20] In addition to Article 5(3) of the ePrivacy Directive, see also Article 6(1)(a), GDPR.

[21] Article 4(11), GDPR; See also M Nouwens et al, 'Dark Patterns after the GDPR: Scraping Consent Popups and Demonstrating Their Influence' in *Proceedings of the 2020 CHI Conference on Human Factors in Computing Systems* (2020).

[22] Article 5(1)(a) GDPR.

[23] Article 12(1) GDPR.

[24] T Htut Soe, O Elise Nordberg, F Guribye and M Slavkovik, 'Circumvention by Design: Dark Patterns in Cookie Consent for Online News Outlets' in *Proceedings of the 11th Nordic Conference on Human-Computer Interaction: Shaping Experiences, Shaping Society (NordiCHI' 20)* (2020, ACM, New York) doi.org/10.1145/3419249.3420132.

[25] I Sanchez-Rola et al, 'Can I Opt Out Yet? GDPR and the Global Illusion of Cookie Control' in *Proceedings of the 2019 ACM Asia Conference on Computer and Communications Security (AsiaCCS' 19)* (2019, ACM, New York) 340 doi.org/10.1145/3321705.3329806 at 344.

[26] M Toth, N Bielova and V Roca, 'On Dark Patterns and Manipulation of Website Publishers by CMPs' (2022) 2022(3) *Proceedings on Privacy Enhancing Technologies* 478 doi.org/10.56553/popets-2022-0082.

[27] A Stöver et al, 'Website Operators Are Not the Enemy Either: Analyzing Options for Creating Cookie Consent Notices without Dark Patterns' (2022) dl.gi.de/server/api/core/bitstreams/cf9c34b9-2708-4008-bc98-946df0844f59/content.

[28] C Santos et al, 'Consent Management Platforms under the GDPR: Processors and/or Controllers?' in *Annual Privacy Forum 2021* (Springer, Cham) 47, arxiv.org/pdf/2104.06861.

[29] Article 7(2) and Recital 42 GDPR.

[30] F Nyquist and T Hildebrand, 'Cookies, GDPR and Dark Patterns: Effect on Consumer Privacy' (2021) Bachelor of Science in Computer Science Thesis, Blekinge Institute of Technology, Karlskrona, Sweden, example.com.

[31] H Habib et al, '"Okay, Whatever": An Evaluation of Cookie Consent Interfaces' in *Proceedings of the 2022 CHI Conference on Human Factors in Computing Systems* (ACM, New York, 2022) 1 dl.acm.org/doi/pdf/10.1145/3491102.3501985.

[32] A Mathur et al, 'Dark Patterns at Scale: Findings from a Crawl of 11K Shopping Websites' (2019) 3 *Proceedings of the ACM on Human-Computer Interaction* CSCW 81, doi.org/10.1145/3359183, especially at 81:26, which discusses how dark patterns violate legal requirements under laws like the Unfair Commercial Practices Directive and damage user trust.

[33] RY Wong, A Chong, and RC Aspegren, 'Privacy Legislation as Business Risks: How GDPR and CCPA Are Represented in Technology Companies' Investment Risk Disclosures' (2023) 7(CSCW1) *Proceedings of the ACM on Human-Computer Interaction* 1 doi.org/10.1145/3579515 at 5.

[34] Toth, Bielova and Roca (n 26) 4.

[35] W Khan, *Digital Deception and the Illusion of Choice: How Dark Patterns Undermine Informed Consent Despite GDPR* (MSc thesis, North Dakota State University 2023) library.ndsu.edu/ir/items/0875b585-b8ba-4902-813c-7069f3a11fe4 at 12.

[36] J Kessler, 'Data Protection in the Wake of the GDPR: California's Solution for Protecting "The World's Most Valuable Resource"' (2019) 93 *Southern California Law Review* 99 heinonline.org/HOL/Page?handle=hein.journals/scal93&div=7&g_sent=1&casa_token=weBBS9d_DVYAAAAA:8Ae1ENNDOr_et6DbYZNwDlVBBJl0rlrnotaOyfE1Tut53Ae-49RDknLNDwZl0gceSidZiVvg, especially at 101.

[37] *Commission Nationale de l'Informatique et des Libertés (CNIL) v Google LLC* (Decision of 21 January 2019) www.edpb.europa.eu/news/national-news/2019/cnils-restricted-committee-imposes-financial-penalty-50-million-euros_en.

[38] CNIL, 'Deliberation of the Restricted Committee SAN-2020-012 of 7 December 2020 concerning Google LLC and Google Ireland Limited' (CNIL, 2020) www.cnil.fr/sites/cnil/files/atoms/files/deliberation_of_restricted_committee_san-2020-012_of_7_december_2020_concerning_google_llc_and_google_ireland_limited.pdf.

[39] CNIL, 'Deliberation of the Restricted Committee SAN-2020-013 of 7 December 2020 concerning Amazon Europe Core' (CNIL, 2020) www.cnil.fr/sites/cnil/files/atoms/files/deliberation_of_restricted_committee_san-2020-013_of_7_december_2020_concerning_amazon_europe_core.pdf.

[40] On 31 December 2021, CNIL fined Facebook €60 million for not providing users with an equally simple method to refuse cookies as to accept them.

[41] Belgian Data Protection Authority, 'IAB Europe Held Responsible for a Mechanism That Infringes the GDPR' (Belgian Data Protection Authority, 2023) www.dataprotectionauthority.be/citizen/iab-europe-held-responsible-for-a-mechanism-that-infringes-the-gdpr#:~:text=The%20Litigation%20Chamber%20therefore%20imposed,into%20compliance%20with%20the%20GDPR.

[42] European Data Protection Board, 'Guidelines 05/2020 on Consent under Regulation 2016/679' (Version 1.1, 13 May 2020) 7 www.edpb.europa.eu/sites/default/files/files/file1/edpb_guidelines_202005_consent_en.pdf.

[43] Autoriteit Persoonsgegevens, 'AP past boetebeleidsregels aan' (Autoriteit Persoonsgegevens, 2025) autoriteitpersoonsgegevens.nl/actueel/ap-past-boetebeleidsregels-aan.

[44] Case C-210/96 *Gut Springenheide GmbH and Rudolf Tusky v Oberkreisdirektor des Kreises Steinfurt – Amt für Lebensmittelüberwachung* ECLI:EU:C:1998:369, [1998] ECR I-4657, para 31; Recital 18 UCPD.

[45] Section 5 of the Federal Trade Commission Act (FTC Act), codified at 15 U.S.C. § 45(a)(1) states: 'Unfair methods of competition in or affecting commerce, and unfair or deceptive acts or practices in or affecting commerce, are hereby declared unlawful.'

[46] 15 U.S.C. § 41, which states: 'A commission is hereby created and established, to be known as the Federal Trade Commission, which shall be composed of five commissioners [...]'.

[47] 5 U.S.C. § 46, which provides that the Commission may: 'Require, by general or special orders, persons, partnerships, and corporations, engaged in or whose business affects commerce, to file with the Commission [...] annual or special [...] reports or answers in writing to specific questions'; 'Investigate, from time to time, trade practices in commerce'; 'Issue subpoenas, and require the attendance and testimony of witnesses and the production of all documentary evidence relating to any matter under investigation'.

[48] 5 U.S.C. § 57a; 15 U.S.C. § 46(i); 5 U.S.C. § 46(j).

[49] Directive 2005/29/EC of the European Parliament and of the Council of 11 May 2005 concerning unfair business-to-consumer commercial practices in the internal market and amending Council Directive 84/450/EEC, Directives 97/7/EC, 98/27/EC and 2002/65/EC of the European Parliament and of the Council and Regulation (EC) No 2006/2004 of the European Parliament and of the Council ('Unfair Commercial Practices Directive')[1] [2005] OJ L 149/22, recitals 7–9.

[50] Council Directive 93/13/EEC of 5 April 1993 on unfair terms in consumer contracts [1993] OJ L95/29, arts 6(1), 7(1).

[51] Articles 6 and 7 UCPD.

[52] Articles 8 and 9 UCPD.

[53] Article 6 UCPD.

[54] Article 7 UCPD.

[55] Authority for Consumers & Markets, 'ACM confronts online stores using misleading countdown timers with their practices' (*ACM*, 6 July 2023) www.acm.nl/en/publications/acm-confronts-online-stores-using-misleading-countdown-timers-their-practices; Macfarlanes LLP, 'The CMA's increasing scrutiny of online businesses' use of urgency claims' (*Macfarlanes*, 8 November 2022) www.macfarlanes.com/what-we-think/102eli5/the-cma-s-increasing-scrutiny-of-online-businesses-use-of-urgency-claims-102ic7m/.

[56] W-T Yang and M Leiser, 'Illuminating Manipulative Design: From "Dark Patterns" to Information Asymmetry and the Repression of Free Choice under the Unfair Commercial Practices Directive' (2022) 34 *Loyola Consumer Law Review* 484.

[57] Article 5 UCPD.

[58] Note 56 above; Note this taxonomy is also cited by European Commission, Directorate-General for Justice and Consumers, F Lupiáñez-Villanueva, A Boluda, F Bogliacino and G Liva et al, *Behavioural study on unfair commercial practices in the digital environment – Dark patterns and manipulative personalisation – Final report* (Publications Office of the European Union, 2022) data.europa.eu/doi/10.2838/859030 at 31–32.

[59] European Parliament and Council, 'Directive (EU) 2019/2161 of the European Parliament and of the Council of 27 November 2019 amending Council Directive 93/13/EEC and Directives 98/6/EC, 2005/29/EC and 2011/83/EU of the European Parliament and of the Council as regards the better enforcement and modernisation of Union consumer protection rules (Text with EEA relevance) '[2019] OJ L328, 7.

[60] European Commission, 'Fitness Check of EU Consumer Law on Digital Fairness' (2023) p 2.

[61] Directive (EU) 2020/1828 of the European Parliament and of the Council of 25 November 2020 on representative actions for the protection of the collective interests of consumers and repealing Directive 2009/22/EC [2020] OJ L409/1.

[62] Directive 2009/22/EC of the European Parliament and of the Council of 23 April 2009 on injunctions for the protection of consumers' interests (Codified version) Text with EEA relevance OJ L 110, 1.5.2009, pp 30–36; Regulation (EU) 2017/2394 of the European Parliament and of the Council of 12 December 2017 on cooperation between national authorities responsible for the enforcement of consumer protection laws and repealing Regulation (EC) No 2006/2004 (Text with EEA relevance)OJ L 345, 27.12.2017, pp 1–26; Directive (EU) 2020/1828 of the European Parliament and of the Council of 25 November 2020 on representative actions for the protection of the collective interests of consumers and repealing Directive 2009/22/EC (Text with EEA relevance) OJ L 409, 4.12.2020, pp 1–27.

[63] 15 U.S. Code § 45 – Unfair methods of competition unlawful; prevention by Commission.

[64] European Data Protection Board, 'Binding Decision 5/2022 on the Dispute Submitted by the Irish SA Regarding WhatsApp Ireland Limited (Art 65 GDPR) '(EDPB, 5 December 2022) edpb.europa.eu/system/files/2023-01/edpb_bindingdecision_202205_ie_sa_whatsapp_en.pdf.

[65] Note 10, EDPB.

[66] Article 5(1)(c) GDPR.

[67] Competition and Markets Authority, *Online Hotel Booking Sites: Commitments to Improve Information Clarity, Accuracy and Presentation* (2019) www.gov.uk/cma-cases/online-hotel-booking.

[68] X Gabaix, D Laibson, D Li, H Li, S Resnick and CG de Vries, 'The impact of competition on prices with numerous firms' (2016) 165 *Journal of Economic Theory* 1–24; M Hunt and E Lindemann, 'Dark Patterns – Where Privacy, Consumer and Competition Laws Meet' (2023) *Bristows* www.bristows.com/news/dark-patterns-where-privacy-consumer-and-competition-laws-meet/.

[69] Competition and Markets Authority, 'Online Choice Architecture: How Digital Design Can Harm Competition and Consumers' (April 2022) 29 assets.publishing.service.gov.uk/media/624c27c68fa8f527710aaf58/Online_choice_architecture_discussion_paper.pdf.

[70] Khaitan & Co, 'Dark Patterns: Shedding Light on Potential Competition Law Implications' (2024) *Lexology* www.lexology.com/library/detail.aspx?g=c994cdde-a6d8-4a7f-b77d-f8ae911ed1e5.

[71] M Tripathi, 'Dark Patterns and Antitrust Laws: Shedding the Light on the Artificial Barriers' (2023) *NLIU CBCL* cbcl.nliu.ac.in/competition-law/dark-patterns-and-antitrust-laws-shedding-the-light-on-the-artificial-barriers/.

[72] Hunt and Lindemann (n 68).

[73] Tripathi (n 71).

[74] S Chitranshi, 'Contextualising Dark Patterns as Unfair Trade Practices Under the 2023 DCA' (2023) *The RMLNLU Law Review Blog* rmlnlulawreview.com/2024/02/04/contextualising-dark-patterns-as-unfair-trade-practices-under-the-2023-dca/.

[75] Khaitan & Co (n 70).

[76] Sherman Antitrust Act 1890, 15 USC §§ 1–7; Federal Trade Commission Act 1914, 15 USC §§ 41–58.

[77] Embodied in the Treaty on the Functioning of the European Union (TFEU), specifically Articles 101 and 102.

[78] Competition and Markets Authority, 'Hotel Booking Sites to Make Major Changes After CMA Probe' (GOV.UK, 2019) www.gov.uk/government/news/hotel-booking-sites-to-make-major-changes-after-cma-probe.

[79] Competition and Markets Authority, 'CMA Leads Europe-Wide Action on Car Hire' (GOV.UK, 2015) www.gov.uk/government/news/cma-leads-europe-wide-action-on-car-hire.

[80] Khaitan & Co (n 70).

[81] Federal Trade Commission, 'FTC Takes Action Against Amazon for Enrolling Consumers in Amazon Prime Without Consent and Sabotaging Their Attempts to Cancel' (Federal Trade Commission, 21 June 2023) www.ftc.gov/news-events/news/press-releases/2023/06/ftc-takes-action-against-amazon-enrolling-consumers-amazon-prime-without-consent-sabotaging-their.

[82] MR Leiser and MM Caruana, 'Dark Patterns: Light to Be Found in Europe's Consumer Protection Regime' (2021) 10(6) *Journal of European Consumer and Market Law*.

[83] Directive (EU) 2019/2161 of the European Parliament and of the Council of 27 November 2019 amending Council Directive 93/13/EEC and Directives 98/6/EC, 2005/29/EC, and 2011/83/EU as regards the better enforcement and modernisation of Union consumer protection rules [2019] OJ L328/7, art 1.

[84] Directive (EU) 2019/2161 of the European Parliament and of the Council of 27 November 2019 amending Council Directive 93/13/EEC and Directives 98/6/EC, 2005/29/EC, and 2011/83/EU as regards the better enforcement and modernisation of Union consumer protection rules [2019] OJ L328/7, art 4.

[85] European Commission, 'Fitness Check on EU Consumer Law on Digital Fairness' (2024) ec.europa.eu/info/law/better-regulation/have-your-say/initiatives/13413-Digital-fairness-fitness-check-on-EU-consumer-law_en.

[86] European Commission, 'Fitness Check of EU Consumer Law' (ibid); European Commission, 'Study to support the Fitness Check of EU Consumer Law on Digital Fairness and the Modernisation Directive (EU) 2019/2161 – Final Report Part 2' (2024).

[87] Chitranshi (n 74).

[88] BEUC, *Dark Patterns and the EU Consumer Law Acquis* (Position Paper, BEUC-X-2022-013, February 2022) www.beuc.eu/sites/default/files/publications/beuc-x-2022-013_dark_patters_paper.pdf.

[89] Bureau Européen des Unions de Consommateurs, 'Dark Patterns and the EU Consumer Law Acquis: Recommendations for Better Enforcement and Reform' (BEUC 2022) www.beuc.eu/sites/default/files/publications/beuc-x-2022-013_dark_patters_paper.pdf.

[90] V Xynogalas and MR Leiser, 'The Metaverse: Searching for Compliance with the General Data Protection Regulation' (2024) 14(2) *International Data Privacy Law* 89, DOI: doi.org/10.1093/idpl/ipae004.

[91] Hunt and Lindemann (n 68).

[92] Chitranshi (n 74).

[93] EASA, 2022.

[94] *Planet49 GmbH* (n 17).

[95] Leiser and Caruana (n 82).

[96] F Di Porto and A Egberts, 'The collective welfare dimension of dark patterns regulation' (2023) 29(1–2) *European Law Journal* 114–41. onlinelibrary.wiley.com/doi/pdf/10.1111/eulj.12478.

Chapter 4
Emerging Digital Design Laws and Regulations

[1] J Van Hoboken, A Arnbak, and N Van Eijk, 'The Proposed EU Digital Services Act: Challenges and Opportunities for Platform Regulation' (2019).

[2] Regulation (EU) 2022/2065 of the European Parliament and of the Council of 19 October 2022 on a Single Market for Digital Services (Digital Services Act) and amending Directive 2000/31/EC [2022] OJ L277/1.

[3] Regulation (EU) 2022/1925 of the European Parliament and of the Council of 14 September 2022 on contestable and fair markets in the digital sector and amending Directives (EU) 2019/1937 and (EU) 2021/2161 (Digital Markets Act) [2022] OJ L 265/1.

[4] Regulation (EU) 2023/1542 of the European Parliament and of the Council of 13 July 2023 on harmonised rules on fair access to and use of data (Data Act) [2023] OJ L130/1.

[5] Directive 2002/58/EC of the European Parliament and of the Council of 12 July 2002 concerning the processing of personal data and the protection of privacy in the electronic communications sector (Directive on privacy and electronic communications) [2002] OJ L 201/37.

[6] Regulation (EU) 2016/679 of the European Parliament and of the Council of 27 April 2016 on the protection of natural persons with regard to the processing of personal data and on the free movement of such data, and repealing Directive 95/46/EC (General Data Protection Regulation) [2016] OJ L 119/1.

[7] Directive 2005/29/EC of the European Parliament and of the Council of 11 May 2005 concerning unfair business-to-consumer commercial practices in the internal market and amending Council Directive 84/450/EEC, Directives 97/7/EC, 98/27/EC and 2002/65/EC of the European Parliament and of the Council and Regulation (EC) No 2006/2004 of the European Parliament and of the Council (Unfair Commercial Practices Directive) [2005] OJ L 149/22.

[8] P Voigt and A Von dem Bussche, *The EU General Data Protection Regulation (GDPR): A Practical Guide*, 1st edn (Springer, 2017) www.scirp.org/reference/referencespapers?refer enceid=2996831.

[9] European Commission, 'The Digital Services Act: Ensuring a Safe and Accountable Online Environment' (2022) commission.europa.eu/strategy-and-policy/ priorities-2019-2024/europe-fit-digital-age/digital-services-act_en.

[10] European Commission, 'Proposal for a Regulation of the European Parliament and of the Council on a Single Market for Digital Services (Digital Services Act) and Amending Directive 2000/31/EC' COM (2020) 825 final.

[11] European Parliament, 'Amendments Adopted by the European Parliament on 20 January 2022 on the Proposal for a Regulation of the European Parliament and of the Council on a Single Market for Digital Services (Digital Services Act)' (2022) P9_TA (2022)0014.

[12] Dr J Jaursch, 'Strengthening EU Proposals on Deceptive Platform Design: Ideas on How to Improve the Draft Digital Services Act' (Stiftung Neue Verantwortung, Policy Brief, March 2022) www.stiftung-nv.de/en.

[13] European Commission, 'European Commission Welcomes the Agreement on New Rules to Improve the Energy Efficiency of Buildings' (Press Release, 10 July 2023) ec.europa. eu/commission/presscorner/detail/en/ip_23_6709.

[14] Article 3(i) DSA.

[15] Article 34 DSA.

[16] Article 27 DSA.

[17] Article 32 DSA.

[18] C Santos, N Bielova, S Ahuja, C Utz, CM Gray and G Mertens, 'Which Online Platforms and Dark Patterns Should Be Regulated under Article 25 of the DSA?' (2024) *SSRN Electronic Journal*, ssrn.com/abstract=4899559.

[19] Recital 78 DSA.

[20] P Siciliani and H Gamper, 'Should a Finding of Material Distortion under Art 6 Para 1 UCPD Raise an Unrebuttable Presumption of Breach of the Duty of Professional Diligence' (2013) 2 J Eur Consumer & Mkt L 225.

[21] Case C-210/96 *Gut Springenheide GmbH and Rudolf Tusky v Oberkreisdirektor des Kreises Steinfurt – Amt für Lebensmittelüberwachung* ECLI:EU:C: 1998:102, [1998] ECR I-04657, para 37.

[22] M Husovec, 'Rising Above Liability: The Digital Services Act as a Blueprint for the Second Generation of Global Internet Rules' (2023) 38(3) *Berkeley Technology Law Journal* 118.

[23] Santos, Bielova, Ahuja, Utz, Gray and Mertens (n 18).

[24] Recital 37 DMA.

[25] Article 3 DMA.

[26] Article 13(6) DMA.

[27] F Di Porto and A Egberts, 'The collective welfare dimension of dark patterns regulation' (2024) 29(1–2) *European Law Journal* 114–41. doi.org/10.1111/eulj.12478.

[28] H.R. 6083, 'Deceptive Experiences to Online Users Reduction (DETOUR) Act', 117th Congress (2021–2022), reintroduced in the 118th Congress on 27 July 2023, available at www.congress.gov/bill/118th-congress/senate-bill/2708.

[29] H.R. 3816, 'American Innovation and Choice Online (AICO) Act', 117th Congress (2021–2022), available at www.congress.gov/bill/117th-congress/house-bill/3816/ text paired with S.2992, 117th Congress (2021–2022), available at www.congress.gov/ bill/117th-congress/senate-bill/2992.

[30] M Brenncke, 'Regulating Dark Patterns' (2024) 14 *Notre Dame J Intl Comp L* 44.

[31] Regulation (EU) 2023/1542 of the European Parliament and of the Council of 12 July 2023 on harmonised rules on fair access to and use of data (Data Act) [2023] OJ L191/1.

[32] S De Conca, 'The Present Looks Nothing Like the Jetsons: Deceptive Design in Virtual Assistants and the Protection of the Rights of Users' (2023) 51 *Computer Law & Security Review* 105866.

[33] KD Moller et al, 'Dark Designs: Patterns, Privacy, and a Paradigm Shift for HCI' (2023) *Proceedings of the 2023 CHI Conference on Human Factors in Computing Systems* doi. org/10.1145/3544548.3581432.

[34] Brenncke (n 30) 39.

[35] Article 3(i) DSA.

[36] ibid.

[37] ibid.

[38] ibid.

[39] Article 2 DMA.

[40] ibid.

[41] ibid.

[42] ibid.

[43] Recital 27 DMA.

[44] Article 3(p); Recital 30 DMA.

[45] Article 7(2) UCPD.

[46] ibid, Article 7(2); Article 25 DSA.

[47] Article 3(i) DSA.

[48] ibid.

[49] ibid.

[50] ibid.

[51] Recital 27 DSA.

[52] Article 3(p) DSA.

[53] Recital 27 DSA.

[54] Article 3(i) DSA.

[55] Recital 70 DSA.

[56] ibid.

[57] ibid.

[58] Recital 42 GDPR.

[59] Article 2(d) UCPD.

[60] Article 3(i) DSA.

[61] ibid.

[62] ibid.

[63] Article 3(p) DSA.
[64] ibid.
[65] Article 3(i) DSA.
[66] Recital 70 DSA.
[67] Article 13 DSA.
[68] Article 25 DSA.
[69] Article 6(1)(a) GDPR.
[70] Article 7 GDPR.
[71] ibid.
[72] Article 9(2)(a) DSA.
[73] Article 25 DSA.
[74] Recital 18 UCPD.
[75] Article 8 UCPD.
[76] Article 8(1) GDPR.
[77] Article 8(2) GDPR.
[78] ibid.
[79] Article 7(1) GDPR.
[80] Recital 38 GDPR.
[81] Articles 12 and 13 GDPR.
[82] Recital 18 UCPD.
[83] Article 5(3) UCPD.
[84] Article 5(3) UCPD.
[85] Article 8 UCPD.
[86] Article 6 UCPD.
[87] Article 7 UCPD.
[88] ibid.
[89] ibid.
[90] Article 7(2) UCPD.
[91] Article 6(1)(b) UCPD.
[92] Recital 70 DSA.
[93] Article 3(i) DSA.
[94] ibid.
[95] Article 2 DSA.
[96] Article 25 DSA.
[97] Article 4(11) GDPR.
[98] Article 7 GDPR.
[99] Article 4(11) GDPR.

Chapter 5
System Architecture Patterns and
the Personalisation of Exploitation

[1] Regulation (EU) 2022/2065 of the European Parliament and of the Council of 19 October 2022 on a Single Market for Digital Services and amending Directive 2000/31/EC (Digital Services Act) [2022] OJ L277/1.

[2] Regulation (EU) 2024/1689 of the European Parliament and of the Council of 12 July 2024 laying down harmonised rules on artificial intelligence (Artificial Intelligence Act) and amending certain Union legislative acts [2024] OJ L206/1.

[3] 'Understanding System Architecture: Types & Benefits' (*Brainium Infotech*,13 September 2022) www.brainiuminfotech.com/blog/understanding-system-architecturetypes-benefits/.

[4] 'What is UI design? A complete introductory guide' (UX Design Institute) www.uxdesigninstitute.com.

[5] 'What is User Interface (UI) Design?' (Interaction Design Foundation) www.interaction-design.org.

[6] AS Tanenbaum and M Van Steen, *Distributed Systems: Principles and Paradigms*, 2nd edn (Pearson Education, 2007) ch 2.

[7] I Sommerville, *Software Engineering*, 10th edn (Pearson Education, 2016) 182–85.

[8] M Sipser, *Introduction to the Theory of Computation*, 3rd edn (Cengage Learning, 2012) 29–35.

[9] California Privacy Rights Act of 2020, Cal. Civ. Code § 1798.100 et seq.

[10] C Lallemand and G Gronier, 'A Design Space for Supporting User's Navigation in Complex Websites' (2007) 5(1) *Journal of Web Engineering* 5, 23.

[11] Sipser (n 8) 29–35, 231–40.

[12] ibid.

[13] F Ricci, L Rokach and B Shapira, *Recommender Systems Handbook*, 2nd edn (Springer, 2015) 1–35.

[14] J Burrell, 'How the Machine "Thinks": Understanding Opacity in Machine Learning Algorithms' (2016) 3 *Big Data & Society* 1.

[15] A Adadi and M Berrada, 'Peeking inside the black-box: A survey on Explainable Artificial Intelligence' (XAI, 2018). IEEE Access, 6, 52138-52160.

[16] G Păun, 'Computing with membranes' (2000) 61(1) Journal *of Computer and System Sciences* 108–43.

[17] Burrell (n 14).

[18] N Diakopoulos, 'Algorithmic accountability: Journalistic investigation of computational power structures' (2015) 3(3) *Digital Journalism* 398–415.

[19] E Bozdag, 'Bias in algorithmic filtering and personalization' (2013) 15(3) *Ethics and Information Technology* 209–27.

[20] J Cobbe, 'Regulating Recommending: Legal and Policy Directions for Governing Platforms' (*Verfassungsblog*, 2021) verfassungsblog.de/roa-regulating-recommending/.

[21] FJ Zuiderveen Borgesius, 'Improving search engine neutrality: A comparative analysis of regulatory approaches' (2016) 12(2) *Utrecht Law Review* 72–89.

[22] FJ Zuiderveen Borgesius and J Poort, 'Online Price Discrimination and EU Data Protection Law' (2023) 60(2) *Common Market Law Review* 523–58.

[23] For a case study about a provider who showed more expensive hotel results to users on mac devices vs PC devices, see J Angwin, 'On Orbitz, Mac Users Steered to Pricier Hotels' (*The Wall Street Journal*, 23 August 2012).

[24] E Bozdag, 'Bias in algorithmic filtering and personalization' (2013) 18(1) *Ethics and Information Technology* 15, 20.

[25] European Parliament, Consumer Protection in Online Video Games: A European Single Market Approach, Wednesday, 18 January 2023, www.europarl.europa.eu/doceo/document/TA-9-2023-0008_EN.html.

[26] House of Lords, Gambling Harm – Time for Action (HL Paper 153, 2020) paras 115–130; SM Gainsbury et al, 'A systematic review of internet gambling: Prevalence, predictors of harm, and policy implications' (2013) 17(4) *Addiction* 835, 853.

[27] N Seaver, 'Captivating Algorithms: Recommender Systems as Traps' (2019) 24(4) *Journal of Material Culture* 421.

[28] CA Lehmann, CB Haubitz, A Fügener and UW Thonemann, 'The Risk of Algorithm Transparency: How Algorithm Complexity Drives the Effects on the Use of Advice' (2022) 31(9) *Production and Operations Management* 3419.

[29] ND Goodman, VK Mansinghka, DM Roy, K Bonawitz and JB Tenenbaum, 'Church: a language for generative models. In Proceedings of the 24th Conference on Uncertainty in Artificial Intelligence' (UAI, 2016).

[30] BJ Fogg, 'Persuasive Technology: Using Computers to Change What We Think and Do' (2003) 5(1) *Ubiquity* 2. 1.

[31] C Nodder, *Evil by Design: Interaction Design to Lead Us into Temptation* (New Riders, 2013) 55–80.

[32] S Zuboff, *The Age of Surveillance Capitalism: The Fight for a Human Future at the New Frontier of Power* (PublicAffairs, 2019).

[33] A Oulasvirta et al, 'Long-Term Use and Trust in Persuasive Computing Systems' (2019) 13 *ACM Transactions on Interactive Intelligent Systems* 1.

[34] RH Thaler and CR Sunstein, *Nudge: Improving Decisions about Health, Wealth, and Happiness* (Penguin Books, 2009).

[35] N Eyal, *Hooked: How to Build Habit-Forming Products* (Portfolio, 2014).

[36] A Tversky and D Kahneman, 'Judgment under Uncertainty: Heuristics and Biases' (1974) 185 *Science*.

[37] RB Cialdini, *Influence: The Psychology of Persuasion* (Harper Business, 2007).

[38] E Pariser, *The Filter Bubble: How the New Personalized Web is Changing What We Read and How We Think* (Penguin Press, 2011).

[39] M Cinelli et al, 'The Echo Chamber Effect on Social Media' (2021) 6 *Proceedings of the National Academy of Sciences* 1.

[40] D Susser, B Roessler and H Nissenbaum, 'Technology, Autonomy, and Manipulation' (2019) 8 *Internet Policy Review* 1.

[41] S Mills and K Ball, 'Surveillance and Conformity in the Digital Age: A Critical Analysis' (2019) 9 *Digital Culture & Society* 2.

[42] K Yeung, 'Hypernudge: Big Data as a Mode of Regulation by Design' (2017) 20 *Information, Communication & Society* 118; M Taddeo and L Floridi, 'How AI Can Be a Force for Good' (2018) 24(1) *Science and Engineering Ethics*.

[43] DA Norman, *The Design of Everyday Things*, Revised and expanded edn (Basic Books, 2013) 45–66.

[44] G Chen and DR Karger, 'Less is More: Probabilistic Models for Retrieving Fewer Relevant Documents' (2006) 29(1) *ACM SIGIR Forum* 429, 436.

[45] G Kostygina et al, 'Nudging and Informed Consent: Reflections on "Libertarian Paternalism"' (2021) 21 *International Journal of Law and Information Technology* 1, 15.

[46] DL King et al, 'Gamification: The effect of rewards and incentives on online consumer engagement' (2014) 46(4) *Journal of Business Research* 529, 537; House of Lords, Gambling Harm – Time for Action (HL Paper 153, 2020) paras 115–130.

[47] A Alter, *Irresistible: The Rise of Addictive Technology and the Business of Keeping Us Hooked* (Penguin Press, 2017) 55–80.

[48] J Van Dijck, 'Social media and the platform society' (2018) 20(4) *Television & New Media* 347, 352.

[49] A Schuster et al, 'Real-time analysis of user behavior in online social networks' in CC Aggarwal (ed), *Social network data analytics* (Springer, 2011) 323–48.

[50] N Eyal and R Hoover, 'Hooked: A Guide to Building Habit-Forming Products' (2014) 2(1) *Nir and Far* 1, 10.

[51] *Understanding DAU/MAU: Key Metrics for Product Success* (Statsig, 2023).

[52] Seaver (n 27) 42, 50.

[53] KC Laudon and CG Traver, *E-commerce: Business, Technology, Society*, 13th edn (Pearson, 2016) 150–75.

[54] PD Berger and NI Nasr, 'Customer lifetime value: Marketing models and applications' (1998) 32(2) *Journal of Interactive Marketing* 17, 33.

[55] T Bucher, 'Want to be on the top? Algorithmic power and the threat of invisibility on Facebook' (2012) 3(3) *New Media & Society* 318, 337.

[56] D Helbing et al, 'Will Democracy Survive Big Data and Artificial Intelligence?' in D Helbing et al (eds), *Digitalization and Global Futures* (Springer, 2021) 85–112.

[57] King et al (n 46) 529, 537.

[58] W Schultz, 'Dopamine reward prediction error coding' (2016) 23(1) *Dialogues in Clinical Neuroscience* 23, 30; MD Griffiths, 'The role of cognitive bias and skill in fruit machine gambling' (1994) 9(1) *British Journal of Psychology* 351, 369; Alter (n 47) 40–65.

[59] Fogg (n 30) 1–25.

[60] J Susskind, 'Digital Nudges and the Law: On the Ethics of Persuasive Technology in the Digital Age' (2020) 33(1) *Ratio Juris* 1, 15.

[61] D Zendle and P Cairns, 'Video game loot boxes are linked to problem gambling: Results of a large-scale survey' (2018) 13(11) *PLoS ONE* e0206767 doi.org/10.1371/journal.pone.0206767.

[62] I Montiel, A Basterra-González, JM Machimbarrena, J Ortega-Barón and J González-Cabrera, 'Loot box engagement: A scoping review of primary studies on prevalence and association with problematic gaming and gambling' (2022) 17(1) *PLoS ONE* e0263177 doi.org/10.1371/journal.pone.0263177.

[63] D King, P Delfabbro and M Griffiths, 'Video game structural characteristics: A new psychological taxonomy' (2010) 8(1) *International Journal of Mental Health and Addiction* 90–106.

[64] LY Xiao, LL Henderson, RKL Nielsen, P Grabarczyk and PWS Newall, 'Loot Boxes: Gambling-Like Mechanics in Video Games' in N Lee (ed), *Encyclopedia of Computer Graphics and Games* (Springer, 2024); L Nakamura, (2009). 'Don't hate the player, hate the game: The racialization of labor in World of Warcraft' (2009) 26(2) *Critical Studies in Media Communication* 128–44 doi.org/10.1007/978-3-031-23161-2_459; J Mills, M Milyavskaya, N Heath and J Derevensky, 'Problem Gambling and Gaming in Adolescents: Relationships with Psychological Needs, Self-Concept, and Impulsivity' (2018) 87 *Computers in Human Behavior* 155.

[65] Zendle and Cairns (n 61).

[66] D Bavelier and CS Green, 'The Role of Video Games in the Formation of Gaming Addiction' (2019) 10 *Frontiers in Psychology* 1136.

[67] DJ Kuss and MD Griffiths MD, 'Internet Gaming Addiction: A Systematic Review of Empirical Research' (2012) 10 *International Journal of Mental Health and Addiction* 278.

[68] King, Delfabbro and Griffiths (n 63) 90.

[69] ibid 90–106.

[70] A Drummond and JD Sauer, 'Video Game Loot Boxes Are Psychologically Akin to Gambling' (2018) 2 *Nature Human Behaviour* 530; Zendle and Cairns (n 61).

[71] MD Griffiths, 'Is the Buying of Loot Boxes in Video Games a Form of Gambling or Gaming?' (2018) 22 *Gaming Law Review* 52.

[72] AK Przybylski and K Murayama, 'Fear of Missing Out, Need for Touch, and Time on Facebook: Prospective Predictors of Problematic Social Media Use' (2013) 29 *Computers in Human Behavior* 1814.

[73] JP Zagal, S Björk and C Lewis, 'Dark Patterns in the Design of Games' in Foundations of Digital Games (Foundations of Digital Games, 2013) 39.

[74] J Hamari and V Lehdonvirta, 'Game Design as Marketing: How Game Mechanics Create Demand for Virtual Goods' (2010) 5 *International Journal of Business Science & Applied Management* 14.

[75] Zendle and Cairns (n 61).

[76] H Wardle and D Zendle, 'Loot boxes, gambling, and problem gambling among young people: Results from a cross-sectional online survey' (2021) 24(4) *Cyberpsychology, Behavior, and Social Networking* 267–74.

[77] Bavelier and Green (n 66).

[78] Griffiths (n 71).

[79] Zendle and Cairns (n 61).

[80] H Nicklin, E Spence and T Grimes, 'The Ethics of Dark Patterns in Games' (2021) 36 *Journal of Media Ethics* 25.

[81] B Abarbanel and BJ Bernhard, 'The Commercialisation of Online Social Gaming and the Gambling Convergence' (2012) 28 *Journal of Gambling Studies* 455.

[82] Zendle and Cairns (n 61).

[83] DL King, PH Delfabbro and MD Griffiths, 'The Role of Structural Characteristics in Problematic Video Game Play: A Review' (2011) 14 *Cyberpsychology, Behavior, and Social Networking* 341.

[84] Kuss and Griffiths (n 67) 278.

[85] Zendle and Cairns (n 61).

[86] Mills, Milyavskaya, HeatN and Derevensky (n 64) 155.

[87] JR Hauser et al, 'Website Morphing 2.0: A Framework for Online Testing and Experimentation' (2020) 53 *Journal of Business Research* 725, 735.

[88] Kostygina et al (n 45) 1, 15.

[89] PS Fader and BG Hardie, 'Probability Models for Customer-Base Analysis' (2009) 23(1) *Journal of Interactive Marketing* 61.

[90] P Weinberg and W Gottwald, 'Impulsive consumer buying as a result of emotions' (1982) 10(1) *Journal of Business Research* 43–57.

[91] K Suk, J Lee and DR Lichtenstein, 'The Influence of Price Presentation Order on Consumer Choice' (2012) 49(5) *Journal of Marketing Research* 708.

Chapter 6
AI-Powered Deceptive Design

[1] C O'Neil, *Weapons of Math Destruction: How Big Data Increases Inequality and Threatens Democracy* (Crown, 2017); F Pasquale, *The Black Box Society: The Secret Algorithms that Control Money and Information* (Harvard University Press, 2015).

[2] European Commission, 'Commission Guidelines on Prohibited Artificial Intelligence Practices Established by Regulation (EU) 2024/1689 (AI Act)' C(2025) 884 final (4 February 2025) 18–50, digital-strategy.ec.europa.eu/en/library/commission-publishes-guidelines-prohibited-artificial-intelligence-ai-practices-defined-ai-act.

[3] L Weissinger, 'AI, Complexity, and Regulation' (SSRN, 14 October 2021) ssrn.com/abstract=3943968.

[4] PS Park, S Goldstein, M Chen and D Hendrycks, 'AI Deception: A Survey of Examples, Risks, and Potential Solutions' (2023) arXiv arxiv.org/abs/2308.14752; See also N Bontridder and Y Poullet, 'The Role of Artificial Intelligence in Disinformation' (2021) 3 *Data & Policy* e32 doi.org/10.1017/dap.2021.20.

[5] J McCarthy, ML Minsky, N Rochester and CE Shannon, 'A Proposal for the Dartmouth Summer Research Project on Artificial Intelligence' (1955).

[6] SJ Russell and P Norvig, *Artificial Intelligence: A Modern Approach*, 4th edn (Pearson, 2021).

[7] H Surden, 'Artificial Intelligence and Law: An Overview' (2019) 35(4) *Georgia State University Law Review*.

[8] On page 1247, Pasquale discusses the 'older, "symbolic" school of AI' and how it relies on 'explicitly programmed rules.' On page 1248, he contrasts this with machine

learning, where 'algorithms are '"trained" on massive datasets' and can adapt over time. F Pasquale, 'Toward a Fourth Law of Robotics: Preserving Attribution, Responsibility, and Explainability in an Algorithmic Society' (2017) 78 *Ohio State Law Journal* 1243, 1247–48.

[9] I Goodfellow et al, *Deep Learning* (MIT Press, 2016) 110–15, 115–20, 10–11.

[10] T JM Bench-Capon and F Coenen, 'Isomorphism and Legal Knowledge Based Systems' (1992) 1(1) *Artificial Intelligence and Law* 65, 66, 68–70, 79–80.

[11] E Clark, 'How Retailers Are Using AI to Manipulate Consumer Shopping' (*Forbes*, 28 November 2023) www.forbes.com/sites/elijahclark/2023/11/28/how-retailers-are-using-ai-to-manipulate-consumer-shopping/.

[12] 'Exploring the Role of Artificial Intelligence in Consumer Experience and Brand Relationship' (2020) Spanish Journal of Marketing – ESIC, www.emerald.com/insight/content/doi/10.1108/SJME-01-2020-0021/full/html.

[13] High-Level Expert Group on Artificial Intelligence, *Ethics Guidelines for Trustworthy AI* (European Commission 2019) 12–13, 14, 16.

[14] 'How Machine Learning Can Improve the Customer Experience' *Harvard Business Review* (March 2023) hbr.org/2023/03/how-machine-learning-can-improve-the-customer-experience.

[15] K Cukier, 'How AI Shapes Consumer Experiences and Expectations' (2021) *Journal of Marketing* journals.sagepub.com/doi/abs/10.1177/0022242920972932.

[16] European Union, *Consolidated Version of the Treaty on the Functioning of the European Union* [2008] OJ C115/01; See also European Commission, Communication from the Commission on the Precautionary Principle (COM(2000) 1 final, 2 February 2000) eur-lex.europa.eu/LexUriServ/LexUriServ.do?uri=COM:2000:0001:FIN:EN:PDF; see also C Sunstein, *Laws of Fear: Beyond the Precautionary Principle* (Cambridge University Press, 2005) 14.

[17] Article 191(2) of the TFEU states that Union environmental policy shall be based on the precautionary principle; Principle 15 of the Rio Declaration states: 'To protect the environment, the precautionary approach shall be widely applied by States according to their capabilities. Where there are threats of serious or irreversible damage, lack of full scientific certainty shall not be used to postpone cost-effective measures to prevent environmental degradation.'; The EU's REACH regulation (Registration, Evaluation, Authorisation, and Restriction of Chemicals) embodies this principle, requiring companies to identify and manage the risks linked to the substances they manufacture and market in the EU; The WTO's Agreement on the Application of Sanitary and Phytosanitary Measures (SPS Agreement) incorporates the precautionary principle in allowing countries to set their standards for food safety and animal and plant health. While the SPS Agreement encourages scientific evidence as a basis for standards, it recognises that preventive measures may be adopted provisionally in cases of insufficient scientific evidence. See also World Health Organization, *The Precautionary Principle: Protecting Public Health, the Environment and the Future of Our Children* (2004) iris.who.int/handle/10665/346211.

[18] *Artegodan GmbH and Others v Commission*, 26 November 2002, ECR II-04945, para 184.

[19] European Commission, Communication on the Precautionary Principle (COM(2000) 1 final, 2000).

[20] Consolidated Version of the Treaty on the Functioning of the European Union [2012] OJ C326/47, art 191(2).

[21] OECD, *Risk and Regulatory Policy: Improving the Governance of Risk* (OECD Publishing, 2010) 19–23.

[22] J Black and AD Murray, 'Regulating AI and Machine Learning: Setting the Regulatory Agenda' (2019) 10(3) *European Journal of Law and Technology* 1, 1–2.

[23] European Parliamentary Research Service, *The Precautionary Principle: Definitions, Applications and Governance* (2015) www.europarl.europa.eu/RegData/etudes/IDAN/2015/573876/EPRS_IDA(2015)573876_EN.pdf.

[24] Black and Murray (n 22) 1, 4–5.

[25] Resolution (2020/2012) by European Parliament: 'considers that building an approach should be in line with the precautionary principle that guides Union legislation and should be at the heart of any regulatory framework for AI …' p 7.

[26] A Adimi Gikay, 'Risks, Innovation, and Adaptability in the UK's Incrementalism Versus the European Union's Comprehensive Artificial Intelligence Regulation' (2024) 32(1) *International Journal of Law and Information Technology* eaae013 doi.org/10.1093/ijlit/eaae013.

[27] D Castro, 'Ten Ways the Precautionary Principle Undermines Progress in Artificial Intelligence' (Information Technology and Innovation Foundation, 4 February 2019) itif.org/publications/2019/02/04/ten-ways-precautionary-principle-undermines-progress-artificial-intelligence/.

[28] OECD (n 21) 16–20, 32–37.

[29] MK Sparrow, *The Regulatory Craft: Controlling Risks, Solving Problems, and Managing Compliance* (Brookings Institution Press, 2000) 14–18; MK Sparrow, *The Character of Harms: Operational Challenges in Control* (Cambridge University Press, 2008) 31–52.

[30] Sunstein (n 16) 18–22 and 110–20; see also NN Taleb, R Read, R Douady, J Norman and Y Bar-Yam, 'The Precautionary Principle (with Application to the Genetic Modification of Organisms)' (2014) arXiv:1410.5787.

[31] P Carvão, 'The Dual Imperative: Innovation and Regulation in the AI Era' (2024) arXiv preprint arXiv:2407.12690, 1–17.

[32] Black and Murray (n 22) 1, 7.

[33] M Botes, 'Regulating Scientific and Technological Uncertainty: The Precautionary Principle in the Context of Human Genomics and AI' (2023) 119 (5/6) *South African Journal of Science* 1–6 at 3–5.

[34] Regulation (EU) 2024/1689 of the European Parliament and of the Council of 13 June 2024 laying down harmonised rules on artificial intelligence and amending Regulations (EC) No 300/2008, (EU) No 167/2013, (EU) No 168/2013, (EU) 2018/858, (EU) 2018/1139 and (EU) 2019/2144 and Directives 2014/90/EU, (EU) 2016/797 and (EU) 2020/1828 (Artificial Intelligence Act) (Text with EEA Relevance).

[35] I Ayres and J Braithwaite, *Responsive Regulation: Transcending the Deregulation Debate* (Oxford University Press, 1992).

[36] Article 6 AI Act.

[37] While not explicitly defined in a specific article, minimal-risk AI systems are essentially those that fall outside the other three categories. They are generally considered to pose minimal, or no health, safety, or fundamental rights risk.

[38] Article 52 AI Act.

[39] T Cohen, 'They are regulating manipulative artificial intelligence' (SCRIPTed, 2023) 20, 203.

[40] Directive 2010/13/EU of the European Parliament and of the Council of 10 March 2010 on the coordination of certain provisions laid down by law, regulation or administrative action in Member States concerning the provision of audiovisual media services (Audiovisual Media Services Directive) (Text with EEA relevance).

[41] Article 9 AVMSD.

[42] Communications Act 2003, c 21.

[43] Ofcom Broadcasting Code (Ofcom, July 2019) www.ofcom.org.uk/tv-radio-and-on-demand/broadcast-codes/broadcast-code.

[44] France's Code of Public Health Code de la santé publique (France) www.legifrance.gouv.fr/.

[45] Germany's Interstate Treaty on Broadcasting and Telemedia Interstate Treaty on Broadcasting and Telemedia (Germany) www.die-medienanstalten.de/.

[46] Spain's General Law on Audio-visual Communication Ley General de Comunicación Audiovisual (Spain) www.boe.es/.

[47] Testo Unico dei Servizi di Media Audiovisivi e Radiofonici (Italy) Testo Unico dei Servizi di Media Audiovisivi e Radiofonici (Consolidated Text of Audiovisual Media Services and Radio Services) Decreto Legislativo 31 Luglio 2005 n. 177, as amended by Decreto Legislativo 15 Marzo 2010 n. 44 www.normattiva.it/.

[48] M Franklin, PM Tomei and R Gorman, 'Strengthening the EU AI Act: Defining Key Terms on AI Manipulation' (2023) arXiv preprint arXiv:2308.16364.

[49] RJ Neuwirth, *The EU Artificial Intelligence Act: Regulating Subliminal AI Systems* (Routledge, 2023) www.routledge.com/The-EU-Artificial-Intelligence-Act-Regulating-Subliminal-AI-Systems/Neuwirth/p/book/9781032333755. Available at SSRN: ssrn.com/abstract=4135848 or dx.doi.org/10.2139/ssrn.4135848.

[50] Unlike (a) and (b), these cues are imperceptible to the conscious senses but can still be processed by the brain. [a] and [b] might still be partially detectable under certain conditions, but [d] ensures complete imperceptibility.

[51] Franklin, Tomei and Gorman (n 48).

[52] Neuwirth (n 49).

[53] C Boine, 'AI-enabled Manipulation and EU Law' SSRN: ssrn.com/abstract=4042321 or dx.doi.org/10.2139/ssrn.4042321.

[54] ibid.

[55] D Susser, B Roessler and H Nissenbaum, 'Technology, Autonomy, and Manipulation' (2019) 8(2) *Internet Policy Review* 26.

[56] AW Wood, 'Coercion, Manipulation, Exploitation' in C Coons and M Weber (eds), *Manipulation: Theory and Practice* (Oxford University Press, 2014) 18–21 doi.org/10.1093/acprof:oso/9780199338207.003.0002.

[57] R Noggle, 'Manipulation, Salience, and Nudges' (2018) 32 *Bioethics* 164; TRV Nys and B Engelen, 'Judging Nudging: Answering the Manipulation Objection' (2017) 65 *Political Studies* 199.

[58] Article 50.

[59] LM Van Swol and MT Braun, 'Deception detection and decision making: A review of cognitive and social factors' (2019) 55 *New Ideas in Psychology* 100732; A Ito, N Abe, T Fujii and E Mori, (2019). 'Neural correlates of spontaneous deception' (2019) 14(9) *Social Cognitive and Affective Neuroscience* 978–88.

[60] This chapter leans on Lex Zard's theoretical framework for understanding 'persuasion'. Persuasion can be understood in two ways. Broadly, it is an umbrella term encompassing all forms of influence, from rhetoric to coercion. More narrowly, it refers to 'changing someone's mind by providing reasons that they can consciously reflect upon and evaluate'. See L Zard, *Power & Dignity: The Ends of Online Behavioral Advertising in the European Union*, Dissertation (Leiden University, 2024).

[61] Case C-210/96 *Gut Springenheide and Tusky v Oberkreisdirektor Steinfurt* ECLI:EU:C:1998:369, [1998] ECR I-4657, paras 31, 32, 36 and 37. See also Case C-220/98 *Estée Lauder Cosmetics GmbH & Co. ORG v Lancaster Group GmbH*, opinion of Advocate General Fennelly, ECLI:EU:C: 1999:425, para 28.

[62] Article 5(2) UCPD.

[63] Articles 6 and 7 UCPD.

[64] Article 8 UCPD.

[65] Case C-281/12 *Trento Sviluppo srl, Centrale Adriatica* ECLI:EU:C:2013:859, [2014] 1 All ER (Comm) 113.

[66] *Toyota Sweden AB v Volvo Personbilar Sverige AB* [2010] MD 8 (Marknadsdomstolen, 12 March 2010).

[67] J Trzaskowski, (2016). 'Lawful distortion of consumers' economic behaviour – collateral damage under the Unfair Commercial Practices Directive' (2016) 27(1) *European Business Law Review*.

[68] Case C-210/96 *Gut Springenheide GmbH and Rudolf Tusky* (n 61).

[69] Case C-281/12 *Trento Sviluppo srl and Centrale Adriatica* (n 65).

[70] M Leiser, 'Psychological Patterns and Article 5 of the AI Act: AI-Powered Deceptive Design in the System Architecture and the User Interface' (2024) 1 *Journal of AI Law and Regulation* 5.

[71] Recital 29 AI Act.

[72] Council Directive 85/374/EEC of 25 July 1985 on the approximation of the laws, regulations and administrative provisions of the Member States concerning liability for defective products [1985] OJ L210/29.

[73] Regulation (EU) 2023/988 of the European Parliament and of the Council of 10 May 2023 on general product safety, amending Regulation (EU) No 1025/2012 and Directive (EU) 2020/1828, and repealing Directive 2001/95/EC and Council Directive 87/357/EEC [2023] OJ L135/1.

[74] Directive 2000/60/EC of the European Parliament and of the Council of 23 October 2000 establishing a framework for Community action in the field of water policy.

[75] Under Articles 6(3) and (4), any plan or project likely to have a 'significant effect' on a protected site must undergo an appropriate assessment. The directive's implementation guidelines clarify that significance is evaluated in terms of the site's conservation objectives and the degree of impact on the integrity of the site.

[76] Arguably, Article 5(1) of the UCPD [2005] OJ L 149/22.

[77] Regulation (EU) No 596/2014 of the European Parliament and of the Council of 16 April 2014 on market abuse (Market Abuse Regulation) and repealing Directive 2003/6/EC of the European Parliament and of the Council and Commission Directives 2003/124/EC, 2003/125/EC and 2004/72/EC Text with EEA relevance.

[78] Directive 2000/60/EC of the European Parliament and of the Council of 23 October 2000 establishing a framework for Community action in the field of water policy [2000] OJ L327/1.

[79] Council Directive 92/43/EEC of 21 May 1992 on the conservation of natural habitats and of wild fauna and flora [1992] OJ L206/7.

[80] Article 11(3)(i) Water Framework Directive.

[81] Article 6(3) and (4) Habitats Directive.

Chapter 7
The Illusion of Control: Who is Truly Vulnerable?

[1] J Williams, 'Freedom and Persuasion in the Attention Economy' (DPhil thesis, University of Oxford, 2017) 151 at 5 ora.ox.ac.uk/objects/uuid:8065d7b0-4125-4b1f-9218-8623380e03d7/download_file?safe_filename=James%2BWilliams%2B-%2BDPhil%2BThesis%2B-%2BFINAL.pdf&file_format=application%2Fpdf&type_of_work=Thesis.

[2] European Parliament, 'Addictive Design of Online Services and Consumer Protection in the EU Single Market' [2023] OJ C 4164 www.europarl.europa.eu/doceo/document/TA-9-2023-0459_EN.html.

[3] C Mackenzie, W Rogers and S Dodds, 'Introduction: What Is Vulnerability, and Why Does It Matter for Moral Theory?' in C Mackenzie, W Rogers and S Dodds (eds), *Vulnerability: New Essays in Ethics and Feminist Philosophy* (Oxford University Press, 2013) 1, doi.org/10.1093/acprof:oso/9780199316649.003.0001.

[4] F Luna, 'Elucidating the Concept of Vulnerability: Layers not Labels' (2009) 2(1) *International Journal of Feminist Approaches to Bioethics* 121, utppublishing.com/doi/10.3138/ijfab.2.1.121.

[5] G Malgieri, 'The Concept of Fairness in the GDPR: A Linguistic and Contextual Interpretation' in Proceedings of the 2020 Conference on Fairness, Accountability, and Transparency (ACM, January 2020) 154, 160 dl.acm.org/doi/abs/10.1145/3351095.3372868.

[6] G Malgieri and J Niklas, 'Vulnerable Data Subjects' (2020) 37 *Computer Law & Security Review* 105415, 8, doi.org/10.1016/j.clsr.2020.105415.

[7] ibid.

[8] L Jarovsky, 'Transparency by Design: Reducing Informational Vulnerabilities Through UX Design' (25 May 2022) SSRN ssrn.com/abstract=4119284.

[9] Article 5(1)(a) GDPR.

[10] E Fosch-Villaronga and G Malgieri, 'Queering the Ethics of AI' in DJ Gunkel (ed), *Handbook on the Ethics of Artificial Intelligence* (Edward Elgar Publishing, 2024) 301, citing R Xenidis and L Senden, 'EU Non-Discrimination Law in the Era of Artificial Intelligence: Mapping the Challenges of Algorithmic Discrimination' in U Bernitz et al (eds), *General Principles of EU Law and the EU Digital Order* (Kluwer Law International, 2020) 151–82, arxiv.org/pdf/2308.13591.

[11] Malgieri (n 5).

[12] S Mahomed et al, 'AI, Children's Rights, & Wellbeing: Transnational Frameworks: Mapping 13 Frameworks at the Intersections of Data-Intensive Technologies, Children's Rights, and Wellbeing' (The Alan Turing Institute, 2023) www.turing.ac.uk/news/publications/ai-childrens-rights-wellbeing-transnational-frameworks; 5Rights Foundation, *Disrupted Childhood: The Cost of Persuasive Design* (April 2023); 5Rights Foundation, *Feedback on the European Commission Proposal for the Artificial Intelligence Act, COM/2021/206 Final* (August 2021) 2, 5rightsfoundation.com/wp-content/uploads/2024/10/AIAct-5RightsfeedbacktoEC.pdf.

[13] A Krogh Ravna and T Iversen, 'Getting Played: The True Cost of Virtual Currency' (*Forbrukerrådet*, September 2024,) 13 storage02.forbrukerradet.no/media/2024/09/getting-played-2024-compressed-komprimert-sept24-1.pdf; BEUC, 'Consumer Groups Denounce Video Games' Manipulative Spending Tactics' (12 September 2024) 2 www.beuc.eu/sites/default/files/publications/BEUC-PR-2024-030_Consumer_groups_denounce_video_games_manipulative_spending_tactics.pdf.

[14] M Leiser and V Xynogalas, 'The Metaverse: Searching for Compliance with the General Data Protection Regulation' (2024) 14(2) *International Data Privacy Law* 89.

[15] Council of Europe, 'The Metaverse and its Impact on Human Rights, the Rule of Law, and Democracy' (September 2024) 7 rm.coe.int/the-metaverse-impact-on-and-its-impact-on-human-rights-the-rule-of-law/1680ae6bce.

[16] European Parliament, 'The Impact of Disinformation on Democratic Processes and Human Rights in the World' (2021) v www.europarl.europa.eu/RegData/etudes/STUD/2021/653635/EXPO_STU(2021)653635_EN.pdf.

[17] N Helberger, M Sax, J Strycharz and H-W Micklitz, 'Choice Architectures in the Digital Economy: Towards a New Understanding of Digital Vulnerability' (2022) 45 *Journal of Consumer Policy* 176 doi.org/10.1007/s10603-021-09500-5.

[18] ibid.

[19] R Bellan, 'How Amazon Uses AI: From "Rufus" to Personalized Movie Recommendations' (*Business Insider*, 7 July 2024) www.businessinsider.com/how-amazon-is-using-ai-from-rufus-to-movie-recommendations-2024-7.

[20] A Rosenblat, *Uberland: How Algorithms Are Rewriting the Rules of Work* (University of California Press, 2018); see also S Wachter, B Mittelstadt and C Russell, 'Why Fairness Cannot Be Automated: Bridging the Gap Between EU Non-Discrimination Law and AI' (2021) 41(4) *Computer Law & Security Review* 105560.

[21] OECD, *Artificial Intelligence in Society* (OECD Publishing 2019) doi.org/10.1787/eedfee77-en, 59.

[22] Directive (EU) 2019/882 of the European Parliament and of the Council of 17 April 2019 on the accessibility requirements for products and services [2019] OJ L151/70.

[23] Recital 2 EAA.

[24] Joined Cases C-335/11 and C-337/11 *HK Danmark (Ring)* ECLI:EU:C:2013:222, [2013] 3 CMLR 21 at paras 37–39; Case C-363/12 *Z v A Government Department* ECLI:EU:C:2014:159, [2014] 3 CMLR 20; Case C-354/13 *Fag og Arbejde (Kaltoft)* ECLI:EU:C:2014:2463, [2015] 2 CMLR 19.

[25] Recital 29.

[26] Centre for Data Ethics and Innovation, *Review into Bias in Algorithmic Decision-Making* (*gov.uk*, 27 November 2020) www.gov.uk/government/publications/cdei-publishes-review-into-bias-in-algorithmic-decision-making/main-report-cdei-review-into-bias-in-algorithmic-decision-making.

[27] UNESCO, *Beijing Consensus on Artificial Intelligence and Education* (2019) unesdoc.unesco.org/ark:/48223/pf0000368303.

[28] S Barocas and AD Selbst, 'Big Data's Disparate Impact' (2016) 104 *California Law Review* 671; C O'Neil, *Weapons of Math Destruction: How Big Data Increases Inequality and Threatens Democracy* (Crown, 2016); Amnesty International and Access Now, 'The Toronto Declaration: Protecting the Right to Equality and Non-Discrimination in Machine Learning Systems' (16 May 2018) www.torontodeclaration.org/.

[29] Z Obermeyer et al, 'Dissecting Racial Bias in an Algorithm Used to Manage the Health of Populations' (2019) 366(6464) *Science* 447, doi.org/10.1126/science.aax2342.

[30] For example, the United Nations Convention on the Rights of Persons with Disabilities (CRPD) calls for States Parties to 'promote and protect the human rights of all persons with disabilities, including children with disabilities'; Convention on the Rights of Persons with Disabilities (adopted 13 December 2006, entered into force 3 May 2008) 2515 UNTS 3, art 4(1)(h).

[31] Article 22(1) GDPR recognises the potential for harm when algorithmic systems make decisions that significantly impact individuals without human intervention; See also High-Level Expert Group on Artificial Intelligence, 'Ethics Guidelines for Trustworthy AI' (European Commission, 2019) digital-strategy.ec.europa.eu/en/library/ethics-guidelines-trustworthy-ai; Council of Europe, 'Framework Convention on Artificial Intelligence and Human Rights, Democracy and the Rule of Law' (opened for signature 5 September 2024) CETS No. 225 www.coe.int/en/web/artificial-intelligence/the-framework-convention-on-artificial-intelligence.

[32] G Malgieri and M-L Rebrean, 'Vulnerability in the EU AI Act: Building an Interpretation' (28 November 2024) SSRN, ssrn.com/abstract=5058591 or dx.doi.org/10.2139/ssrn.5058591.

[33] United Nations Educational, Scientific and Cultural Organization (UNESCO), 'Recommendation on the Ethics of Artificial Intelligence' (2021) 6, 8 unesdoc.unesco.org/ark:/48223/pf0000380455. This Recommendation emphasises inclusivity and fairness in AI development and deployment. It calls for special attention to vulnerable groups, including children, older people, and people with disabilities.

[34] 5Rights Foundation, *Shedding Light on AI: A Framework for Algorithmic Oversight* (2024) 12, 5rightsfoundation.com/wp-content/uploads/2024/08/Shedding-light-on-AI-a-framework-for-algorithmic-oversight.pdf.

[35] OECD, *Gap Analysis and Implementation Roadmap for Enhancing the Digital Skills of Seniors During and Beyond the RRP Implementation Timeline* (OECD Publishing, 2024) www.oecd.org/content/dam/oecd/en/about/programmes/dg-reform/slovak-republic/Gap-analysis-and-implementation-roadmap-for-enhancing-the-digital-skills-of-seniors-during-and-beyond-the-RRP-implementation-timeline.pdf.

[36] European Pillar of Social Rights, Proclaimed by the European Parliament, the Council and the European Commission on 17 November 2017.

[37] Council Directive 2000/78/EC of 27 November 2000 establishing a general framework for equal treatment in employment and occupation [2000] OJ L 303/16.

[38] Article 2 Council Directive 2000/78/EC establishing a general framework for equal treatment in employment and occupation [2000] OJ L303/16.

[39] General Equal Treatment Act (Allgemeines Gleichbehandlungsgesetz – AGG), enacted 14 August 2006, Federal Law Gazette I 2006, 1897.

[40] French Labour Code (Code du travail) (France) Article L1132-1, last amended by Law No. 2019-486 of 22 May 2019.

[41] Legislative Decree No. 206 of 6 September 2005 (Codice del Consumo), as amended.

[42] Case C-144/04 *Mangold v Helm* ECLI:EU:C:2005:709, [2005] ECR I-9981 at paras 75–77.

[43] Article 5(3) TEU (Principle of Subsidiarity): confirms that the EU acts only when Member States cannot sufficiently achieve objectives; Article 4(2) TEU (Respect for National Identity): Protects national identities, permitting flexibility in implementation; See also Directive (EU) 2011/93 on Combatting Sexual Abuse and Exploitation of Children – Sets minimum standards while allowing stricter national measures; Case C-60/00 *Carpenter v Secretary of State for the Home Department* [2002] ECR I-06279 – highlights the need for balancing national measures with EU standards in child protection.

[44] Article 5(3); Annex I, Point 28 UCPD.

[45] Council Directive 2000/78/EC of 27 November 2000 establishing a general framework for equal treatment in employment and occupation [2000] OJ L303/16, arts 1 and 5.

[46] Directive (EU) 2019/882 of the European Parliament and of the Council of 17 April 2019 on the accessibility requirements for products and services [2019] OJ L 151/70.

[47] Article 4(1); Annex I, Sections I and II Accessibility Directive.

[48] Article 4(2) Accessibility Directive.

[49] Recital 5 Accessibility Directive.

[50] United Nations Educational, Scientific and Cultural Organization (UNESCO), *Recommendation on the Ethics of Artificial Intelligence* (2021) 30, unesdoc.unesco.org/ark:/48223/pf0000381137.

[51] Council Directive 2000/43/EC of 29 June 2000 implementing the principle of equal treatment between persons irrespective of racial or ethnic origin [2000] OJ L180/22, art 2(2)(b).

[52] R Blakely, 'Warnings Over Digital Hauntings by AI Replicas of Dead Relatives' *The Times* (London, 30 November 2024) www.thetimes.com/uk/science/article/warnings-over-digital-hauntings-by-ai-replicas-of-dead-relatives-c9bzl7tpg.

[53] M Field, 'Period-Tracking Apps Investigated over Data Harvesting Fears' *The Telegraph* (7 September 2023) www.telegraph.co.uk/business/2023/09/07/period-tracking-apps-investigated-fears-data-harvesting/.

[54] A Alutaybi, D Al-Thani, J McAlaney and R Ali, 'Combating Fear of Missing Out (FoMO) on Social Media: The FoMO-R Method' (2020) 17 *International Journal of Environmental Research and Public Health* 6128.

[55] Children's Commissioner for England, 'Loot Boxes and Gambling' (Children's Commissioner for England, 22 October 2019) www.childrenscommissioner.gov.uk/blog/loot-boxes-and-gambling/.

[56] Federal Trade Commission, 'FTC Report Shows Rise in Sophisticated Dark Patterns Designed to Trick and Trap Consumers' (FTC, 14 September 2022) www.ftc.gov/news-events/news/press-releases/2022/09/ftc-report-shows-rise-sophisticated-dark-patterns-designed-trick-trap-consumers.

[57] Federal Trade Commission, 'Getting In and Out of Free Trials, Auto-Renewals, and Negative Option Subscriptions' (FTC, 14 September 2022) consumer.ftc.gov/articles/getting-and-out-free-trials-auto-renewals-and-negative-option-subscriptions.

[58] American Psychological Association, 'Protecting Teens on Social Media' (APA, September 2023) www.apa.org/monitor/2023/09/protecting-teens-on-social-media.

[59] European Parliament, 'Loot Boxes in Online Games and Their Effect on Consumers, in Particular Young Consumers' (European Parliament, 2020) www.europarl.europa.eu/thinktank/en/document/IPOL_STU(2020)652727.

[60] V Charisi, S Chaudron, R Di Gioia, R Vuorikari, M Escobar-Planas, I Sanchez and E Gómez, *Artificial Intelligence and the Rights of the Child: Towards an Integrated Agenda for Research and Policy*, EUR 31048 EN (Publications Office of the European Union, 2022) ISBN 978-92-76-51837-2, doi:10.2760/012329 publications.jrc.ec.europa.eu/repository/handle/JRC127564.

[61] Royal Society for Public Health, *Status of Mind: Social Media and Young People's Mental Health and Wellbeing* (RSPH, 2017) 8, www.rsph.org.uk/static/uploaded/d125b27c-0b62-41c5-a2c0155a8887cd01.pdf; for a more recent reference, see JT Hancock, S Xun Liu, M Luo and H Mieczkowski, 'Social Media and Psychological Well-Being' in SC Matz (ed), *The Psychology of Technology: Social Science Research in the Age of Big Data* (American Psychological Association 2022) 196 doi.org/10.1037/0000290-007.

[62] Mental Health Foundation, 'Body Image in Childhood' (Mental Health Foundation, 2019) www.mentalhealth.org.uk/explore-mental-health/articles/body-image-report-executive-summary/body-image-childhood.

[63] BEUC, '"Dark Patterns" and the EU Consumer Law Acquis' (European Consumer Organisation, 2022) www.beuc.eu/sites/default/files/publications/beuc-x-2022-013_dark_patters_paper.pdf 6.

[64] European Consumer Organisation, '"Dark Patterns" and the EU Consumer Law Acquis' (BEUC, 2022) www.beuc.eu/sites/default/files/publications/beuc-x-2022-013_dark_patters_paper.pdf.

[65] J Lewallen and E Behm-Morawitz, 'Pinterest or Thinterest? Social Comparison and Body Image on Social Media' (2016) 2 *Social Media + Society* 2056305116640559, doi.org/10.1177/2056305116640559.

[66] S Kumar Muppalla, S Vuppalapati, A Reddy Pulliahgaru and H Sreenivasulu, 'Effects of Excessive Screen Time on Child Development: An Updated Review and Strategies for Management' (2023) 15(6) *Cureus* e40608, doi.org/10.7759/cureus.40608.

[67] C Montag, B Lachmann, M Herrlich and K Zweig, 'Addictive Features of Social Media/Messenger Platforms and Freemium Games against the Background of Psychological and Economic Theories' (2019) 16(14) *International Journal of Environmental Research and Public Health* 2612, doi.org/10.3390/ijerph16142612.

[68] Information Commissioner's Office, 'Safeguard and Empower the Public: Annual Action Plan October 2022 – October 2023' (ICO, 2022) ico.org.uk/about-the-ico/our-information/our-strategies-and-plans/ico25-strategic-plan/annual-action-plan-october-2022-october-2023/safeguard-and-empower-the-public/?q=child.

[69] S Livingstone, M Stoilova and R Nandagiri, 'Children's Data and Privacy Online: Growing Up in a Digital Age' (London School of Economics and Political Science, 2018) 30, 31 www.lse.ac.uk/media-and-communications/assets/documents/research/projects/childrens-privacy-online/Evidence-review-final.pdf.

Chapter 8
Toward a Future Free of Manipulation

[1] Inside Privacy, 'The EU Stance on Dark Patterns' (*Inside Privacy*, 3 May 2023) www.insideprivacy.com/eu-data-protection/the-eu-stance-on-dark-patterns/; 'Dark Patterns, Online Ads Will Be Potential Targets for the Next Commission, Reynders Says' (*Euractiv*, 4 October 2023) www.euractiv.com/section/digital/interview/dark-patterns-online-ads-will-be-potential-targets-for-the-next-commission-reynders-says/; European Commission, Directorate-General for Justice and Consumers, F Lupiáñez-Villanueva et al, *Behavioural Study on Unfair Commercial Practices in the Digital Environment – Dark Patterns and Manipulative Personalisation – Final Report* (Publications Office of the European Union, 2022) data.europa.eu/doi/10.2838/859030.

[2] OECD, *Dark Commercial Patterns* (OECD Digital Economy Papers No. 336, October 2022) 26–27 www.oecd.org/en/topics/sub-issues/dark-commercial-patterns.html.

[3] Cognitive Bias Codex, upload.wikimedia.org/wikipedia/commons/6/65/Cognitive_bias_codex_en.svg.

[4] N Bielova, L Litvine, A Nguyen, M Chammat, V Toubiana and E Hary, 'The Effect of Design Patterns on (Present and Future) Cookie Consent Decisions' in *33rd USENIX Security Symposium (USENIX Security 24)* (2024) 2813–30.

[5] Cognitive Bias Codex (n 2).

[6] R Sin, T Harris, S Nilsson and T Beck, 'Dark Patterns in Online Shopping: Do They Work and Can Nudges Help Mitigate Impulse Buying?' (2022) *Behavioural Public Policy* 1–27 doi.org/10.1017/bpp.2022.11.

[7] M Potel-Saville and M Da Rocha, 'How to Solve the Dark Pattern Issue: A Human-Centred Approach' in R Leenes et al (eds), *Data Protection and Privacy, Volume 16: Ideas That Drive Our Digital World* (Bloomsbury, 2023).

[8] European Data Protection Board (EDPB), *Guidelines on Deceptive Design Patterns in Social Media Platform Interfaces, Version 2* (EDPB, 2023) 4 www.edpb.europa.eu/system/files/2023-02/edpb_03-2022_guidelines_on_deceptive_design_patterns_in_social_media_platform_interfaces_v2_en_0.pdf.

[9] Article 5(1)(a) GDPR.

[10] Article 5(2) GDPR.

[11] Article 25 GDPR.

[12] C Utz, M Degeling, S Fahl, F Schaub and T Holz, '(Un)informed Consent: Studying GDPR Consent Notices in the Field' in Proceedings of the 2019 ACM SIGSAC Conference on Computer and Communications Security (ACM, November 2019) 973–90.

[13] Case C-646/22 *Compass Banca SpA v AGCM* ECLI:EU:C:2024:957.

[14] ibid paras 51–60.

[15] D Haije, 'Balancing Rationality and Reality: Insights from the CJEU's Compass Banca Judgment' (Lexology, 15 November 2024) www.lexology.com/library/detail.aspx?g=61c4f171-059d-42f6-afc4-25b6a3458033.

[16] Deceptive Design Cases' (Deceptive Design) www.deceptive.design/cases?authorities=Spanish+DPA+%28AEPD%29.

[17] LG Passau, final judgment of 9 April 2024–4 O 260/23 GRUR-RS 2024, 8093 www.gesetze-bayern.de/Content/Document/Y-300-Z-GRURRS-B-2024-N-8093?hl=true.

[18] V Nuijens, 'Turning Dark Patterns into Honest Patterns: Insights from Cases of EU Data Protection Authorities on ePD and GDPR Violations in Cookie Banners to Inform the Design of "Honest Patterns"' (unpublished Master of Laws thesis, Vrije Universiteit Amsterdam 2024).

[19] M Potel-Saville and M Francois, 'From Dark Patterns to Fair Patterns? Usable Taxonomy to Contribute Solving the Issue with Countermeasures' (Annual Privacy Forum, June 2023); R Schäfer et al, 'Fighting Malicious Designs: Towards Visual Countermeasures Against Dark Patterns' in Proceedings of the 2024 CHI Conference on Human Factors in Computing Systems (CHI '24) (Association for Computing Machinery, 2024) doi.org/10.1145/3613904.3642661. www.researchgate.net/publication/371314839_From_Dark_Patterns_to_Fair_Patterns_Usable_Taxonomy_to_Contribute_Solving_the_Issue_with_Countermeasures.

[20] V Krauss et al, 'Create a Fear of Missing Out – ChatGPT Implements Unsolicited Deceptive Designs in Generated Websites Without Warning' (arXiv, 2024) arxiv.org/pdf/2411.03108.

[21] Potel-Saville and Francois (n 19) 145–65.

[22] Note 8 at 65.

[23] Note 8 at 65.

[24] Note 8 at 67.

[25] Note 8 at 68.

[26] Note 8 at 69.

[27] Note 8 at 69.

[28] European Data Protection Board, Guidelines 03/2022 on Deceptive Design Patterns in Social Media Platform Interfaces: How to Recognise and Avoid Them (Version 2.0, 14 February 2023) 28 edpb.europa.eu.

[29] Note 8 at 12.

[30] Article 5(2) GDPR.

[31] Note 8 at 3, 8–10, 12, 28.

[32] Note 8 at 3, 12, 13–14, 17.

[33] Note 17.

[34] Note 17 at 45, 49.

[35] Note 17 at 49.

[36] Note 17 at 49–50.

[37] Court of Justice of the European Union, *X v Commission* (Case T-354/22, *Bindl* ECLI:EU:T:2025:4) curia.europa.eu/juris/document/document.jsf?text=&docid=294090&pageIndex=0&doclang=EN&mode=lst&dir=&occ=first&part=1&cid=397223.

[38] ibid para 191.

[39] ibid para 197.

[40] Case C-243/05 P *Agraz and Others v Commission* ECLI:EU:C:2006:708, [2006] ECR I-10833, para 27.

[41] Article 26 GDPR.

[42] L Rostock, *Cookie Banner Is Illegal* (Case 3 O 762/19, 15 September 2020) www.online-und-recht.de/urteile/cookie-banner-ist-rechtswidrig-landgericht-rostock-20200915/.

[43] L Rostock, *Decision of 15 September 2020, Case No. 3 O 762/19*, paras 1–3, 26–27.

[44] Articles 12, 13 GDPR.

[45] Article 13(1)(f) GDPR.

[46] Articles 45–49 GDPR.

[47] Article 26(2) GDPR.

[48] Case C-40/17 *Fashion ID GmbH & Co KG v Verbraucherzentrale NRW eV* ECLI:EU:C:2019:629, [2020] 1 WLR 969.

[49] Note 37 at 3 and 27.

[50] Article 5(2) UCPD.

[51] Point 5, Annex I UCPD.

[52] Point 7, Annex I UCPD.

[53] Point 22, Annex I UCPD.

[54] Point 20, Annex I UCPD.

[55] Point 31, Annex I UCPD.

[56] Point 11, Annex I UCPD.

[57] Point 26, Annex I UCPD.

[58] Directive (EU) 2019/2161 of the European Parliament and of the Council of 27 November 2019 amending Council Directive 93/13/EEC and Directives 98/6/EC, 2005/29/EC and 2011/83/EU as regards the better enforcement and modernisation of Union consumer protection rules [2019] OJ L328/7.

[59] Directive (EU) 2019/2161 of the European Parliament and of the Council of 27 November 2019 amending Council Directive 93/13/EEC and Directives 98/6/EC, 2005/29/EC and 2011/83/EU as regards the better enforcement and modernisation of Union consumer protection rules [2019] OJ L328/7, recitals 22–27, arts 1(4), 3, and 7(4a).

[60] Recital 67 DSA.

[61] Lupiáñez-Villanueva et al (n 1).

[62] European Commission, '*Commission Opens Formal Proceedings Against X (Formerly Twitter) Under Digital Services Act* '(25 September 2023) digital-strategy.ec.europa.eu/

en/news/commission-opens-formal-proceedings-against-x-under-digital-services-act; European Commission, '*Commission Opens Formal Proceedings Against TikTok Under Digital Services Act* '(28 September 2023) digital-strategy.ec.europa.eu/en/news/commission-opens-formal-proceedings-against-tiktok-under-digital-services-act.

[63] Forbrukerrådet, '*Complaint Against Amazon Prime*' (January 2021) storage02.forbrukerradet.no/media/2021/01/complaint-against-amazon-prime.pdf; see also European Commission, '*Consumer Protection: Amazon Prime Changes Its Cancellation Practices to Comply with EU Consumer Rules*' (Press Release, 16 January 2022) ec.europa.eu/commission/presscorner/api/files/document/print/en/ip_22_4186/IP_22_4186_EN.pdf.

[64] Federal Trade Commission Act, 15 USC §§ 41–58 (1914, as amended) www.law.cornell.edu/uscode/text/15/chapter-2.

[65] Children's Online Privacy Protection Act (COPPA), 15 USC §§ 6501–6506 (1998, as amended).

[66] Restore Online Shoppers' Confidence Act, 15 USC §§ 8401–8405 (2010).

[67] 15 U.S.C. § 6502: Children's Online Privacy Protection Act, 15 USC § 6502 (1998, as amended).

[68] Epic Games Complaint: *United States of America v Epic Games, Inc.*, Complaint for Permanent Injunction, Civil Penalties, and Other Relief, Case No. 5:22-CV-00518-BO (US District Court, Eastern District of North Carolina, 19 December 2022) www.ftc.gov/system/files/ftc_gov/pdf/2223087EpicGamesComplaint.pdf.

[69] 15 U.S.C. § 45.

[70] Epic Games Settlement: *United States of America v Epic Games, Inc.*, Stipulated Order for Permanent Injunction and Civil Penalty Judgment, Case No. 5:22-CV-00518-BO (US District Court, Eastern District of North Carolina, 19 December 2022) www.ftc.gov/system/files/ftc_gov/pdf/2223087EpicGamesSettlement.pdf.

[71] *Perkins v LinkedIn Corporation* [2014] 53 F Supp 3d 1222 (ND Cal).

[72] California Business and Professions Code § 17200: California Business and Professions Code § 17200 (2023).

[73] Note 71 at 92–93, 99–100, 50.

[74] Note 71 at 50, 92–93, and 99–100.

[75] Complaint: Federal Trade Commission, 'Complaint for Permanent Injunction, Monetary Relief, and Other Relief' (3 November 2022) www.ftc.gov/system/files/ftc_gov/pdf/Vonage-Complaint.pdf.

[76] Restore Online Shoppers' Confidence Act, 15 USC § 8404 (2010).

[77] Section 5(a) FTC Act.

[78] Stipulated Final Order: 'Stipulated Order for Permanent Injunction, Monetary Judgment, and Other Relief' (3 November 2022) www.ftc.gov/system/files/ftc_gov/pdf/Vonage-Stipulated-Final-Order.pdf.

[79] *Federal Trade Commission v Vonage Holdings Corp, Vonage America LLC, and Vonage Business, Inc*, Stipulated Order for Permanent Injunction, Monetary Judgment, and Other Relief (US District Court for the District of New Jersey, 3 November 2022) Case No 3:22-cv-6435, section V, para A, www.ftc.gov/system/files/ftc_gov/pdf/Vonage-Stipulated-Final-Order.pdf.

[80] J King and A Stephan, 'Regulating Privacy Dark Patterns in Practice: Drawing Inspiration from the California Privacy Rights Act' (2021) 5(2) *Georgetown Law Technology Review* 250–76.

[81] BJ Fogg, *The Fogg Behavior Model* (Behaviour Design Lab, Stanford University 2019) Technical Report.

[82] Potel-Saville and François (n 19).

[83] Article 25 GDPR.

[84] Article 5(1)(c) GDPR.

[85] Recital 38 GDPR.

[86] 5Rights Foundation, *Disrupted Childhood: The Cost of Persuasive Design* (Publications Office of the European Union, 2023) 5rightsfoundation.com/wp-content/uploads/2024/08/5rights_DisruptedChildhood_G.pdf.

[87] docsend.com/view/ds5254d3rnyucyw3.

[88] Consumer Reports Digital Lab, *The Princeton Ad Observatory* innovation.consumer-reports.org/initiatives/the-princeton-ad-observatory/.

[89] ST Khanna, A Johri and V Tangri, 'Detecting Deception: An AI-Driven Approach to Identify Dark Patterns' (2024) 12(4) *International Journal of Intelligent Systems and Applications in Engineering* 1658–69 www.ijisae.org.

[90] S Mills and R Whittle, 'Detecting Dark Patterns Using Generative AI: Some Preliminary Results' (2023) *SSRN* ssrn.com/abstract=4614907; A Ramteke, S Tembhurne, G Sonawane and RN Bhimanpallewar, 'Unmasking Dark Patterns: A Machine Learning Approach to Detecting Deceptive Design in E-commerce Websites' (2024) arXiv preprint arxiv.org/abs/2406.01608.

[91] S Savarese, 'What Are Large Action Models (LAMs)?' (*Salesforce*, 27 June 2023) www.salesforce.com/blog/large-action-models/.

[92] M Leiser, 'Weapons of Mass Distraction: Large Action Models (LAMs) and Their Legal Implications' (17 December 2024) SSRN ssrn.com/abstract=5061723 or dx.doi.org/10.2139/ssrn.5061723.

[93] D Ivanov, 'What Are Large Action Models and How Do They Work?' (*Trinetix*, 29 March 2024) www.trinetix.com/insights/the-what-why-and-how-of-large-language-models.

[94] N Mathes, '5 Ways Agentforce Can Elevate Your Marketing Strategy' (*Salesforce*, 3 December 2024) www.salesforce.com/blog/agentforce-for-marketing/; Y Zhang, P Tokmakov, M Hebert and C Schmid, 'A Structured Model for Action Detection' (2019) 2019 IEEE/CVF Conference on Computer Vision and Pattern Recognition (CVPR); D Shah, B Osiński, B Ichter and S Levine, 'LM-Nav: Robotic Navigation with Large Pre-Trained Models of Language, Vision, and Action' (2022) 6th Conference on Robot Learning (CoRL 2022).

[95] TA Salthouse, 'The processing-speed theory of adult age differences in cognition' (1996) 103(3) *Psychol Rev.* 403–28. doi: 10.1037/0033-295x.103.3.403. PMID: 8759042.

[96] European Commission, 'Commission Guidelines on Prohibited Artificial Intelligence Practices Established by Regulation (EU) 2024/1689 (AI Act)' C(2025) 884 final (4 February 2025) 18–50 digital-strategy.ec.europa.eu/en/library/commission-publishes-guidelines-prohibited-artificial-intelligence-ai-practices-defined-ai-act.

INDEX